Gender and American Law

The Impact of the Law on the Lives of Women

Series Editor

Karen J. Maschke

GARLAND PUBLISHING, INC.
New York & London
1997

Contents of the Series

Educational Equity

Edited with introductions by
Karen J. Maschke

GARLAND PUBLISHING, INC.
New York & London
1997

Library of Congress Cataloging-in-Publication Data

Educational equity / edited with introductions by Karen J. Maschke.
    p.   cm. — (Gender and American law ; 4)
    Includes bibliographical references.
    ISBN 0-8153-2518-5 (alk. paper)
    1. Educational equalization—Law and legislation—United States.
2. Women—Education—Law and legislation—United States. 3. Sex
discrimination in education—Law and legislation—United States.
I. Maschke, Karen J. II. Series.
KF4155.A2E36 1997
344.73'0798—dc21   96-51812
                                                            CIP

Printed on acid-free, 250-year-life paper
Manufactured in the United States of America

Contents

Series Introduction

From colonial times to the present, the law has been used to both expand and contract the rights of women. Over the last two decades, a body of literature has emerged that examines the ways in which the law has had an impact on the lives of women in the United States. The topics covered in this series include the historical development of women's legal rights, matters surrounding reproduction, sexuality and the family, equal employment opportunity, educational equity, violence against women, pornography, sex work, hate speech, and developments in feminist legal thought. The articles represent multidisciplinary approaches in examining women's experiences with the law and provide theoretical insights about the nature of gender equality.

A unifying theme in these articles is that women have been constructed historically as "different," and that this characterization "has had implications in regard to the way in which women are understood as objects and subjects of law" (Fineman 1992, p. 1). Biological differences between women and men and assumptions about the different "nature" of women and men have provided the basis for legal restrictions on women's ownership of property, guardianship of their children, ability to control their reproduction, and access to the workplace and educational institutions.

Even though women have more legal rights now than at any other time in history, many of the articles show that the law can both eradicate and reinforce women's subordination. Nineteenth-century child custody law is a telling example. While "judges granted women new legal power in family affairs," they also placed "severe limits on married women's overall legal rights" (Grossberg 1983, p. 235). On the one hand, by claiming the authority to determine which parent should be granted custody, judges dismantled the practice of fathers possessing unquestioned domain over matters of child custody and guardianship. Yet judges also "ensured that women's domestic powers did not translate into extensive external political and economic authority" (Grossberg 1983, p. 237).

The limitations of legal reform are also revealed by contemporary attempts to achieve gender equality. For example, in the 1970s many local governments adopted comparable worth wage policies. Such policies were "designed to correct historically discriminatory wages of female- and minority-dominated jobs" (Evans and Nelson 1989, p. 172). However, when some local communities were forced to raise women's wages to correct discriminatory practices, they eliminated or modified various jobs and social programs. Many of these programs, such as after school latchkey programs, were developed in response to the needs of two-paycheck and female-headed families. "In other words," note Evans and Nelson, "local governments are reacting to comparable worth with threats to renege on the emerging social commitment to policies addressing what have been traditionally defined as *women's* problems" (Evans and Nelson 1989, p. 183).

Other articles provide additional evidence of how legal reforms may actually disadvantage women in ways that are unanticipated. Furthermore, they reveal the problems in employing the model of equality as a basis for achieving gender justice. The emerging "difference theories" in feminist legal thought focus on the ways in which women and men live "gendered lives," and the ways in which legal and social institutions are shaped and operate according to gendered constructs (Fineman 1992).

The articles in this series also show how the law affects women in different ways. Women of color, poor women, and single mothers may experience the power of the law in ways that are different from the experiences of white, middle-class women. Poverty reform discourses are laden with images of single mothers as "bad" and often lump these women together "with drug addicts, criminals, and other socially-defined 'degenerates' in the newly-coined category of 'underclass'" (Fineman 1992, p. 283). Consequently, current welfare policies are not designed so much to help single mothers as they are to punish them for their bad behavior.

Several authors show how in the legal matters concerning male violence against women, "the experiences of women of color are frequently the product of intersecting patterns of racism and sexism" (Crenshaw 1991, p. 1243). These authors contend that theories of gender oppression must acknowledge the intersection of race and sex, the ways in which women have contributed to the social construction of race, and the oppression of black women. They also point out that the analyses of the law's role in women's oppression must take account of the intersectional identities of women and of how the law responds to, reinforces, and stigmatizes those identities.

The articles in this series bring together an outstanding selection from a growing body of work that examines how the law treats women and gender difference. They represent some of the most intriguing theoretical writing on the subject and reflect the strong multidisciplinary character of contemporary research on women and the legal order.

Notes

Cited works are contained in volumes five, three, seven, and two, respectively.

Crenshaw, Kimberle. 1991. Mapping the Margins: Intersectionality, Identity Politics, and Violence Against Women of Color. *Stanford Law Review* 43:1241–99.

Evans, Sara M. and Barbara J. Nelson. 1989. Comparable Worth: The Paradox of Technocratic Reform. *Feminist Studies* 15:171–90.

Fineman, Martha. 1992. Feminist Theory in Law: The Difference it Makes. *Columbia Journal of Gender and Law* 2:1–23.

Grossberg, Michael. 1983. Who Gets the Child? Custody, Guardianship, and the Rise of a Judicial Patriarchy in Nineteenth-Century America. *Feminist Studies* 9:235–60.

Volume Introduction

Women's access to education has changed dramatically since the colonial period, when dame schools provided one of the only opportunities available for middle-class white women and girls to obtain schooling (Lindgren and Taub 1993). Since then, questions have been raised about whether women should be admitted to the public schools, about whether they should be admitted to coeducational schools, about the types of programs they should take, about the quality and purpose of their education, and about their access to the same programs and services that are offered to men and boys. As the 20th century draws to a close, these and other issues continue to shape the debate over educational equity for women and girls.

It was after the American Revolution that higher education in academies became available to middle-class women. These academies emerged for the purpose of providing a certain type of schooling: to prepare "women to be better mothers and wives, especially for their role in shaping the moral and civic character of the citizens of an expanding new nation" (Lindgren and Taub 1993, p. 266).

Women made great advances in higher education after the Civil War. Between 1875 and 1925, women gained access to many educational institutions, such as state colleges and normal schools for women, as well as professional schools and universities that traditionally were all-male institutions (Lindgren and Taub 1993). Yet by 1925, many coeducational institutions began to adopt policies restricting women's access to their programs. For example, women could make up only 5 percent of the students at medical schools. This quota continued to shape medical school admission policies until 1945 (McGlen and O'Connor 1995). Although recent research shows that there have been differences in women's educational experiences depending on the type of institution they attended (Ogren 1995), the U.S. educational system has been and continues to be shaped by gendered practices and structures.

Victoria Brown's study of high schools in Los Angeles during the progressive era illustrates the ways in which education was highly gendered. What emerged in the Los Angeles school system, like elsewhere throughout the country, was a growing concern for the "boy problem." Obsessed "with the fact that girls comprised 60 percent of the high school population," Los Angeles educators debated how to prevent their schools from being taken over and feminized "by the weaker sex" (Brown 1990, pp. 496–97). As a result of this growing trend, educators in Los Angeles attempted to make high school more attractive to boys. Their efforts included expanding the number of science and technical courses, establishing "parental" schools for boys who were truants and staffing them with male teachers, hiring more male teachers in the regular classrooms, and implementing policies that resulted in the "thorough masculinization of inter-scholastic sports and student government" (Brown 1990, p. 506–10).

By the middle of the 20th century, a variety of policies and practices that denied women and girls access to certain programs and that stigmatized them in the classroom were prevalent at all levels of the U.S. educational system. In 1970, both houses of Congress held hearings "that documented the pervasiveness, perniciousness, and long-range consequences of sex discrimination in educational policy, practices, and attitudes" (Lindgren and Taub 1993, pp. 276–77). Two years later, Congress passed Title IX of the Educational Amendments of 1972. Title IX declares that no person, on the basis of sex, can "be excluded from participation in, be denied the benefits of, or be subjected to discrimination under any education program or activity receiving Federal financial assistance." Federal regulations that were issued to enforce Title IX covered admissions and recruitment, curriculum standards, "research, extracurricular activities, student aid, student services, counseling and guidance, financial aid, housing, and athletics" (Lindgren and Taub 1993, p. 277).

Although Title IX has expanded women's access to educational institutions and programs, it has not eliminated sex discrimination in education. Nor has it fundamentally altered gender role values that permeate the U.S. educational system. The practices of two powerful institutions in the U.S., collegiate sports and all-male military academies, exemplify how far women have yet to go in achieving educational equity and in altering traditional gender roles.

For most of the 20th century, women participating in sports have had to overcome the myth that they are "simply too fragile to engage in strenuous physical contests" (Olson 1991, p. 109). This myth shaped the policies that kept women and girls from participating in a wide range of athletic activities taking place in public parks, elementary, secondary, and collegiate institutions, the Olympics, and professional sports teams. Women and girls have filed dozens of lawsuits challenging discriminatory practices in educational institutions that prohibited women and girls from playing on certain men's and boys' teams, that paid female coaches less than their male counterparts, and that failed to provide women and girls with the same opportunities for team sports (Olson 1991; Wong and Ensor 1985–86).

Litigation has also been used to challenge restrictive admissions policies at the nation's two remaining state-supported, all-male military academies: the Citadel in South Carolina and the Virginia Military Institute (VMI). In 1994, the Citadel was ordered to admit Shannon Faulkner, a female who was admitted by mistake because the academy assumed her name was that of a male applicant. Although Faulkner eventually dropped out of the academy, several females entered the Citadel in the fall of 1996.

VMI fought longer and harder than the Citadel to keep women out of the ranks of its cadets. In 1992, the U.S. Court of Appeals for the Fourth Circuit ruled that the state of Virginia had violated the equal protection clause of the 14th Amendment by refusing to admit women to VMI. The court determined that the state could remedy this violation by admitting women, by establishing a parallel program for women, or by giving up its state funding. Virginia responded by establishing the Virginia Women's Institute for Leadership. This program was lodged at Mary Baldwin College, a private women's college. Then in September 1996, the Board of Visitors of VMI voted to admit women to VMI by a vote of 9-8. The vote was prompted by a U.S. Supreme Court decision in which the Court held that VMI's male-only admission policy violated the equal protection clause of the 14th Amendment.

The controversy over the male-only admissions policy at VMI reflects the extent to which traditional gender roles and expectations continue to shape educational policies. VMI's program at Mary Baldwin College was designed to be supportive and encouraging, rather than an "adversarial" program like the one at its male-only institution. As pointed out in an *amicus* brief filed by Carol Gilligan, the women's program was based on

> classic, time-worn generalizations picturing women as passive, men as aggressive; women as peaceful, men as violent; women as cooperative, men as competitive; women as 'connected,' men as independent; women as consensus-builders, men as authoritarian (Women's Rights Law Reporter 1994, p. 10).

These stereotypes are powerful reminders that despite the gains women and girls have made in achieving access to education, gender values and structures will continue to play a role in their educational experiences and opportunities.

Notes

Articles marked with an asterisk (*) are included in this volume.

*Brown, Victoria Bissell. 1990. The Fear of Feminization: Los Angeles High Schools in the Progressive Era. *Feminist Studies* 16:493–518.

Lindgren, J. Ralph and Nadine Taub. 1993. *The Law of Sex Discrimination*, 2d ed. Minneapolis: West Publishing Co.

McGlen, Nancy E. and Karen O'Connor. 1995. *Women, Politics, and American Society*. Englewood Cliffs, N.J.: Prentice-Hall.

*Ogren, Christine A. 1995. Where Coeds Were Coeducated: Normal Schools in Wisconsin, 1870–1920. *History of Education Quarterly* 35:1–26.

*Olson, Wendy. 1991. Beyond Title IX: Towards an Agenda for Women and Sports in the 1990s. *Yale Journal of Law and Feminism* 3:105–51.

Women's Rights Law Reporter. 1994. Opposing All-Male Admission Policy at Virginia Military Institute: *Amicus Curiae* Brief of Professor Carol Gilligan and the Program on Gender, Science, and Law. *Women's Rights Law Reporter* 16:1–16.

*Wong, Glenn M. and Richard J. Ensor. 1985–86. Sex Discrimination in Athletics: A Review of Two Decades of Accomplishments and Defeats. *Gonzaga Law Review* 21:345–93.

Educational Equity

An Interview on Title IX with Shirley Chisholm, Holly Knox, Leslie R. Wolfe, Cynthia G. Brown, and Mary Kaaren Jolly

Title IX of the Education Amendments of 1972 specifically prohibits discrimination on the basis of sex in elementary and secondary schools, colleges, and universities. It states: "No person in the United States shall, on the basis of sex, be excluded from participation in, be denied the benefits of, or be subjected to discrimination under any education program or activity receiving federal financial assistance. . . ." Conflict over the formulation and interpretation of the regulation erupted immediately after the passage of Title IX, and its statutory limits continue to be tested, increasingly in the courts, across the country. This interview explores the effects of Title IX and the controversy surrounding its implementation. Five women, each uniquely involved with the short but volatile history of Title IX, discuss its implications and potential for ensuring a more equitable educational system. The interview participants include The Honorable Shirley Chisholm, Democratic Congresswoman from New York; Mary Jolly, Staff Director and Counsel to the Senate Subcommittee on the Constitution chaired by Senator Birch Bayh; Leslie Wolfe, Director of the Women's Educational Equity Act Program, and formerly Special Assistant to the Assistant Secretary for Education, who earlier had been Deputy Director of the Women's Rights Program of the Commission on Civil Rights; Cindy Brown, Principal Deputy Director of the Office for Civil Rights in HEW; and Holly Knox, Director of PEER, the Project on Equal Education Rights of the NOW Legal Defense and Education Fund, and former Legislative Specialist in the United States Office of Education.

Shirley Chisholm: First let's give a definition of what Title IX is all about. The purpose of Title IX is to guarantee equal access for women in the academic world and in athletics. In reality, it is part of an affirmative action program. Women have always occupied a secondary status in the United States. And in the same way that it was necessary for Blacks to get recognition by virtue of the Voting Rights Act and the Civil

Interviewers were Neal Baer, Donna Hulsizer, and Lauri Perman of the HER Editorial Board. Photographs were taken by Michael Moser.

Harvard Educational Review, Vol. 49, No. 4, November 1979.
Copyright © 1979 by President and Fellows of Harvard College.
0017-8055/79/1100-0504$01.86/0

2

I think that while racial discrimination has been looked at as one of the social blights in our society, I believe that many of our citizens still do not believe that sexism is a problem.

Rights Act—Title IX is of the same import to women. I think that while racial discrimination has been looked at as one of the social blights in our society, many of our citizens still do not believe that sexism is a problem. Consequently, the necessity for having on the record, once and for all, the fact that women must not be discriminated against on the basis of their sex, and particularly where federal funds are involved, is one of the main reasons why we felt that Title IX would be so important.

Unfortunately, there have been many misinterpretations of Title IX. This, of course, is to be expected, primarily from white men, specifically the college presidents and college coaches who descended on Washington to let everybody know what a deleterious effect the Title IX sports policy would have if it were implemented. But we have to understand that these particular persons in our society have been the beneficiaries of the status quo, and anything that poses a threat, or anything that seems to be a little disconcerting to them—propels them to get into the act and try to block progress. However, I'd like to say that it was very unfortunate that back in 1972, when the legislation was enacted, President Nixon did not enforce many pieces of progressive legislation. The regulations finally came out three years later, and here we are, still attempting to see whether or not we can get them implemented.

I personally feel that a great deal of education has to be done so that those persons in our universities and colleges who oversee our athletics programs understand the importance of Title IX. For me, the question of women's equal access to sports is especially interesting because of its importance to black women. The woman who happens to be black faces a double barrier and the entire sports policy, especially with respect to scholarships, is most important. As a black woman, the potential access to college education for black and other minority women is of priority value.

*What would you say are now the urgent issues affecting
the implementation of Title IX?*

Chisholm: I think one of the major issues, of course, is the role of society. Women have been given prescribed roles from the moment of their birth; now they are moving in another direction. The tradition women were supposed to follow in that particular scheme of things runs contrary to what Title IX is all about. We talk of a dynamic, changing, moving society, and quite often it's very difficult to get people to accept change, because change is very frightening. Change is somewhat threatening.

I also think there are a great many confusions about Title IX outside of Washington. The very fact that so many college presidents and football coaches came to Washington because they perceived that something was going to be detrimental to their specific interests is a clear indication that they misinterpreted the policy. The policy really attempts to develop some type of equity. It is not a literal policy in terms of dollar for dollar; there are so many other factors that enter into the picture.

505

Mrs. Chisholm, what do you see as the role of the legislature now with respect to Title IX?

Chisholm: I think the role of the legislature is to monitor the implementation of Title IX. But I personally cannot see the legislative bodies implementing, enforcing, or monitoring Title IX until there is a clearcut understanding of the legislation by those who are in positions of authority and have the power to see that the policies are carried out.

Holly Knox: Shirley, as you mentioned, there's a major assault on Title IX's coverage of athletics, backed by the male college establishment. We've had some very damaging amendments introduced recently, which have been aimed at Title IX, and I'm sure there will be more. To whom in Congress can we look to lead the fight to defend women's rights under Title IX?

Chisholm: To be very truthful, we have to look to the women on the House side. I don't know to whom we look in the Senate. I think there are many senators who, on the basis of their past patterns of political behavior, have indicated a clear interest and concern with issues pertaining to women. We have to look to Senators Bayh and Ken-

Congresswoman Shirley Chisholm

nedy — those gentlemen who have always indicated by their behavior and by their actions that they have a commitment to women's rights.

An unfortunate thing happened recently on the Hill. A few months ago many college coaches from all over the country came down and got the gentlemen's ears — they got the "old-boy" network going. It is very hard to get around that sort of thing. The women on the House side will have to be very persuasive and will have to find techniques to convince the gentlemen that this is an issue that deals with human rights and equal rights. I have found that unless we are able to convince them in two specific ways — that economically something is going to happen and that constitutionally this is a basic right — other tactics don't usually work.

We, as seventeen women in the House, find it difficult to go up against all these men especially when men have been the lobbyists, have been the male presidents, and have been the male coaches. It becomes very difficult. But we have handled the ball in the House, and although few in number, we have succeeded. It's not easy, but we accept the challenge.

What exactly is Congress's role in appropriating funds for Title IX?

Chisholm: I foresee the role of Congress as appropriating the necessary funds to carry out the intent of the Title IX regulation. Of course, we have to remember that again the Appropriations Committee and the subcommittees are headed by gentlemen — gentlemen who may or may not be sympathetic or have any empathy for women's issues. We also have a great deal of lobbying to do with the appropriate committees.

Leslie Wolfe: I feel I should interject something here as the new Director of the Women's Educational Equity Act Program. As you all know, there is a new mandate to that program, a new authorization. Any appropriation over $15 million is automatically targeted primarily to local school districts and local groups, and to institutions of higher education, to fund projects that they develop themselves to implement Title IX. If the Congress were able to appropriate more than $15 million in 1981, we could begin the process of awarding grants for local Title IX activities. That would be a kind of appropriation for Title IX that is not earmarked for Title IX enforcement. Instead, it really focuses on the need to involve the local school districts in caring about Title IX implementation. It means they will have to begin thinking about the kinds of projects they need to develop for themselves and planning specific activities related to Title IX compliance. Then we will hold out the promise of a few dollars to help them. We hope that it will be an effective mechanism for ensuring compliance with Title IX, going beyond compliance with the "letter" of the law to compliance with the "spirit" of the law.

Chisholm: I know that Secretary Califano put together a team out of the Office for Civil Rights — I have to call it a "road show" for want of a better term — to visit different campuses to talk with the presidents and coaches, to get a feeling about what was happening. This had to be done as a result of the furor that developed around Title IX, and I was wondering whether a report is ready.

Cindy Brown: I was the one whom Secretary Califano charged with leading that series of visits to a number of universities to look at how their athletic programs worked.

507

5

Particularly, we looked at what steps they've taken to develop their women's athletic programs and how the proposed athletic policy, which we published in December, would actually work in practice at a number of diverse institutions. We also talked with college officials about possible revisions in that proposal.

Mary Jolly: Cindy, can we have on record the eight universities you visited?

Brown: They were Duke University, University of California at Los Angeles, Stanford University, Ohio State University, University of Richmond, Lincoln University in Missouri, Villanova University, and the University of Maryland. I don't know how familiar you are with the range of universities this list represents, but they're very different. Some are private, some are public. They offer different kinds of academic programs. They vary in size, in the nature of their athletic programs, and in how those athletic programs are funded.

Every university we visited has taken major steps in upgrading their women's athletic programs. Some have done more than others. The schools that have big, successful programs for men tend to be the ones that are making the greatest efforts in developing programs for women. And they seem committed to developing their women's programs to the same level of competition and excellence as their men's. That's not to say that, even at those schools that are doing a lot, there aren't some problems that need to be dealt with. There are problems with coaches' salaries; the basic notion of equal pay for equal work has not been universally followed in athletic programs at our universities. There are also problems in recruiting. While women's programs have been developed quickly, I'd say that the effort to recruit highly skilled women athletes has lagged behind. At some of the schools I visited there are serious problems in scholarship equity. As Mrs. Chisholm said, direct benefits to students, like scholarship aid, affect their whole educational and economic futures as well as their abilities to excel in athletics.

Chisholm: I think college presidents and a few coaches became quite perturbed over Title IX because they saw it primarily in terms of the fact that women were going to be invading their territory. They didn't even take it a step further, which is what I did with them. I said, "All right, if it's a possibility that you feel women are going to be invading your territory, you haven't even thought about black women, who also should be able to benefit from some of these scholarships. They're at the very bottom of everything, and here's an opportunity for them not only to get an education, but also to become involved in the sports program of a particular university." Many of them smiled rather sheepishly. I persuaded some of them. I don't know how effective that persuasion was, nor how long it's going to last.

Brown: I think one of the indications of discrimination in athletics is that so many women who have been able to excel have done it through their parents' help. The middle-income kids have been able to find the resources outside the high schools and the colleges to develop their skills, whereas low-income women, often minority women, have not received that kind of assistance because their families don't have the economic means to go outside the public institutions. You can see that minority women are not present in large numbers in intercollegiate athletic programs, and that's another indication that there is discrimination in intercollegiate athletics.

Mrs. Chisholm, what do you think people at the local level can do to help the seventeen women in the House of Representatives?

Chisholm: I have come to the conclusion that in order to secure equity of employment and academic opportunities for women in this country there is a necessity for more women to be in the legislature. To the extent that there are more women in the legislative bodies, women's issues and priorities will be given real consideration. The gentlemen are usually so terribly busy with other kinds of issues that the fact that women do not have equity doesn't even enter some of their minds. And so I feel that it is important that women run for public office on the city level, the state level, and on the national level.

The seventeen of us now in the Congress have done fantastically well ever since we pulled ourselves together into a women's caucus. In this caucus we have the most conservative woman to the most progressive woman. But we have found common avenues and common instruments that bind us together on women's issues. We plan our strategies, just like the gentlemen plan their strategies. We parcel out certain gentlemen to certain women legislators on the basis of their personalities. We have a fantastic time; we're few in number, but we have a lot of fun. Just as the Civil Rights Act and the Voting Rights Act made the Fourteenth Amendment a reality in the twentieth century, I happen to believe that Title IX and the ERA will make equal rights a reality for women in the twentieth century.

Knox: One line of argument used against Title IX on specific issues, but also used against Title IX in general, is the local-control or states-rights argument. I hear echoes of the argument the southern governors and the southern white establishment used in the fifties and sixties to fight civil rights legislation—"leave us alone, we know best." What do you think of that issue and the way that argument is being used now?

Chisholm: Oh, yes, we hear that argument in the cloak room where the gentlemen are constantly saying the federal government is entering into too many spheres of our lives. The states-right versus federal-rights issue becomes a real excuse for persons not doing the moral thing in a presumably democratic society. I think what we constantly have to try to do is to remind these gentlemen that if we had depended solely upon the states for black people to acquire basic civil rights in this country, we never would have gotten them. If it were not for the federal government intervening to protect the rights of all the people in this nation, this nation would not be what it is today. Some of the gentlemen don't like to hear that argument, but that is the truth, and that's what we have to emphasize.

Wolfe: We especially hear the states-rights argument in education because education has always been reserved to the states, and there's a sacredness about the state and local district's right to control education. Traditionally, the federal role in education has been to provide funding to the states to achieve certain national purposes. The current federal purposes, in terms of access, equality, and desegregation, are making some of the states uncomfortable. But, nonetheless, they are at least as important as the national purpose that was served by, for example, the National Defense Education Act Programs. We keep hearing that argument regularly and, of course, with the athletics issue in Title IX, it's becoming a good deal more strident. I think we need to

509

7

... women just cannot give up fighting for their rights, whether it's on an economic, social, political, or academic level ... women have to become revolutionaries.

---

persuade the states, partly by giving them a few dollars, that indeed this national purpose is their own. It's what the Congress tried to do with the Vocational Education Act. It's a very painful, difficult issue.

Chisholm: It's very interesting to me that even though the number of women in college athletics has risen almost 400 percent between 1971 and 1976, some legislators don't even look at that statistic. It shows a remarkable insensitivity and lack of attunement to the specific and unique needs of 52 percent of the population of this country that is female. This lack of sensitivity and understanding has caused women to move out to develop the women's movement. We realized that we could not rely on the gentlemen to recognize that we are totally, 100 percent, human beings. But it has been very interesting to me that the remarkable increase in the percentage of women entering athletics for a period of four or five years didn't even cross the minds of these gentlemen who run the universities. Perhaps this is a barrier we have to look at.

Wolfe: I also think we might be able to persuade university administrators that it's to their advantage to serve women students, since enrollments in higher education are consistently declining, with two exceptions — older students and women students. If the universities and the small colleges wish to survive, they must start serving the needs of that population.

Mrs. Chisholm, since you have to leave, do you have any final statement you want to make?

Chisholm: The final statement I have to make is that women just cannot give up fighting for their rights, whether it's on an economic, social, political, or academic level. We must remember the old adage that God helps those who help themselves. We have to remember that the way into the corporate boardroom is usually through the locker room.

Wolfe: Do you remember several years ago in a speech you said that women must become revolutionaries? I have always been grateful to you for saying so succinctly what many of us believe.

Chisholm: Yes, women have to become revolutionaries.

Thank you very much, Mrs. Chisholm. Going back to when Congress first passed Title IX in 1972, we'd like to talk briefly about the three years it took HEW to write the implementation guidelines. Why was there such a long delay between the passage of Title IX and the final draft of the regulation in 1975?

Knox: I think the reason is very simple. The people who ran HEW were afraid of Title IX. They were afraid of the controversies that they knew would arise over Title IX, and, in classic bureaucratic fashion, they buried it in the hope that it might go away.

8

At that time the issues that were talked about as the most explosive were things like fraternities and sororities. People in the Office for Civil Rights and the Secretary's Office often were so afraid of those issues that they preferred simply to do nothing. It was a year after the enactment of Title IX before the first comprehensive draft of the regulation was circulated. The Office for Civil Rights sat on it for a full year. Finally, Congress did pass an amendment that exempted fraternities and sororities, and I think that took some of the pressure off.

Jolly: I think that we have to keep in mind that those people who are appointed by the President to be the directors of these agencies, like the Secretary of HEW, and all of the other political appointees, really do not have that much power. You're dealing with a bureaucracy that is overwrought and uncoordinated. Our government usually isn't run by the President and the Cabinet. It's usually run by all the people who are below them. There is so much bureaucratic red tape that if the people below don't want to do the work required, a program can easily be scuttled. You know, it's very easy to pull the plug on a President or on a Cabinet Secretary, very easy. If you have an agency like HEW that is so large—it's the largest in our national government—you have a lot of people in mid-level and upper mid-level positions who can very easily just not do their jobs and scuttle a project for years and years. And so that's another reason why you don't get a lot of things done.

When President Carter took office a couple of years ago, there were over 1,400 sex-discrimination complaints filed with HEW that had not been investigated. There were also 800 unanswered letters. So you can see that the working folks weren't doing their jobs, and by not doing their jobs, they impeded the whole progress of civil rights and equal rights for both men and women. Califano requested and received from Congress more than 800 new positions. The agency was reorganized to assure consistency in enforcement and better management. Civil rights attorneys were assigned to each of the ten regional offices to provide immediate support and collaboration on cases.

Mary Kaaren Jolly

511

Knox: I couldn't disagree more that the problem was ever staff, money, or organization. In the first four years of Title IX, HEW received only six complaints per investigator per year, including race, sex, and national-origin discrimination complaints. That is hardly an overwhelming case load for that staff. They had plenty of staff in the beginning. The addition of 800 staff people was never necessary to enforce Title IX. The problem was that there was no political will to use those staff people to investigate and resolve cases. In the first four years of Title IX, HEW investigators resolved only three-tenths of one complaint per investigator per year. Why? It was not inefficiency, although that agency has been one of the most inefficient bureaucracies. It is because at the top levels, the leadership of HEW would not allow those cases to be resolved. They would not issue rulings saying that certain practices were in violation of the law. It wasn't really the fault of the investigators. Their hands were tied, and they were tied all up and down the line.

Jolly: I think one thing that we can never forget is that this whole process is going to take the efforts of men as well as women, because we're going to have to work for years and years to get women legislators in key positions on appropriations, judiciary, and education committees before they can do anything. No matter how many women from now until twenty years from now are elected, they still won't be in positions of power in Congress. We're not going to win this thing just with women. I think that we cannot forget the men we're going to need in order to help women get one step ahead. I've never believed that just because a woman is a judge, a lawyer, a social worker, a psychologist, or an educator, that you're going to get something for women's rights. I've seen too many women in powerful positions who are not ERA people.

Wolfe: I think one of the things you said, Mary, about bureaucrats, is generally true. However, if we go back to the "olden days" when the regulations were being drafted, it was just the opposite. As I understand it, in HEW, orders came down from the very top, from the Secretary's office, to bureaucrats to just "cool it" on Title IX. I have been told that then-Secretary Weinberger asked, "What is this? What are we doing here?" It's my sense, from having been both a political appointee and a "bureaucrat," that quite often the real problem is at the top, as Holly said. The same bureaucrats are in HEW now as were there during the Nixon Administration. The new layer on top of them has been able to move and shape them a little bit, which is why Cindy has had so much success in getting letters answered and the backlog of complaints reduced.

We're talking about two different things here. First, we're talking about the Title IX regulations that implement the statute. We're also talking about the policy interpretation issued by the Office for Civil Rights last December on intercollegiate athletics. This policy interpretation covers only one area of Title IX — intercollegiate athletics. It does not cover ordinary physical education classes in elementary and junior high schools. It also doesn't cover a lot of other important issues which the regulation does. One thing we were concerned about in the United States Commission on Civil Rights was the fact that there was very little attention given to using Title IX to eliminate sex bias in the schools. One example of that is the passage in the preamble to the regulation about textbooks and curriculum.

Leslie R. Wolfe

Could you expand on the textbook and curriculum issue?

Wolfe: Well, textbooks and curriculum were not covered by the regulation.

They're excluded?

Wolfe: HEW excluded textbooks from the regulation because of alleged First Amendment problems.

So we have no legal recourse for textbooks that are blatantly sexist?

Wolfe: Absolutely not, under the current Title IX regulation.

Knox: That depends on an interpretation in court. Let me give a little bit of history on that issue. We were talking before about the tone of decision making, and this is a very interesting case study. Textbook discrimination was one of the main issues women's groups had been looking at before Title IX passed. It was also one of the few issues concerning the rights of elementary and secondary students included in the

513

11

hearings on Title IX. So it was an issue Congress had addressed. Despite that, HEW excluded textbooks from its regulation. The argument was that it was a First Amendment issue. That was not true. HEW never defended that position legally. It was a political decision.

The issue is not whether an individual has the legal right to read any book that he or she wants to, nor whether a publisher has the legal right to publish the book. The issue is whether public school boards can be required to choose nonsexist textbooks. The courts have consistently said that parents and students do not have a right to use any textbook that they want in a public school: In fact, the Supreme Court has said that a school board can take certain books out of the school library. School boards act as censors, they do select the textbooks that are to be used in the schools, and they have a right to do that. The issue is simply whether the federal government can ask them, as a condition for getting federal money, to include certain criteria in their selection process.

Wolfe: Now, however, under the Title IX regulation, you cannot say that a school district is in noncompliance with Title IX if it imposes sexist or racist materials on students. This is unfortunate and, I think, violates the "spirit" of the law.

Knox: The decision was made because one influential college president from the same state as the Secretary of HEW wrote a letter to the Secretary protesting the coverage of textbooks. Secretary Weinberger had already approved a draft of the regulation that included a provision covering textbooks, asking school districts to review their textbooks and to make sure they were not sex-biased. No federal standards. He had approved that. He got a letter from the president of Stanford University expressing shock and horror at the intrusion into academic freedom. The orders came down immediately from Secretary Weinberger that there was to be no such provision in the regulation, and that was that.

Wolfe: That's the operation of the old-boy network.

Knox: I'd like to tell one other anecdote about the decision-making process in HEW when this regulation was taking shape. The internal debates in 1974-75 on the proposed regulation were carried out chiefly by those who were special assistants and assistants to the heads of a variety of HEW agencies and units. Most of these people were women—they were not all feminists, but they were women. When the crunch came and the final decisions had to be made about what was going to be published in the Federal Register, those decisions were made at a meeting with the Secretary and his senior officials. At that meeting, staff members of those senior officials were barred. That was virtually unprecedented; the instructions were "no staff." That meant that the room held seven men and not a single woman, and that's the reason they did it. When they sat down to hash out what was really going to go into the regulation, they did not want any women in the room.

Why did HEW accept complaints before the regulation was issued on Title IX, and what happened to the complaints that were filed betwen 1972 and 1975?

Brown: As soon as the statute was passed, the law went into effect. Usually an agency will enforce a law if it's clear on its face. I believe HEW determined that there was not enough guidance in the statute of law, so they accepted complaints and just held them until the regulation was final. Unfortunately they never really did mount a comprehensive enforcement program on Title IX. We have now nearly eliminated our complaint backlog with the exception of some problems involving intercollegiate athletics. We are investigating and issuing letters and negotiating settlements in physical education on the elementary and secondary level and in interscholastic athletics and coaches' salaries at the secondary level. But we're not investigating complaints in the intercollegiate athletic area; we're waiting until our athletic policy is out in final form.

The other area in which we've had significant difficulty is Title IX employment, where at least eight district courts and three courts of appeal have ruled that we do not have jurisdiction. This has caused tremendous problems, because institutions have refused to negotiate with us. In some instances, they have refused to let us investigate complaints.

What we're doing is taking an approach under Title IX that we are required by statute to take under Title VI. In 1964, Title VI limited jurisdiction on employment discrimination to those areas where we could show that by discriminating against employees of an institution, you were directly, or at least demonstrably, discriminating against the beneficiaries—in the case of school systems, the students. It works somewhat differently in the sex-discrimination area than in the race-discrimination area, because some pools of employees are largely made up of women—school teachers, for example. In such cases, we're going to have to show a systemic or class violation, discrimination against a class of teachers or administrators. We think by definition that class discrimination is discriminatory against students. It's going to be harder in the university area. It's going to be very hard to show that discrimination against one woman who was denied tenure has discriminatory effect on students.

Wolfe: What you will be able to show is a pattern in every school district in the country, in which most classroom teachers are women and most of the administrators are men—the people who run the schools in this country are white men and that's true in every school district in the country.

Jolly: Congress and the Office for Civil Rights have turned down the NCAA's attempts to exempt football at least four times, and now we're going for a fifth or sixth time.

Wolfe: When Weinberger did introduce the regulation to the Congress, an attorney for the NCAA said, in an hysterical way, "This will be the end of intercollegiate football as we know it!" The *Washington Star* wrote an editorial in which they said, "Not a bad idea."

Also, speaking as someone concerned about education, I think the attitude toward athletics is one of the most damaging in our schools. Children are encouraged to believe that if they cannot be a football hero, they can't be athletes, and that they are failures. There is the sense in the schools that the emphasis ought to be on competitive athletics rather than on lifetime physical fitness and physical-education activities. Individual sports like swimming, things you can do yourself, are ignored. We learn team playing in the most vicious and malicious ways. Women do not, of course, but the men do. Quite often one sees the legacy of that in the operation of both the Congress and

515

13

Cynthia G. Brown

the Administration. Team-playing means something very negative in a lot of ways. I think that if we were to end intercollegiate athletics as we know it, we might be able to substitute something a little more humane and equitable that would also be educationally valuable.

Jolly: It would definitely be a little healthier.

14

You have to ask serious questions about values in this country when a major subcommittee chairman of the House of Representatives can say that if it comes down to a fight between football and women: "I'm sorry, ladies, but women are going to lose."

Knox: Football has become the essence of the macho mystique. You have to ask serious questions about values in this country when a major subcommittee chairman of the House of Representatives can say that, if it comes down to a fight between football and women, "I'm sorry, ladies, but women are going to lose."

Wolfe: Football prepares men to become president and chairman of the board at General Motors, senator from such-and-such a state, or secretary of a department. The imagery of team-playing is used in the operation of departments, and sports images govern our thinking too much.

Brown: I have to disagree with you a little bit, Leslie. The discipline and opportunity to excel at something, like highly competitive athletics, should also be available to women. There are a lot of negative things about team competition in certain sports, but there are also positive things, and I think we have to take a balanced view. There should be lots of different kinds of educational and athletic opportunities in our higher education system open to women, and women ought to have the same chance to participate and to get coaching that will allow them to excel. It's important for any individual to realize the heights of his or her ability, whether academic or athletic. These things are all related to self-concept and to your ability to function successfully in a wide variety of areas. Women really haven't had that opportunity.

Given the history of enforcement problems, what's happening now? We've talked about clearing up the complaint backlog—how do these cases get cleared up? To our knowledge, HEW has never withdrawn federal funds. How do you resolve these cases?

Brown: We receive many, many complaints. They're increasing in magnitude tremendously. As soon as we receive a complaint, we acknowledge it and schedule an investigation. We are obligated to complete the investigation 105 days after we've received it. After we issue a "letter of finding" we are obligated to try to negotiate a voluntary resolution of the problem within ninety days. If we are not able to negotiate a settlement within those ninety days, then we have an additional thirty days to initiate enforcement action. In the vast majority of the investigations we undertake, whether they're complaints or compliance reviews, we initiate on our own, we are able to get a voluntary settlement. We have a higher level of findings of violation in the Title IX area, I think, than in any other.

Jolly: How many investigators do you have?

Brown: We have twelve or thirteen hundred.

Jolly: How many cases does each investigator handle each year?

517

Brown: Over twelve investigated cases. We have sent notices to about five districts for failure to comply with Title IX. There were two for failure to file Title IX assurances, and there were two where we initiated enforcement proceedings. Both were engaged in employment discrimination and both have gone into Federal Court and enjoined the proceedings.

Can you explain what it means to initiate enforcement proceedings?

Brown: When we determine that attempts to voluntarily settle the case have not succeeded, we send them two documents. One is a notice of an opportunity for a hearing. They're contacted about a hearing date before an impartial administrative-law judge. He or she makes a ruling, and there are several appeal opportunitites to an HEW reviewing authority. From the reviewing authority, it goes to the Secretary to make a decision about fund termination. At any time an institution can appeal under the federal court system. We also send what's called the deferral letter. We defer new funds, which means that during the course of the administrative hearing process and the appeals process, an institution cannot receive additional federal funds.

How often have you taken these actions of either terminating funds or sending a deferral letter?

Brown: As an old civil rights advocate, I used to be highly critical of the Office for Civil Rights for not initiating enforcement proceedings or terminating federal funds with the kind of frequency it did in the sixties when approximately 200 school districts lost their federal funds over southern school desegregation, and another 600 or so had enforcement proceedings initiated against them. Right now there's only one school system that has had its federal funds terminated—a school district in Michigan which is failing to desegregate.

I'm sorry I don't have the figures with me today about the number of enforcement proceedings we've initiated. But, generally, in my view, the Office for Civil Rights has been very successful in negotiating settlements. We've made major findings of violation in vocational education, in physical education, and in extracurricular activities in elementary schools in which we've been able to negotiate settlements. I don't think anything has been as difficult to achieve through voluntary negotiation as school desegregation was in the South.

We do find now that we are not able to negotiate compliance in employment areas under Title IX. We could initiate hearings in thirty or forty employment cases tomorrow, but it would be foolish because school systems have gone to court and enjoined us and won. We don't have one court ruling in our favor about Title IX employment jurisdiction, but we've been able to negotiate compliance in almost all other Title IX areas. I think it's going to be interesting to see what happens in athletics. We do have a case now that we're close to winding up involving admission to a graduate school, and I hope we take action very soon. That would be a very important issue.

Jolly: Cindy, don't you and Holly believe that the use of federal funds is an effective mechanism to get schools to comply? Or do you feel there might be better mechanisms?

Brown: I don't know that Holly and I agree. I think the federal-fund termination sanction is extremely important and can be very effective. I do not feel it is too harsh a sanction. In my two and a half years at the Office for Civil Rights I do not feel that any decision has been made because of the feeling that such a sanction is too harsh.

Knox: I think cutting off funds is the only way to get school districts and colleges to stop discriminating against women or anybody else. There's no evidence that they will act for any other reason except under court order, under massive monetary damages, or under the threat of losing federal money. Clearly it works; that was the way the back of the dual school system in the South was broken. Although the 1954 Supreme Court decision said school systems must desegregate, desegregation did not happen until Congress passed the 1964 Civil Rights Act giving the government that weapon. It took that weapon to make it happen; it's going to take that weapon to make it happen for women in education.

We've talked a lot about past problems with enforcement, now we'd like you to comment on whether things have changed. Are the obstacles still the same? Is it still bad will on the part of people in power? Or do you think different forces are operating now?

Wolfe: I think a lot of the same things are still operating and will continue to operate. I think Holly and Cindy are right that to promote the possibility of real enforcement, fund termination is the only effective sanction. There's still a great fear of change, especially in times of possible recession and inflation. As unemployment gets higher, there will be a desire to keep women somewhat limited, very similar to what happened in the fifties—you know, back to the hearth and out of the factory—because there were too many returning veterans who needed jobs. That policy was supported by a tremendous ideological and media blitz, and similar things may happen again. I think we've gone too far to stop, though. But the obstacles in terms of attitudes and consciousness will continue to exist; the economic situation makes it even more difficult. For example, we have limited slots in vocational education, and we are asking for them to be open to women, to minorities, and to handicapped persons—people who have traditionally been excluded. There's a good deal of resistance to this based on economic realities as well as on simple sexism and racism.

Brown: Technical assistance, like the Women's Educational Equity Act Program, is important to help institutions comply, but I agree with Leslie that it has to go with a strong enforcement program. WEEA is an important source of HEW funds that can help in Title IX enforcement.

Knox: As long as decisions are made at the federal level, the state level, and the local level predominantly by men, we are going to have to struggle to win equal rights for women. It will be interesting to see the effect of having a woman, a black woman, as Secretary of HEW, and whether she will be a more sympathetic ear to the cries for equal rights for women under Title IX and other issues. The last Secretary of HEW, despite his push to show better results from the Office for Civil Rights from a management point of view, has been notoriously unsympathetic to equal rights for women and has personally been, to my mind, the main obstacle at HEW for the last two-and-one-half years.

519

17

You're hopeful?

Knox: Naturally, I'm hopeful. We'll see what will happen. Also, Carter has announced a shift of power towards the White House. He is trying to consolidate power in the White House and particularly in the hands of Hamilton Jordan, who is best known to the American public for doing rude and offensive things to women. So we'll see what influence that has.

Does anyone else want to comment on the question about obstacles?

Wolfe: If we look at what has happened to the consciousness of the country in the last ten years, we might want to feel a little more optimistic. I'm always accused of being too optimistic, but, indeed, the consciousness of the country is changing. Not the powerful people, not the people who, as Holly says, run the government and so on, but regular folks in the media. We don't see "women's libbers" in the media, we see the word "feminist" used with a certain amount of respect. These are small things that are significant. A few weeks ago there was an article in the *Washington Post* about the high school boys who were members of Future Homemakers of America. These seventeen-year-old adolescents said remarkably feminist things. This could not have happened five, six, or seven years ago. I think Title IX is largely responsible, at least in educational circles, and so is WEEA — which has funded numerous activities which have increased public awareness of sex-equity issues.

Knox: We're talking about signs of progress and where we've had progress and where we haven't. I'd like to give you a summary of that. The greatest area of progress in the schools as far as women's opportunities are concerned has been in sports. We've seen a tremendous explosion of sports opportunities for girls. I see sports as a very important frontier for women. In 1972, when Title IX passed, for every one girl on a high school interscholastic team there were twelve boys. Now the ratio is down to two-to-one male-to-female. Women are now 33 percent of the high school students in interscholastic sports, a tremendous rate of progress.

In two other areas, though, we've seen virtually no progress, and they are very important. One is in vocational education where we've seen only token changes. There has been virtually no change in the last seven or ten years in the percentage of girls training for traditionally male occupations. Today PEER has just finished an analysis of state data on vocational education and we found that only 11 percent of the students in traditionally male vocational courses are women. The biggest change has been in the movement of boys into traditionally female areas, such as home economics. There is no comparable movement of girls into traditionally male vocational courses.

The second area where we've seen virtually no progress has been in the crucial area of who runs the schools. Eighty-eight percent of the school administrators in this country today are men. More than 65 percent of the teaching force is female. Most administrators come from the ranks of teachers. We have not begun to crack that and, until we do, we're going to have the same struggle in every school district in the country to try to get school administrators to deal with the issue of women's rights. Since 1972, the increase of women administrators has been less than 1 percent.

Jolly: It's interesting to note that seven years ago when Title IX was enacted, women had one percent of the total athletic budget. Now it's about 21 percent, even though the participation of women in the sports area has increased so dramatically. And yet, the men's athletic budget over those same seven years has risen 65 percent, despite little change in the number of men going into athletics.

Leslie, could you describe what you've called the three-tiered approach toward Title IX and its implications for the future?

Wolfe: Congress essentially enacted a triple strategy. The first part, of course, is Title IX, a civil rights statute that prohibits sex discrimination. Sex discrimination is defined differently from sex stereotyping and sex bias, and is a very specific legal concept. The second part of the strategy is the Women's Educational Equity Act. It is a specific program geared to provide funds for eliminating sex bias, stereotyping, and discrimination in schools, colleges, universities, and vocational education. It is a tiny program compared to the total education budget, but it is the only program that provides funds exclusively to try to eliminate sexism in education.

The third congressional strategy is exemplified by the recent amendments to the Vocational Education Act. The Education Amendments of 1976 established many requirements for state vocational education programs regarding sex equity, elimination of sex bias, discrimination and stereotyping, and the provision for vocational education resources to disadvantaged inner-city youth. In other words, the third strategy would "mainstream" sex-equity concerns into all major Federal education programs.

(left to right) Cynthia G. Brown, Neal Baer, Holly Knox, Lauri Perman, Mary Kaaren Jolly, Congresswoman Shirley Chisholm, Leslie R. Wolfe, and Donna Hulsizer.

521

One of the crucial roles legislators can play is to protect Title IX from amendments that would weaken it. How vulnerable is Title IX to amendments that could weaken it? What can be done to see that Title IX remains intact?

Jolly: Most of our civil rights laws have been quite vulnerable, especially at the appropriations level. Whenever we try to provide funds to implement these laws, they're constantly gutted by people on both sides, House and Senate, who don't want them implemented. They vote against funds or try to attach riders onto the appropriations bill or any bill that happens to come down the road. We therefore need a strong grassroots effort from the same states that house these major universities. People need to write and call their senators and representatives in Congress to vote against erosions of Title IX and other civil rights acts.

One question that confuses many people is why the Equal Rights Amendment is needed and what the Equal Rights Amendment would do that Title IX would not do. Title IX is restricted to education, but could someone comment on the ways in which the ERA might also strengthen equal opportunity in education?

Wolfe: Title IX is merely a statute. The Equal Rights Amendment would provide the constitutional basis for all such statutes that provide equality for women. It provides a constitutional basis for determining whether laws or policies discriminate against women, which is why it is opposed so strongly. Under the ERA, women will be defined as full and equal participants in the life of the country, they will be defined by the Constitution as full citizens, and they will then see themselves and be seen as free and equal persons. It will not change Title IX. It will not make Title IX unnecessary because the ERA will never be a specific statute applying to specific federally funded programs.

Knox: Under the ERA we can count on the courts to be tougher than HEW has been under Title IX on a number of issues, for instance, athletics. We are no longer fighting for "half a loaf" in athletics for women. We're fighting over whether women are going to get a slice of the loaf. That is the issue that is being debated now. The courts have been stronger under the Fourteenth Amendment already and will be even stronger under the ERA on the athletics issue. For instance, in Pennsylvania, under a state ERA, we have a court ruling that school districts may not bar girls from playing contact sports with boys. That's much farther than HEW has gone under the regulation, and I think we'll see more rulings like that.

Jolly: One purpose of the Equal Rights Amendment is to avoid piecemeal legislation. Most of the nondiscrimination statutes were needed because we did not have an Equal Rights Amendment at the federal level.

Wolfe: It is true that at the federal level we have piecemeal legislation. Some people allege, "Well, now that you have Title IX, equal-credit opportunity, and an active fair-housing law, for example, you don't really need the ERA." But we do indeed, because we need to be included in the Constitution and need that constitutional support basis for equal-rights legislation and litigation.

We want to be clear about the roles of all three branches of government with respect to

Title IX and the rules of Congress, the Department of HEW, and the courts. Could someone expand on the role of the courts?

Brown: I think it's important to note that civil rights is a very controversial area in this country and that all branches of government get involved with it. Whether HEW enforcement is effective or not effective, Congress is going to debate the key civil rights issues. Athletics is going to be debated by the Congress whether HEW sends up its final policy officially or not. People should always be aware that Congress is going to consider these things over and over again with every new controversial issue. Actually, HEW has not had its appropriations cut for civil rights enforcement. What has been much more the case are amendments on authorization and appropriations bills which limit our enforcement power. The three branches are entwined. The courts have entered into the Title IX enforcement area now in an important way with the recent Supreme Court decision in the *Cannon* case.

Could someone describe the Cannon *case and its significance?*

Knox: The Supreme Court recently ruled under *Cannon* that there is a private right to sue under Title IX. That has been an issue for many years, and it's been debated in various ways in the courts. Now we have it from the Supreme Court that people are free to bring lawsuits under Title IX. It's terribly important. School districts and colleges will comply with court orders, for the most part, and insofar as we can get good,

Holly Knox

523

The more tightly controlled the Department of Education is by the education establishment, the less likely it is going to be to challenge that establishment in women's rights, civil rights, or any other issue.

strong court orders on equal rights in education, the *Cannon* case is going to be influential.

I note several reservations about the impact of that ruling, though. First of all, litigation is very expensive. I see no organizations right now that have a great deal of money to do extensive litigation under Title IX. Most private individuals cannot afford to sue and will not sue. Also, the Supreme Court has ruled rather consistently of late that the only discrimination that it recognizes to be unconstitutional is intentional discrimination. We've had the best court cases under the Fourteenth Amendment in areas like sports, where discrimination is absolutely blatant and unquestionable. When vocational courses are explicitly barred to girls, we can get somewhere under Title IX in the courts. But those practices have been on the decline since Title IX passed and the discrimination we're now facing is subtle and more difficult to prove.

Finally, we have the same problem in the courts that we have everywhere else—there are very few judges who are women. Male judges have a difficult time seeing sex discrimination. Not too long ago, the Supreme Court said that discrimination against pregnant employees is not discrimination against women. The fact that 100 percent of the employees who are disadvantaged are female has apparently nothing to do with it. That problem is repeated at all levels of the judiciary.

Would the creation of a Department of Education make any difference in Title IX enforcement?

Wolfe: Well, that depends. If the Department of Education bill gets out of conference and passes the House and the Senate with anti-civil-rights amendments, it will have a very serious negative effect on civil rights enforcement. If, however, a Department of Education bill passes which does not include those amendments, then there's a very good chance that the Department of Education, under vigorous leadership, could indeed do an extraordinarily effective job of Title IX enforcement.

Knox: Some of the opposition to the Department of Education has come from civil rights and women's rights organizations for this reason: civil rights enforcement in the federal government has always depended on taking money away from the educational establishment. That is always a problem because federal administrators are usually heavily influenced by the education establishment and don't like to take punitive action against it. A Department of Education is going to intensify that problem. In the long run, the Department of Education is going to be more tightly controlled by education interests than HEW has been. After all, HEW's leadership comes from many different places. The more tightly controlled the Department of Education is by the education establishment, the less likely it is going to be to challenge that establishment in women's rights, civil rights, or any other issue. So I think we have, over the long run, nothing but more trouble to look for from the Department of Education as far as civil rights and women's rights are concerned.

The NCAA claims that Title IX only covers federally funded programs, not institutions that receive the funds. Does the Office for Civil Rights agree with that interpretation?

Brown: We do not agree with that interpretation of jurisdiction for Title IX, and it comes up, not just in Title IX, but in all civil rights laws we enforce. We have an Office of General Counsel's legal opinion that defends our interpretation that athletic programs are an integral part of the educational offerings of our postsecondary system and are therefore covered by Title IX. It's not a matter of whether the program is directly financed by federal funds; that's not the principle of Title VI or Title IX. It has to do with an institution receiving federal funds for any of its programs on the theory that they are all integrally related to accomplishing its educational objective.

What can parents and teachers do at the local level to indicate their support for Title IX?

Wolfe: Enormous things can be done by parents and PTAs who are concerned about their children's futures. They can have an impact on the school board by electing feminists, whether male or female. They can urge their school boards to take action to ensure that, for example, curricula are not deliberately sexist and that the history of women and minorities is not omitted from textbooks.

They can put pressure on us, which we need desperately. They can see that their concerns for women's equality are conveyed to their local representatives in the state legislature and to their members of Congress particularly. Also, maybe more of the parents who get into the struggle for equity for their children will start running for office themselves. Why shouldn't they be members of the school board? Why shouldn't they run for the state legislature? Why shouldn't they become members of the Congress and continue that struggle?

What should a parent, child, or teacher do to file a complaint of sex discrimination in the schools?

Wolfe: Of course, there is the appropriate route of filing an official complaint under Title IX with HEW. I think that's always something that should be done, but I don't think anyone who has a complaint should stop there. They should probably mobilize support for whatever larger issues their complaint reflects.

Brown: They should also confront the institution that is discriminating against them. The best and fastest way to solve problems is to fight them at the local level.

Wolfe: One of the best ways they can confront the institutions is with a formal complaint. Once they have filed a formal complaint and have done a good analysis of the issues, then they can try to deal with the institution. One strategy is to say to the institution, "We would rather not have to go through all these administrative proceedings and we hope that we can work this out as reasonable adults together." But the complaint strategy always has to be part of it. A lot of cases are resolved at the local level when the principal of the school says, "Oh, dear me, I didn't know that. I'm sorry, let's fix that right away." That does happen.

525

Brown: Every institution is supposed to establish a grievance procedure for handling complaints of discrimination under Title IX. That does not have to be exhausted before a complaint can be filed with HEW, but it is an affirmative step that every institution must take.

We believe the public needs to be better informed about Title IX. Could you explain the role of PEER in disseminating Title IX information?

Knox: PEER is a privately financed advocacy group, part of the NOW Legal Defense and Education Fund, that works for equal rights for women in education. We serve many functions. We have been monitoring the federal government's role in either holding back progress or promoting it, and we have put pressure on the federal government to do more. In 1974, PEER drew together a group of feminists from a variety of national organizations to form the National Coalition for Women and Girls in Education. Since then, we have sought, very successfully, to bring together other national organizations and constituencies in this country who work for equal education for women and girls. We've published information for parents, teachers, and school administrators who are concerned about the issues.

PEER is beginning to organize community groups and parents to look at their own school districts and find out what the problems are. We have a local action kit called "Cracking the Glass Slipper" which helps community organizations work through what questions to ask. What does the law say? Where do you go for information to find out what your school district is doing? That's the first thing that local community people need to do. And then the second thing is, voters and taxpayers have to start standing up and saying, "We want equal education for our kids, male and female." When that happens, things are going to change and where that has happened, things have changed.

"The Ladies Want to Bring About Reform in the Public Schools": Public Education and Women's Rights in the Post-Civil War South

KATHLEEN C. BERKELEY

AS THE REGULAR monthly meeting of Memphis, Tennessee's Board of Education drew to a close on the evening of February 10, 1873, Judge J. O. Pierce, a new member, rose to his feet. Speaking in behalf of the city's corps of female teachers, the representative from the tenth ward introduced the following resolution:

Resolved, that it is the opinion of this board and will hereafter be its policy, that women employed as teachers in the Memphis city schools, are for the same services and in the same grade, entitled to the same salary as men employed as teachers.

Resolved, that the superintendent be appointed to a committee to prepare and report to this board at its next meeting, a schedule of salaries equalized upon the basis of the foregoing resolution for consideration.[1]

Pierce's petition neither shocked nor surprised his fellow board members. On at least one occasion during the last six years, a past superintendent and current board member included in his annual school report a recommendation to revise and upgrade the "disproportionate compensation" paid to women employed by the board.[2] Moreover, in recent months the women teachers had grown more vocal and persistent in communicating their dissatisfaction with the discriminatory wages they received to the board and to the public.[3]

Realizing that the issue could no longer be avoided, the board reluctantly

---

Ms Berkeley is a member of the History Department of the University of North Carolina at Wilmington.

voted to reserve its next public meeting for a full discussion of the judge's resolution. The ensuing debate would rock the very foundations of Memphis society by quickly spilling beyond the confines of the March meeting. In the weeks following the February board meeting Pierce and the women teachers continued to press their cause. The ground swell of support for the women's cause led several board members to suggest that the women teachers not show up at the March meeting unless they wished to lose their teaching positions. Heeding the advice offered, not a single female teacher attended the March meeting. Instead, the women sent a petition thanking Judge Pierce for supporting their cause.[4] Over the next four months a lengthy, emotionally-charged exchange of letters and editorials appeared in the *Memphis Appeal*. The controversy which the newspaper's editors dubbed the "Woman's Question" even drew heated responses from interested parties living in surrounding counties.[5]

The intensity of the arguments advanced either in favor of or in opposition to Pierce's resolution suggests that Memphians perceived the women's issue as much broader than a request for "equal pay for equal work." An editorial comment by the *Memphis Appeal* succinctly defined the dilemma the women teachers' request caused:

Arising out of the simple proposal that the women teachers of our public schools shall, for the same labor, receive the same wages as men, the discussion has widened, broadened, and deepened until it embraces the question of woman's capacity to enter the lists against men and sustain herself by successive competition.[6]

The women's demand for treatment and compensation equal to that which their male counterparts received, as well as the hostility which their demands engendered, were symptomatic of a society in transition. While the roles of women were changing rapidly in the post-Civil War South, societal expectations governing those roles remained static.[7] Viewed in this light, the controversy over the "Woman's Question' in Reconstruction Memphis illuminates the emerging conflict between the socioeconomic changes underway in the bluff city and the prevailing cultural and political norms.

Tracing the roots of this "revolution in the woman's sphere" one locates them embedded in the widening opportunities women experienced as a result of the war.[8] The Civil War, to paraphrase one historian, was fought in the front yard of Southern housewives.[9] Thus, it had an indelible effect on their lives. Responding to war-time "manpower" shortages, Southern white women committed themselves to the war effort. In so doing, they narrowed the gap between women's private domestic duties and their public civil obligations.[10] Middle and upper-class women not only assumed the management of family farms and businesses but also coordinated voluntary soldiers' and civilians' relief societies like the "Southern Mothers" which organized during the summer of 1861 in Memphis, Tennessee.[11] Meanwhile, laboring-class women combined self-preservation with civic responsibilities by entering the paid labor force as nurses and factory operatives.[12]

The Civil War represented more than a temporary crisis in the lives of Southern white women. Despite the scanty attention paid "to the ladies" in the well-tilled field of Civil War-Reconstruction history enough evidence exists to suggest that the economic and human war-losses forced abrupt and permanent changes in their lives.[13] In the aftermath of the war, Southern society witnessed a dramatic increase in the number of white women seeking gainful employment.[14] Anne Scott documented this trend in her study of Southern women published a decade ago.

In Virginia, for example, the total of 5,000 women in maufacturing in 1870 doubled by 1890 though the total population had increased by less than a third. In Mississippi 700 professional women were counted in 1870 and over 3,000 in 1890; a fourfold increase in a population which had increased only by 25 percent. Georgia had 5,000 women in manufacturing and mechanical jobs in 1870 and 12,000 in 1890; and so it went in the whole South.[15]

Tennessee too recorded an increase in the number of female breadwinners. In 1870, census enumerators listed a total of 45,402 women gainfully employed. By 1890 that number had increased to 80,582.[16]

In their search for work, many Southern women marketed traditional domestic skills. Native-born white women appeared most frequently on the census rolls as dressmakers, milliners, seamstresses, mantua makers, dairy-women, nurses, housekeepers, and hotel and boardinghouse matrons. Mill operators and clerks were two other occupational categories in which white women found employment. Black women largely remained in the same positions they had served under the institution of slavery: agricultural workers, laborers (not specified), cooks, laundresses, ironers, and servants.[17]

The striking increase in women entering the paid labor force coincided with the rapid proliferation of county, municipal and state public school systems across the post-war South.[18] Although public education for white children was not an innovation of Congressional Reconstruction, the constitutional and legal provisions which established tax-supported education for blacks revitalized and strengthened existing programs for whites.[19] Increased enrollment after the war necessitated the refurbishing of old dilapidated schools if not the building of new ones.[20] The abundant supply of women able to teach and in need of gainful employment allowed school boards to ease their strained budgets by hiring females and paying them roughly half the wages earned by male teachers.[21] Nonetheless, despite the wage disparities between men and women, each decade after the Civil War the number of Southern white women entering the field of teaching increased. By 1900 teaching had become the leading occupation for female breadwinners from the more "educated" classes.[22]

Public school administrators such as the Memphis, Tennessee Superintendent of Education, W. Z. Mitchell, justified the disproportionate wages paid to women upon two premises. First, men and women did not provide the same services even when they taught in the same grades. Second, and more important, the salaries paid to women were sufficient to maintain a competent corps of female teachers.

The physical separation of boys and girls in the grammar and secondary grades allowed school board members to argue that male and female teachers served different functions in the school system.[23] In the opinion of educators like Mitchell, boys were more difficult to control and educate than girls.

A school of boys at the intermediate period of youth—ten to twelve—requires a male teacher to govern it, as this age is more uncontrollable than when younger or older. At a more advanced age, an appeal may be successfully made to the judgment or honor, or pride of the pupil while the rod, held *in terrorem*, exerts the best effect upon *young America*.[24]

Men were needed to maintain order and serve as appropriate role models for young boys. Thus, "the positions in the corps assigned to male teachers are those which cannot be filled by females, and as a matter of course, the labor of the man is no more to be compred with that of the woman in the schoolroom than that of the sexes in other departments of labor."[25] Mitchell, for example, disapproved of substituting women for men in the boys' classrooms. When that happened, he claimed, not only the quality of education but also the management and order of the schools declined.[26]

Satisfaction with the caliber of the female teaching staff led public school administrators to conclude that the remuneration offered to women teachers was more than adequate.[27] Two factors supported this position. Relative to the wages women earned in other sectors of the labor force, teaching was a lucrative occupation. Competition for a teaching position was stiff for females, with more applicants than vacancies occurring at the anual July hiring sessions.[28]

At the same time, public school officials worried that teaching was not a profitable venture for ambitious men. The Memphis Board of Education, like others around the country, strove to be competitive with other professional and business occupations in order to entice "men with high attainments, moral worth and eminence"[29] into the teaching field. After a careful survey nation-wide in 1867, Memphis' ubiquitous Superintendent W. Z. Mitchell succinctly summed up the axiom governing male salaries:

The policy pursued in other cities in paying more than double to male teachers is founded on sound principle and the law of supply and demand. . . . Liberal salaries to your male teachers, will call to your service ability and enterprise, low salaries will give you only such as labor for anything and give in return a very low order of talent.[30]

In presenting his recommendations to the board to raise the salaries earned by men, Mitchell expressed some concern about the city's ability to attract and retain high caliber male teachers.

The salaries paid our male teachers are lower than in any other city of the same character where a system of free schools are [sic] supported with the regularity with which they are in Memphis. You may find a man at times out of employment who will consent to serve you at any price, but men of ability, such as you should elect, can earn more in business or another profession. A clergyman, physician or lawyer, if competent, can earn three or four times the amount [paid to male teachers] and the teacher will very soon leave your employ to engage in such activities as will be more remunerative.[31]

Did Superintendent Mitchell and those following him have cause to worry about the attrition of their male teaching staff? If the answer is yes, then was it because ambitious men viewed the teaching profession as a temporary stepping stone to more lucrative and satisfying ventures?

My analysis of the men hired by the Memphis public school system both before and after the Civil War lends some support to the interpretation offered above. Approximately two-thirds (68.8 percent) of the men hired between 1855 and 1860 taught in the public schools for one year, while the remaining third (31.2 percent) taught for only two consecutive years. Forty-four percent of the pre-war male teachers could be traced beyond their employment in the public schools. All of these men apparently found more "rewarding" occupations in Memphis. According to subsequent listings in the city directories, these former teachers found employment in the following areas: bookkeeper, portrait painter, cotton factor, a sawmill owner, a grocer, a principal/teacher in a private academy, and as superintendent of public instruction. During the post-war era, of the men hired between 1865 and 1875 three-fourths of them taught for only one year before leaving the field of teaching. Those men who remained in public education tended to assume supervisory positions.[32]

Memphis school officials' concern for improving the retention rate of male instructors led board members to vote consistently during the early post-war era to increase the wages paid to men at the expense of the women. During the 1868–69 school year, for example, men earned on the average of $111.25 per month as compared to the women's monthly average of $80.62.[33] Then in 1870, following the withdrawal of state revenues with the return of Southern Democrats to state government, the municipal school board gathered to pare down its annual expenditures.[34] The board scrapped construction of two new schools and reduced the teaching staff of the black schools from twenty-three instructors to eleven. The women teachers found their wages slashed to a monthly average of $68.11. Yet even during this period of retrenchment Colonel Leath, the current superintendent, recommended that board members vote to increase the wages paid to male teachers. The board complied: men's salaries reached an average of $123.57 during the 1870–71 school year.[35]

What factors accounted for the school board's ability to pursue a discriminatory salary policy which favored men over women? Why was it not until the 1870s that an organized, collective struggle by women for "equal pay for equal work" appeared in Memphis? After all, from its inception as a state-chartered institution in 1856, the public schools depended upon the city's "native daughters" to staff the classrooms.[36] Between 1855 and 1869 women comprised between two-thirds to three-fourths of the city's teaching corps. During the decade of the women's protest, those figures rose only slightly. Women accounted for approximately four-fifths of the public school instructors during the 1870s.[37]

The conjunction of two interrelated factors best explains the absence of an organized protest among women teachers in Memphis until the decade following the Civil War. First, although women comprised a majority of the teaching staff before the war they, along with their male counterparts, did not remain as permanent members of that paid labor force. Prior to 1860 roughly half (51.6 percent) of the female instructors taught for only one year in the public school system. Five of the thirty-one women hired by the school board between 1856 and 1860 taught for two consecutive years while slightly less than a third (32.2 percent) remained in the employ of the public schools for three consecutive years.[38] Although only a few more married women (56.2 percent) than single women (43.7 percent) engaged in public school teaching prior to the war, marital status significantly affected the longevity of a woman's teaching career. Over two-thirds of the married women left public education after one year while almost the same proportion of single women persisted in the teaching field for at least two to three years.[39] Second, the ready availability of new recruits when combined with the rapid turnover of female teachers undoubtedly inhibited collective action. The temporary nature of women's work made the women teachers either reluctant or unable to protest against the more privileged status of their male counterparts.[40]

The Civil War represented a watershed in the working lives of Southern white women. As previously noted, the number and percentage of women entering the paid labor force increased through each decade after the war.[41] At the same time, my analysis of the careers of women teachers in Memphis indicates that at least in one city, the Civil War radically altered working force participation among women of the educated classes. After 1865, women seeking gainful employment in the public schools did not view teaching as a temporary pastime. No longer a brief interlude in one's lifework, teaching became a career for women after the war; especially for those women who remained single. Thus, the city's first permanent teaching force would consist of unmarried women.[42]

Between 1865 and 1875 the demographic and labor force persistence patterns of women entering the teaching field in Memphis underwent a marked transformation from their pre-war configurations. In the postwar era, over three fourths (77.7 percent) of the females employed by the school board were single.[43] Not surprisingly, more single women persisted in the labor force than did married women. This fact, however, does not indicate that married women refrained from seeking steady employment. If one examines the persistence pattern of the married population, one finds that for every married woman who left the teaching field after one year, another one remained in the labor force for at lest five consecutive years.[44]

Overall, the persistence rate of women teachers in Memphis rose after the Civil War. Less than one-third (30.6 percent) of the eighty-eight women hired by the Memphis School Board between 1865 and 1875, left after one year. Of the roughly two-thirds (69.4 percent) persisting beyond that first year, almost half of the women taught consecutively for a period of two to four years. The other half remained with the school system anywhere from five to eight years. Finally, slightly over one-fourth (26.5 percent) of the female teachers corps persisted in the labor force for at least eight years.

What then enabled the women teachers in Memphis to overstep the bounds of female propriety during the 1872–73 school year by agitating for "equal pay for equal work?" By the early seventies, a significant body of women had been in the work force for several years. In 1870 women teachers collectively experienced first-hand the material consequences of their subordinate position in the teaching profession. That year in the interest of economy, the male school board had slashed the women's wages while simultaneously voting to increase the men's wages. More, however, than simply their common identity as helpless victims could sustain the women's protest throughout the winter of 1872 and the spring of 1873. The women teachers supported one another not only because their economic plight drew them together, but also because they formed a close-knit community bound by ties of friendship and family. Educated at Court Street Female High School, a significant number of women graduated and entered the teaching profession together after the war. Finally, their sense of sisterhood grew out of the fact that six local families had a combined total of twelve sisters as well as a mother-daughter team employed in the public schools.[45]

Arising out of the simple request that women, for the same work, are entitled to the same pay tha men receive, the controversy surrounding the "Woman's Question" bore only a slight resemblance to the original proposal. Opponents questioned whether women were mentally and physically capable of competing equally with men. This line of reasoning, as advanced by school board member G. W. F. Cook, argued that women were inferior to men. The female of the species, Cook proclaimed during the heat of the March debate, could perform no task equal to or better than a male save that of suckling babies! Women outside the home, Cook insisted, were interlopers who usurped the place and function of men.[46]

Proponents of the women's cause responded by disputing the doctrine of female inferiority and its corollary of male superiorty. Led by "sensible mothers and keen-eyed schoolmarms," according to the editorial wit of the *Memphis Appeal*, this group challenged male authority and ability by criticizing the school board's management of the public schools. Representatives from public female community as well as from female teachers offered the following suggestions in their four point reform program:

1. To organize the school board on the basis of equal representation by members of both sexes.

2. To pay teachers on the basis of merit and experience rather than on the basis of sex.
3. To institute a split session school-day to ease overcrowded classrooms which contributed to a decline in the quality of education.
4. A critique of the rote method of instruction currently in vogue with the board of education.[47]

Responding to the gibes that the women's reforms sought to dilute the authority and power of men, one spokeswoman wrote, "when men assume to themselves the whole management of school-rooms and school-children, they are plainly usurping the natural place of women and are pushing themselves into our peculiar sphere."[48] Thus, maternal experience and feminine instinct provided the fodder for the women's campaign against the exclusive right of men to wield power in the public arena.

Despite the support of scores of citizens and one of the two leading conservative Democratic newspapers, the school board voted against Pierce's resolution on April 14, by a three to two margin. Two reasons informed the majority report's conclusions which read in part, "at this time it was not expedient to disturb the present state of affairs pertaining to salaries."[49] Conducted by Superintendent H. S. Slaughter, a nation-wide survey of fifteen cities of comparable size and stature convinced board members that women teachers in Memphis received as much compensation as women teachers of other cities. And, in a blatant effort to negate the significance of the women's collective protest, an official spokesman for the board publicly stated that the board was not aware of any dissatisfaction with the wages presently received by women employed in the Memphis public schools.[50] The actions of the board in a private meeting scarcely a week after Pierce's resolution lost suggests that, contrary to the statement above, the board was well aware of female discontent with the present salary schedule. After threatening for months to dismiss anyone involved with the protest activities, the board summarily fired two women known for their association with the women's cause.[51]

An unknown number of women teachers and several of their supporters from the community-at-large made one last attempt during the 1872–73 school year to win the battle for equal pay. A week before the annual July board meeting where members would vote on the teaching staff, salary schedule and superintendent for the upcoming year, the following editorial appeared in the *Memphis Appeal:*

We are in receipt of several letters from persons connected with the public school system of Memphis and others who have a direct personal interest in them, advocating the election of Miss Clara Conway to the position of Superintendent of the Public Schools, and the only reason we have for rejecting them is their length. They all exceed the limits we have named for correspondence. To the election of Miss Conway to so high and responsible a position we can see no objection. She possesses all the ability requisite for it with the experience of several years as an educator [Clara Conway was principal of the Alabama Street schools for several years]. To the gentleness and refinement of a cultivated lady she invites all the firmness requisite to the director of our schools. . . .

We do not know a man in our city who can surpass her in fitness. If Miss Clara Conway will accept the position, she has the hearty support of the *Appeal* and we hope she will be elected.[52]

The effort to elect a woman as superintendent of the public schools collapsed and ended in failure. It arose, undoubtedly, more out of a determination to demonstrate a continued commitment to the women's cause than out of an attempt to pursue direct political action. The school board controlled both the nomination and election of the school superintendent. At the July seventh meeting, Clara Conway's name was not brought forth during the nominating procedures. Finally, not only were the women's protest activities of the past several months ignored, but also the board approved a new salary schedule which maintained the wage inequities based on gender.[53] Nonetheless, the call for a female superintendent was a brilliant tactical maneuver, for its failure exposed the absolute powerlessness of women to protect their interests as long as they lacked the right to participate in the electoral process.

The "equal pay for equal work" issue eventually was resolved in Memphis, but not because of an enlightened sense of justice which demanded equity in the market place. When school board officials met in July of 1878 to revise the salary schedule, the need to economize was uppermost in their minds. A series of calamities had struck Memphis during the five years since the teachers' protests and the city's tax base had begun to erode in response to municipal woes.[54] Confronted with a budget crisis, school board members took two steps towards equalizing teachers' salaries. Staff positions in the public schools were collapsed into the following categories—principal, high school teacher, grammar teacher, primary teacher, and supernumerary teacher—and all wages were lowered to the levels previously paid only to the women. Rank and salary were to apply equally to both white and black school systems.[55]

The salary reductions had the effect of removing any financial incentive for men to remain in the field of teaching. With amazing rapidity, men abandoned the profession and it became the domain of women. When contracts were handed out for the 1878–79 school year, only four men were hired to staff the white public schools and all of them were principals.[56] Of the forty-eight teachers employed in the white schools, thirty-seven were single women and the remaining eleven were married women. The city not only depended upon its native daughters to staff the public schools, but also provided for their education. Over half (25) of the teachers had graduated from the local high school.[57]

One final point. There is perhaps a wider political context within which one may view the women's struggle for equity in Memphis. Its larger historic significance lies in what it reveals about a burgeoning movement among Southern white women during the post-Reconstruction era. By the late 1870s,

Southern white women had begun to organize to obtain political rights in order to promote and secure their economic and familial concerns. By 1900 state suffrage associations proliferated across the South.[58] What factors had promoted this shift in consciousness?

In Memphis, the economic oppression female teachers suffered when combined with the school board's response to their demands politicized women both within the public school system and beyond in the wider community. Women awoke to the realization that they could not continue to rely upon the honesty and integrity of a few fair-minded men to safeguard women's interests. Prior to the controversy over the "Woman's Question," for example, Elizabeth Avery Meriwether and her sister-in-law, Lide Meriwether, were the lone voices in Memphis speaking out on a multitude of issues of vital concern to women.[59]

In the aftermath of the uproar over the teachers' demands, the Meriwether women carefully nurtured the budding interest in "women's issues" such as suffrage, temperance, married women's property rights, equity in the wage scale and liberal divorce laws. By the late seventies, Elizabeth and Lide Meriwether were conducting suffrage and temperance meetings in their respective parlors. These local societies became the springboards from which both women would launch successful state and national careers during the eighties in the National Women Suffrage Association and the Women's Christian Temperance Union.[60]

Thus, the 1872-73 debate over the "Woman's Question" in Memphis provides an important link between the "bold assertion of a handful of women" like the Meriwethers to a national suffrage organization during the last two decades of the nineteenth century.[61] Incidents like the teachers' protest in Memphis would lay the foundations for raising up a corps of women (the rank and file) interested in and committed to working collectively for women's rights. Thrust into the paid labor force for the first time after the Civil War, thousands of "respectable" Southern white women came face to face with the difficulties women encountered when they lost the "protection" of their fathers and husbands. The women's persistence in the market place challenged existing ideas about what constituted women's proper sphere. The full implication of this change in consciousness would be felt in 1920 by men and women when Tennessee's ratification assured the successful passage of the Nineteenth Amendment.[62]

NOTES

1. Memphis, Tennessee, *Memphis Appeal*, February 11, 1873.
2. W. Z. Mitchell was Superintendent of Public Instruction for the 1866-67 and 1868-69 school years. From 1871 to 1874 he represented ward nine of the school board. The following men, all members of the board during the year of the women's protest were board members during Mitchell's tenure as superintendent: Michael Gavin, H. C. Connell, and H. S. Slaughter. See the following annual reports of the Memphis Board of Education: *The Fifteenth Annual Report of the Board of Education of the City of Memphis, Tennessee, 1866-67* (Memphis, Tennessee, 1867); the *Seventeenth Annual Report of the*

Board of Education for the City of Memphis, Tennessee, 1868-69 (Memphis, Tennessee, 1969); the *Twentieth Annual Report of the Board of Education for the City of Memphis, Tennessee, 1871-72* (Memphis, Tennessee, 1872); the *Twenty-First Annual Report of the Board of Education of the City of Memphis, Tennessee, 1872-73* (Memphis, Tennessee, 1873).

3. *Memphis Appeal*, December 6, 27, 1872 and February 2, 1873. The women initiated a letter campaign, a program of reform for the management of the city schools, ad even suggested that women be allowed to represent their interests on the school board by seeking public office.

4. See the *Memphis Appeal*, March 1, 6, 7, 10, 11, 14, 1873.

5. *Memphis Appeal*, December 27, 1872. From mid-March to the end of April and then during June and July, letters and editorials poured forth on the "Woman's Question." At one point the editors of the *Memphis Appeal* threatened to stop printed letters pertaining to the women's controversey because other topics of community concern were being squeezed out of the available space. *Memphis Appeal*, March 28, 1873.

6. *Memphis Appeal*, March 28, 1873.

7. See John Carl Ruoff "Southern Womanhood, 1865-1920: An Intellectual and Cultural Study." (Ph.D. dissertation, University of Illinois, 1976) for an analysis of cultural attitudes regarding Southern white women.

8. Anne F. Scott, *The Southern Lady, From Pedestal to Politics, 1830-1930* (Chicago, 1970).

9. *Bessie Jones, ed., Hospital Sketches,* reprint edition (Cambridge, MA, 1960).

10. One aspect of recent feminist scholarship has been the relationship between war and social change. Within this context a controversy rages. On the side of "progress" are those scholars who suggest that wars and/or revolutions have "liberated" women from prevailing patriarchal attitudes which governed appropriate female behavior. Opponents of this thesis argue for a continuity of conventional values concerning women's proper socioeconomic responsibilities rather than a change. Interestingly, both positions take as their linchpin the expansion of the "female sphere" during such crises when manpower shortages and increased production needs are met by women performing tasks previously done by men. The progressive school equates this shift in female responsibilities with a corresponding redistribution of power between men and women, while critics focus on the temporary nature of wartime changes.

    The following representes a partial list of studies which focus on this issue: Mary Beth Norton, *Liberty's Daughters: The Revolutionary Experience of American Women, 1750-1800* (Boston, 1980); Linda K. Kerber, *Women of the Republic: Intellect and Ideology in Revolutionary America* (Chapel Hill 1980); Catherine Clinton, *The Plantation Mistress: Women's World in the Old South* (N.Y., 1983); William Chafe, *The American Woman: Her Changing Social, Economic and Political Roles, 1920-1970* (New York, 1972); Maurine Weiner Greenwald, *Women, War and Work: the Impact of World War I on Women Workers in the United States* (Westport, Conn., 1980); Karen Anderson, *Wartime Women: Sex Roles, Family Relations, and the Status of Women During World War II* (Westport, Conn. 1982); Suzanne B. Lebsock, "Radical Reconstruction and the Property Rights of Southern Women" *Journal of Southern History* V. 43 (1977):195-216 and Scott, *Southern Lady.*

11. Scott, *Southern Lady*, pp. 81-102; Kathleen Berkeley "'Like a Plague of Locusts': Immigration and Social Change in Memphis, Tennessee, 1850-1880" (Ph.D. University of California, 1980), Chapter 2 "And the War Came."

12. Scott, *Southern Lady*, pp. 81-102; Berkeley, "'Like a Plague of Locusts,'" Chapter 2 and Carol Hymowitz and Michaele Weissman, *A History of Women in America* (New York, 1978), Ch. 9, "Homespun Blue and Gray."

13. See Gavin Wright, *The Political Economy of the Cotton South: Households, Markets and Wealth in the Nineteenth Century* (New York, 1978); David Potter, *Division and the Stress of Reunion, 1845-1876* (Glenview, Ill., 1973); and Carl N. Degler, *The Age of Economic Revolution, 1876-1900* (Glenview, Ill., 1967) for information on the social and economic dislocation experienced by the South as a result of the Civil War.

    Anne Scott argued that the "Civil War created a generation of women without men." With a quarter of a million men dead, large numbers of women would be left single or widowed. To them would fall the burden of caring for themselves and dependents. According to Scott's research, manuscript sources were "filled with references to young women school teachers. From these sources it seems that half the young women in the post-war South must have taught school at least briefly." Scott, *Southern Lady* pp. 106, 112.

14. Dept. of Commerce and Labor, Bureau of the Census, *Statistics for Women at Work* (Washington, D.C., 1907); Scott, *Southern Lady* pp. 106-133; Wilmington, North Carolina, *The Semi-Weekly Messenger*, April 13, 1897.

15. Scott, *Southern Lady*, p. 123.

16. See the *Ninth Census of the United States, Statistics of the Population*, V.1 (Washington, D.C., 1872) and the *Eleventh Census of the United States, Statistics of the Population*, V.1 (Washington, D.C., 1892).

17. These occupation categories appeared most frequently in the census schedules. See the *Ninth Census; the Tenth Census of the United States, Statistics of the Population* V.1 (Washington, D.C. 1882) and the *Eleventh Census*.

18. For information on the development of public education in the post-Civil War South see the following: Berkeley, "'Like a Plague of Locusts'", Ch. 5, "Education is the First Element of Our Advancement"; Henry Bullock, *A History of Negro Education in the South from 1619 to the Present* (Cambridge, Mass., 1967); Charles W. Dabney, *Universal Education in the South*, 2 vols. (Chapel Hill, 1936); Edgar Knight, *The Influence of Reconstruction on Education in the South* (N.Y., 1913) and William P. Vaughn, *Schools for All: The Blacks and Public Education in the South, 1830-1877* (Lexington, Ky., 1974).

19. Berkeley, "'Like a Plague of Locusts'", Ch. 5 "Education."

20. Ibid, and Vaughn, *Schools for All*, pp. 50-76. In addition to strained finances Southern opposition to public education turned on a fear of "mixed" schools where white and black children would be taught together.

21. Women teachers consistently earned almost half of what men teachers earned both before and after the Civil War. See the following for more information: Mary P. Ryan, *Womanhood in America: From Colonial Times to the Present*, second edition (N.Y., 1975) p. 94; Lillian Faderman, *Surpassing the Love of Men* (N.Y., 1980), p. 184-185; Memphis, Tennessee, *Seventeenth Annual Report of the Board of Education, 1868-69*, pp. 65-67. A survey of twenty cities across the country found that men employed in the field of public education generally earned two to three times the amount women teachers earned. The Memphis survey estimated the average yearly wage for male teachers in 1868 at $1,752 as compared to the female's average yearly salary of $535.

   Also see Robert E. Doherty's article, "Tempest on the Hudson: The Struggle for 'Equal Pay for Equal Work' in the New York City Public Schools, 1907-1911," in *History of Education Quarterly* 19:4 (Winter 1979):413-434.

22. In 1900, nine out of every ten adult women engaged in teaching were white women born in the United States. In all states, native-born white women with both parents also native-born, formed the most numerous class of teachers; this group was especially well-represented in the Southern states. See *Women at Work*, "Teachers" pp. 109-121.

23. Memphis, Tennessee, *The Eighteenth Annual Report of the Board of Education for the City of Memphis, Tennessee, 1869-70* (Memphis, Tennessee, 1870).

24. Ibid, p. 14.

25. *Seventeenth Annual Report of the Board of Education, 1868-69*, pp. 65-66.

26. Ibid, pp. 66-67.

27. Thomas Dublin, *Women At Work: The Transformation of Work and Community in Lowell, Massachusetts, 1826-1860* (N.Y., 1979); Ryan, *Womanhood in America; Fifteenth Annual Report of the Board of Education, 1866-67*, pp. XXXIX and *Seventeenth Annual Report of the Board of Education, 1868-69*, pp. 64-67.

28. A careful reading of annual reports of the Memphis, Tennessee Board of Education between 1865-1878 indicates that there was an abundance of women presenting credentials for teaching certificates each year.

29. *Seventeenth Annual Report of the Board of Education, 1968-69*, p. 65.

30. Ibid, p. 67.

31. Ibid, p. 66. Also see Doherty, "Tempest on the Hudson," pp. 419-20.

32. The statistics on male employment in the public schools are based on an analysis of the persistence patterns of men hired by the Memphis Board of Education from 1855-1860 and 1965-1875.

33. *Seventeenth Annual Report of the Board of Education, 1968-69*, p. 67.

34. See Berkeley, "'Like a Plague of Locusts'", ch. 5, "Education" for the effect reconstruction politics had upon the state and local public school system in Tennessee.

35. Memphis, Tennessee, *Memphis Avalanche*, September 17, 1870 and the *Eighteenth Annual Report of the Board of Education, 1869-70*.

36. See David Moss Hilliard, "The Development of Public Education in Memphis, Tennessee, 1848-1948" (Ph.D. University of Chicago, 1946) and Berkeley, "'Like a Plague of Locusts'", ch. 5, "Education" for the history of public education in Memphis.

37. This data is based on the analysis of the men and women hired by the Memphis Board of Education between 1855-1869.
38. The statistics on female employment in the public schools are based on analyzing the persistence pattern and marital status of women employed by the Memphis Board of Education from 1855-1860.
39. Only one woman, Mrs. Henrietta Hampton, taught both before the war and after. She was employed in the public school system as late as 1878. Her teaching career spanned at least twenty-three consecutive years.
40. The assumption made in the text about the availability of new female recruits is based on a careful reading of the *Annual Reports of Superintendents of Memphis Public Schools* between 1864 and 1879. See Dublin, *Women at Work* and Alice Kessler-Harris, "Where Are the Organized Women Workers?" *Feminist Studies* 3 (Fall 1975): 92-100 for discussions of the factors which inhibited and promoted collective female labor protests.
41. See, *Statistics for Women at Work*, "Teachers" pp. 109-121; Wilmington, North Carolina, *The Semi-Weekly Messenger*, April 13, 1897 and the *Memphis Appeal*, March 28 and 30, 1873.
42. The statistics on the marital status of Memphis female teachers are drawn from an examination of the eighty-eight women hired by the school board between 1865 and 1875.
43. By 1900, nine out of every ten white women teachers were single. While the average age of women teachers ranged between 25-34, the proportion of women over 44 still engaged in teaching was greatest in New England and in the South Atlantic and South Central states. See *Statistics for Women at Work* p. 117.
44. Of the eighty-eight women employed by the Memphis School Board between 1865-1875, fourteen were married. Six of the married women left teaching after one year (two of those six women had husbands employed in the public schools). One married woman taught for two consecutive years, one for three years, one for five years, and five women for eight successive years.
45. See the *Seventeenth Annual Report of the Board of Education, 1868-69; the Nineteenth Annual Report of the Board of Education for the City of Memphis, Tennessee, 1870-71* (Memphis, Tennessee, 1871) and the *Twenty-Second Annual Report of the Board of Education for the City of Memphis, Tennessee, 1972-73* (Memphis, Tennessee, 1873) for the names of both the female graduates of the Court Street Female High School and the names of women hired as teachers by the board.

    Miss Jeannie Higbee, the principal of Court Street Female High School issued the following statement in her report on the "success" of the female high school to the superintendent: "In contemplating the work accomplished by our high school, that good work has been done is best proven by the fact that of the eleven graduates of last year, eight were examined in the regular teachers' examination, all receiving a high average and of these, five have been successfully employed as teachers in our graded schools since September making an aggregate of eleven graduates of the female high school now in the employ of your board." *Twenty-Second Annual Report, 1872-73*, p. 26. Four Cairnes sisters, two Ennis sisters, two Knunkle sisters, two Belcher sisters, and two Reudelhuber sisters taught in the public schools between 1866 and 1875. Mrs. Henrietta Hampton's daughter, Mary, also taught in the public schools.
46. *Memphis Appeal*, March 14, 21, 22, 28, 1873.
47. See the *Memphis Appeal*, February 2, March 1, 7, 10, 18, 21, 22, and April 11, 1873.
48. See Elizabeth Avery Meriwether's letter in the *Memphis Appeal*, February 2, 1873.
49. *Memphis Appeal*, April 15, 1873.
50. Ibid.
51. The private meeting in which two women teachers were fired was held on April 21, 1873 and reported in the *Memphis Appeal* on the twenty-second of April and the tenth of June, 1873. Also see Elizabeth Cady Stanton, Susan B. Anthony and Matilda Joslyn Gage, eds. *The History of Woman Suffrage* Vol. 3, 1876-1875 (N.Y., 1970), p. 882.

    On the sixth of June, Judge Pierce presented a resolution to the board urging that the two dismissed teachers be given an additional month's salary because they did not receive any prior notice before they were dismissed. The resolution failed; only Pierce supported it. See the *Memphis Appeal*, June 10, 1873.
52. *Memphis Appeal*, July 3, 1873.
53. *Memphis Appeal*, July 8, 1873.
54. See Berkeley, "'Like a Plague of Locusts'", ch. 6, "'By Eschewing All Personal Politics or Sectional Needs': Redemption Politics and Urban Reform in the Bluff City, 1865-1879," pp. 298-373.
55. *Twenty-Seventh Annual Report of the Board of Education of the City of Memphis, For The Scholastic Year 1878-79*. (Memphis, 1880), pp. 56, 77-78. Principals earned $100.00 per month; high school teachers, $75.00 per month; primary and grammar and supernumerary teachers earned $60.00 per month. An additional category of special teachers earned $30.00 per month.

56. In 1877, the Memphis city school system employed six principals (four men and two women) and thirty-nine teachers (two men and thirty-seven women). The two male instructor taught at the high school. Dr. C. J. Hunter earned $125 per month while the two women instructors earned $100 per month. Professor E. Westzman, who taught only the French and German classes, earned $36 per month.

The previous year, in addition to Hunter and Westzman, there was a third male teacher employed at Market Street school. He earned $115 a month, while the six female teachers at the school earned $72 a month. The principal of Market Street school, Miss Clara Conway, earned $120 per month; five dollars more than the male teacher on her staff and five dollars less than what Hunter, the high school instructor earned.

In 1878, after the revised salary schedule reduced the principal's pay to $100 per month, Clara Conway tendered her resignation and opened her own private school for girls. Four years earlier, (1874), the city school system had lost another long-time employee. Miss Jeannie Higbee, principal of the female high school since 1871, resigned her position one year after the women teachers' protest failed. Jeannie Higbee taught at a private church school for a few years and then she too opened her own high school. By 1881 Miss Higbee's High School employed seven women teachers. See the *Memphis City Directory* for the years 1871-1881.

57. *Twenty-Seventh Annual Report* pp. 14, 78-79. In this report, the superintenent proposed awarding two positions in the white schools each year to "members of the graduating high school class as a prize for the best average in scholarship, attendance and deportment during the three years' course in the High School" (p. 21).

By 1878, the black public schools were staffed by blacks only. For the 1878-79 school year, fourteen full-time members were employed in the black schools (four men and ten women). Three of the men were teachers, while the fourth was the principal of the entire black school system. Seven of the women teachers were married while the remaining three were single. Unlike white Southern women who married, black married women tended to persist in the paid labor force. According to the data compiled in *Statistics for Women at Work*, the marital condition of black women teachers was significantly higher than for white women teachers. See *Statistics for Women at Work*, p. 118, also see Berkeley "'Like a Plague of Locusts'", ch. 5 "Education", for an analysis of the evolution of the black public school system in Memphis.

58. Scott, *Southern Lady*, pp. 165-183. *Woman Suffrage in Tennessee* (N.Y., 1950) by Elizabeth Taylor is but one of the many studies published by Taylor on the Woman Suffrage Movement in the South.

59. *Memphis Appeal*, January 25, and March 10, 1873; Stanton, et al., *History of Woman Suffrage*, vol. 3, pp. 20, 27, 153-154, 180-81, 183, 192-193, 197, 822, 955-956; Elizabeth Avery Meriwether, *Recollections of 92 Years* (Nashville, Tennessee, 1958).

60. *Memphis Appeal*, May 2-6, 1873; Meriwether, *Recollections*; Stanton, et. al. *History of Woman Suffrage* and Francis Elizabeth Willard and Mary A. Livermore, eds., *A Woman of the Century* (N.Y., 1893), pp. 498-499.

61. Scott, *Southern Lady*, p. 176.

62. See Eleanor Flexner's discussion of how Tennessee's crucial vote put the pro-suffrage forces "over the top" on August 18, 1920. Eleanor Flexner, *Century of Struggle: The Woman's Rights Movement in the United States*, (N.Y., 1974) pp. 320-324.

SEX DISCRIMINATION IN ATHLETICS: A REVIEW OF TWO DECADES OF ACCOMPLISHMENTS AND DEFEATS

Glenn M. Wong,* Richard J. Ensor**

I. INTRODUCTION

As women's athletics enters into a mid-life growth pattern, following an initial explosion in women's intercollegiate programs in the 1970's and early 1980's, it faces great uncertainties. The absorption of the defunct Association of Intercollegiate Athletics for Women (AIAW) by the NCAA,[1] the effects of the Supreme Court's *Grove City College v. Bell* decision[2] on enforcement of Title IX in athletics,[3] the loss of football television revenues by the NCAA,[4]

---

*Glenn M. Wong is Professor of Sport Law at the University of Massachusetts-Amherst. He is a lawyer, and has co-authored a book entitled LAW AND BUSINESS OF THE SPORTS INDUSTRIES. He has published numerous articles on sports law, sports finance and business and sports labor relations. He is a graduate of Brandeis University, Boston College Law School, and is a member of the Massachusetts Bar.

**Richard J. Ensor is on the faculty of the Sport Management Department at the University of Massachusetts-Amherst. He is a former Assistant Athletic Director of Marketing and Promotions at Seton Hall University, and has also served as Sports Information Director at Saint Peter's College in Jersey City, New Jersey and Assistant Athletic Director at St. Louis University. A final year law student at Seton Hall University School of Law, Mr. Ensor is student director of its Sports Law Forum.

1. The National Collegiate Athletic Association (NCAA) is a private organization made up of a voluntary membership of approximately 800 four-year colleges and universities located throughout the United States. Member schools agree to be bound by NCAA rules and regulations and are obligated to administer their athletic programs in accordance with NCAA rules. Over half of the NCAA's members are state-subsidized universities, and most receive some form of federal financial assistance. *See* 1986-87 NCAA Manual, NCAA Publications (Mission, Kansas 1986); *See also* Association For Intercollegiate Athletics For Women v. NCAA, 558 F. Supp. 487 (D.D.C. 1983), *aff'd*, 735 F.2d 577 (D.C. Cir. 1984).

2. *See* Grove City College v. Harris, 500 F. Supp. 253 (W.D. Pa. 1980), *rev'd* Grove City College v. Bell, 687 F.2d 684 (3d Cir. 1982), *aff'd* 465 U.S. 555 (1984).

3. *See Title IX Not a Dead Issue, But It's Mellowing*, NCAA News, July 14, 1982, at 1, 3, col. 1, 1; *NCAA Attorney Discusses Changes in Title IX*, NCAA News, July 28, 1982, at 3, col. 1 (the two articles cited above are reprints of a speech entitled "Is Title IX a Dead Issue?" presented by Attorney Mr. William D. Kramer at the annual workshop of the College Sports Information Directors of America in Dallas, Texas on June 29, 1982); *After Grove City*, Athletic Business, May, 1985, at 10, col. 1.

4. NCAA v. Bd. of Regents of Oklahoma and Univ. of Georgia Athletic Ass'n, 546 F. Supp. 1276 (W.D. Okla. 1982), *modified* 707 F.2d 1147 (10th Cir. 1984), *aff'd* 468 U.S. 85

and its potential effect on the funding of non-revenue producing sports championships,[5] and the failure to ratify the Equal Rights Amendment to the federal Constitution[6] all pose serious questions to those individuals concerned with continued development of women's athletic programs. With little time to reflect on how far and how fast they have come with their programs,[7] women's athletic program administrators and the legal experts who represent their interests face new and increasingly difficult problems to solve.[8]

Many indicators, including increases in participation, specta-

---

(1984); *See also Court Voids NCAA's TV Contracts, But Joy Doesn't Reign Supreme,* Washington Post, June 26, 1984, at C7; *College Football Set Free,* Boston Globe, June 26, 1984, at 45; *Fewer Appearances for Smaller Schools,* USA Today, June 28, 1984, at C2; *Ruling is Expected to Increase Number, Variety of College Football Teams on TV,* Wall St. J., June 28, 1984, at 4; *NCAA Pacts to Televise College Football Violate Antitrust Law, High Court Rules,* Wall St. J., June 28, 1984, at 4; *Fat Cats Win Again; Amateurs The Losers,* Washington Times, June 28, 1984, at B1; Barbash, *Supreme Court Breaks NCAA Hold on Televised College Football Games,* Washington Post, June 28, 1984, at 1; *NCAA's Reeling, But Don't Expect a KO Any Time Soon,* (AP Wireservice), Jacksonville Times-Union and Journal, July 1, 1984, at D13; *NCAA Setback on TV Poses Threat of Disorder,* N.Y. Times, July 15, 1984, at 56; *College Football TV in Disarray as Groups Scramble for Contracts,* NCAA News, July 18, 1984, at 1; *Supreme Court Rules NCAA's Limits on TV Football Games Are Illegal,* Chronicle of Higher Educ., July 25 1984, at 1; *Uncertain Times Ahead for NCAA,* USA Today, September 17, 1984, at C1; *Big TV Revenues Now Tougher to Get, Most College Football Powers Discover,* Chronicle of Higher Educ., January 9, 1985, at 37; *Financial Report in the Black, But Budget Restraints Urged,* NCAA News, January 9, 1985, at 1.

    5. Wong and Ensor, *The Impact of the U.S. Supreme Court's Antitrust Ruling on College Football,* 3 Entertainment & Sports Law., 3 (Winter 1985).

    6. For information on the Equal Rights Amendment, *see,* the following: *The Equal Rights Amendment, Hearings Before the Senate Subcomm. on Constitutional Amendments,* 91st Cong., 2d Sess. (1970); *Equal Rights 1970, Hearings Before the Senate Comm. on the Judiciary,* 91st Cong., 2d Sess. (1970); S. Rep. No. 92-689, Senate Comm. on the Judiciary, 92d Cong., 2d Sess. (1972); *Equal Rights for Men and Women, Hearings Before Subcomm. No. 4. of the House Judiciary Comm.,* 92d Cong., 1st Sess. (1971); H.R. Rep. No. 92-259, House Judiciary Comm., 92d Cong., 1st Sess. (1971). *See also Discrimination Against Women, Hearings on Section 805 of H.R. 16098 Before the Special Subcomm. on Education of the House Comm. on Education and Labor,* 91st Cong., 2d Sess. (1970). *See also,* DAVIDSON, GINSBURG AND KAY, SEX-BASED DISCRIMINATION, (1974); *ERA Dies,* Time, July 5, 1982 at 29; *What Killed Equal Rights?,* Time, July 12, 1982 at 32-33.

    7. *See generally* Visser, Lesley, *They're Playing To Rave Notices,* Boston Globe, Nov. 11, 1985, at 49, 64, col. 1, 1.

    8. *See Women's Progress in Athletics May Be Slowing, Leaders Fear,* Chronicle of Higher Educ., November 6, 1983, at 23, 26, col. 2, 1; *see generally* TOKARZ, KAREN L., *Women, Sports, and the Law: A Comprehensive Research Guide to Sex Discrimination in Sports,* (August, 1986), and Tokarz, *Separate but Unequal Eductional Sports Programs: The Need For a New Theory of Equality,* 1 BERKELEY WOMEN'S L.J. 1 (Fall 1985).

tors, and local and national media coverage, point to growth in women's athletics.[9] The development of athletic opportunity for women may be attributed, to a large extent, to Title IX of the Education Amendments of 1972,[10] a federal statute which prohibits sex discrimination. Before Title IX, women comprised only fifteen percent of the total number of athletic participants in college.[11] By 1984, thirty and eight-tenths percent of all participants in NCAA intercollegiate athletics were women.[12]

As compiled by the NCAA, the average number of women's varsity sports operated in a member institution's athletic program had risen from 5.61 in 1977 to 6.9 in 1984, while aggregate expenditures for women's intercollegiate athletics have increased from $24.7 million in 1977 to $116 million in 1981.[13] The AIAW studied the relative amounts of financial aid given to male and female athletes from 1973 to 1982. The AIAW estimated that for 1973-74, NCAA Division I schools spent an average of $1.2 million on men's athletic programs but only $27,000 in women's programs.[14] By the 1981-82 academic year, the institutions expended an average of $1.7 million on men and $400,000 on women.[15] This result was contrary to the predictions made by many opponents of Title IX, who generally thought increased money spent on women's programs would decrease the amount of money provided for men's programs.[16]

---

9. *See generally* Summary, Miller Lite Report on Women in Sports, Milwaukee, WI (December 1985).

10. P.L. 93-380, 88 Stat. 484, (1974); *see generally* Alfano, *Coach's Career Reflects Rise in Women's Sports*, N.Y. Times, Dec. 16, 1985, at C6, col. 1; Alfano, *Pioneer Immaculata Recalls a Simpler Era*, N.Y. Times, Dec. 17, 1985, at B17, B18, col. 1. *See also Many Women Link Anti-Sex-Bias Law to Outstanding Olympic Performances*, Chronicle of Higher Educ., August 29, 1984, at 31, 32, col. 2, 1.

11. Fields, *Title IX at IX*, Chronicle of Higher Educ., June 23, 1982, at 1, 12, col. 2, 1.

12. *Id.*

13. *See Women's Programs List Legislative Priorities*, NCAA News, June 6, 1984, at 1, 12, col. 1, 1.

14. *Supra* note 11, at 1.

15. *Supra* note 11, at 12. The average women's athletic budget for a Big Ten Conference school in 1974 was $3,500. In 1977-78 that amount had increased on an institution by institution basis to anywhere between $250,000 to $750,000 per year. *Supra* note 11, at 1.

16. *See* Koppett, *Moaning Colleges Map Defenses Against Title IX*, Sporting News, January 27, 1979, at 39, col. 1; *Hot Issues on NCAA Agenda* Sporting News, January 31, 1979, at 19, col. 1; Neinas, *Title IX Now a Money Issue*, NCAA News, September 30, 1979, at 2, col. 3. *See also*, Crowe, *NCAA Members Increase Budgets by 75 Pct. in 4 Years, Study Finds*, Chronicle of Higher Educ., Sept. 22, 1982, at 9, col. 2.

Participation in and funding of women's athletics have increased for many reasons. One major factor is the drastic change in society's attitudes toward women, including women's own perception about their athletic capabilities and participation.[17] These attitudinal changes have helped increase athletic opportunities for women.[18] Second, the NCAA has repeatedly indicated it is committed to equal athletic opportunity without regard to sex.[19] Despite its late entry into providing athletic opportunities for women, the NCAA has made significant strides in doing so since 1981.[20] In 1982-83, its subsidy of thirty women's championships was $2.2 million and exceeded its support of 28 men's championships that were nonrevenue producing by eight and four-tenths percent.[21] Within its ranks, however, there is disagreement concerning the direction the association should take following the dissolution of the AIAW and NCAA's assumption of control over women's intercollegiate athletics.[22]

For instance, at a May 1984 meeting of administrators of NCAA women's athletic programs, representatives present requested the meeting's minutes indicate a show of support for House Rule 5490.[23] This civil rights legislation, with Senate Bill 2568[24] was proposed as a response to the *Grove City College* deci-

---

17. *Supra* note 9.

18. *See The Changing Face of Girls' Sports* Boston Globe, March 11, 1980, at 48, col. 1.

19. *See NCAA Files Statement Regarding Civil Rights Legislation*, NCAA News, June 6, 1984, at 1, 3, col. 2; *Association Files Title IX Comments*, NCAA News, March 8, 1979, at 4, 7, col. 1, 1.

20. *See, e.g. Association Expands Staff For Women's Programs*, NCAA News, Sept. 13, 1982, at 1, 11, col. 2, 3.

21. *Supra* note 11.

22. *See* Goodman, *Women's AD's Worried*, Boston Globe, February 29, 1984; at 61, 65, col. 6, 1.

23. H.R. 5490, *A Bill to clarify the application of Title IX of the Education Amendment of 1972, section 504 of the Rehabilitation Act of 1973, the Age Discrimination Act of 1975, and Title VI of the Civil Rights Act of 1964*, 98th Cong., 2d Sess., April 12, 1984, *see also Civil Rights Act of 1984*, House Report 98-829, part 1 and 2, 98th Cong. 2d Sess. The report noted in part that, "The purpose of this legislation is simple and straight-forward: to reaffirm pre-*Grove City College* judicial and enforcement practices which provided for broad coverage of these antidiscrimination provisions." *Id.* at 1.

24. S. 2568, *To clarify the application of Title IX of the Education Amendments of 1972, section 504 of the Rehabilitation Act of 1973, the Age Discrimination Act of 1975, and Title VI of the Civil Rights Act of 1964*, 98th Cong., 2d Sess., April 12, 1984.

sion,[25] which ruled that Title IX applies only to the individual programs receiving federal funding at an institution of higher education and not to an entire institution. The proposed bills that would have ensured athletic programs still fell within the parameters of Title IX.[26] Despite the representative's request, the NCAA filed a statement supporting the objectives of House Rule 5490 but objecting to the bill's construction.[27] In general, the NCAA indicated[28] the impact of *Grove City College* was overstated, the bill's authority would be overinclusive, and the demands of inspection and enforcement would be too burdensome and costly.[29]

Beyond Title IX concerns, athletic administrators are increasingly worried about continued funding of women's intercollegiate programs.[30] Some worry the NCAA made commitments to attract women's athletic programs into the Association in the early 1980's it will find hard to maintain.[31] Especially in light of the reduced

---

25. *Supra* note 2; *See also Shelving of Civil Rights Bill Leaves Women's Athletics in Lurch*, Wall St. J., November 9, 1984, at 14, col. 1; Weir, *A Threat to Women in Sports*, USA Today, November 3, 1983, at C1, 2, col. 3, 1.

26. Legislation to overturn the Supreme Court's *Grove City College* decision failed to pass through Congress in 1984. The House of Representatives had passed the legislation (H.R. 5490) by a vote of 375-32 in June 1984. However, the Senate version of the legislation (S. 2568) failed to gain passage. Similar legislation was introduced in 1985. *See Bill to Overturn Grove City Rule Killed in Senate*, Chronicle of Higher Educ., October 10, 1984, at 1, 22, col. 2, 4, 1; *Bill to Reverse High Court's* Grove City *Decision Gets Bipartisan Support*, Chronicle of Higher Educ., April 18, 1984, at 21, col. 1; *House Passes Civil Rights Bill*, NCAA News, July 4, 1984, at 7; *House Backs Bill to Counter Supreme Court Ruling in Grove City Case; and Senate Unit Postpones Action*, Chronicle of Higher Educ., July 5, 1984, at 13.

27. *Supra* note 19.

28. *Supra* note 19.

29. In response to the Supreme Court's *Grove City College* decision, the Women's Sports Foundation instituted a letter-writing campaign to have its membership influence passage of Senate bill 2568. The foundation stressed the importance of Title IX in the development of women's intercollegiate athletics and its continued need for future progress. *See Title IX Needs You*, Women's Sports, September 1984, at 49, col. 1.

30. Indicative of the financial concerns of athletic administrators is that since the emergence of the NCAA as the dominant organization in both men's and women's collegiate sports, there has been a tendency toward combining championships (for example, indoor track and skiing) to cut costs. *See Intercollegiate Skiing Halts Its Downhill Slide—NCAA Combines Men's and Women's Championships to Make Sure Enough Will Be Competing*, Chronicle of Higher Educ., March 9, 1983, at 18, col. 1.

31. However, at the 1985 NCAA Convention, Division 1A institutions (105 major football playing institutions) voted to require themselves to each sponsor at least eight women's and eight men's sports programs by the 1986-87 academic year. The vote on the requirement was 74 to 37. Approximately 30 Division 1A member institutions did not meet the

funding from college football television contracts due to the *Board of Regents of University of Oklahoma v. NCAA.*[32] For instance, at the May 1984 meeting of NCAA women's athletic program administrators, John Toner, who was then president of the NCAA and who chaired the session, stated:

> It seems to many who are responsible for generating the dollars to pay intercollegiate athletics costs that there must be some correlation between added program costs and increased revenues to support those costs. It seems to me that it is time for women leaders to concentrate on how they can stimulate and enlarge the income from women's programs.[33]

As women reach the competitive level of men's athletics, they also begin to face the same pressures to succeed, market, and control corruption in their programs. Merrily Dean Baker, University of Minnesota women's athletic director notes: "The potential for corruption is there and may already by employed in some places. I think our greatest challenge will be to avoid the pitfalls of the men."[34] The NCAA's director of enforcement David Berst notes further "We already have the worst example in men's programs. We hope that women conclude it's intolerable to end up in this same situation."[35]

Another concern is that while participants[36] and fans[37] interest in women's intercollegiate athletics continues to grow in the 1980's, there is a steady erosion in the number of women holding positions as administrators, and especially, coaches.[38] From 1973 to 1984 the

---

qualifications at the time of the vote and faced being dropped from the division and being ineligible for championships in 1986. *See Major Football-Playing Universities Must Field Teams in at Least 8 Women's Sports by 1986, New Rule Says,* Chronicle of Higher Educ., January 30, 1985, at 29, 31, col. 2, 1. Significantly, at the Fifth Special NCAA Convention during the summer 1985, the Division 1A membership reduced the above requirements to six women's sports in 1986, and seven women's sports in 1987. *See* 1986-87 NCAA Manual, bylaw 11-1(g)-(1), at 141.

    32. 546 F. Supp. 1276.

    33. *Supra* note 13.

    34. *Id. See also The Fine Art of Recruiting Superstars for Big-Time Women's Basketball,* Chronicle of Higher Educ., Mar. 30, 1983 at 21, col. 2; and *Recruiting Now Favors the Rich,* Boston Globe, May 5, 1983, at 67.

    35. *Id.*

    36. *Supra* note 9.

    37. *Supra* note 9.

    38. Alfano, *Signs of Problems Amid the Progress,* N.Y. Times, Dec. 15, 1985, sec. 5, at 1, 6, col. 1.

percentage of men coaching women's sports on the NCAA's division I level rose from ten percent to fifty and one-tenth percent.[39] While this problem may be in part a reflection of the limited experience of women in the coaching ranks,[40] some women also contest it is because they have a limited role in the governing procedures of the NCAA.[41]

As women's athletics faces these challenges, it may no longer rely on once available legal options. Title IX and other legislation, initially, were vanguards of changing societal attitudes, as well as legal factors, that helped bring about substantial change in sex discrimination in the United States. Women brought complaints about unequal treatment to court and, even more importantly, were often successful in their litigation. Recently, however, a number of setbacks have besieged the women's movement. Failure to enact the Equal Rights Amendment, and limitations the United States Supreme Court imposed on Title enforcement have caused concern among promoters of women's athletics.[42] A direct result of the *Grove City College* decision was the immediate termination of

---

39. *Id. See also* Acosta and Carpenter, *Women in Athletics—A Status Report,* Brooklyn College (1985); *Women's Coaching Opportunities Dwindling, Report Says,* NCAA News, Oct. 14, 1985, at 3, col. 1.

40. The lack of professional sport leagues for women, especially in basketball, may contribute to the lack of experienced women head coaches, because in part it provides no feeder system by which talented players may go through a transition from player to coach. *See generally Miller Time in Pros? Not Likely,* N.Y. Daily News, Feb. 2, 1986, at 58, col. 1; *New League for Women,* N.Y. Times, Oct. 28, 1984, sec. 5, at 4; and, *Proud Pioneers,* Boston Herald, Mar. 9, 1979, at 12.

41. Donna DeVarona, President of the Women's Sports Foundation and 1964 Olympic Gold Medalist, has noted that the loss of the Title IX is significant:

> I think everyone knows that women's athletics made tremendous strides under Title IX. But I don't think too many people realize that Title IX is no longer effective for us. They've taken that away, and if we just stand by, they'll take away a lot more.

> . . . Right now there is no visible pressure on athletic administrators and women have no recourse. Title IX did not come with dollar requirements, but there was a heavy understanding that if schools discriminated, they might lose federal funding. Without that, who knows what they'll do?

> . . . Unfortunately, people do not always do the right things voluntarily.

See Dodds, *Title IX In With a Fury, Exits to Anger of Women,* L.A. Times, Nov. 5, 1985, at E2, col. 2.

42. Judith Holland, associate athletic director at UCLA, has noted that: "Title IX had a big influence . . . you had to expect that sooner or later it would die out or be ignored . . . our history is replete with issues that are big one day and put aside the next." *See* Dodds, *supra* note 41.

twenty-three Title IX investigations.[43] At the forefront of concerns facing women's athletics in the 1980's are the retrenchment of programs so instrumental in the progress achieved in women's athletics, the absence of an organization such as the AIAW to champion the movement's specific issues, and potential funding problems.[44]

This Article attempts to distinguish among the various legal theories and principles utilized in sex discrimination cases over the last two decades and identify those that are currently most viable.[45] The legal principles discussed include equal protection, Title IX, and state equal rights amendments.[46] The following section examines theories in detail, with particular concern given to courts' applications of legal precedent in sports related litigation.

In section three the authors review Title IX's development as a potent weapon for those who sought expansion of playing opportunities for women. The section addresses standing, scope and applicability of Title IX, and Office of Civil Rights Title IX compliance reviews. Section four examines sex discrimination suits' impact on student-athletes with emphasis on the difference courts have given to suits involving "contact" and "non-contact" sports. Psychological, physiological, and competitive arguments are reviewed. Section five focuses on sex discrimination in athletic em-

---

43. *See 23 Cases on Civil Rights Closed After Court Rules*, N.Y. Times, June 3, 1984, at 36, col. 1.

44. For further information, *see also* Carpenter, *Title IX: After Grove City*, Sports and Law: Contemporary Issues, 48 (1985).

45. For further information on sex discrimination in athletics, *see* BERRY AND WONG, LAW AND BUSINESS OF THE SPORTS INDUSTRIES, (1986); and, R. YASSER, SPORTS LAW, (1985).

46. For further information on sex discrimination in athletics, *see* Sipleins & Popovich, *Sex Equity in the Public School*, 12 URB. LAW. 509 (1980); Ingram & Bellaver, *Sex Discrimination in Park District Athletic Programs*, 64 WOMEN'S L.J. 33 (Winter 1978); Comment, *A Litigation Strategy on Behalf of the Outstanding High School Female Athlete*, 8 GOLDEN GATE L. REV. 423 (1979); Comment, *The Female High School Athlete and Interscholastic Sports*, 4 JOURNAL OF LAW AND ED. 285 (1975); Comment, *Sex Discrimination in Interscholastic High School Athletics*, 25 SYRACUSE L. REV. 535 (SPRING 1974); Comment, *Sex Discrimination in Athletics*, 21 VILL. L. REV. 876 (October, 1976); Note, *Legal Problems of Sex Discrimination*, 15 Alberta L. Rev. 122 (1977); Note, *Sex Discrimination in High School Athletics*, 6 IND. L. REV. 661 (1973); Note, *Sex Discrimination and Intercollegiate Athletics*, 61 IOWA L. REV. 420 (December 1975); Note, *Sex Discrimination in High School Athletics: An Examination of Applicable Legal Doctrines*, 66 MINN. L. REV. 1115 (1982); Note, *Sex Discriminination in High School Athletics*, 57 MINN. L. REV. 339 (1972); Note, *Title IX: Women's Intercollegiate in Limbo*, 40 WASH. & LEE L. REV. 297 (1983); Note, *Emergent Law of Women and Amateur Sports: Recent Developments*, 28 WAYNE L. REV. 1701 (1982).

ployment. This examines sex based bias in the hiring of coaches and personnel in related athletic positions such as game officials and media access to locker rooms.

II. Legal Principles

Sex discrimination in athletics has been challenged using a variety of legal arguments, including state equal rights amendments[47] and the Equal Pay Act,[48] but have relied mainly upon equal protection laws or Title IX.[49]Sharpe, 347 U.S 497 (1954).

A state equal rights amendment can also be used to attack alleged sex discrimination; however, not all states have passed such legislation. The fourth argument concerns two separate statutes: the Equal Pay Act and Title VII of the Civil Rights Act of 1964.[50] Although neither statute was passed to deal specifically with sex discrimination, both have been used to challenge employment-related discrimination.

Equal protection arguments are based on the fifth and fourteenth amendments to the United States Constitution, which guarantees equal protection of the law to all persons found within the United States.[51] Title IX is a relatively recent method of attacking sex discrimination. Although the original legislation was passed in 1972, implementation was delayed for the promulgation of regulations and policy interpretations.[52] Even with the delays, many have claimed the rise in participation by women in athletics was directly related to the passage of Title IX.[53]

Regardless of whether a plaintiff employs an equal protection or Title IX approach, he or she usually contends there is a fundamental inequality. When the court attempts to deal with these

---

47. *See supra* note 6.
48. Equal Pay Act of 1963, 29 U.S.C. § 206 (1976).
49. *See supra* note 10.
50. *Supra* note 48.
51. U.S. Const. amend. XIV, § 1. The fourteenth amendment provides, in relevant part, that no state shall "deny any person within its jurisdiction the equal protection of the laws." This prohibition on the states applies to the federal government through the process of "reverse" incorporation of the fourteenth amendment into the fifth amendment. *See, e.g.* Bolling v. Sharpe, 347 U.S 497 (1954).
52. *See* Comment, *HEW's Final "Policy Interpretation" of Title IX and Intercollegiate Athletics*, 6 J.C. & U.L. 345 (1980).
53. *Supra* note 41.

claims, it considers three factors. The first is whether the sport from which women are excluded is one involving physical contact. Total exclusion from all sports or from any non-contact sport is considered a violation of equal educational opportunity. The second factor the courts consider is the quality and quantity of opportunities available to each sex as well as the amount of money spent on equipment, the type of coaches provided, and the access to school-owned facilities. The third factor the courts consider is age and level of competition involved in the dispute. The younger the athletes involved, the fewer the actual physiological differences that exist. Without demonstrable physiological differences, the justification of inherent biological differences as a rational basis for the exclusion of one sex from athletic participation is negated.

For instance, in *Pavey v. University of Alaska*,[54] female student athletes brought against the University of Alaska for discrimination in the operation of its athletic program in violation of Title IX, and the fourteenth amendment's due process and equal protection clauses. The University filed a third party suit against the NCAA and the AIAW that charged the two association's inconsistent rules required the institution to discriminate in its athletic program in violation of federal laws. The NCAA and AIAW moved for dismissal of the suit. The district court denied the motions. It held the University's suit stated a valid claim, the University was reasonably trying to avoid a confrontation with the two association's rules that could cause a disruption in the school's student athletes' participation in intercollegiate athletics, and the facial neutrality of the association's rules did not negate the University's claim that those rules, in combined effect, forced the institution to discriminate in its athletic program.[55]

A. Equal Protection

Historically, sex has been an acceptable category for classifying persons for different benefits and burdens under any given law.

---

54. 490 F. Supp. 1011 (D. Alaska 1980).

55. For further information on *Pavey* and like cases involving intercollegiate athletics, see *Suits Focus on Men's, Women's Rules Differences*, NCAA News, March 31, 1980, at 3, col. 1; *Courts Decide in Three Rules Difference Cases*, NCAA News, June 15, 1980, at 1, 3, col. 1, 1.

In 1872, the United States Supreme Court, in *Bradwell v State*,[56] noted "The paramount destiny and mission of a woman are to fulfill the noble and benign offices of wife and mother. This is the law of the Creator."[57] In 1908, the Supreme Court stated[58] that a classification based on gender was constitutionally valid. It was not considered to be a violation of equal protection, whether based on actual or imagined physical differences between men and women. Modern equal protection theories have now gained preeminence, and the use of gender to classify persons is considered less acceptable.

Under traditional equal protection analysis, the legislative gender-based classification must be sustained unless it is found patently arbitrary and/or bears absolutely no rational relationship to a legitimate governmental interest.[59] Under this traditional rational basis analysis, overturning discriminatory laws is extremely difficult. In sex discrimination sports litigation this implies women may be excluded from athletic participation upon a showing of a rational reason for their exclusion and by providing comparable options for those who are excluded. The rational reason must be factually supported and not be based on mere presumptions about the relative physical and athletic capabilities of women and men. It remains, however, a relatively easy standard for the defendant to meet as it invokes only the lowest standard of scrutiny by the court.

The courts have not found sex to be a suspect class, which would elevate it to the status held by race, national origin, and alienage. If the courts were to decide sex is a suspect class, it would make all rules that classify on the basis of gender subject to strict

---

56. 83 U.S. (16 Wall) 130 (1873).
57. *Id.* at 141.
58. Muller v. Oregon, 208 U.S. 412 (1908).
59. In Ridgefield Women's Political Caucus, Inc. v. Fossi, 458 F. Supp. 117 (D. Conn. 1978), plaintiff girls and taxpayer parents brought claims against town selectmen seeking to enjoin the town from offering public property at a nominal price to a private organization that restricted membership to boys. The district court found for the plaintiffs, ruling that the defendants had no right to offer land at less than fair value to the private organization in question as long as this organization restricted membership and the town failed to offer to girls recreational opportunities comparable or equivalent to those provided by the organization in question. Until such services are offered, any conveyance of the property at a nominal fee would constitute governmental support of sex discrimination in violation of the equal protection clause of the fourteenth amendment.

scrutiny analysis. Under this standard, the rule makers would have to prove there are compelling reasons for the classification and there is no less restrictive alternative. They would also have to prove the classification was directly related to the constitutional purpose of the legislation and this purpose could not have been achieved by any less objectionable means. Many rules and laws would fail to meet this high standard, and hence would be judged to be discriminatory.

Some courts have moved away from the broad interpretation of the rational relationship test by increasing the burden on the defendant. This intermediate test, between the rational basis and strict scrutiny test, was established by the United States Supreme Court in *Reed v. Reed*.[60] The court established therein that sex-based classifications "must be reasonable, not arbitrary, and must rest upon some ground of difference having a fair and substantial relation to the object of the legislation, so that all persons similarly circumstanced shall be treated alike."[61] Mere preferences or assumptions concerning the ability of one sex to perform adequately are not acceptable bases for a discriminatory classification. The United States Supreme Court again addressed this issue in *Frontiero v. Richardson*.[62] In a plurality opinion, Justice Brennan reasoned that ". . . although efficacious administration of governmental programs is not without some importance, 'the Constitution recognizes higher values than speed and efficiency'. . . there can be no doubt that 'administrative convenience' is not a shibboleth, the mere recitation of which dictates constitutionality."[63] A factual basis for any gender classification must exist. This intermediate test is still one step away from a declaration by the courts that sex is an inherently suspect class.

Because no majority opinion has applied a strict scrutiny analysis in a case challenging a gender-based classification, courts may opt to apply either a rational basis test or the intermediate standard of review. The intermediate standard requires more than an easily achieved rational relationship but less than a strict scrutiny standard for compliance. The class must bear a substantial rela-

---

60.   404 U.S. 71 (1971).
61.   *Id*. at 76.
62.   411 U.S. 677 (1973).
63.   *Id*. at 690.

tionship between a classification and a law's purpose must now be founded on fact, not on general legislative views of the relative strengths and/or abilities of the two sexes.

Three key elements commonly are considered in an equal protection analysis of athletic discrimination cases. The first is state action which must be sufficiently present, before any claim can be successfully litigated. Without it an equal protection argument under the United States Constitution does not apply. This factor has significant ramifications in cases in which the athletic activity is conducted outside the auspices of a state or municipal entity or a public educational institution. One example would be a youth sport league, such as little league baseball.[64]

The second factor is whether the sport involves physical contact. In contact sports the courts have allowed separate men's and women's teams. This "separate but equal" doctrine is based on considerations of the physical health and safety of the participants. When separate teams do not exist, however, both sexes may have an opportunity to try out and meet the necessary physical requirements on an individual basis. A complete ban on participation of one sex will not be upheld if based on generalizations about characteristics of an entire sex rather than on a reasonable consideration of individual characteristics.[65]

The third factor to be considered is whether both sexes have equal opportunities to participate in athletic competition. This "equal opportunity" usually requires the existence of completely separate teams or an opportunity to try out for the one available team. If there are separate teams, however, it is permissible for the governing organization to prohibit co-ed participation. Unlike classifications based on race, when gender is a determining factor "separate but equal" doctrines may be acceptable. The issue then may become whether the teams are indeed equal.[66] Other factors that have been taken into consideration are the age of the participant and the level of the competition. Physical differences between boys

---

64. *See e.g.*, King v. Little League Baseball, Inc., 505 F.2d 264 (6th Cir. 1974) and *infra* note 141.

65. *See, e.g.*, Clinton v. Nagy, 411 F. Supp. 1396 (N.D. Ohio 1974).

66. *See, e.g.*, O'Connor v. Bd. of Educ. of School Dist. No. 23, 645 F.2d 578 (7th Cir. 1981); *cert. denied.*, 454 U.S. 1084, (1981); Ritacco v. Norwin School Dist., 361 F. Supp. 930 (W.D. Pa. 1973).

and girls below the age of twelve are minimal. Therefore, health and safety considerations that might be applicable to older athletes have not constituted legitimate reasons for restricting young athletes' access to participation.[67]

The legal analysis of any particular case, however, will depend on the philosophy of the court and the particular factual circumstances presented.[68] Some courts are reluctant to intervene in discretionary decisions made by an association governing athletic events unless there are obvious abuses.[69] Other courts have been reluctant to intervene in discretionary decisions because they do not believe they have the administrative knowledge or time necessary to oversee the administration of sport programs effectively.

Historically, challenging sex discrimination based on the equal protection laws has not been totally effective. The constitutional standard of rational relationship has been a very difficult one for a plaintiff to overcome. The use of the intermediate standard, a more stringent test, has led to some of the recent successful challenges of alleged sex discrimination. However, the plurality decision of the United States Supreme Court in *Frontiero v. Richardson*[70] lessens the impact of the intermediate standard. A strong decision by the court to apply the intermediate standard or find that sex should be included as a suspect category would greatly assist plaintiffs in attacking alleged sex discrimination.

Another disadvantage of the equal protection laws is that they constitute a private remedy. Therefore, the plaintiff must be in a position to absorb the costs of litigation. This reduces the number of complaints filed and encourages settlement before final resolution of a number of equal protection claims.[71]

67. *See, e.g.,* Bednar v. Nebraska School Activities Ass'n, 531 F.2d 922 (8th Cir. 1976).

68. *See, e.g.,* Brenden v. Indep. School Dist. 742, 342 F. Supp. 1224 (D. Minn. 1972), *aff'd,* 477 F.2d 1292 (8th Cir. 1973).

69. *See, e.g.,* for situations where the courts decided to review the discretionary decisions of different types of amateur athletic associations, Kentucky High School Athletic Ass'n v. Hopkins County Bd. of Educ., 552 S.W.2d 685 (Ky. Ct. App. 1977); Missouri *ex rel* Nat'l Junior College Athletic Ass'n v. Luten, 492 S.W.2d 404 (Mo. Ct. App. 1973); Colorado Seminary v. NCAA, 417 F. Supp. 885 (D. Colo. 1976) *aff'd* 570 F.2d 320 (10th Cir. 1978).

70. 411 U.S. 677.

71. For further information on athletic participation and equal protection, *see* Note, *Constitutional Law-Equal Protection-Sex Discrimination in Secondary School Athletics,* 46 TENN. L. REV. 222 (Fall 1978).

III. Title IX

Section 901(a) of Title IX of the Education Amendments of 1972 provides: "No person in the United States shall, on the basis of sex, be excluded from participation in, be denied the benefits of, or be subjected to discrimination under any education program or activity receiving federal financial assistance. . . ."[72]

Title IX became law on July 1, 1972.[73] It specifically and clearly recognizes the problems of sex discrimination and forbids such discrimination in any program, organization, or agency that receives federal funds. A long process of citizen involvement preceded the first set of regulations. In July 1975, the Department of Health, Education & Welfare (HEW) issued the regulations designed to implement Title IX.[74] The regulations were criticized as vague and inadequate.[75] In December 1978, HEW attempted to alleviate the criticism by releasing a proposed policy interpretation that attempted to explain, but did not change, the 1975 requirements.[76] However, not until December 1979, seven years after the original passage of Title IX, did the Office of Civil Rights (hereinafter OCR)[77] release the policy interpretation for Title IX.[78] These final guidelines specifically included intercollegiate athletics. Developed after numerous meetings and countless revisions, they reflected comments from universities, legislative sources, and the public.

The policy interpretation contained some very strict guidelines for OCR to apply in assessing Title IX compliance, including the following:

---

72. Education Amendments of 1972, P. L. 92-318, Title IX—Prohibition of Sex Discrimination, July 1, 1972 (now codified as 20 U.S.C. § 1681(a)).

73. *Id.*

74. 45 CFR § 86 A-F.

75. *See* Note, *Judicial Deference to Legislative Reality: The Interpretation of Title IX in the Context of Collegiate Athletics,* 14 N.C. Cent. L.J. 601 (1984).

76. For an examination of the legislative history of Title IX in respect to athletics, *see* Comment, *The Evolution of Title IX: Prospects for Equality in Intercollegiate Athletics,* 11 Golden Gate L. Rev. 759 (1981); Note, *Title IX and Intercollegiate Athletics: Adducing Congressional Intent,* 24 B.C.L. Rev. 1243 (1983); Gaal, DiLorenzo Evans, *HEWS's Final "Policy Interpretation" of Title IX and Intercollegiate Athletics,* 6 J.C. & U.L. 345 (1980).

77. The Department of Health, Education and Welfare (HEW) was divided into two agencies, the Department of Education and the Department of Health and Human Services. The Office of Civil Rights (OCR) is part of the Department of Education.

78. *Supra* note 52.

1. The inclusion of football and other revenue-providing sports;

2. "Sport-specifics" comparisons as the basis for assessing compliance;

3. "Team-based" comparisons (grouping sports by levels of development) as the basis for compliance assessments;

4. Institutional planning that does not meet the provisions of the policy interpretation as applied by OCR.[79]

The policy interpretation also outlined "nondiscriminatory factors" to be considered when assessing Title IX compliance. These factors include differences that may result from the unique nature of particular sports, special circumstances of a temporary nature, the need for greater funding for crowd control at more popular athletic events, and differences that have not been remedied but which an institution is voluntarily working to correct. In the area of compensation for men's and women's coaches, OCR assessed rates of compensation, length of contracts, experience, and other factors, while taking into account mitigating conditions such as nature of duties, number of assistants to be supervised, number of participants, and level of competition.[80]

The major issues Title IX raises revolve around the scope of the legislation and the programs to which it applies. The July 1975 policy regulations issued by HEW covered three areas of activity within educational institutions: employment, treatment of students, and admissions. Several sections of the regulations concerned with the treatment of students included specific requirements for intercollegiate, intramural, and club athletic programs.

One important issue is whether Title IX applies to an entire institution or only to the programs within an institution that receive direct federal assistance. The United States Supreme Court ruled in *Grove City College v. Bell*[81] that only those programs

---

79. Memorandum, "HEW Final Policies on Title IX/Athletics," To: AIAW Executive Committee, From: Renouf & Polivy, Attorneys at Law, Dec. 6, 1979, at 9-10 (document on file with the author); *see also,* Gaal & DiLorenzo, *Legality and Requirements of HEW's Proposed "Policy Interpretation" of Title IX and Intercollegiate Athletics,* 6 J.C. & U.L. 161 (1980), and *supra* note 52.

80. *See supra* note 52.

81. 687 F.2d 684. *See also U.S. Asks Supreme Court to Reject Plea by College to*

within an institution that receive direct financial assistance from the federal government should be subject to Title IX strictures. This interpretation is often referred to as the "programmatic approach" to the Title IX statute.[82] Other lower courts have reached the opposite conclusion, that the receipt of any federal aid to an institution, whether it be limited to only certain programs or indirect (for example, student loan) programs, should place the entire institution under the jurisdiction of Title IX. This interpretation is called the "institutional approach" to Title IX.[83]

While Title IX does not require the creation of athletic programs or the same sport offerings to both sexes—for example, a football program for women or a volleyball program for men—it does require equality of opportunity in accommodation of interests and abilities, in athletic scholarships, and in other benefits and opportunities.[84]

Athletics and athletic programs were not specifically mentioned in Title IX when it first became law in 1972. Congress was generally opposed to placing athletics programs under the realm of Title IX. Taking the position that sports and physical education are an integral part of education, however, HEW specifically included athletics, despite strong lobbying efforts to exempt revenue-producing intercollegiate sports from the Title IX requirements. This specific inclusion of athletics occurred in 1974 and extended from general athletic opportunities to athletic scholarships. Among the principles governing inclusion of athletic scholarships was the idea that all recipients of federal aid must provide "reasonable opportunities" for both sexes to receive scholarship aid. The existence of "reasonable opportunities" was determined by examining the ratio of male to female participants. Scholarship aid would

---

Review Sex-Bias Law, Chronicle of Higher Educ., February 2, 1983, at 13, col. 2.

82. For an examination of this approach in an athletic related case, *see* Othen v. Ann Arbor School Bd., 507 F. Supp. 1376 (E.D. Mich. 1981), *aff'd*, 699 F.2d 309 (1983).

83. For further information concerning the institutional and programmatic approaches to Title IX application, *see* The Application of Title IX to School Athletic Programs, 68 CORNELL L. REV. 222 (1983); *The Program-Specific Reach of Title IX*, 83 Colum. L. Rev. 1210 (1983). *See also* Haffer v. Temple Univer., 524 F. Supp. 531 (E.D. Pa. 1981), *aff'd* 688 F.2d 14 (3rd Cir. 1982), (interpreting the "institutional approach" to Title IX.) *See also Temple Won't Challenge Court Ruling that Sex:-Bias Law Applies to Sports*, Chronicle of Higher Educ., November 24, 1982, at 13, col. 2.

84. *See* Othen v. Ann Arbor School Bd. 507 F. Supp. 1376 (E.D. Mich. S.D. 1981).

then be distributed according to this participation ratio.[85]

Another section of the ORC Title IX regulations specified requirements for athletic programs.[86] Contact sports were subject to regulations distinct from those governing noncontact sports. The regulations in this section state that separate teams were acceptable for contact sports and for teams in which selection was based on competition skill. For noncontact sports, if only one team existed, both sexes must be allowed to compete for positions on the team.[87] The Office of Civil Rights, which monitors compliance of Title IX, has considered many factors in determining the equality of opportunity, and as was noted by one court included:

> In assessing the totality of athletic opportunity provided, institutions shall be guided by regulations implementing Title IX of the Educational Amendments of 1972, and shall assess at least the following:
> a. Appropriateness of equipment and supplies.
> b. Games and practice schedules.
> c. Travel and per diem allowances.
> d. Opportunity for coaching and academic tutoring.
> e. Coaches and tutors.
> f. Locker rooms, practice and competitive facilities.
> g. Medical and training services.
> h. Housing and dining facilities and services.
> i. Publicity.
> Athletic expenditures need not be equal but the pattern of expenditures must not result in a disparate effect on opportunity. Institutions may not discriminate in the provision of necessary equipment, supplies, facilities, and publicity for sports programs.[88]

As noted by the court, equal expenditures were not required, but comparative budgets could be considered in relation to those factors listed.[89]

The procedures of Title IX analysis were established in special administrative guidelines, which listed specific factors that should be examined in athletic programs. The guidelines reviewed the number of sports, the type of arrangements, and benefits offered to women competing in athletics. When teams of one sex were fa-

---

85.   45 C.F.R. § 86.13 (c).

86.   *Id.* at § 86.41 (c).

87.   *Id.* at § 86.

88.   *See* Aiken v. Lievallen, 39 Or. App. 779, 593 P.2d 1243 (1979).

89.   *Id.* See also 45 C.F.R. § 86.41 (c).

vored in such areas as funding, coaching, and facilities, resulting in severely reduced opportunities for the other sex to compete, the courts would closely examine program expenditures, number of teams, and access to facilities to determine if the school was fulfilling the requirements of Title IX. As a general rule, although Title IX did not require the adoption of programs and equivalent funding, increases in either or both were often necessary to redress past discrimination.

The final area the regulations covered the Title IX method of enforcement. Compliance with the dictates of the law is monitored by the Office of Civil Rights (OCR) located in the Department of Education. OCR initiates the procedure that makes random compliance reviews and investigates complaints submitted by individuals. The first step in the process is to examine the targeted institution's records to review its attempted compliance with Title IX. Following a preliminary review, the OCR has the option of conducting a full hearing or dropping the case.

If the OCR calls a full hearing, the institution has the right to have counsel present and to appeal any adverse decision; the complainant has neither of these rights. The affected individual is not a party involved in the hearing. Instead, the OCR becomes the complainant and pursues the claim. If the OCR finds the institution has not substantially complied, it may turn its finding over to federal or local authorities for prosecution under the appropriate statutes.

Since 1979, there have been a number of attempts to change Title IX. Many of the proposals would lessen the impact of Title IX. Senator Hatch of Utah introduced one of these proposed changes on June 11, 1981. His amendment would have specifically restricted the scope of Title IX to those programs that receive direct funding from the federal government.[90] It was also designed to specify that money received by students in the form of scholarships, grants, or loans does not constitute federal aid for Title IX purposes.[91] Passage of this amendment would have effectively eliminated claims by women in the areas of athletics and other ex-

---

90. S. 1361, as reported in *Courts, Congress Challenge Title IX* WEAL (Women's Equity Action League) Washington Report June-July, 1981 at 3, Washington, D.C.
91. *Id.*

tracurricular activities, health care, guidance counseling, and residential housing, since these programs do not generally receive direct federal funding. It would have also restricted application of Title IX to employment discrimination claims, thereby relegating these problems to the less inclusive legislation of Title VII of the Civil Rights Act of 1964.[92] Supporters of the amendment found merit in the proposal because it advocated the lessening of federal involvement in education. Furthermore, some educators argued that the lack of governmental restraint would not necessarily create a situation in which women's athletic programs would suffer. Instead, they claimed, administrators would become more innovative in terms of women's programs once they were freed from threats of legal action if these programs did not immediately meet the standards of men's programs.[93] Senator Hatch's proposal was not passed, and he subsequently withdrew the legislation.

Another proposed amendment, commonly referred to as the Family Protection Act, advocated the repeal of Title IX.[94] Its provisions would have removed from the jurisdiction of federal courts the right to determine whether the sexes should be allowed to intermingle in athletics or in any other school activity.

A third effort to restrict the power of Title IX involved a bill introduced by Senators Hatch and Edward Zorinsky of Nebraska.[95] It proposed the OCR reimburse institutions for expenses incurred during any OCR investigation of institutional programs or activities.[96] Opponents of this bill argued that should the OCR be required to reimburse schools without a corresponding increase in its own budget, the total budget actually available for enforcement would diminish.[97] Opponents also argued less money for enforcement would restrict the number of investigations the OCR initiated, thereby limiting the potential deterrent value of the threat of such an investigation.[98] None of the proposed amendments to Title

---

92. *Id.*

93. *Id.*

94. Introduced on June 17, 1981 as companion bills by Rep. Albert Smith (R-AL), H.R. 3955, and Sens. Roger Jepsen (R-IA) and Paul Laxalt (R-NV), S. 1378. As reported in WEAL Washington Report, *supra* note 90.

95. S. 1091, as reported in WEAL Washington Report, *supra* note 90, at 3.

96. WEAL, Washington Report, *supra* note 90.

97. *Id.*

98. *Id.*

IX have been enacted.[99]

A. *Equal Rights Amendment*

There has been no federal legislation enacted prohibiting sex discrimination to date. Supporters of the Equal Rights Amendment (ERA)[100] argued that passage of a constitutional amendment would have remedied the lack of such a general prohibition.[101] In order to amend the United States Constitution, the proposed amendment must first be passed by a three-quarters vote of both the United States Senate and the House of Representatives.[102] Then it must be ratified by at least 38 state legislatures.[103] The ERA was passed in both Houses of Congress in 1972[104] but it did not receive the necessary 38 ratifications from state legislatures by the required deadline of July 1, 1982.[105]

In some instances, individual states have adopted equal rights amendments to their state constitutions. Thus, equal rights amendments have impacted athletics at the state level, but not at the federal level. Several cases have been decided in the complainant's favor on the basis of a state ERA.[106] All of these cases, how-

---

99. For further information on Title IX, *see* Cox, *Intercollegiate Athletics and Title IX*, Geo. Wash. L. Rev. 34 (1977-1978); Tashjian-Brown, *Title IX: Progress Toward Program Specific Regulation of Private Academia*, 10 J.C. & U.L. 1 (1983); Kadzielski, *Title IX of the Education Amendments of 1972: Change or Continuity?* 6 J. L. & Educ. 185 (1977); Kadzielski, *Postsecondary Athletics in an Era of Equality: An Appraisal of the Effect of Title IX*, 5 J.C. & U.L. 123 (1978-79); Martin, *Title IX and Intercollegiate Athletics: Scoring Points for Women*, 8 Ohio N.U.L. Rev. 481 (1981); Comment, *Sex Discrimination in Athletics: Conflicting Legislative and Judicial Approaches*, 29 Ala. L. Rev. 390 (1977-1978); Comment, *Half-Court Girls' Basketball Rules: An Application of the Equal Protection Clause and Title IX*, 65 Iowa L. Rev. 766 (1980); Comment, *Title IX's Promise of Equality of Opportunity in Athletics: Does It Cover the Bases?* 64 Ky. L.J. 432 (1975-76); Comment, *Title IX and Intercollegiate Athletics: HEW Gets Serious About Equality in Sports?* 15 New Eng. L. Rev. 573 (1979-80); Comment, *Title IX: Women's Collegiate Athletics in Limbo*, 40 Wash. & Lee L. Rev. 297 (1983); Comment, *Sex Discrimination and Intercollegiate Athletics: Putting Some Muscle on Title IX*. 88 Yale L.J. 1254 (Apr.-July); Note, *The Application of Title IX to School Athletic Programs*, 68 Cornell L. Rev. 222 (Nov. 1982-Aug. 1983); *Women and Athletics: Toward a Physicality Perspective*, 5 Harv. Women's L.J. 121 (1982).

100. *Supra* note 6.

101. *Supra* note 6.

102. U.S. Const. art. V.

103. *Id.*

104. *Supra* note 6.

105. *Supra* note 6.

106. *See, e.g.*, Darrin v. Gould, 85 Wn. 2d 859, 540 P.2d 882 (1975). *See also*, Packel v.

ever, could have been decided based on other legal arguments in states without ERA's.[107]

In general, the proposed federal ERA absolutely prohibited gender discrimination and required any law using gender as a basis for classification be subject to a strict scrutiny analysis by the courts. ERA opponents claimed this prohibition was an unnecessary step. They believed women's rights are sufficiently protected by the United States Constitution, state equal protection laws, and other federal legislation such as the Equal Pay Act, Title VII, and Title IX.[108]

ERA supporters argued that without proper enforcement, neither Title IX nor Title VII would alleviate the basic problems of sex discrimination.[109] The strength of Title IX, in particular, was and remains dependent on federal funding, since a reduction in funding could effectively diminish OCR's enforcement capabilities. In addition to this financial vulnerability, sex discrimination statutes are also subject to congressional revisions, which may lessen or even negate much of the available protection. It has been argued that a constitutional amendment would be more sheltered from political interests.[110] Supporters of a constitutional amendment argue the effectiveness and importance of an equal rights amendment can be demonstrated in *Darrin v. Gould*.[111] In *Darrin*, the lower court considered the equal protection argument and ruled in favor of the defendant. The Washington Supreme Court,

---

Pennsylvania Interscholastic Athletic Ass'n, 18 Pa. Commw. 45, 334 A.2d 839 (1975), in which the State of Pennsylvania, as plaintiff, claimed the PIAA's bylaws denied female athletes the same opportunity to practice and compete in interscholastic sports afforded male athletes. Citing the Pennsylvania ERA as authority, the court found a PIAA rule that prohibited mixed competition a practice "unconstitutional on its face under the ERA." *See also*, 60 Op. Cal. Att'y. Gen. 326 (1977).

107. *But see* MacLean v. First Northwest Indus. of America, Inc., 24 Wn. App. 161, 600 P.2d 1027 (1979) *rev'd* 96 Wn. 2d 338, 635 P.2d 633 (1981), where a class action was brought against the City of Seattle and the corporation operating a professional basketball team alleging "Ladies Night" price-ticketing policies were violative of the state's equal rights amendment and of the state law that prohibited sex discrimination. The court of appeals reversed a lower court decision and found the ticket practice a violation of the amendment.

108. *Supra* note 6.

109. *Supra* note 6.

110. *Supra* note 6.

111. 85 Wn. 2d 859. *See* Comment, *Sexual Equality in High School Athletics: The Approach of Darrin v. Gould*, 12 Gonz. L. Rev. 691 (Summer 1977).

however, reversed the decision in favor of the plaintiffs, based on the state's equal rights amendment argument.[112] Regardless of the precarious position in which protection against sex discrimination exists, an equal rights amendment on the state level is often helpful and may be crucial to the success of sex discrimination cases[113] and greater athletic opportunities for women.[114]

IV. Title IX and Athletics Programs

A. Standing

The first legal challenge to Title IX was brought by the NCAA. The NCAA sought declaratory and injunctive relief for the invalidation of the Title IX regulations promulgated by HEW in *National Collegiate Athletic Association v. Califano.*[115] The NCAA specifically sought relief for the invalidation of the Title IX regulations promulgated by HEW with respect to sex discrimination in athletics.[116] Summary judgment was granted to HEW as the district court held the NCAA did not have standing as an association representing its member schools to pursue the suit.[117] The NCAA appealed the district court decision.[118] The appeals court reversed the lower court ruling and held that while the NCAA does not have standing to sue in its own right, it does have standing to sue on behalf of its members.[119]

---

112. According to information supplied by the National Organization for Women, (NOW) as of 1984, 16 states had enacted their own individual equal rights amendments. (Telephone interview with authors September, 1984).

113. Four states responded to Title IX by opening all teams to both sexes. The result was that boys dominated all the teams, and fewer girls than before could compete. For instance in Indiana, the first and second-place volleyball teams (previously all female) had one and three boys, respectively. In West Virginia, the first-place girls' bowling team was composed of five boys. Michigan was forced to change its rule so that boys could not compete on a statewide level on girls' teams. This information came from reports sent to member organizations by the National Federation of State High School Athletic Associations. *See* NATIONAL FED'N PUBLICATION, Summer 1975 (in-house publication).

114. For further information on individual state's ERAs, *see* Broder and Wee, *Hawaii's Equal Rights Amendment: Its Impact on Athletic Opportunities and Competition for Women*, 2 U. HAWAII L. REV. 97 (1979).

115. 444 F. Supp. 425, 428 (D. Kan. 1978) *rev'd* 622 F.2d 1382 (10th Cir. 1980); *see also Appeals Court Ruling Favors NCAA*, NCAA News, Apr. 30, 1980 at 1, b, col., 3, 3.

116. 444 F. Supp. 425, 428.

117. 444 F. Supp. 425.

118. 622 F.2d 1382 (10th Cir. 1980).

119. *Id.*

B. Scope and Applicability of Title IX

A major issue in Title IX litigation centers on arguments concerning its scope. The specific question is whether Title IX applies only to the specific departments receiving direct funding (commonly referred to as the "programmatic approach") or extends to any department within an institution that benefits from federal assistance (commonly referred to as the "institutional approach").[120] The dilemma is often expressed as whether Title IX is, or is not, program-specific. An integral factor in the resultant litigation has been the determination of what constitutes qualifying federal assistance. In some cases, it has been argued federal student loan programs constitute federal aid to an institution, while other interpretations define federal aid as only those funds specifically earmarked or directly given to a particular program. Therefore, in terms of the scope of Title IX, the questions become very complex: What constitutes federal aid? Is indirect aid or direct aid required by the statute? Once federal assistance is found, is only the particular program that benefits directly from the aid subject to Title IX regulation, or is the entire institution?

The decision in *Grove City College v. Bell*,[121] has answered some of these questions, but other issues remain to be clarified through further litigation or legislation. Many of the cases preceding *Grove City College v. Bell* dealt with the "programmatic" versus "institutional" issue.[122] The resolution of certain issues in

---

120. *See supra* note 83 and accompanying text.

121. 687 F.2d 684 (3d Cir. 1982).

122. Various federal district courts had taken a programmatic approach. *See, e.g.,* Hillsdale College v. Dep't of Health, Educ., and Welfare, 696 F.2d 418 (6th Cir. 1982) *vacated and remanded* 466 U.S. 901 (1984) (for further consideration in light of Grove City College v. Bell, 465 U.S. 555 (1984)); Bennett v. W. Texas State Univ. 525 F. Supp. 77 (N.D. Tex. 1981) *rev'd without published opinion* 698 F.2d 1215 (N.D. Tex. 1983).

In University of Richmond v. Bell, 543 F. Supp. 321 (E.D. Va. 1982), the University of Richmond, a private institution, refused to give the (OCR) investigator access to data requested in conjunction with the investigation of a complaint alleging sex discrimination in the institution's athletic program. The university argued the agency had no authority to request any information because the athletic department received no federal funding. The OCR argued that because the athletic department benefits from other federal funding received by the university, specifically federal student loan and grant programs, it falls under Title IX jurisdiction.

In its opinion, the court redefined federal student funding as payment for services rendered to the college and as such was not deemed direct assistance to the institution. Even if these funds were construed as aid to educational institutions, the court decided they do not

Grove City College was extremely important, not only in terms of the potential ramifications for hundreds of schools whose only federal assistance exists in the form of indirect aid or student participation in loan programs, but also because it established a precedent and settled contradictory approaches and decisions among the circuit courts.[123]

The decision in *North Haven Board of Education v. Bell*[124] had particularly important ramifications for Title IX litigation. While the case did not specifically deal with athletics, the Supreme Court resolved two fundamental questions about the scope of Title IX applicable to athletics. First, it decided Title IX prevented discrimination against employees as well as against students. Second, it determined both the power to regulate and to terminate federal assistance are program-specific. Thus, Title IX sanctions are limited to particular programs receiving federal financial assistance.[125]

The issue of "programmatic" versus "institutional" was ultimately decided by the Supreme Court in *Grove City v. Bell*.[126] This 1984 decision had an immediate and dramatic impact on then-pending litigation initiated by the Department of Education (successor to HEW and responsible for Title IX enforcement) against colleges and school systems allegedly violating Title IX.

---

constitute the requisite direct aid necessary for Title IX jurisdiction as was determined by North Haven Bd. of Educ. v. Bell 456 U.S. 512 (1982), which established the program-specific interpretation of the statute. *See also Univ. of Richmond Sues to Halt U.S. Probe of Its Sports Programs,* Chronicle of Higher Educ., May 11, 1981, at 8, col. 1; *Judge Bars Civil Rights Office's Probe of Richmond Athletic Department,* Chronicle of Higher Educ., July 21, 1982, at 9, 10, col. 2, 1; *Court Bars Title IX Athletics Probe,* NCAA News, July 14, 1982, at 3, col. 3; *Decision That Limits Title IX Will Stand,* NCAA News, Sept. 20, 1982, at 1, 12, col. 1, 1, and *Civil-Rights Office Dropping Sex-Bias Investigation at William and Mary,* Chronicle of Higher Educ., Dec. 15, 1982, at 23, col. 1.

An institutional approach was originally taken by the court in Haffer v. Temple Univ., 524 F. Supp. 531 (E.D. Pa. 1981) *aff'd* 688 F.2d 14 (3d Cir. 1982) and by the court of appeals in *Othen,* 699 F.2d 309 (6th Cir. 1983).

123. *See also,* Yellow Springs Exempted Village School Dist. Bd. of Educ. v. Ohio High School Athletic Ass'n, 443 F. Supp. 753 (S.D. Ohio, 1978), *rev'd* 647 F.2d 651 (6th Cir. 1981), which involved OHSAA rule excluding girls from participation contact sports. The district court found the rule unconstitutional based on the Due Process clauses of the fifth and fourteenth amendments. On appeal, parts of the lower court's decision were reversed and the case was remanded for further proceedings although an injunction against the rule was maintained.

124.   456 U.S. 512 (1982).

125.   *Id.*

126.   465 U.S. 555 (1984).

The Department of Education had to drop cases in which policies in an athletic department were being challenged if it could not be established that the athletic departments[127] or programs directly received federal funds. Cases against the University of Alabama, University of Maryland, Penn State University, the New York City school system, and at least 19 other institutions were immediately discontinued or severely narrowed when no such connection could be found.[128]

The Office of Civil Rights (OCR) commenced a proceeding in March 1984, which may indicate the strategy the OCR will employ in future Title IX actions.[129] The OCR informed Auburn University that an investigation had revealed Title IX violations in the Auburn athletic department.[130] The OCR conceded that it no longer had jurisdiction over the athletic department, but charged

---

127. *Id.* Although the *Grove City College* decision did not directly involve the application of Title IX to athletics, Justice Brennan (with whom Justice Marshall joined, concurring in part and dissenting in part) noted at 595 n.9:

> . . . Congress has consistently endorsed the Department's regulation of college athletic programs, and indeed has affirmatively required such regulations. *See, e.g.,* Pub. L. 93-380, Sec. 844, 88 stat. 612 (1974) ("The Secretary shall prepare and publish . . . proposed regulations implementing the provisions of Title IX . . . relating to the prohibition of sex discrimination in federally assisted education programs which shall include with respect to intercollegiate athletics reasonable provisions considering the nature of particular sports.") See also Brief for Council of Collegiate Women Athletic Administrators as Amicus Curiae 4-16. *Cf.* Haffer v. Temple Univ.. . . . The opinion for the Court, limited as it is to a college that receives only "(s)tudent financial aid . . . (that) is *sui generis*", *ante,* at 16, obviously does not decide whether athletic programs operated by colleges receiving other forms of federal financial assistance are within the reach of Title IX. *Cf.* 688 F.2d, at 15, n.5 (discussing the many forms of federal aid received by Temple University and its athletic department).

Brennan's concurring dissent in Grove City College v. Bell, 104 S. Ct. 1211, 465 U.S. at ___.

128. *Supra* note 45.

129. Immediately following the *Grove City College* decision, the OCR dropped its efforts to cut off federal aid to the University of Maryland and Auburn University for Title IX violations in their athletic departments. The OCR decided it did not have jurisdiction to investigate the departments because they received no direct federal funding. However, in the case of Auburn University, the OCR decided it would still seek to pursue enforcement on the student financial aid program at Auburn since that program recieved federal aid. Financial aid was involved because the OCR charged that the institution had failed "to award athletics scholarships and grants-in-aid so as to provide reasonable opportunities for such awards for students of each sex in proportion to the number of students of each sex participating in intercollegiate athletics." For further information, *see Grove City Decision Spurs OCR Actions,* NCAA News, March 21, 1984, at 1, 16, col. 1.

130. *Id.*

that its investigation also revealed Title IX violations in the awarding of financial aid.[131] The OCR therefore commenced proceedings to terminate all federal funding for the Auburn financial aid program.[132] Concentration on athletic scholarship policies may be the most effective legal tool remaining for the OCR unless and until federal legislation is passed reaffirming Title IX's applicability to all of a school's or college's programs.

Such legislation was introduced by a bipartisan coalition of senators and congressmen in April 1984.[133] The legislation proposed to change the wording in Title IV, Title IX, the Rehabilitation Act (rights of the handicapped), and the Age Discrimination Act, to state that discrimination was prohibited in the programs and activities of any "recipient" of federal funds. The bill further defined "recipient" as "any state or political subdivision thereof, . . . or any public or private agency, institution or organization, or other entity . . . to which federal financial assistance is extended (directly or through another entity or a person)."[134] As of 1985, however, no legislation has been enacted to reverse the Supreme Court's decision.[135]

C. *Office of Civil Rights Title IX Compliance Reviews*

The Office of Civil Rights is responsible for conducting compliance reviews of Title IX. It selects schools at random to review for Title IX compliance and also reviews schools based on complaints brought by individuals. The OCR begins a Title IX investigation by notifying the school and then collecting data on the over-

---

131. *Id.*
132. *Id.*
133. *Supra* note 26.
134. *Supra* note 26.
135. For articles concerning Title IX court decisions, *see Even Colleges That Get Only Indirect Aid Must Obey U.S. Bias Laws, Court Says,* Chronicle of Higher Educ., September 1, 1982, at 19, col. 2; *Ruling Could "Decimate" Protection Against Sex Bias, Official Says,* Chronicle of Higher Educ., September 1, 1982, at 20, col. 1; *Sports Not Covered by Bias Law Unless U.S. Pays, A Judge Rules,* Chronicle of Higher Educ., March 9, 1981, at 5, col. 1; *Bell Unveils "flexible" Approach to Settling Complaints of Sex Bias in College Athletics,* Chronicle of Higher Educ., April 27, 1982, at 1, col. 1; *First Circuit Takes Programmatic View of Title IX,* Sports Law Reporter, Vol. 4, No. 10, February 1982, at 1, col. 1; *Judge Says Title IX Doesn't Cover College's Sports Program,* Chronicle of Higher Educ., September 9, 1981, at 8, col. 1, 2, and, *Court to Decide Case on Title IX and Student Aid,* Chronicle of Higher Educ., March 2, 1981, at 1, 12, col. 6. 3.

all athletic program. The information may include the number of teams, scheduling of games and practice times, travel and per-diem allowances, compensation of coaches, provision of facilities, and publicity. Based on a review of the data, the OCR will determine whether the equivalent treatment, benefits, and opportunities mandated by Title IX have been afforded to both sexes.

A finding of inequality in a single component of the program is not a basis in and of itself for the OCR to find a school in noncompliance with Title IX. The OCR's approach in investigating and determining compliance with Title IX has been to focus on the *overall* provision of equivalent opportunities in the athletic program. Therefore, the OCR will look to other components of the athletic program before it finds the school to be in noncompliance. In addition, Secretary Terrel H. Bell of the Department of Education adopted a nonconfrontation approach in 1981. Under this policy, the OCR may find schools in compliance with Title IX if the schools agree to rectify any violations of Title IX found through the OCR's investigation.

OCR officials will meet with the administrators of an investigated institution and review the OCR's proposed findings before issuing a letter of noncompliance. If the institution voluntarily forms a committee to adopt a plan to rectify its violations within a reasonable period of time, the institution will be granted a letter of compliance for implementing a corrective plan. The Department of Education is then responsible for monitoring the progress of the plan. If the plan is not implemented within the time specified or proves to be an inadequate remedy, the OCR may find the institution in noncompliance and take further legal action.[136]

---

136. The Office of Civil Rights had issued decisions after Title IX compliance reviews on a number of institutions, including the following: University of Akron; Bentley College; University of Bridgeport; Central Michigan University; Central Missouri University; University of Hawaii at Manoa; University of Illinois, Urbana Campus; University of Iowa; University of Kansas; Kansas State University; Michigan State University; University of Missouri, Kansas City; University of Nevada, Reno; Northwest Missouri State University; Pensacola Junior College; St. Olaf College; Texas A & M University; University of Texas at Arlington; and Yale University.

V. Sex Discrimination Cases And The Student-Athlete

The following section discusses cases concerning the presence or absence of teams available to either sex. Within each category, the cases have been further divided into those dealing with contact and those dealing with noncontact sports. This was done because the litigants' approach—and sometimes the Courts' result—differ due to the type of sport and resulting physical contact involved.

The division of cases is not by legal theory, since very often the litigation makes use of several prominent theories—for example, equal protection, Title IX, and state equal right amendments (in certain states). Therefore, to distinguish between the cases would entail too much repetition without sufficiently differentiating the decisions.

The courts generally view contact sports and noncontact sports differently. Thus, in cases involving sex discrimination in athletics, the arguments used will vary depending on whether or not the particular sport is designated a contact sport. Under Title IX, contact sports include boxing, wrestling, rugby, ice hockey, football, basketball, and other sports in which the purpose or major activity involves bodily contact. In some jurisdictions, baseball and soccer have also been labeled contact sports. For contact sports certain arguments are commonly propounded. The most frequent defense raised is that women, as a group, lack the physical qualifications necessary for safe and reasonable competition against men in a sport in which bodily contact is expected to occur. It is argued that women are more susceptible to injury because they have a higher percentage of adipose (fatty) tissues and a lighter bone structure. Because of these physiological differences, the argument goes, contact sports are more dangerous for all women.

Plaintiffs in such litigation counter this argument by insisting that physical capability should be determined on a case-by-case basis. When there is no opportunity for participation in a certain sport, a blanket prohibition is overinclusive and violates equal protection by assuming that all women have identical physical structures and that all men are stronger and more athletically capable than women. Indeed, the health and safety rationale behind such total exclusion may fail a court challenge, as has been demonstrated in some cases. In one case, a women who was 5'9" tall and weighed over 200 pounds was denied a chance to play football because her supposedly lighter bone structure would render her more susceptible to injury. There was, however, no height or weight requirements for men, and the court thus found exclusion from participation to be unacceptable.[137]

Although the most important consideration used to substantiate separate teams for contact sports is the health and safety of the participants, this argument does not apply to noncontact sports. Since there is no legitimate and important state interest for allowing exclusion from noncontact sports, citing sex as the sole exclusionary factor would constitute a violation of United States constitutional guarantees of the equal protection clause. Thus, defendants make different arguments in noncontact sport sex discrimination cases. The most common argument is that if men and women are allowed to compete together and/or against each other, the psychological development of both would be impaired. This stance is generally based on a variation of the "tradition" argument, which says that allowing men and women to compete as equals will irreparably disturb the innate nature of relationships between the sexes.

Another commonly made argument is that if all men and women are allowed to compete together, men will dominate the co-ed teams. The underlying rationale here is that since men are inherently stronger and more physically capable than women, co-ed teams will actually limit womens opportunities. Plaintiffs in such cases argue this justification does not account for individual differences among participants. Additionally, it does not recognize the argument that if women are given opportunities to compete against men from the beginning of their athletic careers, their capabilities would improve and men may not be able to totally dominate the athletic field.

A. One Team Only

The general rule in both contact and noncontact sports is that when only one team is available, both sexes must be allowed to try out for and play on that team. The student-athlete's capability and

---

137. Clinton v. Nagy, 411 F. Supp. 1396 (N.D. Ohio 1974).

risk of injury must be determined on an individual basis, with recognition that the contact or noncontact sports designations only matter if there is opportunity for athletes of both sexes to compete. If there is ample opportunity for women to compete on their own, courts appear less apt to allow women to compete with men in contact sports.[138]

B. Contact Sports

In cases where contact sports are involved and there is no women's team, there is a split in decisions as to whether to allow a female to play on the men's team. In the majority of cases, as represented by *Clinton v. Nagy*,[139] the courts have upheld the women's sex discrimination claim and have allowed participation on the men's team.[140] In some cases, the plaintiff-female was not successful because of the lack of state action or there was no violation of the sex discrimination laws.[141]

---

138. For further information, *see The Case for Equality in Athletics*, 22 CLEV. ST. L. REV. 570 (Fall 1973); *Female High School Athlete and Interscholastic Sports*, 4 J. L. & EDUC. 285 (April 1975); *The Emergent Law of Women and Amateur Sports: Recent Developments*, 28 WAYNE L. REV. 1701 (Summer 1982).

139. *See supra* note 137 and accompanying text.

140. For further information *see Irrebuttable Presumption Doctrine: Applied to State and Federal Regulations Excluding Females from Contact Sports*, 4 U. DAYTON L. REV. 197 (1979); *Title IX of the Education Amendment of 1972 Prohibits All-Female Teams in Sports Not Previously Dominated by Males*, 14 SUFFOLK U.L. REV. 1471 (Fall 1980); *Girls' High School Basketball Rules Held Unconstitutional*, 16 J. FAM. L. 345 (Fall 1978).

141. *See also*, the following decisions:

(a) Lavin v. Chicago Bd. of Educ. 73 F.R.D. 438 (1977), Lavin v. Illinois High School Ass'n 527 F.2d 58 (7th Cir. 1975), in which the trial court denied the class action claim because plaintiff was no longer a member of the "class" after graduation and because plaintiff did not present an argument that showed she was qualified enough to make the boy's squad, so was not a member of that particular "class" of girls either. The court did allow plaintiff's individual claim for damages.

(b) Muscare v. O'Malley, Civil No. 76-C-3729 (N.D. Ill. 1977), where in ruling for the plaintiff, a 12-year-old girl, the court reasoned that offering tackle football for males, and only touch football to females, was a violation of equal opportunity under the fourteenth amendment.

(c) Lincoln v. Mid-Cities Pee Wee Football Ass'n, 576 S.W.2d 922 (Tex. Civ. App. 1979), where an action was brought by an eight-year-old female who wanted to play on a Pee Wee Football team. The appeals court stated that the discrimination complained of must be state action or private conduct that was encouraged, or closely interrelated in function with state action. The court found neither and held that the Texas ERA did not cover purely private conduct.

(d) Hoover v. Meiklejohn, 430 F. Supp. 164 (D. Colo. 1977), where the district court held for the plaintiff, based on an equal protection analysis. The court held that the appro-

For instance, in *Junior Football Ass'n of Orange County, Texas v. Gaudet*,[142] the trial court granted a temporary injunction allowing plaintiff to play football in the Junior Football Association until she reached puberty. This decision was based on article 1, section 3a of the Texas Constitution, which provides: "Equality under the law shall not be denied or abridged because of sex, race,

---

priate analysis requires a triangular balancing of the importance of the opportunities being unequally burdened or denied against the strength of the state's interests and the character of the group being denied the opportunity. The court found that the complete prohibition by CHSAA violated Hoover's rights to equal protection and that the school had three options: allow co-ed teams; discontinue the sport for males; or field a second, all-female team.

(e) Leffel v. Wisconsin Interscholastic Athletic Ass'n, 444 F. Supp. 1117 (E.D. Wis. 1978), where plaintiffs were granted the right to participate in a varsity interscholastic program in any sport in which only a boys' team was provided. The court awarded summary judgment finding that:

> . . . exclusion of girls from all contact sports in order to protect female high school athletes from unreasonable risk of injury was not fairly or substantially related to a justifiable government objective in the context of the Fourteenth Amendment, where demand for relief by the instant plaintiffs would be met by establishing separate girls' teams with comparable programs. *Id.* at 1118-19.

(f) Simpson v. Boston Area Youth Soccer, Inc., Case No. 83-2631 (Super. Ct. Mass. 1983) (settled), where defendant soccer association excluded plaintiff, a sixth-grade female, from the all-male soccer team in her town. Plaintiff had played for three years on co-education teams, and many of her former teammates were on the team. Although the defendant also maintained a girls' league, no team in that league was readily accessible to the plaintiff. Plaintiff was also considered an above-average soccer player and maintained that the girls' league would present inferior competition. The case was settled when defendant soccer league agreed to change its constitution and bylaws to allow females to play on male teams, with such teams being entered in the boys' league.

(g) Force v. Pierce City R-VI School Dist., 570 F. Supp. 1020 (W.D. Mo. 1983), where the court granted injunctive relief for the plaintiff, a 13-year-old female seeking to play on the interscholastic football team, and held that:

> (1) no sufficiently substantial relationship was shown between blanket prohibition against female participation on a high school football team and Title IX of the Educational Amendments of 1972, high school activities association rules and regulations, maintaining athletic educational programs which are as safe for participants as possible, or administrative ease, and (2) under the circumstances, rules and regulations of high school activities association and manner of promulgation and enforcement thereof constituted "state action," thus subjecting association's actions to equal protection clause requirements and, as such, enforcement of rule which effectively prohibited members of opposite sex from competing on same team in interscholastic football would be enjoined. *Id.*

(h) Morris v. Michigan State Bd. of Educ., 472 F.2d 1207 (6th Cir. 1973), in which plaintiff tennis player brought suit against a state high school association because of its rule barring mixed competition in interscholastic sports when no girls team existed at her school. The trial court granted an injunction against enforcement of the rule. On appeal, the decision was affirmed, but the suit was remanded to the lower court to specify that the rule be barred only in noncontact sport situations.

142. 546 S.W.2d 70 (Tex. Civ. App. 1976).

color, creed or national origin."

The Amateur Athletic Association in *Gaudet* appealed, contending there was not sufficient state action to authorize the injunction. The association argued there was insufficient evidence of state involvement to authorize the temporary injunction and the court agreed. The court noted: "Not every subversion by the federal or state government automatically involves the beneficiary in 'state action,' and it is not necessary or appropriate in this case to undertake a precise delineation of the legal rule as it may operate in circumstances not now before the court."[143]

C. Noncontact Sports

In cases involving noncontact sports where there is no women's team, the trend and majority of cases allow the women to participate on the men's team. Cases such as *Gilpin v. Kansas State High School Activities Association, Inc.*[144] *Brenden v. Independent School District 742*[145] and *Reed v. Nebraska School Activities Association*[146] allowed women to participate on men's cross-country, tennis, and golf teams where there were no women's teams.[147] Other courts have reached an opposite result and have

---

143. Simkins v. Moses H. Cone Memorial Hosp. 323 F.2d 959, 967 (4th Cir. 1963).

144. 377 F. Supp. 1233 (D. Kan. 1974), in which plaintiff, a junior high school cross country runner, was held to be effectively deprived of an opportunity to compete. The court held that the KSHSAA rule prohibiting mixed competition was unconstitutional and noted: "Thus, although the Association's overall objective is commendable and legitimate, the method employed to accomplish that objective is simply over-broad in its reach. It is precisely this sort of overinclusiveness which the Equal Protection Clause disdains." *Id.* at 1243.

145. 342 F. Supp. 1224 (D. Minn. 1972), *aff'd*, 477 F.2d 1292 (8th Cir. 1973), in which plaintiffs protested as a rule prohibiting mixed tennis and cross country ski race competitions. The court found the application of the rule arbitrary, unreasonable, and unconstitutional.

146. 341 F. Supp. 258 (D. Neb. 1972), in which plaintiff challenged a state high school athletic association's practice of providing a public school golf program for boys, while providing none for the girls and prohibiting girls from participation with or against boys. The district court held for plaintiff reasoning that her interest to compete and receive coaching outweighed the association's concerns.

147. For further cases, *see* Carnes v. Tennessee Secondary School Athletic Ass'n. 415 F. Supp. 569 (E.D. Tenn. 1976), involving a girl who wanted to play on the boys' high school baseball team. The court granted a preliminary injunction from a rule barring mixed competition in contact sports. The district court held that there was a likelihood that Carnes would prevail on the merits of the claim and a denial of injunction would result in irreparable harm to Carnes. *See also* Morris v. Michigan State Bd. of Educ., 472 F.2d 1207 (6th Cir.

prevented females from participating on the men's team.[148] Again, where private organizations are involved, the plaintiff-women may have difficulty proving the necessary state action.[149]

One area of amateur sports, Little League Baseball, has been a frequent party to lawsuits involving noncontact sports and sex discrimination.[150] In 1984, a number of lawsuits involving such issues were also brought against the International Olympic Committee before the 1984 Summer Olympic Games were held in Los Angeles.[151]

1973); Haas v. South Bend Community School Corp., 259 Ind. 515, 289 N.E.2d 495 (1972); Bednar v. Nebraska School Activities Ass'n., 531 F.2d 922 (8th Cir. 1976).

148. *See, e.g.,* Harris v. Illinois High School Ass'n, No. S-Civ. 72-75 (S.D. Ill. 1972), involved an action brought by a girl who wanted to play on her high school boys' tennis team. There was no girls' team. The court held that gender classifications were rational. Plaintiff's claim that she had a "right" to participate in interscholastic sports was denied. *See also,* Gregoria v. Bd. of Educ. of Asbury Park, No. A-1277-70 (N.J. Super Ct. 1971); Hollander v. Connecticut Interscholastic Athletic Conf., Inc., Civil No. 12-49-27 (Conn. Super. Ct. 1971) *appeal dismissed,* 164 Conn. 658, 295 A.2d 671 (1972).

149. 208 U.S. 412 (1908).

150. *See,* the following cases which involved suits against Little League Baseball: Rappaport v. Little League Baseball, Inc., 65 F.R.D. 545 (1975), which involved a group of parents and plaintiff girls who filed suit against Little League Baseball because of its policy of excluding girls from participation. The Little League changed its policy after the complaint was filed. The court ruled the case moot; King v. Little League Baseball, Inc., 505 F.2d 264 (6th Cir. 1974); Magill v. Baseball Conference, 364 F. Supp. 1212 (W.D. Pa. 1973); Magill v. Avonworth Baseball Conference, 516 F.2d 1328 (3rd Cir. 1975); Fortin v. Darlington Little League, Inc., 376 F. Supp. 473 (D.R.I. 1974), *rev'd* 514 F.2d 344 (1st Cir. 1975); Nat'l Org. for Women Essex County Chapter v. Little League Baseball, Inc., 127 N.J. Super. 522, 318 A.2d 33 (1974).

151. See, in particular, Martin v. Int'l Olympic Comm., 740 F.2d 670 (9th Cir. 1984), which involved Mary Decker, Grete Waitz, and 50 other leading female runners who filed in August 1983 a sex discrimination suit against the International Olympic Committee, the Los Angeles Olympic Organizing Committee, the International Amateur Athletic Federation, the Athletics Congress, and others. The suit was filed in Los Angeles Superior Court, and sought an order that would force the defendants to include 5,000-and 10,000-meter runs for women at the 1984 Olympic Games in Los Angeles. These events are part of the men's events and were historically excluded from the women's program because of the belief that women could not physically handle the distances. The request for injunctive relief was denied by the court. The International Olympic Committee later added these events to the women's program for the 1988 Olympic Games in Seoul, S. Korea. *See also Female Runners Sue to Add Long Events,* N.Y. Times, August 12, 1983, at A18, col. 1; *Female Runners Lose Appeal,* N.Y. Times, June 22, 1984, at A19, col. 1; *Olympic Challenge: Women Sue for 5 and 10-K Races,* 70 A.B.A. J. 42 (March, 1984).

D. Women's Team, No Men's Team

The all-women, no-men type of case has arisen only with non-contact sports. In cases where there is a women's team and no men's team for noncontact sports, there is a split in decisions as to whether to allow a male to play on the women's team. In *Gomes v. Rhode Island Interscholastic League*,[152] the courts upheld the male's sex discrimination claim and allowed him to play on the women's volleyball team. In *Clark v. Arizona Interscholastic Ass'n*,[153] the court refused to allow boys to compete on the girls' volleyball team.[154] The male-plaintiff may not succeed for a variety of reasons, including lack of state action where a private organizatuon is involved,[155] prohibition of males on women's teams to redress disparate treatment of females in interscholastic athletic programs,[156] interscholastic programs to promote athletic opportunities for females,[157] and the fact that there are more general ath-

---

152. 469 F. Supp. 659 (D.R.I. 1979), *vacated as moot*, 604 F.2d 733 (1st Cir. 1979).

153. 695 F.2d 1126 (9th Cir. 1982, *cert. den.* 104 S. Ct. 79 (1983).

154. For further information on Clark v. Arizona Interscholastic Ass'n, *see Constitutional Law—Equal Protection—Sex Discrimination Against Males in Athletics—Physiological Differences are Valid Reasons to Exclude Boys from Girls' Athletic Teams*, (Clark v. Arizona Interscholastic Ass'n, 695 F.2d 1126 (9th Cir. 1982), *cert. den.*, 104 S. Ct. 79 (1983)), 6 WHITTIER L. REV. 151 (1984); *Equal Protection Scrutiny of High School Athletics*, (Clark v. Arizona Interscholastic Ass'n, 695 F.2d 1126 (9th Cir. 1982), *cert. den.* 104 S. Ct. 79 (1983)), 72 KY. L.J. 935 (1983-1984).

155. *See* White v. Corpus Christi Little Misses Kickball Ass'n, 526 S.W.2d 766 (Tex. Civ. App. 1975). On appeal, plaintiff argued that denial of right to play in the girls' kickball because of his sex was a denial of equal protection under both the federal and state constitutions. The appeals court held the plaintiff failed to establish the requisite state action, because his participation was denied by a private organization acting without any connection to government except that the games were played in a public park.

156. *See* Forte v. Bd. of Educ. North Babylon Union Free School Dist., 431 N.Y.S.2d 321 (1980), which involved an action which was brought by plaintiff Forte on behalf of his son, a 17-year-old high school student who wanted to play on the North Babylon High School volleyball team, which was all female. The court held for the defendant. The court reasoned that the rule the school district had enacted as a discernible and permissible means of redressing disparate treatment of females in interscholastic athletic programs.

157. *See* Petrie v. Illinois High School Ass'n, 75 Ill. App. 3d 1980, 31 Ill. Dec. 653, 394 N.E.2d 855 (1979), an action brought by plaintiff Petrie, who wanted to play on the girls' high school volleyball team since the school had no boys' team. The Illinois High School Association would not allow Petrie to play on the girls' team. The appeals court, affirmed a lower court decision which upheld the association's rule. The court found no violation of state law and reasoned the association's rule "substantially related to and served the achievement of the governmental objective of maintaining, fostering, and promoting athletic opportunities for girls."

letic opportunities for males.[158]

E.   Women's Teams and Men's Teams

In sex discrimination cases involving athletes in which there are existing teams for both sexes, four different types of arguments are generally raised. The first is that "separate but equal is not equal." In these cases, the women sue to participate on the men's teams because the competition may be better and the women are far superior to the participants on the women's teams. As *O'Connor v. Board of Education of School Dist. No. 23*[159] illustrates, the court will generally approve "separate but equal" teams and rule against plaintiff-females who want to play on boys' teams and their arguments on playing ability. The second type of argument is that the separate teams are not equal, especially with respect to the benefits and opportunities provided to the teams. In *Aiken v. Lieuallen*,[160] plaintiff-female athletes contended they were discriminated against in the areas of transportation, officiating, coaching, and the school's commitment to competitive programs. In a similar case, a court awarded damages to plaintiff-female athletes and ordered equivalent funding for the men's and women's athletic programs.[161]

---

158.   *See*, Mularadelis v. Haldane Central School Bd., 74 A.D.2d 248, 427 N.Y.S.2d 458 (1980), an action brought by plaintiff Mularadelis, a member of the high school's girls' tennis team who was told by the school board he could no longer play on the team. The appeals court reversed a lower court decision and held for the school board on the basis that Title IX allowed for the exclusion of boys from the girls' team when there were, overall, more athletic opportunities for boys in the community; *see also* Attorney Gen. v. Massachusetts Interscholastic Athletic Ass'n Inc., 378 Mass. 342, 393 N.E.2d 284 (1979).

159.   645 F.2d 578 (7th Cir. 1981), *cert. denied*, 454 U.S. 1084, (1981), in which a junior high school girl sought to try out for the boys' team despite the existence of a separate but equal girls' team. The district court granted a preliminary injunction to the plaintiff holding the school's classification violated plaintiff's fundamental right to develop as an athlete. The appeals court reversed holding the plaintiff had not demonstrated a reasonable likelihood that the two-team approach for this contact sport was not substantially related to the objective of maximizing participation in sports.

160.   39 Or. App. 779, 593 P.2d 1243 (1979), in which plaintiff taxpayers and parents of student-athletes on the University of Oregon women's basketball team appealed a ruling of the chancellor of the Board of Higher Educ. that the university was not violating OR. REV. STAT § 659.150, that prohibited discrimination based on sex. On appeal, the court, after reviewing allegations of discrimination in areas of transportation, officiating, coaching, and university commitment, remanded the case to the chancellor for further review. For further information on *Aiken, see* Aiken v. Lievallen and Peterson v. Oregon State Univ.: *Defining Equity in Athletics,* 8 J.C. & U.L. 369 (1981-82).

161.   Blair v. Washington State Univ. No. 28816 (Super. Ct. Wash. 1982), in which a

The third type of case occurs when two teams exist but the women compete under different playing rules than the men. These situations, challenged on equal protection grounds, have produced mixed results. The trend seems to be to disallow different rules when those rules are based purely on the gender of the athletes, especially when those rules place those who play under a disadvantage if they want to continue in the sport.

The fourth type of case involves different seasons for the same men's and women's sport. The courts have generally held separate seasons of play are not a denial of equal protection of the law.

F. *Separate But Equal*

The sexes are generally separated when it comes to participation in sports, and the challenges to this practice have been largely unavailing. The doctrine of "separate but equal" remains applicable to sex distinctions, even though it has been rejected for discrimination based on race. Thus, if separate teams exist for men and women, there may be a prohibition against co-ed teams or against women competing against men. The doctrine raises the critical question of whether or not such separate teams are substantially equal. The fact that two teams exist does not necessarily satisfy the doctrine. "Separate but equal" is based on the concept that the exclusion of a group is not unconstitutional if the excluded group is provided with comparable opportunities. If women are excluded from the men's basketball team but are provided with an equal one of their own, the school district will not be in violation of Title IX under the "separate but equal" theory. When the sexes are segregated in athletics, there must be an overall equality of expenditures, coaching, and access to facilities. Without this substantial equality, the existence of separate teams and the prohibition of women competing with men is unconstitutional.

Apart from these circumstances, the segregation of the sexes in athletics is generally upheld, although the courts are usually careful to examine the specific circumstances in each case before

---

class action brought by present and former student-athletes at Washington State University alleged sex discrimination in its athletic programs. The claim was based on the Washington State Equal Rights Amendment. The court held for the plaintiffs and ordered in part increased financial support for women's athletics.

making a determination. As under an equal protection analysis, a court usually considers whether or not the particular sport in question is a contact[162] or a noncontact sport.[163] Physiological differences between the sexes have been found to be a valid reason for the exclusion of one sex from a contact sport. When dealing with noncontact sports, the courts have allowed co-educational partici-

---

162. *See* the following cases:

(a) Hutchins v. Bd. of Trustees of Michigan State Univ. No. G79-87 (W.D. Mich. 1979), which involved a Title IX complaint brought by the women's basketball team from the Michigan State East Lansing campus against Michigan State University and the Board of Trustees, alleging the men's team was receiving better treatment. The alleged better treatment included more money for traveling and better facilities. The court held for the plaintiffs and issued a temporary restraining order barring the better treatment of the men's team.

(b) Peterson v. Oregon State Univ. (settled 1980), which involved two student-athletes who filed a complaint with the Board of Education of the State of Oregon which alleged Oregon State Univ. (OSU) offered athletic programs of lesser quality to female student-athletes than were offered to their male counterparts. A settlement was reached, OSU Conciliation Agreement for Sex Equality in Intercollegiate Athletics, in July, 1980, that implemented a five-year plan at OSU designed to put the men's and women's athletic programs on an equal competitive basis.

163. *See* the following cases.

(a) Michigan Dep't of Civil Rights, *ex rel.* Forton v. Waterford Township Dep't of Parks and Recreation, 355 N.W.2d 305 (Mich. Ct. App. 1983), in which a plaintiff brought a Civil Rights Act claim based on defendant's policy of maintaining a gender-based elementary level basketball program. The appeals court reversed the district court's decision and ruled in favor of the plaintiff. The court reasoned that: (1) separate leagues involved were not equal and could not withstand equal protection analysis, and consequently violated the Civil Rights Act, and (2) subsequent modification of policy to allow up to two girls to participate on each boys' basketball team and two boys on each girls' basketball team did not cure the statutory violation.

(b) Ritacco v. Norwin School Dist., 361 F. Supp. 930 (W.D. Pa. 1973), in which the plaintiff, a high school graduate, brought a class action suit against The Pennsylvania Interscholastic Athletic Association for its rule which in effect required separate girls' and boys' teams in contact sports. The court noted plaintiff no longer belonged to the class and was not a proper party. It also noted the rule did not unfairly discriminate against females and had in fact caused a "virtual mushrooming of girls' interscholastic sports teams."

(c) Ruman v. Eskew, 343 N.E.2d 806 (Ind. Ct. App. 1976), in which plaintiff, Ruman, wanted to play on the high school boys' tennis team, even though there was a girls' team at her school. The Indiana High School Athletic Association prohibited girls from playing on boys' teams if there were girls' teams in the same sport. The court upheld the defendant's rule since it was reasonably related to the objective of providing athletic opportunities for both males and females. It further stated that "until girls' programs comparable to those established for boys exist, the rule cannot be justified." However, in this case, since the trial court had already decided the issue of "whether the tennis program for girls at Munster High School during the school year 1974-75 was and is comparable to that for boys," the appellate court believed it was in no position to "review the evidentiary basis upon which the facts rest."

pation when only one team is sponsored and athletic opportunities for the excluded sex have previously been limited.

G. Same Sport, Different Rules

Cases and issues in this section have traditionally arisen in basketball because, in that sport, women's playing rules are sometimes different. As evidenced by the *Bucha v. Illinois High School Association*,[164] cases have also evolved from generally disparate treatment of female student-athletes rather than from different rules of a sport. In cases where there are different playing rules for women's and men's teams in contact sports, there is a split in decisions whether the women's rules should be changed to conform with the men's. The plaintiff-females in these cases generally have alleged sex discrimination based on the rule differences with men's sports and also the reduced opportunity to compete against other women (who had the advantage of playing under men's rules) for college scholarships. In *Dodson v. Arkansas Activities Association*,[165] the court ruled for the plaintiff-women student-athletes,

---

164.   351 F. Supp. 69 (N.D. Ill. 1972), in which plaintiff female-students brought a class action against the Illinois High School Association (IHSA) because of its bylaws that placed limitations on girls' athletic contests that were not applied to boys' athletics. The district court held for the association reasoning the traditional equal protection standard "requires this court to defer to the judgment of the physical educators of the IHSA once a rational relationship has been shown to exist. . ." *Id.* at 75. The court found a factual basis for the IHSA's claim that physical and psychological differences existed to warrant the different standards.

165.   468 F. Supp. 394 (E.D. Ark. 1979), in which plaintiff, a junior high school basketball player, brought a suit challenging the constitutionality of different playing rules for boys and girls. The court held for the plaintiff, citing the Arkansas' rules for six-on-six girls' basketball that put female basketball players at a tremendous physical and psychological disadvantage in the transition from high school to college basketball since only three other states in the country played half-court basketball at the secondary school level, and all intercollegiate and international competition followed full-court rules. The court found that, "none of the reasons proffered (for the rule differentiation) is at all relevant to a gender-based classification." *Id.* at 397. Defendant stated that "no physiological differences between males and females . . . prohibit females from playing five-on-five basketball," *Id.* and the primary justification given for the sex-based distinction between rules was simply that of tradition. The court noted that:

> The point here is that Arkansas boys are in a position to compete on an equal footing with boys elsewhere,. while Arkansas girls, merely because they are girls, are not. . . . Arkansas schools have chosen to offer basketball. Having taken that step, they may not limit the game's full benefits to one sex without substantial justification.

Id. at 398.

while in *Jones v. Oklahoma Secondary School Activities Association*,[166] and *Cape v. Tennessee Secondary School Athletic Association*,[167] the courts ruled for the defendant-athletic associations.[168]

A different aspect of the season-of-play type lawsuit is illustrated in *Striebel v. Minnesota State High School League*,[169] where the plaintiff-females brought litigation to move the girls' interscholastic swimming season. The defendant athletic association scheduled men's swimming in a different season (e.g., fall) than the women's season (e.g., winter), and was challenged on their scheduling decision based on sex discrimination grounds. The plaintiffs wanted both the girls' and boys' swim season to be in the fall. The athletic association's decision was upheld. The court held the lack of available pool time for both women's and men's teams to practice and compete during the same time of the year provided a reasonable basis for the decision.

---

166. Jones v. Oklahoma Secondary School Activities Ass'n, 453 F. Supp. 150 (W.D. Okla. 1977), where plaintiff Jones sought an injunction to suspend the association's split-court basketball rules, arguing they created an arbitrary and unreasonable distinction between boys and girls that violated her right to equal protection. The court held for the defendant. Plaintiff's Title IX arguments were dismissed because she did not follow administrative procedures. Her fourteenth amendment argument was seen as faulty because her allegations concerning her reduced opportunity to compete in the future and a reduced likelihood for college scholarships did not rise to the level of an equal protection interests. Her claims such rules interfered with her enjoyment of the game as well as her physical development also did not establish a cognizable equal protection claim.

167. Cape v. Tennessee Secondary School Athletic Ass'n, 424 F. Supp. 732 (E.D. Tenn., N.D. 1976), *rev'd per curiam*, 563 F.2d 793 (6th Cir. 1977), involved plaintiff Cape, a high school student, who challenged the "split-court" rules used in women's basketball. These rules, she claimed, denied her the full benefits of the game, as well as an athletic scholarship to college. The court held for the defendant and dismissed the plaintiff's aguments that were based on a private right of action under Title IX and the fourteenth amendment. The court held the plaintiff who sought to challenge regulations must first exhaust all administrative remedies within the Dep't of Health, Educ. and Welfare before her suit could be addressed in federal court.

168. *See also*, Russell, Wolf and Enslav v. Iowa Girls High School Athletic Union (pending), involving three Iowa girls who brought a class action charging the state's six-on-six half-court rules violated their rights under the Equal Protection Clause. Noting that intercollegiate and international competition for women is conducted under five-on-five rules, the plaintiffs argued they were being discriminated against because half-court basketball does not offer the same benefits and experience as the game of basketball available to the boys of Iowa. *See* for further information, Comment, *supra* note 99.

169. 321 N.W.2d 400 (Minn. 1982).

VI. Sex Discrimination in Athletic Employment

This section focuses on sex discrimination in the area of athletic employment. In these cases the plaintiff is generally an employee retained as a coach or physical education teacher. Two separate statutes specifically pertain to discrimination in employment. The first is the Equal Pay Act,[170] which was passed in 1963 and went into effect in 1964. The second is Title VII of the Civil Rights Act of 1964.[171] While the Equal Pay Act deals solely with wages paid to women and men within the same company, Title VII focuses on discriminatory hiring/firing practices and advancement policies within companies. Neither is specific to the issue of sex discrimination, however, as they both encompass discrimination on the basis of race, religion, or national origin. .

The remedies of both injunctive and affirmative relief are available to the winning party in an employment discrimination suit. The prevailing party may be awarded back pay and attorney's fees as well as an injunction prohibiting the employer's unlawful action.

The Equal Pay Act stipulates that an employer must pay equal salaries to men and women holding jobs that require equal skill, effort, and responsibility and are performed under similar working conditions. The jobs done need not be identical; they must only be substantially equal. The employer must still pay equal wages if the variations between jobs are minor. Different salaries are permissible, however, when they are based not on the sex of the employees but on a bona fide seniority system or on merit increases. Consequently, the Equal Pay Act addresses only the most overt wage discrimination cases and does not apply to problems created by prior discrimination in the workplace. The Labor Department's Division of Wages and Hours was initially responsible for enforcement of the Act, but in 1979 enforcement was moved to the Equal Employment Opportunity Commission (EEOC).[172] Enforcement procedures consist of routine checks as well as investigations in response to specific complaints. If a claim is substantiated

---

170. *Supra* note 48.
171. Civil Rights Act of 1964, § 42 U.S.C. 2000(e) (1976).
172. Under the Fair Labor Standards Act, 29 U.S.C. § 201-219 (1982), enforcement was placed in the EEOC.

and a violation found, the complaining party may receive the difference between wages paid to men and women for a maximum two-year period.

Title VII was enacted as a more comprehensive prohibition on private acts of employment discrimination. It forbids discriminatory employment practices based on the race, color, religion, sex, or national origin of the applicant. These categories may, however, be used to differentiate between applicants when sex, religion, or national origin is a bona fide occupational qualification (BFOQ). A BFOQ is very narrowly defined as an actual job requirement, not merely a customer or employer preference. For example, race is never considered a BFOQ. Title VII is applicable to all employers of more than fifteen persons and it specifically covers almost all state and local government employees as well as employees of most educational institutions. It is enforced by the EEOC, which has the authority to process and investigate any complaints. The EEOC may also bring suits in federal court if necessary. Enforcement of Title VII is not limited to EEOC actions, however, because the legislation also has individual and class causes of action.

Both of these approaches have limitations. Even taken together, they are not always sufficient to enforce a prohibition against sex discrimination. Although the Equal Pay Act applies to all employers, Title VII has been limited to employers of more than fifteen people. Thus, many smaller businesses are not under the jurisdiction of Title VII. The Equal Pay Act is limited in other ways. For example, it is directed only to discrepancies in pay levels once on a job. It does not address the problem of discriminatory hiring or advancement policies. The basic weakness of these acts is that neither is all-encompassing. They do not address the overall problems of sex discrimination that exist outside of the workplace. Thus, very few of the problems of discrimination encountered in athletics are addressed by either act. However, this legislation does provide potential relief in the area of athletic employment.

The cost involved in pursuing litigation under these statutes poses another major problem. Neither statute provides any guaranteed basis for the eventual recovery of attorneys fees and/or double or triple damages. Thus, litigation is not an option for many of those who might wish to file claims. Cases may not be pursued, and the effectiveness of the legislation diminishes as the chances that the employer will be punished decreases. One last problem is that until recently, courts have been reluctant to interpret the statutes broadly because hiring and salary decisions are well within the area of management prerogatives allotted to employers. The courts have been reluctant in the past to interfere in any discretionary decision unless there has been a clear abuse of that discretion. Thus, it is very difficult to establish a case based on a complaint regarding practices in either of these areas. Usually, the evidence is open to a variety of interpretations. Such circumstances can make it difficult or even impossible for a plaintiff to prevail in a sex discrimination case under application of the aforementioned statutes.[173]

A. Coaching

Allegations of discrimination based on sex have often been made in the area of coaching. Many of the claims are based on a lack of parity in pay between the coaches of male and female teams. Often, women coaches of women's teams are paid less than coaches of men's teams. The justification most often made by school districts for the pay differential is that coaches of men's teams and coaches of women's teams do not do equivalent work. In order to redress the inequality in salary, women must prove they perform substantially equivalent work. Some factors courts consider in making determinations are the nature of the game, the number of players being supervised, the length of the playing sea-

---

173. *See* for cases involving the Equal Pay Act and Title VII in relation to athletics. Caulfield v. Bd. of Educ. of City of New York, 632 F.2d 999 (2nd Cir. 1980) *aff'g* 486 F.Supp. (E.D.N.Y. 1979), in which a court upheld a decision that Title IX applies to athletic hiring practices because discrimination against women's access to supervisory positions has a discriminating effect on the institution's students, the direct beneficiaries of federal financial aid. Coaching and other supervisory positions in athletic programs must be assigned without discrimination, even if the program receives no direct federal aid for funding the position; Kunda v. Muhlenberg College, 621 F.2d 532 (3rd Cir. 1980) *aff'g* 463 F.Supp. 294 (E.D. Pa. 1978), was an employment gender discrimination case where plaintiff was a female physical education instructor at a private college. She was denied tenure because she lacked a master's degree, whereas three male members of the physical education department who lacked master's degrees were promoted. The court issued an injunction requiring defendant to promote plaintiff with tenure and back pay. The court of appeals affirmed the decision, finding academic institutions' decisions not *ipso facto* entitled to special treatment under federal laws prohibiting discrimination. The court noted that although the educational institution's interest in academic freedom are important, academic freedom is not implicated in every academic employment decision.

son, the time taken up in the practices, the amount of travel required, and any other responsibilities undertaken by the coach — for example — recruiting, scouting, academic counseling, and so forth.[174]

In cases in which it is difficult for the coach of a women's team to meet the standard of "equivalent work," it has been argued the work is more difficult.[175] Plaintiff coaches of women's teams have

---

174. For further information, *see also*, Appenzeller, *Employment of Coaches: Is The Right To Hire The Right To Fire?*, Sports & Law—Contemporary Issues (Charlottesville, Va. 1985).

175. For cases which involved the Equal Pay Act and Title VII in relation to coaching, *see* the following:

a)   Textor v. Bd. of Regents of Northern Illinois Univ., 87 F.R.D. 751 (N.D. Ill. 1980), 711 F.2d 1387 (7th Cir. 1983), where female women's athletic director and coach, Alice Textor, appealed the district court's denial of her motion to amend her complaint alleging the Mid-America Conference had practiced sex discrimination in its operation of the intercollegiate athletic conference. The appeals court remanded the case to the district court to allow the plaintiff to file an amended complaint.

b)   Burkey v. Marshall Country Bd. of Educ., 513 F. Supp. 1084 (N.D. W. Va. 1981), which involved plaintiff coach who had instituted a girl's junior high school basketball program in 1971 and then posted a 31-5 record in the next four years. In keeping with school board policies she was paid one half the amount the boy's team coach received. Plaintiff filed complaints with state and federal authorities alleging sex discrimination. In 1977, HEW found a Title IX violation for the plaintiff and the EEOC also found reasonable cause to believe the board's policies constituted unlawful sex discrimination.

Plaintiff was then removed as coach and transferred to an elementary school. Plaintiff brought suit against the school board based on Title VII, the Civil Rights Act of 1971, and the Equal Pay Act. The court found for Burkey, awarded her $1,260 back pay and the next available teaching position at either junior or senior high school.

c)   California Women's Coaches Academy v. California Interscholastic Fed'n, No. 77-1270 LEW (C.D. Cal. 1980), (settled), involved the California Women's Coaches Academy which in 1977, filed a class action with three individual members alleging unlawful sex discrimination against the league and the California Department of Education. The suit was settled in 1980 and the settlement provisions included more sports for girls, longer seasons, and more and better paid women's officials for girls' interscholastic contests.

d)   Jackson v. Armstrong School Dist., 430 F. Supp. 1050 (W.D. Pa. 1977), involved an action brought by plaintiffs Jackson and Pollick, who were women's basketball coaches. They claimed the school district had violated Title VII and the Pennsylvania Human Relations Act by paying them significantly less than the male coaches of the men's basketball team. Four men and four women within the districts coaching women's basketball were all paid equally. The court ruled in favor of the defendant, finding it lacked jurisdiction under the State Human Relations Act and the plaintiffs' claim was not valid.

e)   Kenneweg v. Hampton Township School Dist., 438 F. Supp. 575 (W.D. Pa. 1977), in which plaintiffs, coaches Kenneweg and Love sued the Armstrong School Dist. on grounds of sex discrimination. They claimed they were paid less because of their sex. The court held that because the charge filed with the Equal Employment Opportunity Commission had dealt only with the question of pay, the complaint could not be amended to allege discrimination with respect to working conditions. The court also held the actions of the school

argued girls have not been exposed to sports as boys; therefore, coaches of women's teams often spend more time actually teaching their players. They do not have the luxury of merely improving on the skills of a player who has participated in that sport for a number of years. Instead, they often coach women who have had no experience in the particular sport at all. However, as women's sports programs proliferate at the youth levels, this argument is becoming less effective.[176]

B. *Other Sports-Related Employment Discrimination*

While Title IX has been available as a basis to contest sex discrimination in coaching, attacks on perceived inequalities in other sports-related employment have consisted largely of allegations of the denial of equal protection rights. Cases regarding discrimination in officiating, refereeing, and media coverage have

---

district in paying female coaches of female sports less than male coaches of male sports did not constitute discrimination based on sex. In deciding for the defendant, the court stated the claim was based on a Title VII argument and "disparity in treatment not based on plaintiff's sex is not a valid claim under Title VII."

f)   State Div. of Human Rights v. Syracuse City Teachers Ass'n, 412 N.Y.S.2d 711 (App. Term 1979), involved an action by two female coaches who filed a complaint with the State Division of Human Rights. The women had agreed to coach the junior high girls' basketball team as volunteers and were not paid. The women later found the male basketball coach was receiving $308 to coach the boys' team. The commissioner of the Human Rights Division found the board of education had discriminated against the women and ordered equal payment. The court overturned the commission's decision. It found no discrimination in employment. The court reasoned that both the male and female coaches were treated equally and the unequal pay schedule was reasonable because the job responsibilities and time commitment differed.

g)   United Teachers of Seaford v. New York State Human Rights Appeal Bd., 414 N.Y.S.2d 207 (App. Div. 1979), the court held a union has an obligation to represent its member coaches fairly and impartially and may not discriminate on the basis of race or sex. The fundamental purpose of a union is to provide for its members the bargaining power that unity creates; when a union fails to exercise that power in the bargaining process and permits an employer to discriminate against union members, it discriminates against them as surely as if it proposed the inequitable agreement. Evidence proved the union was aware of the unduly low salaries and had settled for an agreement that grossly discriminated against female coaches.

h)   Kings Park Central School Dist. No. 5 v. State Div. of Human Rights, 424 N.Y.S.2d 293 (1980), petitioners asked the court to review a decision of the State Division of Human Rights finding unlawful discrimination by the petitioner in paying coaches of boys' teams more than girls' teams. The court granted the petition and found no discrimination by the school district. Although the skill, effort, and responsibility were equal, coaches boys' teams required greater coaching time and travel.

176.   For further information, *See Equal Pay or Coaches of Female Teams: Finding a Cause of Action Under Federal Law*, 55 NOTRE DAME LAW. 751 (June 1980).

stemmed from charges that employment practices, and specifically exclusionary rules, are arbitrary, related to no legitimate purpose, and are therefore violations of the plaintiffs' constitutional rights.[177]

Arbitrary height and weight requirements for umpires and referees may act unlawfully to discriminate against women. When such requirements are not sufficiently related to the job, they may be deemed arbitrary and thus impose unconstitutional restrictions.[178]

One area in particular, women athletes who wish to compete in professional wrestling,[179] has produced a series of decisions in which state athletic commissions were named defendants. The courts, in most cases, have granted the commissions great latitude in granting licenses and have generally upheld their decisions.[180]

---

177. For further information, *see Employment and Athletics Are Outside HEW's Jurisdiction*, 65 Geo. L.J. 49 (October 1976).

178. *See, e.g.,* New York State Div. of Human Rights v. New York-Pennsylvania Professional Baseball League, 36 App. Div. 2d 364, 320 N.Y.S.2d 788 (1971), *aff'd* 29 N.Y.2d 921, 279 N.E.2d 856, 329 N.Y.S.2d 920 (1972), a sex discrimination case in which the plaintiff, acting upon a complaint of female umpire Bernice Gera, charged the defendant with a violation of a state statute (Sec. 296, Executive Law) prohibiting employment discrimination. The New York Supreme Court, Appellate Division, held that league rules requiring an umpire to stand at least 5'10" tall and weigh at least 170 pounds "were not justified by the claim that umpires must command respect of big men or by factors relating to increased size of professional catchers, physical strain, travel conditions and length of games, and that the standard were inherently discriminatory against women." The league was ordered to cease and desist such discrimination.

179. *See* Hesseltine v. State Athletic Comm'n, 126 N.E.2d 631 (Ill. 1955), involving an action in which plaintiff Hesseltine (also known as Rose Roman) applied through normal procedures for a permit to wrestle. The Illinois State Athletic Commission rejected her application. She appealed to the circuit court and won. The commission appealed. The appeals court affirmed the lower court decision. The defendant's adoption of a rule excluding women from wrestling within the state was seen as arbitrary and therefore invalid; State v. Hunter, 208 Ore. 282, 300 P.2d 455 (1956), involving an action in which defendant Hunter, a female wrestler, was prosecuted by the state for competing in a wrestling match held in violation of a statutory ban on women's wrestling. The court ruled in favor of the state, holding the ban on women's participation in wrestling was not unconstitutional; Whitehead v. Krulewitch, 25 A.D.2d 956, 271 N.Y.S.2d 565 (1966), involving an action in which plaintiff Whitehead appealed from a ruling of the New York Special Term Court denying her a professional wrestling license. The New York Supreme Court, Appellate Division affirmed the decision.

180. *See* Calzadilla v. Dooley, 29 A.D.2d 152, 286 N.Y.S.2d 510 (1968), which involved an action brought by a women wrestler, who alleged the refusal by the state's athletic commission to grant her a professional wrestling license constituted a violation of the fourteenth amendment's equal protection clause. In arguing that "a great deal of latitude and discretion must be accorded the State Athletic Commission," the court held the commission's rule

C. The News Media

The barring of news media members from locker rooms has been an area of concern for many sports organizations. If a barred reporter is female,[181] and male members of the news media are not similarly restricted, she may allege a violation of equal protection of the laws under the fourteenth amendment.[182] In all fourteenth amendment cases, the plaintiff must demonstrate state action is involved before relief can be considered. The court in *Ludtke v. Kuhn* found such state action because the New York Yankees had leased their stadium from the city of New York, a subdivision of the state.[183] Private universities that lease stadiums from the state, municipal, or local governments could face a similar result. When public institutions such as state universities are involved,[184] a court is likely to find state action without the need for such a relationship with a facility. A court is likely to have difficulty finding state action when a private institution (for example, the Boston Red Sox) does not lease from a governmental entity but instead owns its playing facility.

The *Ludtke* decision is the only reported case involving a rule

---

against granting wrestling licenses to women was not "unjust and unconstitutional discrimination against women." The court reasoned that no one had an inherent right to participate in public wrestling exhibitions.

181. *See,* for instance, Ludtke v. Kuhn, 461 F. Supp. 86 (S.D.N.Y. 1978).

182. Counsel for Kuhn and Major League Baseball decided not to appeal Ludtke v. Kuhn, since they believed the decision was not a damaging precedent. *See* NCAA Public Relations Manual, NCAA publication, (Mission, Kansas, July, 1983, Appendix C), letter to David E. Canwood, Director of Public Relations, NCAA, from George H. Gangwere, Esg., Swanson, Midgley, Gangwere, Thurlo & Clarke, Kansas City, Mo., July 11, 1979. *See also* NCAA Public Relations Manual, NCAA publication, Mission, Kansas, July, 1985, Appendix A), Postgame Interviews, Equal Access, Bench Area, Memorandum, which notes: "Dressing rooms from NCAA Championship events are open to all reporters . . . the association has encountered few difficulties administering this policy because most arenas utilized also have a designated interview room. . . This arrangement provides equality for male and female reporters, yet maintains privacy in the dressing rooms."

183. Most major league sports teams routinely allow female sports writers into their locker rooms. A few leagues—for example, the National Basketball Association and the United States Football League—have written policies that give women equal access with men to the locker room. Other leagues allow individual teams to set locker-room policies. For further information, *see Women Sports Writers Gaining in Struggle for Equality, Respect,* NCAA News, December 28, 1983, at 3, col. 5.

184. The NCAA requires its championship teams to open locker rooms to all certified members of the media after a 10-minute cooling-off period. *See,* for instance, 1983 Men's and Women's Soccer National Collegiate Championships Handbook, NCAA publication, at 49 (Mission, Kansas, 1983).

barring female reporters from a male locker room. One important issue—the players' right to privacy—remains unanswered after *Ludtke*. In *Ludtke*, the court found the players' right to privacy had been negated by the presence of television cameras in the locker room.[185] If the right of privacy is not negated in a future case, the court will have to strike a balance between the players' right to privacy and the female reporters' right not to be discriminated against.[186]

VII. CONCLUSION

While there is little doubt that women's intercollegiate athletics is well established in this nation's colleges and universities, and will remain so, it is equally likely that any continued growth will hinge on a number of differing factors. These include political and societal attitudes, future court decisions, and the development of a power base within intercollegiate athletic governance associations by women athletic administrators.

Politically, a change in the executive branch's decision not to pursue OCR investigations of inequities involving women's athletic programs could alter the current status quo concerning sex discrimination in athletics.[187] Similarly, passage of a national Equal Rights Amendment or enactment of additional state ERAs could lead to further advancement.[188] Enactment of any legislation designed to blunt the effect of the *Grove City College* decision could also prove important.[189]

Judicially, post *Grove City College* decisions will be important to women's athletics because they will indicate whether that decision will prove to be a strong or weak precedent. Any decision by

---

185. In March 1985, Major League Baseball Commissioner Peter Ueberroth issued a directive to all clubs, "Club/Media Procedures—1985," in which he noted that in the past MLB has had excellent cooperation with the media, but, "an exception has been in the area of access permitted accredited women reporters. We now are saying that clubhouses will be open and all accredited members of the media will be given the same access." For further information, *see Baseball Adopts Open-Door Policy*, N.Y. Times, Mar. 22, 1985, at A23, col. 1.

186. For further information on media access to locker rooms, *See Civil Rights in the Locker Room*, 2 J. COM. & ENTERTAINMENT L. 645 (Summer 1980).

187. *Supra* note 43.

188. *Supra* note 6.

189. *Supra* note 26.

the courts to raise sex discrimination to the higher standard of strict judicial scrutiny in equal protection cases could also lead to a change in the attitude of this nation's courts to any alleged sex discrimination in athletics.[190]

Finally, if women athletic administrators can become more influential in sports governing bodies, especially the NCAA, they might be better situated to effectuate change in those organizations' attitudes towards women in sports. Donna Lopiano, director of women's athletics at the University of Texas, has noted that, "As long as women had control of the rules system, (in the AIAW) they were in control over what happened."[191] It may be then that through the slow process of gaining positions on governing bodies, women athletic administrators may be able to improve what they view as their stalled progress in advancing women's athletic programs and eliminating sex discrimination in sports.

---

190. *See* notes 59-62 and accompanying text.
191. *Supra* note 38.

The Trouble with Coeducation:
Mann and Women at Antioch, 1853–1860

John Rury and Glenn Harper

Olympia Brown came to Ohio's Antioch College in 1856 in search of a liberal education. At Mount Holyoke Female Seminary she had found too many rules and restrictions: "young ladies are not allowed to stand in the doorway"; "young ladies are not allowed to linger in the halls"; and "we never examine young ladies in Algebra." Reared in Michigan under the influence of a mother determined to see her daughters fully educated, Brown was attracted to Antioch "by evidence of a broader spirit." She graduated four years later and went on to become the country's first ordained female Universalist minister, a women's rights activist, and a vice president of the National Women's Suffrage Association. In the 1850s, however, she was particularly interested in what Antioch's first president, Horace Mann, described as its "Great Experiment": coeducation.[1]

In its very first catalogue Antioch announced itself dedicated to the principle of offering "equal educational opportunities . . . for both sexes."[2] Founded in 1853, it was among a handful of colleges at that time, most of them in the Midwest, that had opened their doors to women. Established by the liberal Christian denomination, with substantial support from Unitarians, Antioch also claimed to be nonsectarian and did not require students to belong to a particular denomination. What made the college most distinctive, however, was Horace Mann's decision to leave

---

John L. Rury is assistant professor of education at the Ohio State University. Glenn Harper is a graduate student in the Program in Historical Preservation at Ball State University. The authors would like to thank Jurgen Herbst, Carl Kaestle, and David Tyack for reading and commenting on an earlier draft of this essay, and Nina Myatt, curator of the Antiochiana Collection at Antioch College, for her extraordinary assistance in tracking down sources. The authors assume responsibility, however, for all inaccuracies and other flaws which remain.

[1] Gwendolyn Willis, ed., *Olympia Brown, Autobiography* (Racine, Wis., 1960), 17-18.

[2] *Catalogue of Antioch College, 1853–1854* (Cincinnati, 1853).

Massachusetts to become its first president. Raised in an orthodox Calvinist household (though he later became a Unitarian), Mann was a leading member of a generation of unrepentant reformers dedicated to social perfection; and he served for over a decade as the first secretary of the Board of Education in Massachusetts.[3] He was easily the best-known educator of his age, and his very presence guaranteed the new college's success. Funded with successful subscription drives in Ohio and the northeastern seaboard states, Antioch boasted an impressive physical plant and claimed to be situated at the highest point in the state. But Mann was less concerned with the college's endowment than its mission. He, too, was drawn to Antioch by the vision of a new type of collegiate institution. In a letter to one of the school's trustees, he explained his decision to accept the presidency.

> No event in my life caused me more deep and solemn anxiety than the application to become a candidate for the presidency of your college at Yellow Springs. The two great ideas that woo me towards your place are: First, that of redressing the long-inflicted wrongs of woman by giving her equal advantages of education. I do not mean to say in all respects an identical education but equal advantages of education with men. Second, the idea of maintaining a non-sectarian college.[4]

Both Olympia Brown and Horace Mann were drawn to Ohio to participate in a new and potentially revolutionary undertaking: educating men and women together, and offering women an education substantially equal to that of men. Their experiences at Antioch, and those of other students, the faculty, and the college's trustees, reveal much about the tensions and conflicts that accompanied the appearance of women as students at American colleges in the nineteenth century. Although Antioch was among the first colleges to attempt coeducation, the experience of women and men there in the 1850s was similar to experiences on other campuses in the years that followed. Simply stated, male administrators and faculty members (and occasionally male students) could not agree with women about what their college careers should entail. At Antioch, Horace Mann and Olympia Brown found that there was a world of difference separating them on the question of "equal educational op-

---

[3] The best biography of Mann is Jonathan Messerli, *Horace Mann: A Biography* (New York, 1972); also useful is David B. Tyack and Elisabeth Hansot, *Managers of Virtue: Public School Leadership in America, 1820–1980* (New York, 1982), 56-63. Both of these accounts emphasize the importance of Mann's religious background for his later career, particularly his inability to accept the Calvinist tenet of original depravity.

[4] Mann to Austin Craig, 13 May 1852, comp. Robert L. Straker, Mann Notes, p. 2578 (an unpublished copy of Horace Mann correspondence, available in Antiochiana Collection, Antioch College Archives). For an overview of the early history of Antioch, see Harvard F. Vallance, "A History of Antioch College" (Ph.D. diss., Ohio State University, 1936).

Olympia Brown.
Courtesy of Antiochiana, Antioch College Library.

portunities for both sexes." In this regard the pattern in which coeducation evolved at Antioch was not unique. It simply marked the beginning of a more general process that would change the social context of college life in the United States from that time forward.

Coeducation and Equality

Antioch was not the first American college to adopt coeducation, of course. And there were a number of exclusively female seminaries, like Mount Holyoke, that aspired to collegiate status in 1853. Oberlin admitted women along with men beginning in 1837 with its very first class, and by 1850 there were a number of small denominational colleges in the Midwest that were educating women. All told there were probably several thousand women in the United States studying in colleges, normal schools, and women's seminaries in the midnineteenth century, less than a fifth of all higher education enrollment. Although still novel, coeducation and collegiate study for women were not entirely new ideas at the time of Antioch's founding, and there were a number of models for the school's leaders to consider as they established their college at Yellow Springs.[5]

The fact of coeducation, however, did not always mean that men and women were educated on an equal standing. As Ronald Hogeland has noted, women were admitted to Oberlin primarily to create a social environment at the college more conducive to the education of male ministers. School officials, including evangelist Charles Grandison Finney, advocated coeducation as a means of keeping men students from developing a "fallacious image of the opposite sex," which might lead to a preoccupation with sexual fantasy and "excessive introversion."[6] Although they constituted from a third to half the student body, most women at Oberlin were enrolled in the "Ladies Department," which featured training in religion, French, and literature. By and large, women were exempted from requirements in Greek, Latin, and Hebrew, which formed the core of the classical curriculum intended to prepare men for the ministry. Only about one out of five women students took classes in the more prestigious classical course; the remainder, Hogeland argues, were trained to serve as discrete, genteel, pious, and frugal wives for ministers. Women's education at Oberlin was decidedly different from— and in practical terms inferior to—that of men.[7]

Antioch represented a sharp break from the practices established at Oberlin, at least as regarded the question of a separate women's curriculum. From the outset women were admitted to the same course of study as men, a curriculum that was considerably less preoccupied with training ministers than was the case with Finney's college. The female enrollment at Antioch was small in the 1850s, but women there took courses in classical languages alongside young men. This distinguished the college from all-female schools like the Troy Female Seminary or Mount Holyoke, where classical studies were not available in the 1850s. Unlike other colleges, Antioch employed women faculty members (at Oberlin female instructors were associated with the Ladies Department). Mann brought his niece, Rebecca Pennell, to serve on the college's original faculty, and she taught moral philosophy, civics, and "didactics." Although she was the only female appointed to the new college faculty, Pennell held her position, teaching both men and women, until Mann's death. Another

---

[5] A useful summary of early coeducation programs can be found in Mabel Newcomer, *A Century of Higher Education for American Women* (New York, 1959), 6. For statistics on enrollment see page 46.

[6] Ronald W. Hogeland, "Coeducation of the Sexes at Oberlin College: A Study of Social Ideas in Mid-Nineteenth-Century America," *Journal of Social History* 6 (Winter 1972-73): 168-69.

[7] Ibid., 167-68.

woman, Lucretia Crocker, was appointed "Professor of Mathematics and Philosophy" for a year in 1857–58. And Rebecca Rice, an Antioch graduate, joined the faculty to teach mathematics and physics in 1866.[8] Even though the number of women faculty was small (about three out of a dozen), in this regard Antioch represented a departure from tradition and the promise of a new direction in women's education.

Horace Mann, of course, was a central figure in the coeducational initiative at Yellow Springs. Mann had long been critical of what he thought were appalling deficiencies in the education of women, and devoted a series of lectures to the problem shortly before coming to Antioch. "Why should the sister be debarred from the generous education of the brother?" he asked. "Community improvement demands improved physical, mental and moral conditions of its sisters. . . . The swiftest reform is improved education for women." Mann depicted women as a tremendous untapped resource for national development, and one that men had not permitted to flower. "The female has every right to a full and complete mental development," he declared. And because Mann felt women best suited by temperament and experience to educate children, their access to equal educational opportunities was imperative. Higher education for women, in that case, was a critical dimension of the development of the nation's entire educational system. Coeducation at Antioch was to be a "Great Experiment" in correcting the wrongs that women's education had suffered.[9]

Given Mann's reputation and Antioch's announcement that "equal opportunities" for both sexes would be maintained, the new college had little difficulty attracting students. The first class included just six students, four men and two women; but the Preparatory Department enrolled more than two hundred, ninety-six of whom were women. In the years to follow, Antioch drew students from around the country who were attracted by its liberal spirit and particularly by the principle of coeducation.[10] To this extent the Great Experiment was a success. But it enjoined a process that would lead to conflict and considerable controversy before the decade was out.

---

[8] A study of the Antioch catalogues from the 1850s provides details about enrollment (students were listed by name), the curriculum, and the faculty. See *Antioch College Catalogue, 1853–55; Antioch College Catalogue, 1856–57* (Springfield, Ohio, 1856); *Antioch College Catalogue, 1858–59* (Cincinnati, 1858). Also see Mary Tyler Peabody Mann, *Life of Horace Mann* (Boston, 1865), 427. For a useful account of the curriculum at the female seminaries, see Elizabeth Alden Green, *Mary Lyon and Mount Holyoke: Opening the Gates* (Hanover, N.H., 1979), especially chs. 4, 5, and 6.

[9] Horace Mann, "The Powers and Duties of Women: A Lecture," Feb. 1852, in Straker, Mann Notes, 2530.

[10] *Antioch College Catalogue, 1853–55*, 3-6. Also Vallance, "History of Antioch College," 92.

Equality and Propriety

Whatever Horace Mann's view of the importance of women's education, his support for coeducation was far from unequivocal. Unlike many other nineteenth-century male educators, Mann does not seem to have suffered doubts about the physical ability of women to endure the demands of collegiate study. His deeply Calvinist upbringing, however, had left him with a rather rigid set of moral standards. As a reformer, Mann was dedicated to perfecting society; but this meant changing it in ways that conformed closely to his own conceptions of right and wrong.[11] The possibilities for moral transgression inherent in the coeducational scheme became one of Mann's biggest preoccupations at Antioch. The result was the development of an elaborate system of rules to govern the relationships of men and women students, which abrogated much of the spirit of coeducation even if it did not affect formal matters of curriculum or what occurred in classrooms. While Mann remained committed in word to the fullest possible intellectual development of women, he became increasingly concerned with their moral development in daily interaction with the opposite sex.

Perhaps the best general expression of Mann's concern with the moral context of coeducational institutions came in an 1858 letter to the regents of the University of Michigan, who were considering a plan to admit women to their college in Ann Arbor. In response to a query about the difficulties associated with educating men and women together, Mann warned them that coeducation was a policy laden with "dangers."

> Strongly, therefore, as I am in favor of the joint education of the sexes I should first demand to know what security can be furnished for moral protection. And until this question shall be satisfactorily answered I should not dare vote in favor of my own side of the question and should make such inquiries as these: Can the sexes have separate lodgings? Can they take their meals together and then be separate? For it is well that they should eat together. Can they have opportunities for meeting each other say once a fortnight or three weeks, in general company as people moving in the same circle meet each other at ordinary parties? This is a great safety valve and should be properly provided for. Can you make yourself secure against *clandestine meetings?* and also against clandestine correspondence, reasonably so, for absolute security is impossible. Are your president and faculty in a state of mind to exercise vigilance over the girls committed to their

---

[11] For discussion of this quality in Mann, see Tyack and Hansot, *Managers of Virtue*, 58. For an account of popular and scientific attitudes about women's abilities, see Charles Rosenberg and Carroll Smith-Rosenberg, "The Female Animal: Medical and Biological Views of Woman and Her Role in Nineteenth-Century America," *Journal of American History* 60 (Sept. 1973): 332-56.

Portrait and monument of Horace Mann. Courtesy of Antiochiana, Antioch College Library.

care as conscientiously as they would over their own daughters or sisters? You may think these are collateral matters. I think they are vital to the question.[12]

The principal issue in Mann's eyes, was sexuality. The mere fact of young men and women cohabiting the same campus raised the terrible specter of promiscuity. Mann shared the popular Victorian conviction that women were intended to be especially pure, pious, and genteel, and that they required protection from the forces of aggressive greed and corruption that ran rampant in the world of men. Barbara Welter has described the battery of ideas surrounding this belief as the "cult of true womanhood," and has argued that it was especially prominent among nineteenth-century educators.[13] Mann was no exception. "The freedom which young men enjoy with safety and profit," he declared, "will not do for young women of the same age and professedly the same footing." The lives of women required special attention in this view, and their education demanded careful precautions. Mann specifically warned the Michigan regents against allowing women students to live off the campus, away from collegiate supervision. "If, for instance, they must be permitted in a city like yours to board promiscuously among the inhabitants," he

---

[12] "Report on the Admission of Females," *Proceedings of the Board of Regents, University of Michigan 1837–64* (Ann Arbor, Mich., 1915), 789.

[13] Barbara Welter, "The Cult of True Womanhood: 1820–1860," *American Quarterly* 18 (Summer 1966): 151-74.

said, "I should prefer that the young women of that age should lose the advantages of an education, rather than incur the moral danger of obtaining it in that way." If granting women equal educational opportunities meant allowing them to be exposed to moral compromise, the venture was not worthwhile. Intellect was clearly superseded in this instance by questions of character and propriety.[14]

Such views were perfectly consistent, of course, with Mann's background. A number of historians have noted the importance he assigned to conservative morality in education. And like most other educational reformers of his age, he was an evangelical champion of pious propriety in matters of sexuality.[15] His and the views of other Victorian educators were probably best expressed by James Orton in 1870. "Many a boy is wrecked in his [college] course, many a one stumbles and recovers himself," Orton declared, "but a girl cannot retrace a false step as her brother can. For her once to fall is ruinous." To the Victorian mentality, a fallen woman—like a fallen angel—was beyond redemption.[16] Mann brought with him a like-minded faculty for the college, at least as regarded questions of propriety. Like him, they were New England men (with the exception of Rebecca Pennell) and shared his morally orthodox views (they also were Unitarians). Shortly after setting up his administration, he happily reported that the school's officers and trustees shared a "remarkable coincidence of opinion" on such matters. If coeducation was to succeed and meet the moral standards Mann and the college trustees expected, there could be no room for dissent on the part of those persons who were to govern students' lives.[17]

As was the case at other nineteenth-century colleges, students at Antioch were expected to observe a battery of rules and regulations. Given the novelty of coeducation and Victorian concern for propriety generally, no one could have been surprised that many of these rules dealt with women and their contact with men students. But the college regulations also defined a special sphere of activities acceptable for women, which limited their options for extracurricular learning. Women students generally were not allowed to live off the campus, as male students were, for the reasons Mann cited in his letter to the Michigan regents. Even in tiny Yellow Springs, the risk of impropriety was too great to permit such independence for the "fair sex." Visits to the rooms of men or women by those of the opposite sex, naturally, were strictly forbidden and were

---

[14] Taken from "Report of the Admission of Females," 791.

[15] See, for instance, the account in Mann, *Life of Horace Mann*, 420-21.

[16] James Orton, *The Liberal Education of Women: The Demand and the Method* (New York, 1873), 270.

[17] For an account of the faculty's views, see Mann, *Life of Horace Mann*, 386.

punishable by immediate expulsion. Interestingly, however, a parlor was provided for the women's dormitory, to allow them to receive guests, particularly men. No mention of a parlor was made for the men's quarters. Whatever mingling was to occur would happen in "Ladies Hall," where it could be closely supervised by the matron in charge. Young men were required to arrange such visits with the matron beforehand, and she was empowered to bar anyone of questionable character from even approaching the women's building.[18]

Contact between men and women students outside living quarters was strictly regulated as well. They were not permitted to ride or walk together off the campus unless accompanied by a faculty member. The college Glen was open to males and females on alternate days to prevent them from meeting there. In the chapel and at other public exercises, men and women students sat on opposite sides of the aisle. The point of all such measures was to hold contacts between male and female students outside the classroom to a minimum. More specifically, they were intended to shelter the women students from contact with young men. Because the rules were enforced in large measure through an honor code, and students were expected to report infractions, there was great pressure to maintain both the spirit and the letter of the law.[19] And since women were relatively few in number and were subject to such close supervision, their behavior probably was subject to greater scrutiny than that of men. The result was women living in a world almost certainly more self-contained than that of their male classmates.

In addition to rules in print in the college catalogues, there were a number of unwritten regulations expressed in the attitudes of Mann and other college officers. In the closed environment of the nineteenth-century college, the ideas and social mores of the president and faculty (and for that matter their very personalities) were typically major elements of the collegiate experience.[20] Although such expectations were not official and are difficult for historians to evaluate, students hardly could have missed them and, indeed, may have weighed them as heavily as formal policy. This unofficial set of rules restricted women's roles even further. For instance, while there was no written policy governing students' visits to

---

[18] *Antioch College Catalogue, 1853-55,* 52-54. In the college's early years, apparently some women students were allowed to board with families who had no sons and had been personally screened by Mann. This may have been due to a shortage of space at the college. Mann's letter to the Michigan regents several years later suggests he was then opposed to women living off campus. See Mann, *Life of Horace Mann,* 421. Mann's wife notes that he was ever careful to "throw guards around the young ladies," wherever they lived.

[19] Ibid.; also see *Antioch College Catalogue, 1855-57,* 38-40.

[20] See Frederick Rudolph, *The American College and University: A History* (New York, 1961), ch. 8.

the village, Mann clearly viewed such trips by men and women in a different light. According to Mary Mann, his wife and first biographer, he considered women who wished to "walk into the village to do a little shopping in the evening" to be "wanting" in true womanliness. Similarly, he felt that women students who "exercise on the gymnastic apparatus" next to the men's dormitory were immodest and unfeminine. To meet Mann's expectations for proper feminine behavior, women never would have left the campus unescorted and would have restricted their contact with men to formal occasions.[21]

Although Mann apparently did not feel that women were less intellectually capable than men, he did believe some areas of study simply were not suitable for them. Politics, for instance, was out of the question. "That any mortal who has ever lived within the roar and stench of that black and sulpherous [*sic*] lake," he declared, "should desire to see women embarked upon its tumultuous and howling waters is a mystery past finding out."[22] Thomas Hill, a faculty member who replaced Mann as president in 1858, felt that "male and female minds differ materially and do not crave identical food." He thought women nearly equal in classics, but that male students took more interest in the philosophy of language. Women could master a math or science problem quite well, he said, "but . . . it was much rarer to find among them the power of going on for themselves to construct new problems and make new discoveries."[23] Both Hill and Mann felt the purposes of women's education to be fundamentally different from that of men's, even if men and women followed the same curriculum. For reasons of propriety and because of their different interests, women were to be sheltered from the rough and tumble, competitive world of men. And they were to be permitted to acquire a superficial, rote knowledge of their studies. If women at Antioch were to be educated for a separate sphere all their own, after all, they needed little understanding of the principles that underlay language, mathematics, science, or theology. What mattered most was that they be morally pure and upright, and possess the advantage of collegiate studies for their careers in the feminine domain (and particularly for teaching).

Despite Antioch's claim to "equal opportunities of education to the sexes," the battery of rules and unofficial expectations that governed women's (and men's) lives at the college constituted a variety of "hidden curriculum" designed to prepare women for a distinct set of roles. In this

---

[21] Mann, *Life of Horace Mann*, 526.

[22] Mann, "The Powers and Duties of Women," Straker, Mann Notes, 2532.

[23] Quoted in Sophia Jex-Blake, *A Visit to Some American Schools and Colleges* (New York, 1867), 134-35.

respect college policies anticipated similar developments at other campuses later in the nineteenth century. At Wisconsin, Cornell, California, and doubtlessly elsewhere, women students found themselves educated in a moral and emotional context quite different from that of their male classmates. If men were educated to transform the world through participation in politics, business, and scholarship, women were taught to devote themselves to domestic responsibilities and education. They were to have little to do outside the home and schoolhouse. If coeducation was indeed an experiment at Antioch, it was carefully controlled. The definition of male and female roles in Victorian society, after all, was an explosive issue and was bound up closely with the delicate matter of sexual promiscuity.[24] The very fact of women attending college with men threatened to challenge the Victorian moral order. Horace Mann and his faculty struggled diligently through the 1850s to prevent just such a calamity from occurring.

Lines of Resistance

Coeducation at Antioch, as well as at other midwestern colleges in the 1850s, was more than a system of rules and moral expectations. It also entailed a process in which young women attempted to redefine their lives by forging new roles for themselves and other women. The early women students (and at least one faculty member) at Antioch saw themselves as pioneers in a battle against discrimination and inequality.[25] They quickly came to recognize the double standards that the college rules and regulations represented and pushed the faculty and administration to come to terms with Antioch's reputation for liberalism with regard to women's education. Although they had little success in terms of changing

---

[24] On this issue see Carl N. Degler, *At Odds: Women and the Family in America from the Revolution to the Present* (New York, 1980), chs. 11 and 12. On the experiences of women on other campuses, see Patricia Foster Haines, "For Honor and Alma Mater: Perspectives on Coeducation at Cornell University, 1868–1885," *Journal of Education* 159 (Aug. 1979): 25-37; Lynn Gordon, "Coeducation on Two Campuses: Berkeley and Chicago, 1890–1912," in *Women's Being, Women's Place: Female Identity and Vocation in American History*, ed. Mary Kelley (Boston, 1979), 171-93; and Amy Hague, " 'What If the Power Does Lie within Me': Women Students at the University of Wisconsin, 1875–1900," *History of Higher Education Annual* 3 (1984): 78-100. On all-female campuses see Roberta Frankfort, *Collegiate Women: Domesticity and Career in Turn-of-the-Century America* (New York, 1977).

[25] The faculty member was Rebecca Pennell, Mann's niece, who threatened to resign in late 1853 because she was receiving only half the pay of the male faculty. In asking to be released as an officer of the college and appointed to the Preparatory Department, she noted, "my name would not then be paraded before the world, as a show of anything false or unreal." Letter from Pennell to the Antioch College trustees, 13 Jan. 1854, Straker, Mann Notes, 3124-26. Pennell remained on the college faculty until 1858.

college policies, and they probably changed few minds, their efforts reveal many of the underlying conflicts at play as American higher education began an important period of reform.

Students came to Antioch in the 1850s principally from the rural Midwest or New England. The vast majority were of native origin; an early student could not recall "a single foreign born student or even one of recent American stock."[26] Age data taken from the college registration books indicate that Antioch students were generally older than students at most other colleges. The mean age at initial registration for the first four classes was 21.6 (21.4 for men and 22 for women). Olympia Brown described this first generation of students as "composed not of boys and girls but of men and women who had come to study, many of them with well-defined goals of life and work." Many Antioch students knew just what they wanted from college. And like other mature students in this period, many came from modest family backgrounds and had to work or borrow heavily to meet college expenses.[27] Despite its success at getting Mann to accept its presidency, Antioch was similar to the dozens of small (mainly denominational) colleges that sprang up in the 1840s and 1850s. It was not a wealthy school, and served a clientele of middle- and even lower-class origins.

The number of women enrolled at Antioch increased rapidly, from two in 1853 to more than twenty-five by the end of the decade, nearly a quarter of all the students in the college course.[28] Several of these women were absent part of each year to earn money. Others taught school nearby, some gave private lessons, and still others washed glass and silver in the college dining room. "If a few hours of leisure time were left after all this employment," noted Olympia Brown, "they were likely to be spent upon extra studies."[29] The women who came to Antioch, like the poor, mature students David Allmendinger identified at New England colleges in this period, were earnest about their studies and quite independent— if not downright unconventional—in their life-styles. And like the "new" college students discussed in Allmendinger's study, they too challenged the social and moral order of the antebellum college. In the case of Antioch, however, there was a new wrinkle to the general pattern of

---

[26] Irene Hardy, *An Ohio Schoolmistress: The Memoirs of Irene Hardy*, ed. Louis Filler (Kent, Ohio, 1980), 204.

[27] Willis, ed., *Olympia Brown, Autobiography*, 19. For comparison of the ages of early Antioch students with those from other schools, see the statistics in Colin Burke, *American Collegiate Populations: A Test of the Traditional View* (New York, 1982), ch. 3.

[28] *Antioch College Catalogue, 1859–61* (Springfield, Ohio, 1859), 7-10.

[29] Quoted in Willis, ed., *Olympia Brown, Autobiography*, 20. Also see Anna C. Brackett, ed., *The Education of American Girls. Considered in a Series of Essays* (New York, 1874), 244.

Freshman class of 1861. Courtesy of Antiochiana, Antioch College Library.

mature students attacking the principle of in loco parentis. In this instance, women students rebelled against conventions dictated by Victorian sexual morality.[30]

Like Olympia Brown, many of the women who came to Antioch in the 1850s were attracted by the college's innovative reputation. They came because they had heard it was a place where women could study alongside men unhampered by frivolous and restrictive rules and regulations.[31] Thus, it is little wonder that Antioch's early history is filled with cases of rules being broken and bent, as young men and women explored the opportunities posed by coeducation. On at least one occasion a woman student was caught visiting Gentlemen's Hall, although she was not expelled because of the reputed good character of the men she met there. Mann concluded that her crime was "in support of a theory rather than with any evil intent."[32] In any case, the residence halls were closely supervised and hence a poor choice for private liaison. A

[30] David F. Allmendinger, *Paupers and Scholars: The Transformation of Student Life in Nineteenth-Century New England* (New York, 1975), see chs. 4-6.

[31] See, for instance, the account of Mahala Jay, who came to Antioch from Oberlin in 1853, in her obituary in "Antioch Alumni Number," *College Bulletin* 13 (1 Dec. 1916): 10.

[32] Mann, *Life of Horace Mann*, 526.

better spot was the Glen, which eventually became the favorite meeting place for men and women students. The first college catalogue in 1853 merely stipulated that alternate days were to be used for male and female visitors to the Glen. The next catalogue, issued two years later, pointedly added that members of the opposite sex were restricted from meeting there. Apparently it was a difficult rule to enforce, however. Writing in the 1870s, G. Stanley Hall (then a faculty member at Antioch) remarked that the alternate days rule in the Glen was far and away the most frequently violated regulation in the college. The Glen was always tempting to the students, Hall wrote, "and the chief disciplinary cases which came before the conservative faculty were the results of incessant pairing off."[33]

Of course, the very fact of Mann's complaints about women students visiting the village alone and exercising on the men's gymnastic equipment suggests that at least some of the women at Antioch did not allow administrators' attitudes to dictate their behavior. Years later, Olympia Brown recalled Mann's continued references to the Great Experiment becoming a "great joke" among the students, particularly the women. In an effort to "civilize" the female students Mann hired a matron from Boston noted for her work in a girls' school there. According to Brown, who described the matron as a "prune," the Antioch women refused to cooperate with her, and she left thinking the students there were "quite uncontrollable." Visitors to the college in the 1850s noted the rather unruly character of the students. "There was more noise during meals and some disposition to gather around the [commons] entrance and gossip afterwards, contrary to rules," one wrote. "Matrons were expected to keep such behavior under control."[34] In this regard, of course, Antioch students probably were not unlike college students elsewhere. And women students in particular seemed determined to shape their collegiate experiences in ways that met their own expectations of equality in education.

In the eyes of many women students there was great incongruity in admitting them to classes with men but strictly separating men and women in other areas of college life. This feeling was perhaps most evident in connection with the issue of separate literary societies for men and women in the 1850s. In the fall of 1853 Antioch's first student literary group, the Alethezetean Society, was established.[35] Like similar groups at other

---

[33] Quoted in Robert Straker, "The Apprenticeship of G. Stanley Hall, 1872-76," *Antioch Alumni Bulletin* 5 (May 1934): 6.

[34] See Willis, ed., *Olympia Brown, Autobiography*, 20; Mann, *Life of Horace Mann*, 419-20; and Blake, *A Visit to Some American Schools*, 130.

[35] A good overview of early student societies at Antioch is provided by Geoffrey N. Stein, "Antioch's Literary Societies in the 1850's" (Undergraduate thesis, Antioch College, 1965).

colleges, the Alethezetean Society promised to be an important focal point of student activity and a key element of the collegiate experience at Antioch. The problem was what to do about the issue of male and female involvement. The Alethezetean Society was formed as a single group divided into two branches, one for men and the other for women. At the suggestion of the faculty, the Society members agreed that joint meetings of the two branches would be limited to two per year.[36] This appeared to be a workable arrangement in keeping with the college's emphasis on propriety in matters of coeducation. Within a year, however, it became evident that the women's branch of the Society was too small to carry on an effective program of literary exercises independently. In the fall of 1854 the Alethezetean membership voted to meet together on an extended basis and elected a married woman student, Mahala Jay, as president. At the end of the fall term, in December 1854, the Society petitioned the college faculty to authorize it to meet permanently as a coeducational group.[37]

The petition was refused by the college faculty, apparently because Mann was opposed to it. When Mann read the decision to the Alethezeteans there was "considerable excitement." Five members resigned from the organization immediately, including Mahala Jay. The rest of the students amended the Society's constitution to create two groups—men's and women's Alethezetean societies. The motion to accomplish this occasioned considerable debate, and upon its passage four more students quit the Society, including the new president, Ada Shepard.[38]

The decision not to permit men and women to meet together in the same literary society aroused a good deal of hard feeling, particularly on the part of women students. In the words of Rebecca Rice it was "the old bugbear of 'sex' " that led to the breakup of the Alethezetean Society. "Mr. Mann and the faculty could not quite see the logical results of educating young men and women together in the same classroom," she wrote. "They could not quite put aside the fears and prejudices of the ages." In particular, Rice felt that Mann and the faculty were concerned about the matter of who would supervise young men and women meeting together.

> Why, here were young men and young women, sitting in a classroom
> it is true, but considering together, under the ruling of their own officers
> (not members of the faculty), such questions as the classroom lessons

---

[36] Ibid., 44.
[37] Ibid., 45-46. Also see the Society's minutes, called "The Alethezetean Record," 8 Sept. and 22 Dec. 1854.
[38] "Alethezetean Record," 2, 9, and 10 Mar. 1885.

suggested and such as were stirring in minds and hearts of people out in the world! It was too much! It might lead to danger to the great experiment![39]

Years later Mahala Jay claimed the faculty thought the idea of a coeducational society "too radical" and without precedent at other institutions.[40] But Mary Mann's recollections suggest that there was also some concern that the *women* in the society were too radical. Mrs. Mann claimed the decision to dissolve the group was made because the faculty felt "the union (of men's and women's branches) was taken advantage of for frivolous rather than literary purposes."[41] Dissatisfaction, she later wrote, came from "women's rights women of an ultra stamp. . . . who felt that their rights were being denied them—'right' being sometimes interpreted to mean, *just what I choose to do*" (emphasis in the original).[42] This interpretation of events may have been especially characteristic of Mary Mann (indeed, she seems to have been preoccupied by the specter of women's rights at the college), but it appears to have been shared widely.[43] As other issues became points of controversy for women students at Antioch, the matter of women's rights became more prominent in their thinking.

In the autumn of 1855 several new literary societies were formed. Two of these—the Crescents, a women's group, and the Stars, a men's group—functioned separately but held public exhibitions and addresses jointly. This arrangement apparently met the approval of Mann and the faculty.[44] In 1857 the hitherto moribund women's Alethezetean Society, which was not associated with a men's group, petitioned the faculty for permission to hold an exhibition of its own. After postponing the decision for some time, the faculty eventually refused to permit these women to sponsor a public exhibition.[45] The reasons why are obscure, but at least

---

[39] Rebecca Rice, "Antioch in the Fifties," *Antiochian* 27 (Dec. 1907): 61.

[40] Quoted in Louise Abbott, "History of the Star Society," *Antiochian* 2d ser., 4 (May-June 1915): 20.

[41] Mary Mann to Mrs. M.D. Conway, 2 Mar. 1864, Straker, Mann Notes, 4654.

[42] Mann, *Life of Horace Mann*, 526-27.

[43] In a letter that Mary Mann wrote to her sister, Sophia Hawthorne, she explained that Ada Shepard—a recent Antioch graduate and tutor for the Hawthorne children—had not gotten her women's rights ideas at the college. "Her coming has saved her from being a furious womens rights woman. All the influence exerted here is adverse to the thing. But as this is where women can be fully educated it brings among others that very class of women greatly to Mr. Mann's annoyance. He makes them inexpressibly uncomfortable here but he tries to modify them." Mary Mann to Sophia Hawthorne, 18 May 1858, Straker, Mann Notes, 2026.

[44] Stein, "Antioch's Literary Societies," 51.

[45] Ibid., 52. Also see Nancy M. Leavel to the Antioch College faculty, 19 June 1857, Straker, Mann Notes, 3866.

one contemporary observer felt the decision was associated with the proclivity of Alethezetean Society members toward women's rights. Moses Cummings, editor of a journal associated with the Christian denomination, argued that the Antioch administration did not want to give the impression that the college favored women's rights.[46] Mann and the other officers of the college were extremely sensitive to the charge that coeducation produced women bound to challenge their place in society. The mere possibility that some of the college's women students might use a formal public speaking exercise as a platform for women's rights was abhorrent enough to cause them to deny the women in this group the right to speak at all.

The faculty's decision in this second case produced an even sharper reaction from the women students. The women's Alethezetean Society disbanded altogether, claiming there was no point to their existence as a society if they could not hold public meetings.[47] Beyond that, however, the women conducted a public demonstration to protest the faculty's (and particularly Mann's) refusal to allow them a speaking exhibition; a number of them (reportedly a "dozen or more") attended the college's first commencement exercise dressed in mourning clothes.[48] Although hardly remarkable by today's standards, this silent exhibition of dissatisfaction drew considerable attention to the entire affair. Stories about the college's decision not to allow women to speak appeared in at least two Ohio newspapers, one as far away as Cincinnati.[49] The novelty of coeducation and the college's innovative reputation made it an object of curiosity, and the women's Alethezetean demonstration occasioned even greater attention. But this was hardly the sort of publicity that Mann and other college officers welcomed.

The official college explanation of events, apparently, was that women students had been in pursuit of "women's rights," a charge that drew angry responses from women both on and off the campus. "Many, many among us have wish't for more Lucy Stones," one wrote to Mann. "Men unman themselves in many ways. But women never unwoman themselves by expressing pure thought, either in private or in public."[50] Another letter, entitled "A Wail from One of the Mourners," apparently was sent to a local newspaper. "That woman pursues her studies and endeavors

---

[46] Quoted in the *Christian Palladium*, 1 Aug. 1857, 188.

[47] Stein, "Antioch's Literary Societies," 52; Nancy M. Leavell to Antioch College faculty, 19 June 1857, Straker, Mann Notes, 3866.

[48] See Rice, "Antioch in the Fifties," 63.

[49] See the *Cincinnati Gazette*, 30 June 1857. Events at the college were often featured in local newspapers. See Stein, "Antioch's Literary Societies," 73.

[50] Nancy Nooks to Mann, 1 July 1857, Antioch College Archives.

to develop her God-given powers under difficulties unknown to man I painfully experience," this correspondent wrote in response to the reference to women's rights, "and that I mourn the existence of that public sentiment and private authority that attempts to limit the education of women I freely admit." Once thrown down, the gauntlet of "women's rights" was immediately picked up by several women. The heart of the issue, however, continued to be the matter of equality in education. The "Mourners" correspondent clearly recognized the double standard imposed by the college's Victorian preoccupations: "Antioch College offers to both sexes 'equal opportunities for education': and I had not heretofore learned that the opportunities were to be limited to the classroom, but thought that what pertains to the development of mind was to be shared equally by both sexes, hence my mistake."[51]

By 1857 women at Antioch had grown weary of the restrictions placed on their experiences by the college authorities. Although it is not entirely clear what followed the demonstration, Mary Mann reported that at least one of the women involved left the college as a result of the whole affair.[52] But others remained. The Alethezetean controversy marked only the beginning of women's rights agitation at Antioch in this period. In subsequent years women students invited Antoinette Brown, a prominent feminist, to speak at the college. When the administration refused to support the lecture and closed the campus to them, the women raised money themselves and arranged for Brown to speak in a nearby church.[53] The controversial bloomer outfit became a popular mode of apparel among women at Antioch in the 1860s, and at least one student was prevented from speaking at a commencement because she refused to wear a dress. Consequently, she refused to accept her degree in public.[54] A decade later the Crescent Society entertained speakers advocating women's suffrage.[55] These incidents, among others, cast doubt on Mann's proposition that women's rights was not a concommitant of coeducation. The trouble with coeducation, after all, was that it posed the question of equality for women in a very direct manner. The issue of "women's rights" remained a continuing source of contention at Antioch for decades following Horace Mann's death in 1858.

---

[51] This letter is filed in the Antiochiana Collection, Antioch College Archives.

[52] Mann, *Life of Horace Mann*, 527.

[53] Olympia Brown, *Acquaintances, Old and New among Reformers* (Milwaukee, Wis., 1911), 16.

[54] Ibid., 21.

[55] Address by Mrs. S.W. Dodds of St. Louis, Mo., to Crescent Society of Antioch College, Antiochiana Collection, Antioch College Archives.

Conclusion

Discontented with the restrictions imposed upon them, women students at Antioch in the midnineteenth century challenged the right of Horace Mann and other officers of the college to delimit their education. While there is little direct evidence that they collectively rejected the college's authority to supervise closely their personal lives, they clearly demanded equality with men students in both formal and informal elements of the curriculum. They wanted the same treatment in and out of class. Many of them had come to Yellow Springs, after all, because of Antioch's reputed liberalism and particularly for the promise of higher education without regard for gender. When they found that Mann and the faculty did not share their view of equity in education, they demonstrated their dissatisfaction.

Star Society room. Courtesy of Antiochiana, Antioch College Library.

As indicated from events in the decades following Mann's death, women at Antioch gradually expanded their ability to determine their own education. They did indeed discuss women's rights, invited their own speakers, and eventually even overcame the faculty's refusal to allow them to meet with men in a student literary society (in 1884).[56] No doubt, as coeducation became more commonplace and less controversial, college officials probably grew less anxious about such questions as women's rights and moral propriety. But there can be little doubt that the impetus for these changes came from the students. The generation of women who came to Antioch in the 1850s and 1860s were similar to their sisters at other colleges in this period. Even though their marriage rates were high (about 76 percent had married by the mid-1880s), several pursued professional careers outside of education, and a number were activists in the women's rights movement. About a quarter of the forty-two female graduates registered in an 1884 alumni directory had taken up professional careers, although most were in education (with several conducting their own schools).[57] These statistics are similar to those for the alumnae of other colleges, including all-female institutions. Whatever the differences in the curricula they studied, early women students were all pioneers.[58] In the nineteenth century, women's higher education challenged the very concept of a special female domestic sphere. If women could have the same education as men, why could they not have similar careers?

The early conflicts at Antioch over women's education pointed to problems associated with coeducation in an age of repressive sexual morality. Horace Mann and the college faculty, like most other educators (including women educators) in nineteenth-century America, believed women should be prepared for a limited set of domestic roles. This preoccupation, coupled with Mann's Calvinist disposition, informed their overbearing concern for propriety. This was aggravated, of course, by their interest in making Antioch appear as respectable as possible to the public and to potential supporters. Problems arose when Mann encountered a generation of young women who had altogether different objectives in education. The expectations of women at Antioch were probably different from their counterparts at all-female schools. After all, they could compare themselves directly with men, and this led some to ponder

---

[56] Stein, "Antioch's Literary Societies," 56.

[57] See *Antiochian*, 2d ser., 9 (1884): 29-34.

[58] For information on the marriage rates and careers of collegiate women, see Barbara Miller Solomon, *In the Company of Educated Women: A History of Women and Higher Education in America* (New Haven, Conn., 1985), ch. 8; also see Kathryn Kish Sklar, "The Founding of Mount Holyoke College," in *Women of America: A History*, ed. Carol Ruth Berkin and Mary Beth Norton (Boston, 1979), 177-201. Marriage rates for women from all institutions, coed or all-female, were between 70 to 80 percent in this period, and the overwhelming preponderance of graduates went into education. Women like Olympia Brown, or Oberlin graduate Antoinette Brown, who became ministers were extremely rare.

The Antioch College campus in 1860. Courtesy of Antiochiana, Antioch College Library.

typically male careers. The shock was a rude one for the college administration. Olympia Brown recalled a conversation between Mann and Rebecca Rice, one of the student activists: Mann "ask(ed) if she thought that the education of women would lead to their wishing to enter the professions, [and] she replied that such was her opinion. He told her that if he thought as she did he should think he was doing very wrong in remaining at the head of a coed school." In short, if coeducation should threaten the traditional domestic roles of women—and cause them to seek careers beyond school teaching—it was to be pronounced a failure. For her part, Olympia Brown found this reaction puzzling. "I wondered much that a professed advocate of coeducation," she declared, "was so disinclined to face its obvious results."[59] Had Horace Mann been able to see what would become of his Great Experiment in the decades to follow (or for that matter in the next 125 years), he might have reconsidered embarking on his expedition to Ohio altogether. The adoption of coeducation at Antioch in the 1850s, however, and at other colleges and universities in the following decade let the genie out of the bottle. Forces of change then revealed in higher education continue to affect college life—and American culture generally—today.

---

[59] Brown, *Acquaintances, Old and New among Reformers,* 17.

THE FEAR OF FEMINIZATION: LOS ANGELES HIGH SCHOOLS IN THE PROGRESSIVE ERA

VICTORIA BISSELL BROWN

There was a time, not so very long ago, when historians blithely assumed that women's access to education, especially education alongside males, was a trusty measure of women's progress and their access to wider social opportunities. Since the early 1970s, however, that comfortable assumption has been shaken by educators and historians who began to take a more critical look at women's educational history. Led by Jill K. Conway, Patricia Albjerg Graham, and others, scholars in the 1970s asked what now sounds like an obvious question. If education alongside men gives women equal opportunities, and American women have had access to such education for over 100 years, then why are American women still beating on all the legal, political, and economic doors that education supposedly opens?[1]

In the past fifteen years, historians who have studied women's experience in institutions of higher education have answered that question by demonstrating that, from the very beginning, coeducation at the college level carried implicit contingencies – that female students not threaten men's dominance in the classroom or on campus and that graduates use their college educations either to be better wives and mothers or to be moral, magnanimous spinsters in the social service occupations designated for women. In addition, research on college women has revealed that when these contingencies were not met, there was a backlash against women in higher education.[2] That backlash, which appeared around the turn of the century, reflected, on the one hand, a fear that college was masculinizing women, hence all the furor over low marriage and fertility rates of college women. On the other

Feminist Studies 16, no. 3 (Fall 1990). © 1990 by Feminist Studies, Inc.

111

hand, the backlash reflected a fear that women were feminizing colleges; female enthusiasm for classical and liberal arts courses ran counter to male administrators' desire to project a virile image of the modern university as a place where ambitious young men could train to become engineers, architects, and research scientists. Women's increasing presence on campus compromised that image. As a result, conscious efforts were made, early in the twentieth century, to segregate college women in distinct, gender-specific programs such as teacher training, social work, and home economics. These programs institutionalized women's marginality on campus and insured that access to a college education would not translate into equal employment opportunity for women after graduation. In short, then, recent research has been able to demonstrate that education alongside men did not bring women the emancipation that logic would suggest, because conscious efforts were made to prevent that emancipation.

Although much remains to be done, the quantity and quality of the existing research on sex roles in higher education seem enormously rich when compared with the paucity of research on the history of gender in primary and secondary schools.[3] Toward redressing that imbalance, this study looks at gender consciousness in the public schools of one U.S. city, Los Angeles, California, at the turn of the century. In this context, Los Angeles should not be regarded as an exotic city but as a relatively homogeneous one. In the years between 1880 and 1910, the population of Los Angeles was remarkably similar to that of the Midwestern cities and states from which the bulk of its residents originated. At the turn of the century, the city's total population was 96 percent white and 80 percent native born. The size of the Los Angeles foreign-born population was similar to that in cities like Des Moines, Indianapolis, Milwaukee, and Omaha; but unlike those Midwestern cities, 15 percent of the foreign-born population in Los Angeles was either Mexican or Chinese, and the European residents in Los Angeles were more often middle class rather than working class. The student population in the Los Angeles schools was even more homogeneous than the adult population. Ninety-eight percent of the students enrolled in 1900 were white, less than 2 percent were foreign born, and less than 2 percent were black. The race and ethnicity of high school students in 1900 were not specified in school board reports, but if the yearbooks from Los Angeles High

School are any guide, the number of black, Chinese, and Mexican students in the city's high school was infinitesimal.[4]

Los Angeles enjoyed tremendous growth and economic success at the turn of the century. This was due partly to the climate and suburban comfort it could offer, but it was also because it was geographically far enough away from the problems of immigration, poverty, and crowding (and sufficiently ill-suited for industry) that people who could afford to move there felt the freedom and the power to create a civic life and a school system that reflected their own vision of the future. These residents approached the twentieth century with cheerful, if not smug, confidence that the political and educational programs they were implementing would not only insure the progress of U.S. society but would also preserve the traditional family system and the gender arrangements that they regarded as essential to the upward evolution of the species.[5]

As a family-oriented, middle-class city, Los Angeles made a conscious commitment to its public school system.[6] By 1900, this city of 102,479 residents was enrolling 71 percent of its schoolage children in its fifty-four elementary schools and its one high school.[7] This overall enrollment rate in Los Angeles reflected the national average at the time, but the city's enrollment of 15 percent of its teenagers in high school was more than double the national average of 7 percent of American teenagers enrolled in high school.[8] In fact, Los Angeles in 1900 actually had two high schools, not one, for within the walls of Los Angeles High School, which enrolled 1,159 students, the Board of Education offered a distinctively separate program called Commercial High School, which enrolled 307 students. This innovative program, begun in 1895, offered business courses in typing, bookkeeping, and shorthand. By 1905, Commercial High School had its own building, was renamed Polytechnic High School, and enrolled 1,240 students.[9]

Los Angeles had been part of the first wave of U.S. cities that opened public high schools in the years immediately following the Civil War. Simultaneous with the appearance of public high schools there was a heated debate over whether such schools should be coeducational, as public elementary schools traditionally were. The debate centered on whether it was proper to educate adolescent girls and boys alongside one another, and on whether pubescent girls would exhaust their reproductive energies trying

to keep up with their male classmates. Although the debate continued into the early 1900s, U.S. taxpayers proved unwilling to
provide separate high schools for girls and boys. By 1895, the high
schools in 94 percent of U.S. cities were coeducational.[10]

Disturbing as coeducation had been to many people in the late
nineteenth century, many more were disturbed by the growing
impression, around 1900, that girls were doing better than boys in
the nation's secondary school system. Despite all the predictions
that adolescent girls would be ruined in a coeducational setting,
girls in 1900 outnumbered boys in the nation's high schools. Back
in 1880, 3 percent of America's seventeen-year-old girls, just like 3
percent of its seventeen-year-old boys, graduated from high
school. But by 1900, almost 8 percent of seventeen-year-old girls
and only 5 percent of seventeen-year-old boys did so. Indeed, by
1900, American girls in general, and Los Angeles girls in particular, constituted 60 percent of the high school population.[11]

It is no exaggeration to say that when U.S. educators at the turn
of the century looked at the figures on female and male enrollment
in the high schools, they became obsessed with the specter of
female dominance. In the eyes of these educators, the fact that
girls comprised over one-half the high school population meant
that American high schools were "in danger of losing their coeducational character and becoming exclusively female seminaries."[12]

In national conferences and educational journals, as well as in
local public school systems, there was increasing concern over
what was called "the boy problem" or the problem of "feminization." At one level, educators worried that schools were not serving
boys as well as girls. At a more fundamental level, however, they
worried that girls' greater enthusiasm for education portended
a drastic reordering of the gender system. F.E. DeYoe and C.H.
Thurber articulated these concerns in 1900 in an article for *The
School Review* which asked, "Where Are the High School Boys?"
According to DeYoe and Thurber, a school system that served
more girls than boys was a school system headed for disaster. "Certainly," they wrote, "if we are not to have a comparatively ignorant
[male] proletariat opposed to a female aristocracy, it is time to
pause and devise ways and means for getting more of our boys to
attend the high school." They noted with bitter irony that "we have
the anomaly of schools attended chiefly by girls though planned
exclusively for boys." Girls, they said, had been "reluctantly admit-

ted" to the high schools "as the simplest and most inexpensive way of meeting the cry for justice to women in educational advantages. Now we find the girls apparently driving the boys out of these very schools."[13]

Los Angeles was right in line with other cities in its reaction to the "boy problem." Like their colleagues elsewhere, Los Angeles educators became obsessed with the fact that girls comprised 60 percent of the high school population. Working within an atmosphere of passionate debate over women's place in society and increasing popular concern over the feminization of the whole culture, Los Angeles educators shared the concern of their peers in other cities that the nation's schools were in danger of being taken over by the weaker sex.[14] Moreover, educators in Los Angeles and throughout the United States were working within their own assumption that boys should be the schools' primary clients. As the Los Angeles superintendent of schools explained in 1903, "boys soon become our wage earners, our mechanics, our voters; and to become successful in any one of these lines . . . calls for work to the end of the eighth grade."[15] As a result of these attitudes, educational administrators in Los Angeles and elsewhere were inclined to feel that schools were not serving the public good if they were not attracting the public's future providers and leaders – boys. Furthermore, if the school program attracted more girls than boys, then there must be something weak or wrong with the program.[16]

Drawing from the era's best-known work on sex differences, *The Evolution of Sex* by Patrick Geddes and J. Arthur Thompson, educators agreed with other modern, scientifically inclined progressives that natural selection had produced two sexes so specialized that their cell metabolism was actually different. Male cells were "katabolic"; they were suited for active, energy-expending, innovative efforts. Female cells, on the other hand, were "anabolic" and therefore suited for passive, energy-conserving, instinctive, repetitive efforts.[17] Thus males were, by nature, individual and unique in their interests, talents, and abilities, but females were, by nature, generic and mediocre.[18]

Educators applied these principles of cell metabolism and female mediocrity to the "boy problem" and concluded that girls were staying in school longer than boys because the typical academic regimen was not sufficiently challenging or imaginative

115

to appeal to the masculine mind. "Girls seem better satisfied to do the work from day to day just as the teacher requires it," argued William F. Book in an article in 1905 on high school students' "point of view." Boys, said Book, "are more inclined to be independent, to break away from the customary routine of the school . . . to oppose anything conventional even before they are bored."[19] A. Caswell Ellis had made a similar argument two years earlier at the National Education Association convention, claiming that the adolescent boy was "a changing, high-pressure, destructive-constructive creature, now yearning for the unattainable ideal, now tingling with desire to do things and to count for something in this world." These boys left school, said Ellis, because they were "cramped into the swaddling-clothes of elementary discipline."[20]

By contrast, educators argued, girls excelled in school because their developmental tasks were easier and more instinctive; they reached their more simple, anabolic level of maturity earlier than boys. "This is the reason why . . . the girl of school age will first get ahead of the boy," explained Maximillian Grozzman in an 1896 issue of the *Child-Study Monthly*.[21] G. Stanley Hall explained that girls could "accept with more patience than boys learning that is merely conventional." Indeed, Hall shared the view of many that girls not only benefited from the mediocrity in the nation's schools, they also contributed to it. In a 1908 article on the "femininization" of the schools, Hall charged that whatever subject girls took soon became "hyper-methodic and feminine."[22] At the same time, Julius Sachs worried that girls' numerical dominance in the schools so transformed the educational process that boys were prevented from putting forth "the full intellectual energy of which they are capable." Surrounded by females, lamented Sachs, males simply could not be stimulated to their "highest attainments."[23]

According to those who feared feminization, the result of girls' presence and success in the high schools was that boys automatically lost respect for education.[24] Jesse F. Millspaugh, the president of the Los Angeles Normal School, declared in 1904 that adolescent boys naturally felt that "everything that is distinctly masculine is to be admired . . . [while] everything womanish is to be despised."[25] In fact, one of the great ironies in all these discussions about feminization is that educators began to worry as much over the boys who stayed in school (and did not despise the "womanish" atmosphere) as they did about the boys who left.

There was the sinking fear that boys who were successful in schools dominated by girls would "become themselves effeminate and unfit for the serious business of life in a man's world."[26]

In the eyes of contemporary observers, then, girls were feminizing the schools, and they were able to do so because the generic American school was every bit as dull and methodical as the generic American girl. Looked at from this point of view, sex differences in high school enrollment were the unfortunate result of the schools' own anabolic character.

The cultural power of these perspectives led to highly distorted analyses of sex differences in school enrollment. First of all, contemporary educators greatly exaggerated the extent of girls' numerical dominance and therefore the extent of the "boy problem"; they perceived a major sex difference where there was, in fact, a relatively minor one. Second, contemporary educators ignored the fact that there were a number of other reasons for girls' numerical dominance of the schools, reasons that had everything to do with female socialization and job opportunities and nothing to do with anabolic cell metabolism.

Take, for example, the flurry over "retention rates," that is, the concern that girls were being retained in school longer than boys and thus becoming the majority in the high schools. Discussions of school retention rates at the time created the impression that the majority of adolescent girls were safely enrolled in the schools while the majority of adolescent boys were loose and at large, but this was not the case. Analysis of Los Angeles enrollment figures reveals that, in fact, an identical majority of both girls and boys below the age of fourteen were enrolled in school in the years between 1890 and 1910, and an almost-identical minority stayed in school after age fourteen, when the law no longer compelled school attendance (see table 1). The difference between the sexes did widen after the age of fourteen, but the important point is that the difference was not nearly as dramatic as discussions of the "boy problem" suggested.[27] Even though a higher proportion of girls than boys stayed in school past the age of fourteen, the majority of girls – like the majority of boys – left school after age fourteen. This was the fact that was consistently obscured in contemporary discussions of the "boy problem" and retention rates in America.[28]

A similarly myopic focus on boys' condition, to the exclusion of

Table 1

School Attendance by Sex and Age Group,
United States and Los Angeles, 1890 and 1910

	5-to-9 year-olds in school (%)		10-to-14 year-olds in school (%)		15-to-19 year-olds in school (%)	
	Boys	Girls	Boys	Girls	Boys	Girls
1890						
United States	49	49	79	80	34	32
Los Angeles	56	58	91	92	37	37
1910						
United States	58	58	88	89	37	39
Los Angeles	87	87	93	93	34	37

any consideration of girls, was true in the contemporary analyses of "retardation." In these years, the term "retardation" did not refer to any assessment of students' innate intellectual abilities. Instead, it referred to students' placement in grades below their age level. In the United States in 1909, 33 percent of public school students were "retarded" or working below grade level, but because there was 13 percent more retardation among boys than girls, educators regarded retardation as a key feature of the "boy problem." Indeed, Leonard P. Ayres, whose research on school attendance exposed this sex difference in retardation, concluded that "our schools as presently constituted are far better fitted to the needs of girls than they are to those of boys."[29]

Los Angeles educators saw Ayres's conclusions reflected in their own retardation pattern. There were more boys than girls in Los Angeles working below grade level (see table 2), but a sizable percentage of girls were working below grade level as well. Rather than indicating a profound difference in the ways girls and boys were progressing through the grades, it appears that many Los Angeles girls, like many boys, were struggling to pass from one grade to the next. And this was true in every ward of the city, from working class to upper middle class, and regardless of racial and ethnic concentrations.[30]

Table 2

Percentage of Enrolled Children, Ages Eight to Nineteen,
Working below Grade Level in Los Angeles, by Sex

	Boys	Girls
1896-97	56	52
1900-01	54	49
1902-03	54	47

Although the figures in tables 1 and 2 make clear that the sex differences in retention and retardation rates were not tremendous, the combined effects of those differences were sufficient to produce the sex ratios that appear in table 3. In the lower grades, where the student population was large, Los Angeles boys actually outnumbered girls. But because more boys than girls dropped out after age fourteen, and because more boys than girls who stayed in school were retained in the lower grades, girls outnumbered boys in the higher grades (where the total student population was much smaller).[31]

Table 3

Sex Ratio by Grade Groups in Los Angeles

	Primary Grades 1-5	Grammar Grades 6-8	High School Grades 9-12
1891-92	101	88	86
1907-08	116	96	88

Because these figures on retention and retardation clearly reveal contemporary educators' paranoid exaggeration of the extent of the "boy problem," it is tempting to conclude that gender was irrelevant to school attendance at the turn of the century, that although girls were doing better than boys, they were not doing that much better, and that girls' and boys' school experience was more

similar than not. The fact remains, however, that of the youngsters
who made it through eighth grade, more girls than boys chose to
enroll in high school, more girls than boys stayed in high school,
and more girls than boys graduated from high school. The numbers were small, to be sure; in 1900, the high school population in
Los Angeles represented only 7 percent of all enrolled students,
and only 15 percent of all the city's adolescents.[32] To dismiss these
numbers as insignificant, however, is to lose an opportunity to
understand the precise nature of gender difference among adolescents in this period. It is also to lose an opportunity to witness the
ways in which educators made institutional changes that
heightened gender difference for later generations. The evidence
from Los Angeles indicates that girls at the turn of the century
were reared more carefully than boys for compliance with institutional rules and regimens. Research done at the time in California showed that girls outnumbered boys by three to two in their
desire to please a teacher or parent, and a 1908 report from the
Girls' Self-Government Committee at Los Angeles High School
noted that the committee had less work to do than the boys' committee because of the "remarkably good behavior" of the girls at the
school and because the girls were, in the words of the committee
members, "easier to control than boys."[33]

In addition, girls were more confined in the home than boys and
thus more likely to be pleased by the relative freedom offered by
school. Evidence from the Los Angeles Board of Education shows
that boys in this era were five times more likely than girls to be
truant from school and that, when truant, boys were more likely
than girls to be out carousing on the city streets.[34] Indeed, all the
evidence on children's lives in Los Angeles at the turn of the century indicates that boys enjoyed much greater freedom than girls
to explore the city, free of adult supervision, and that boys had
many more opportunities than girls to participate in adult activities outside the home, either in regular jobs or by assisting
fathers or neighbors with various chores that were not only responsible but remunerative.[35]

Contemporary observers did often note that boys were pulled
away from school by more immediately gratifying activities, but
they did not recognize the lively attraction of school for girls. Instead, they concluded that because school was boring for boys,
and girls liked school better than boys did, girls must naturally be

drawn to boring activities. No one considered the possibility that, compared with the few other things girls were allowed to do, school was not only quite exciting, it was a unique source of self-esteem.

Observers were similarly androcentric in their discussions of the connection between the school dropout rate and paid employment. It was commonplace to argue in these years that boys who dropped out of school were "consumed with the commercial spirit of the day," anxious to "commence business life, to earn money, and thereby to become more or less their own masters."[36] Girls who stayed in school were not credited with the same kinds of goals, and yet preparation for employment is probably the single most important factor to consider when explaining girls' dominance of secondary schools at the turn of the century. As Susan B. Carter and Mark Prus observed in 1982, "access to good jobs for men" in this period "was acquired through on-the-job training, while access to the good jobs for women was acquired in schools."[37]

Surveys done during this period on children's ideas about their future occupations make it clear that U.S. girls understood the limited job choices open to them in the marketplace. When Hattie Willard surveyed 561 girls and boys in San Jose, Santa Cruz, and San Diego, California, in 1896, she found that 87 percent of the girls named one of only ten different occupations as a likely job choice. By contrast, only 46 percent of the boys were clustered in the top ten "masculine" jobs. More to the point, 41 percent of the girls in Willard's California study named teaching as their occupational ambition. This pattern was repeated in similar surveys of children around the country. Girls typically named only a few occupations, and most popular among those occupations was teaching – followed closely by clerical work.[38]

Because they were in daily contact with teachers, girls must have known that teaching positions went only to the educated. Clerical work, too, required literacy at least, and ofteii a great deal more in the way of bookkeeping and typewriting. In fact, the only occupations frequently named by girls in these studies that did not require formal education were dressmaking and millinery work. As one girl explained to her questioner, "girls stay in school until they graduate because they can't do much to earn money until they get a good education." Boys who were interviewed for these occupational surveys did not express similar views.[39]

Schoolgirls in Los Angeles at the turn of the century may not have been sophisticated in their understanding of the job market, but they were basically correct. In the segregated world of women's work, there were more job choices for females with an education. In Los Angeles in 1900, for example, 28 percent of the females but only 18 percent of the males were in jobs requiring an education beyond eighth grade. In these years, men without an education had access to jobs where informal education and apprenticeships were still valuable, but these avenues to job training were closed to most females. As a result of their limited options, 57 percent of Los Angeles women working in jobs not requiring an education in 1900 were confined to domestic and personal service. By contrast, only 22 percent of Los Angeles males who were in jobs not requiring an education were in domestic or personal service; the remaining 78 percent had a wide variety of jobs in agriculture, manufacturing, trade, and transportation.[40]

The typical Los Angeles girl in 1900 did not have access to such figures, of course, but it is quite likely that if she wanted or needed to earn money before marrying, she and her parents could easily figure out that the most "steady and genteel" job she could get was as a schoolteacher or as a clerical worker and that either position required a high school education.[41]

It was undoubtedly these rational economic calculations, rather than any biological passivity, that explain why there were 756 girls enrolled at Los Angeles High School in 1900 and only 403 boys.[42] Girls and boys simply attended high school in 1900 with different motives and goals and as a result often enrolled in different courses of study. High school boys in this era were usually sons of the elite, upper-middle class who planned to attend college, while high school girls represented a wider range of social classes and often planned to attend normal school, the special teacher training institutions that existed at the time. A 1909 survey of recent graduates from Los Angeles High School found that only 34 percent of the girls were in college, compared with 64 percent of the boys; and 44 percent of the girls were in normal school, compared with just 2 percent of the boys.[43] These differences not only reveal the salience of gender after high school graduation, they also point to different experiences for females and males while in high school. Consider the fact that at Los Angeles High School in 1901, the sex ratio among students who were *not* preparing for college was 66 boys to every 100 girls, but the sex ratio among the high school's college preparatory students was 142 boys to every 100 girls.[44] These sex ratios for college and non-college prep students meant that, in these years, 60 percent of the Los Angeles high school boys were taking geometry, but only 40 percent of the girls were doing so; 8 percent of the boys were taking trigonometry, but less than 1 percent of the girls were; and 23 percent of the boys were taking physics, but only 10 percent of the girls were.[45] These were courses required for admission to the California state university at this time, and they were courses that students experienced as masculine. Male teachers, for example, were heavily concentrated in the math and science departments at Los Angeles High, and school officials expected boys to do better in courses taught by men and to do less well in the English and history courses that were typically taught by females.[46] It is likely that these sorts of expectations became self-fulfilling prophecies in the early twentieth-century classroom.

Educators in Los Angeles at the turn of the century did not, of course, engage in any of this sort of analysis when grappling with the "boy problem." From their perspective, more girls than boys were enrolled in high school because high school was impractical and "anabolic"; girls were not there to prepare for work as teachers but because they didn't have anything better to do. The fact that more boys than girls were enrolled in math and science classes only proved that boys were attracted to practical, "katabolic" activities and that the high school should provide more of such activities in order to attract more boys. Indeed, Los Angeles educators' concerted effort, in the decade following 1900, to enact school programs and policies tailored for boys makes clear the significance of gender ideology in U.S. educational history. For what the Los Angeles evidence suggests is that gender ideology, reflected in the exaggerated reaction to the "boy problem," motivated very real changes in gender practices, and those changes increased the significance of gender in high school students' daily lives in the twentieth century.

The effort to make high school more attractive to boys began with the expansion of Commercial High School within Los Angeles High School. As early as 1897, the school board noted that boys constituted over 55 percent of the Commercial population

but only 40 percent of the regular high school population. The
city's school superintendent was able to use Commercial High's
popularity with boys to win taxpayers' support for a separate
building for Polytechnic High in 1904, and when the new school
opened in 1905 the student body was over 50 percent male.
Course offerings at Polytechnic reflected the desire to attract more
boys than girls. There were courses in industrial arts and business
as well as college prep courses leading to the Colleges of Science
and Commerce, or Architecture, or Mining, Civil Engineering, and
Chemistry at the University of California. Polytechnic did not,
however, offer preparatory courses for the California normal
schools or for the University's College of Arts and Letters. Those
girls who went to Polytechnic took either business courses or domestic science courses.[47]

In addition to this effort to attract boys at the high school level in
the first decade of the twentieth century, Los Angeles educators
also tried to help boys who were habitually truant and boys who
were dropouts. The "parental" schools for truants were exclusively
for boys and staffed entirely by male teachers. Apparently, girls'
truancy was not regarded as sufficiently chronic or threatening to
require a special program,[48] nor, for that matter, was girls' dropout
rate. The Los Angeles Evening School, begun in the 1890s, was
specifically for "boys who would otherwise have no educational
advantages."[49] So focused were the city's educators on reaching
boys who had dropped out of daytime school that the hundreds of
girls who dropped out every year were ignored.

Efforts were also made to appeal to boys in the regular classroom by hiring more male teachers. Like educators in many other
U.S. cities at this time who were making similar efforts to attract
male teachers into the high schools, Los Angeles educators
thought that boys were repelled by female teachers and that a
more masculine faculty would give the schools a more virile image.[50] Although local and national statistics prove that male
teachers did not, in fact, attract male students, and that male enrollments in high school rose and fell independent of the faculty
sex ratio, contemporary educators in Los Angeles still believed
there was a connection between the sex composition of the faculty
and that of the student body.[51] They acted on that belief by offering ever-higher salaries to males. In Los Angeles, between 1890
and 1905, the gap between female and male teachers' average salaries quadrupled.[52]

One of the reasons Los Angeles educators wanted male teachers was to provide adults who could "sympathize" with boys' extracurricular interests, especially their interest in sports. Just as colleges expanded their interscholastic sports programs in these years in order to endow higher education with a more virile image, so too, high school administrators embraced the notion that a competitive sports program run by rugged men would hold boys in school. J. D. Graham, the school superintendent in Long Beach, California, told the *Sierra Educational News* that boys would stay in school for two reasons – to increase their earning power and to take part in "well organized sports activities under capable coaches."[53] The superintendent of schools in Pasadena agreed, arguing that high schools needed to "foster a spirit of athletics" in order to "attract young men to their institutions."[54] In order to show boys that the schools were sympathetic to boys' interests and willing to sponsor outlets for those interests, however, public high schools in Los Angeles and elsewhere had to diminish and rechannel girls' sports enthusiasm. This was a particular problem in Los Angeles between 1902 and 1907, because the girls' basketball team at Los Angeles High was one of the school's only winning interscholastic teams and was credited with having done much to build school spirit.[55] By 1910, however, all interscholastic female teams at Los Angeles High had been disbanded, and a new Girls' Gym Club had been formed to play intraschool, rather than interscholastic, games. By 1910, too, the yearbook reflected the effort to distinguish girls' from boys' sports by no longer making girls' sports pictures the same size as the boys' and by no longer describing female athletes as "cool" or "fast," but, rather, "dainty" and "fair."[56]

At the same time that boys' interscholastic competition was expanding and girls' was diminishing, there was a growing emphasis on girls' important role as cheerleaders for the boys. In 1898, the yearbook editors at Los Angeles High had pleaded with the girls to attend more of the boys' games, but by 1903 the editors were praising the girls for making "a charming appearance with banners of green and white," and in 1907 the girls at Polytechnic were extolled for arranging themselves in a "P" formation in the bleachers at the game against cross-town rival, Los Angeles High.[57]

The shift in girls' athletic role from participant to "pal" was repeated in other extracurricular activities. In the 1890s, Los Angeles educators consciously began to endow student clubs with greater

legitimacy and authority, hoping thereby to make clubs an attractive training ground for male leadership skills. For example, when
the Star and Crescent Society first began at Los Angeles High
School in 1879, it was a literary society and the president was
always a girl. In the 1890s, however, the school's new principal,
W. A. Housh, began to delegate more and more student government functions to the society. With that shift, the presidency of
the society became "the most important student body office of its
day," and from 1895 to at least 1910, the president was always a
boy while the secretary was a girl.[58] Indeed, when some students
in the Ionian Society – the Star and Crescent's counterpart at Commercial High School – tried to run a girl for the presidency in 1900,
the school yearbook reported that their "extraordinary" move
failed and "she was, of course, defeated."[59]

Evidence from the Los Angeles High School yearbooks for this
period indicate that this pattern was quite typical. Principal Housh
firmly believed that public schools should prepare boys for political and business leadership, and under his encouragement boys at
Los Angeles High assumed the more active, dominant roles in
school clubs and girls adopted the more passive, supportive roles.
With Housh as principal, a student store and lunch room were
opened under all-male management, Los Angeles High School
boys built an impressive interscholastic athletic record, and a
cadet corps was begun "to study military tactics," because "out in
the business world a man who had military training had an advantage over the civilian." Los Angeles High started a debating society
in the 1890s, but girls were excluded from it until 1902 and denied
the presidency of the society until at least 1910. Boys' dominance
of the school's new extracurricular activities was so thorough that,
by 1908, boys at Los Angeles High chaired the Lunch House,
Grounds, Boys' Athletic, Music, and Debating committees. Girls
chaired only the Decorations and Girls' Athletic committees.[60]

Extracurricular clubs and sports were a key part of the educators' effort to give high schools an active, virile, masculine image
and thereby persuade boys to stay in school. But to be fully
successful in that effort, the Los Angeles schools also had to institute curriculum changes which would appeal to boys' interests
and reduce the feminine threat by segregating girls into a distinct
female sphere. This dual need was not only met with a strong effort to publicize the high schools' science and business courses but

also with the institution of a manual training program for boys and a domestic science program for girls at the high school level. Development of these two programs throughout the Los Angeles school system is a story in itself, but the important point here is how gender ideology dictated differences in the goals of the manual training and domestic science programs.

Like their counterparts on the national scene, advocates of manual training in Los Angeles were quite sensitive to the charge that their program was a specialized, vocational curriculum for boys, that it was a "tracking" system designed to route boys into specific occupations. In response to that charge, supporters of manual training argued that the program had much broader pedagogical aims.[61] "Our purpose can never be to direct the energies of children into some specific channel," insisted C. A. Kunou, Los Angeles's manual training supervisor. "We cannot . . . prepare children for some specific trade or occupation. . . . By what law or authority could we thus determine or choose?"[62] Rather than a vocational program, school superintendent James Foshay envisioned manual training "as an outlet for boys' energies," as well as "for its value in disciplining the intellect and training the hand."[63] Foshay stated many times during his tenure that the purpose of the city's manual training program was "not to turn out mechanics but to make men."[64] And Kunou explained in 1902 that "the purpose of our work is to develop such qualities as will assist children for life in its wholeness."[65]

Comments such as these regarding the general pedagogical aims of the Los Angeles manual training program contrast sharply with the more narrow goals outlined for the city's domestic science program. Unlike the manual training program, the domestic science program did not promise general mental development, improved eye-hand coordination, or preparation for "life in its wholeness." Instead, domestic science was offered because girls needed to know how to "execute the inevitable duties which will fall to their lot."[66] As Los Angeles developer Abbott Kinney put it, education should prepare students "for the destiny that awaits them. The destiny of woman being marriage, she should be thoroughly prepared and educated for its duties."[67] Even though the city's manual training supervisor questioned "by what law or authority" educators could choose a boy's occupation, he and his colleagues hesitated not a moment to choose one occupation for every girl in the city. Superintendent Foshay's predecessor, William Friesner, who struggled with whether manual training was too applied for the public schools, welcomed domestic science as an indisputably valuable dose of practicality. "The desire that all girls should know how to cook and sew is as universal . . . as that they should read and write," declared Friesner in 1893.[68]

In the case of girls, then, it was not necessary for educators to deny that domestic science was a vocational tracking system. Although educators were uncomfortable with the possibility that manual training might channel certain boys into certain jobs, they were quite comfortable with predicting girls' futures and prescribing the needed preparation for that future. It would have offended Americans' democratic sensibilities to prescribe particular training for a particular class of boys, but the universal prescription of domesticity for girls only reinforced the cultural myth that American home life was unaffected by economic class; all American women, rich and poor, were trained to be homemakers. Domestic science in Los Angeles was not confined to schools with particularly high black, Hispanic, or foreign populations, nor was it presented as a way to Americanize females or train a certain class of girls for employment in domestic service. Indeed, domestic science was included in the high school curriculum at a time when few, if any, girls from the servant class attended high school. Yet domestic science was the most specifically vocational of all the curricula offered in Los Angeles in these years—and the city's educators were proud of that fact. E. C. Moore, the city's superintendent of schools in 1908, wondered out loud "why it should ever have been thought that to learn to cipher or to write [was] more important for a girl than to learn to cook or sew. . . . We must all eat," reasoned Moore, "and half of us must assume the responsibility of preparing food. To learn how to do so is to meet a universal demand." Moore voiced the priorities of many when he argued that it "was more important for a girl to know domestic arts than to know how to write well."[69]

It was Los Angeles educators' fear of feminization that fueled their interest in curricular reforms like manual training and domestic science, as well as their enthusiasm for Polytechnic High, salary increases for male teachers, and the thorough masculinization of interscholastic sports and student government. All these changes, designed to delineate girls' subordinate role in school and society, were enacted in the first decade of the twentieth century in direct response to girls' numerical dominance of the high school population. Educators in Los Angeles, as elsewhere, exaggerated the extent and misunderstood the causes of that dominance, but their errors in perception do not diminish the significance of their response. The policies and programs they enacted at this time meant that gender would be not less, but more, salient than it had ever been before in U.S. public schools, and the remarkable endurance of those policies and programs meant that high school students for the subsequent seventy-five years would be affected by their ancestors' fear of feminization.

These conclusions from the Los Angeles experience take on added significance in light of a recent article in which Elizabeth Hansot and David Tyack depicted the public schools in this era as an island of relative androgyny where American students could perch before being launched into the sex-segregated worlds of home and work. According to Hansot and Tyack, schools provided students with an institutional environment in which "gender distinctions were less salient" than they were in adult institutions.[70]

This characterization may be useful for comparative purposes, as well as for understanding how a few females at this time managed to come out of public schools with nontraditional goals in mind. But the Los Angeles data suggest that Hansot and Tyack's characterization is not adequate for capturing the lived experience of the majority of adolescents attending high school at the turn of the century.

It may be that in the actual classroom setting, girls and boys faced similar demands and rewards. However, girls and boys were not always in the same classrooms; did not bring the same attitudes, goals, and expectations with them to their classrooms; and did not experience school only in the classroom. If Hansot and Tyack's argument is that gender has been less salient in the schools than in the home or workplace, then the argument here is that the attempt to separate the effects of these institutions imposes a theoretical artifice that flattens historical reality, for home and work were ever-present influences in the schools. Even though girls and boys attended classes side by side, gender roles at home and work were powerful factors shaping students' social and academic behavior as well as their motives and goals. So, too, ideology about gender roles was also a powerful factor shaping educators' attitudes and plans.[71]

This helps to explain why the establishment of coeducational high schools – which afforded U.S. girls more social and academic opportunities than previously imagined – did not occasion a more rapid change in the U.S. gender system. The Los Angeles data suggest that this was because the architects of the schools consciously enacted policies and programs that would preserve the gender system that students lived under at home and would live under at work. In this way, educators at the start of this century increased gender salience in order to insure boys' place at the center of the schools' mission and thereby quiet the dark fear of feminization.

NOTES

1. Jill K. Conway, "Coeducation and Women's Studies: Two Approaches to the Question of Woman's Place in the Contemporary University," *Daedalus* 103 (Fall 1974): 239-49; Patricia Albjerg Graham, "So Much to Do: Guides for Historical Research on Women in Higher Education," *Teachers College Record* 76 (February 1975): 421-29; Marion Kilson, "The Status of Women in Higher Education," *Signs* 1 (Summer 1976): 935-42; Elizabeth Tidball, "Of Men and Research: The Dominant Themes in American Higher Education Include Neither Teaching Nor Women," *Journal of Higher Education* 47 (July/August 1976): 373-89.

2. Rosalind Rosenberg, *Beyond Separate Spheres: Intellectual Roots of Modern Feminism* (New Haven: Yale University Press, 1982); Roberta Frankfort, *Collegiate Women: Domesticity and Career at the Turn of the Century* (New York: New York University Press, 1977); Barbara Miller Solomon, *In the Company of Educated Women: A History of Women and Higher Education in America* (New Haven: Yale University Press, 1985). See also Joan G. Zimmerman, "Daughters of Main Street: Culture and Female Comunity at Grinnell, 1884-1917," and Lynn D. Gordon, "Co-education on Two Campuses: Berkeley and Chicago, 1890-1912," both in *Woman's Being, Woman's Place*, ed. Mary Kelley (Boston: G.K. Hall, 1979), 154-70 and 171-94.

3. Sally Schwager, "Educating Women in America," *Signs* 12 (Winter 1987): 335.

4. Department of the Interior, *Report of the Population of the United States at the Eleventh Census, 1890*, vol. 1 (Washington, D.C.: GPO, 1895); *Report of the Population of the United States at the Twelfth Census, 1900*, vol. 1 (1901); *Report of the Population of the United States at the Thirteenth Census, 1910*, vol. 1 (1913) (hereafter referred to as the *U.S. Census Report*). See, too, Robert Fogelson, *The Fragmented Metropolis: Los Angeles, 1850-1930* (Cambridge: Harvard University Press, 1967). Los Angeles High School yearbooks for this period are on file in the archives of Los Angeles High School.

5. Victoria Bissell Brown, "Golden Girls: Female Socialization in Los Angeles, 1880-1910" (Ph.D. diss., University of California, San Diego, 1985), chap. 1: "Los Angeles, a City of Homes"; Fogelson; Carey McWilliams, *Southern California Country: An Island on the Land* (New York: Duel, Sloan & Pearce, 1946); Gregory Singleton, *Religion in the City of the Angels: American Protestant Culture and Urbanization, 1850-1930* (Ann Arbor: UMI Research Press, 1979).

6. MaryLou Locke discusses the effect of Los Angeles's middle-class character on the rapid development of its school system in "Out of the Shadows and into the Western Sun: Working Women of the Late-Nineteenth-Century Urban Far West," *Journal of Ur-*

ban History, forthcoming. See, too, Fogelson.

7. School Statistics, *Los Angeles Board of Education Reports, 1900-01*, 41-45 (hereafter referred to as *Board Reports*). The enrollment figures for Los Angeles contrast markedly with the 51 percent of schoolage children who were enrolled in the public schools in San Francisco in 1900. See U.S. Bureau of Education, *Report of the Commissioner of Education for the Year 1900-01* (Washington, D.C.: GPO, 1902) hereafter referred to as *U.S. Commissioner of Education Report*.

8. U.S. Department of Commerce, *Historical Statistics of the United States: From Colonial Times to the Present* (Washington, D.C.: GPO, 1975), 15, 369.

9. *Board Reports, 1896-97*, 74; *Board Reports, 1900-01*, 50; *Board Reports, 1904-05*, 97; *Board Reports, 1905-06*, 78.

10. *U.S. Commissioner of Education Report, 1894-95*, vol. 1, 1115-18.

11. *U.S. Commissioner of Education Report, 1899-1900.*

12. F.E. DeYoe and C.H. Thurber, "Where Are the High School Boys?" *The School Review* 8 (April 1900): 234.

13. Ibid., 240-41.

14. In 1900, Los Angeles High School had 756 girls and 403 boys. See School Statistics, *Board Reports, 1900-01*, 50.

Concern about feminization of American culture can be seen in such articles as Earl Barnes, "The Feminizing of Culture," *Atlantic Monthly* 109 (June 1912): 770-76; G. Stanley Hall, "Femininization in School and Home," *The World's Work* 16 (May 1908): 1037-44; Luther Gulick, "The Alleged Effemination of Our American Boys," *American Physical Education Review* 10 (September 1905): 216-19; Maximilian Grozzman, "Femalization of Education," *Child-Study Monthly* 2 (June 1896): 126-33; Rabbi Soloman Schindler, "Flaw in Our Public School System: The Preponderance of Female Teachers," *Arena* 6 (June 1892): 59-63; and Alfred A. Cleveland, "The Predominance of Female Teachers," *Pedagogical Seminary* 12 (September 1905): 289-303. John Higham discusses the countertrend toward "masculinization" in "The Reorientation of American Culture in the 1890s," in *Writing American History: Essays in Modern Scholarship*, ed. John Higham (Bloomington: Indiana University Press, 1970), 1-35.

15. Annual Report of the Superintendent to the Los Angeles Board of Education, *Los Angeles Board of Education Reports, 1902-03*, 131.

16. E.P. Clark, "How Shall We Keep the Boy in School? Pt. 2," *The Sierra Educational Review* 6 (June 1910): 29. The journal in which this article appeared was the official organ of the California Teachers Association. In the article, Clark quoted from *The World's Work* to argue that "the preponderance of girls among the graduates" was one proof of the failure of the American high school.

17. Patrick Geddes and J. Arthur Thompson, *The Evolution of Sex* (London: W. Scott, 1889). See, too, William K. Brooks, "The Condition of Woman from a Zoological Point of View," *Popular Science Monthly* 15 (June 1879): 143-55 and 347-56, and "Woman from the Standpoint of a Naturalist," *The Forum* 22 (November 1896): 286-96.

For historiographical discussions of this theory of sex metabolism, see Janice Law Trecker, "Sex, Science, and Education," *American Quarterly* 26 (October 1974): 352-66; Elizabeth Fee, "The Sexual Politics of Victorian Social Anthropology," *Feminist Studies* 1 (Winter-Spring 1973): 23-39; Jill Conway, "Stereotypes of Femininity in a Theory of Sexual Evolution," in *Suffer and Be Still: Women in the Victorian Age*, ed. Martha Vicinus (Bloomington: Indiana University Press, 1972), 140-55; and Flavia Alaya, "Victorian Science and the Genius of Woman," *Journal of the History of Ideas* 38 (April-June 1977): 261-80.

18. G. Stanley Hall explained in his two-volume study, *Adolescence*, that female nature "is more generic and less specific" than male nature. For that reason, said Hall, "each woman is a more adequate representative of her sex than a man is of his. . . . An ideal or

typical male is hard to define; but there is a standard ideal woman." See *Adolescence* (New York: D. Appleton & Co., 1904), 1: 505, 567.

19. William F. Book, "The High School Teacher from the Pupil's Point of View," *Pedagogical Seminary* 12 (September 1905): 285.

20. A. Caswell Ellis, "The Percentage of Boys Who Leave High School and the Reasons Therefore," *Proceedings of the National Education Association* 47 (1903), 796 (hereafter referred to as *NEA Proceedings*).

J. E. Armstrong argued similarly that a girl could naturally conform to the petty requirements of the classroom, but a boy was too independent to be bound by rule. See "Limited Segregation," *The School Review* 14 (December 1906): 730.

21. Grozzman said that the boy "will, in the end, in spite of or perhaps because of his slower intellectual development, outstrip the girl the older he becomes and the more complicated the tasks and problems which are given," but in the meantime, the more early-maturing schoolgirl would be more successful at routine work than the schoolboy. See "Femalization of Education," 123.

J. E. Armstrong argued that "the girls' listless, weary period was more brief and occurred one or two years before she entered high school. The boy, during his first two years in high school finds himself unable to carry his work beside his more mature sisters." In Armstrong's opinion, competition between the two sexes at this age was unfair because it put the boy in "an unfavorable light as the girl has herself in better command just at this period of development." Armstrong supported his argument with the claim that in twenty-five years as a high school principal, "twenty percent of the girls who graduated had attained an average of ninety percent in all their studies, while only two percent of the boy graduates during the same period attained such a grade." See "The Advantages of Limited Sex Segregation in the High School," *The School Review* 18 (May 1910): 341-50. See, too, Armstrong, "Limited Segregation," 729.

22. Hall, *Adolescence*, 1: 510, and "Femininization in School and Home," 1039.

23. Julius Sachs, "Coeducation in the United States," *Educational Review* 33 (March 1907): 301-303.

24. James A. Barr, "The Reasons Why Men Are Leaving School Work and Some Remedies for the Same," *Western Journal of Education* 13 (March 1907): 129. Barr quoted Benjamin Ide Wheeler, the president of the University of California, as having said that a boy "is likely to lose his respect for schools if they are represented to him exclusively and predominantly in the person of women."

For additional expressions of the view that women's presence caused education to be held in low esteem, see C. W. Bardeen, "Why Teaching Repels Men," *Educational Review* 35 (April 1908): 351-58; and Duane Mowry, "Why Are There Few Men Teachers?" *Educational Review* 36 (June 1908): 95-98.

25. Jesse F. Millspaugh, "The Need for Male Teachers for Our Public Schools," *Addresses and Proceedings of the Southern California Teachers' Association* (Los Angeles, 1904): 52-53.

26. G. Stanley Hall, "Coeducation," *NEA Proceedings* 48 (1904): 538-42. For similar expressions of concern, see "Editorial Notes," *The School Review* 17 (January 1909): 55; and Reuben P. Halleck, "What Kind of Education Is Best Suited to Boys?" *The School Review* 14 (September 1906): 515. According to Halleck, "some people in the schools sigh that the boys are not all girls, and then go to work and make them girls as fast as possible."

27. Figures provided in table 1 derived from *Board Reports* and *U.S. Commissioner on Education Reports*. Over 30 percent of adolescents between fifteen and nineteen were enrolled in Los Angeles schools at the turn of the century, but only 15 percent of Los Angeles adolescents were in the high schools. This discrepancy is due to the fact that many adolescents were enrolled in grades below high school.

28. Although it is clear that both sexes were dropping out of school in this period, the

educational community devoted its attention solely to the boys. Articles on the retention problem carried titles like, "Where Are the High School Boys?" "How Shall We Keep
the Boy in School?" "How to Increase Attendance of Boys at the High School," and "The
Percentage of Boys Who Leave High School and the Reasons Therefor." Occasionally,
these articles reported on dropout rates for both sexes but then discussed only the
causes and remedies for boys' poor persistence. Even those articles whose titles made
no reference to the sex of dropouts focused their attention solely on boys. There was not
one article to be found in any educational journal in this period that devoted its discussion to the number of girls dropping out of school.

DeYoe and Thurber; E.P. Clark, "How Shall We Keep the Boy in School? Pts. 1 and 2,"
Sierra Educational Review 6 (May and June 1910): 11-17, 23-30; J.K. Stableton, "How to
Increase the Attendance of Boys at the High School," *NEA Proceedings* 47 (1903): 301-7;
Job Wood, Jr., "Why Do Boys Leave School?" *Western Journal of Education* 8 (March 193):
141-43; Ellis.

29. Leonard P. Ayres, *Laggards in Our Schools: A Study of Retardation and Elimination in
City School Systems* (New York: Charities Publication Committee, 1909), 3, 7. See, too,
Stratton D. Brooks, "Causes of Withdrawal from School," *Educational Review* 26
(November 1903): 385.

30. *Board Reports, 1896-97; Board Reports, 1900-01; Board Reports, 1902-03.*

31. *Board Reports, 1891-92; Board Reports, 1907-08.*

32. *Board Reports, 1900-01; U.S. Census Report, 1900.* For the purposes of this calculation, a "teenager" was defined as a person between fifteen and nineteen years of age,
because that is the age category the Census provides. There were an additional 210
students in the Los Angeles high schools in 1900 who were either below fifteen or over
nineteen, but they were not counted into this calculation.

33. Brown, chap. 3: "Female Nurture"; S.B. Hursh, "A Study of Children's Hopes,"
Child-Study Monthly 1 (February 1896): 256-59. See *The Blue and White*, Los Angeles
High School Yearbook, Summer 1908, n.p.; Winter 1910, n.p.

34. Report of the Attendance Officer to the Los Angeles Board of Education, *Board
Reports, 1905-06*, 197; *Board Reports, 1906-07*, 137; *Board Reports, 1907-08*, 118.

Report of the President of the Los Angeles Board of Education, *Board Reports, 1897-98*,
13; Report of the President of the Los Angeles Board of Education, *Board Reports,
1899-1900*, 14.

35. The U.S. Census for 1910 reveals that, among fourteen- and fifteen-year-olds in Los
Angeles, 19 percent of the boys and 9 percent of the girls were working. And although
Los Angeles girls represented about 50 percent of the city's ten- to twenty-year-old
population, girls represented less than 30 percent of those between ten and twenty
years old who were employed in Los Angeles in 1910. These figures, combined with the
truancy figures already reported, suggest that if a girl was not in school, her chances of
being out in public during the day were far less than a boy's. Brown, "Golden Girls,"
303. For a discussion of boys' opportunities to work for fathers or neighbors, see Brown,
chap. 3: "Female Nurture."

36. William Webster, "Report on Attendance in San Francisco Schools," *Addresses and
Record of the Proceedings of the State Teachers' Association of California* (1899): 470.

37. Susan B. Carter and Mark Prus, "The Labor Market and the American School Girl,
1890-1928," *Journal of Economic History* 42 (March 1982): 164.

38. Hattie Willard, "Children's Ambitions," *Studies in Education* 1 (January 1897):
243-53. For studies similar to Willard's but conducted in other parts of the United
States, see John Jegi, "Children's Ambitions," *Transactions of the Illinois Society for Child-
Study* 3 (October 1898): 131-44; Will S. Monroe, "Children's Ambitions," *New England
Journal of Education* 25 (18 June 1896): 414; Adelaide Wyckoff, "Children's Ideals,"
Pedagogical Seminary 8 (December 1901): 482-90; and Hursh.

39. Book, 213.

40. For the purposes of this survey of job titles listed in the *U.S. Census Report*, the following were regarded as jobs that required an education beyond the eighth grade: official government inspector, architect, author, editor, reporter, clergy, college professor, dentist, lawyer, physician, teacher, trained nurse, notary, bookkeeper, accountant, stenographer, banker, transportation proprietor, insurance agent, chemist, metallurgist, and engineer. *U.S. Census Report, 1890,* vol. 1, pt. 2; *U.S. Census Report, 1900,* vol. 2; *U.S. Census Report, 1910,* vol. 4; *U.S. Census Report, 1900,* vol. 2.

41. Emily S. Boulton described teachers' work as "steady and genteel" in "A Plea for Teachers," *California Teacher and Home Journal* 7 (October 1880): 172-75. In this article, Boulton reasoned that because there were few jobs as respectable as teaching open to women, the market would always be glutted, women would always be underpaid and, therefore, female teachers should be socially compensated with "high respect."

The law did not actually require a high school diploma to enter the state's normal schools until 1904, but the record makes it clear that Los Angeles Normal School began to favor high school graduates as early as the 1890s. This added institutional incentive probably explains why girls in Los Angeles were more likely to *graduate* from high school than boys. For example, in 1900, girls constituted only 57 percent of the freshman high school class in 1900 but commanded 67 percent of the senior class. Logic suggests that the girls who persisted were those who recognized, as one Los Angeles school board report put it, "that so few avenues of lucrative employment are open to women and that teaching is one of the most attainable and attractive." *Board Reports, 1883-84,* 35.

For information on the requirements for entrance into California state normal schools, see Henry W. Splitter, "Education in Los Angeles, pt. 2," *Southern California Quarterly* 33 (September 1951): 239-40; Charles Falk, *The Development and Organization of Education in California* (New York: Harcourt, Brace, & World), 176; California State Superintendent of Public Instruction, *Seventeenth Biennial Annual Report* (1895-96): 6-8; and Evelyn A. Clement, "The Evolution of Teacher Training in California As a Phase of Social Change" (Ph.D. diss., University of California, Berkeley, 1937), 140-42.

42. *Board Reports, 1900-01,* 50.

43. *The Blue and White,* Summer 1909, n.p. A report from the principal of Los Angeles High School to the city's superintendent of schools in 1896 suggested a similar trend. In that report the principal noted that twenty-four of the high school's seventy-one graduates that year would be attending college. The report did not specify what percentage of those twenty-four college-bound adolescents were female and male, but it did note that an additional twenty-two females – or 53 percent of the female graduating class – would be going to normal school.

Many of the females who attended college instead of normal school would later become teachers. Fifty-three percent of the female faculty in American high schools in 1905 were college graduates. See Geraldine Clifford, "Eve: Redeemed by Education and Teaching School," *History of Education Quarterly* 21 (Winter 1981): 485.

44. *U.S. Commissioner of Education Report, 1900-1901,* vol. 2: 1916, 1971.

45. *Board Reports, 1902-03,* 54.

46. Millspaugh, 52-53.

47. *Board Reports, 1896-97,* 13; *Board Reports, 1902-03,* 87. See Mary Grace Jensen, "The Rise and Expansion of Public Secondary Education in The Los Angeles City High School District," (Ed.D. diss., University of California at Los Angeles, 1940), 58-62; and Harry Sargent, "The History of Secondary Education in the City of Los Angeles" (Master's thesis in Education, University of Southern California, 1940), 50-51.

48. Report of the Superintendent of Schools to the Los Angeles Board of Education, *Board Reports, 1904-05,* 73. In the six months between January and June of 1905, for example, girls constituted 16 percent of the 646 children apprehended for truancy, but none of the thirty students from this group who were sent to the special school for

truants were girls. See Report of Attendance Officer Arthur C. Ayres to the Superintendent of the Los Angeles Schools, *Board Reports, 1904-05*, 168-69.

According to Superintendent Foshay, candidates for the special school for truants were "boys who had proved themselves ungovernable" and boys who were "unwilling to receive an education because of the distractions of other forms of life." See Report of the Superintendent to the Los Angeles Board of Education, *Board Reports, 1904-05*, 73.

49. Superintendent's Report to the Los Angeles Board of Education, *Board Reports, 1902-03*, 67. Ten years earlier, the school superintendent had reported that the city's evening school was "open only to boys and the class of boys attending are of the best boys who work in day time to support mothers and other dependent members of the family." See *Board Reports, 1892-93*, 56.

50. According to A. H. Yoder, "no half-grown boy is going to develop into his best self under the exclusive teaching of a woman in a school made up largely of girls." See "Sex Differentiation in Secondary Education," *NEA Proceedings* 47 (1903): 789. Benjamin Ide Wheeler, the president of the University of California, believed that boys beyond the age of thirteen needed "the impression of virility, personal strength and creative capacity that they get from a strong man." In Clark, "How Shall We Keep the Boy in School? Pt. 1," 15. And James Barr, the superintendent of schools in Stockton, California, expressed the view that "the problem of holding the boys in school would be largely solved by a larger proportion of stronger men." See Barr, 127.

51. Edward L. Thorndike, "The Influence of the Number of Men Teachers upon the Enrollment of Boys in the Public High Schools," *Educational Review* 37 (January 1909): 75-77. Thorndike concluded from his survey that "the proportion of boys who leave or stay through high school is almost wholly irrespective of the percentage of men on the staff of the school."

Comparable figures from Los Angeles support Thorndike on this point. The percentage of Los Angeles High School students who were male declined from 48 percent in 1890 to 41 percent in 1900 even though the percentage of teachers who were male increased in that decade from 10 to 41 percent. Between 1900 and 1910, the percentage of students who were male increased from 41 to 44 percent while the percentage of teachers who were male decreased from 41 to 29 percent.

52. Information on teachers' salaries in Los Angeles was derived from *Board Reports* for 1890, 1900, and 1905.

53. J.D. Graham, cited in Clark, "How Shall We Keep the Boy in School? Pt. 2," 29, 30.

54. Report of the Superintendent of Schools to the Pasadena Board of Education, *Annual Report of the Pasadena Board of Education*, 12. California's Governor Pardee actually fired President Pierce of the Los Angeles Normal School in 1904 because Pierce disagreed with Pardee on the need for athletics in the Normal School. Pardee replaced Pierce with Jesse Millspaugh, who shared the governor's conviction that athletics and male teachers were necessary to hold boys in school, and athletics were equally necessary to attract young men to teacher training programs.

55. *The Blue and White*, Summer 1903, n.p.; Summer 1905, n.p.; Summer 1906, n.p.; Summer 1907, n.p.

56. *The Blue and White*, Summer 1910, n.p.

57. *The Blue and White*, Summer 1898, n.p. In the 1901 yearbook, the editors bemoaned the absence at games of "those who manipulate the lace handkerchiefs."

The Polytechnic, Souvenir Edition, June 1901, n.p.; *The Blue and White*, Winter 1903, n.p.; *The Polytechnic*, June 1907, n.p.

58. Marshall Stimson, "Fun, Fights, and Fiestas in Old Los Angeles" (Los Angeles: Los Angeles Public Library, 1966), 72. Stimson's recollection of life under Principal Housh makes clear Housh's purpose to elevate boys' status in the high school. See, for example, 78-79.

59. *The Blue and White*, Winter 1900, n.p.

60. *The Blue and White,* February 1910, n.p. *The Blue and White,* Summer 1907, n.p.; Summer 1910, n.p.; Sargent, 48. *The Blue and White,* Summer 1908.

61. Selwyn Troen, "The Discovery of the Adolescent by American Educational Reformers, 1900-1920: An Economic Perspective," in *Schooling and Society,* ed. Lawrence Stone (Baltimore: Johns Hopkins University Press, 1976), 239-51.

62. Report of the Manual Training Supervisor to the Los Angeles Board of Education, *Board Reports, 1901-02,* 108-14.

63. Report of the Superintendent of Schools to the Los Angeles Board of Education, *Board Reports, 1895-96,* 52-54; *Board Reports, 1904-5,* 11.

64. Report of the Superintendent of Schools to the Los Angeles Board of Education, *Board Reports, 1896-97,* 85; *Board Reports, 1901-02,* 61.

Manual training offered school officials another opportunity to show that they were sympathetic to boys' supposed desire for a more active, practical education and yet ready to prepare the ambitious American boy for "any and all vocations." See Ednah A. Rich, "Constructive Work," *Addresses and Record of the Proceedings of the State Teachers' Association of California* 34 (1900): 266; Report of the Superintendent of the Pasadena Schools to the Pasadena Board of Education, *Pasadena Board Reports, 1902,* 11.

65. Report of the Manual Training Supervisor to the Los Angeles Board of Education, *Board Reports, 1901-02,* 110.

66. "What Girls Should Learn," *California Teacher and Home Journal* 2 (September 1883): 121-26.

67. Abbott Kinney, *Tasks by Twilight* (New York: G.P. Putnam's Sons, 1893), 76-77.

68. Report of the Superintendent of Schools to the Los Angeles Board of Education, *Board Reports, 1892-93,* 49.

69. Report of the Superintendent of Schools to the Los Angeles Board of Education, *Board Reports, 1907-08,* 10-11.

70. Elizabeth Hansot and David Tyack, "Gender in American Public Schools: Thinking Institutionally," *Signs* 13 (Summer 1988): 758.

71. Ibid., 744-47 and 757-58. Hansot and Tyack argue that sex role socialization "may be distinct in different institutions" and that "*within the classroom* both boys and girls learned through their institutional socialization that they were expected to follow similar rules of behavior, learn the same subjects, and gain the same rewards for the same degree of achievement." By contrast, the argument presented here is that sex role socialization in one environment is not experienced so distinctly but is, rather, carried over into other environments. And evidence presented here calls into question the claim that girls and boys expected that they would behave the same in school, learn the same subjects, or receive the same rewards.

Beyond Title IX: Toward an Agenda for Women and Sports in the 1990's

Wendy Olson[†]

INTRODUCTION

When I was eight years old, I tucked my braided pigtails under a blue and red baseball cap, reasoning with all of my third-grade wisdom that the disguise would hide my gender, grabbed my Tony Oliva autographed glove and jumped in the family Wagoneer to go to the baseball park. The early April temperatures were climbing into the 50's in Pocatello, Idaho, and snow had been absent for at least a couple of weeks. Undoubtedly, the season was little league.

After idyllic summers of neighborhood pick-up games, where I became convinced that, despite being the only girl, equality reigned, the forces of Bannock Boys Baseball were Phyllis Schlafly incarnate in my own hometown. The coaches and league officials—one of whom was my elementary school vice principal—took one look at me and didn't even give me a chance to let a grounder roll through my legs at tryouts. It was the first time I was the odd "man" out in athletics; it would not be the last.

I was eight years old in the spring of 1973, just one year after the passage of Title IX of the Education Amendments of 1972. Title IX, as it was affectionately known by any woman who had ever laced on a pair of sneakers, prohibited sex discrimination in any program or activity receiving federal funds.[1] While I was out trying to break the gender barrier in Bannock Boys Baseball, thousands of women athletes, coaches and administrators were basking in the glory of the legislation that they were convinced would be the first mighty step toward making them the oncourt, onfield, in-locker room equals of their male counterparts. After all, colleges, universities and high schools, the loci of female athletes' most visible exclusion and inferiority, were

---

† J.D. Stanford, 1990; B.A. in News Editorial Journalism, Drake University, 1986. The author is currently a law clerk to Judge Barbara J. Rothstein, U.S. District Court, Seattle, Washington and was a member of the women's varsity tennis team at Drake University.

1. Education Amendments of 1972, 20 U.S.C. §§ 1681-1688 (1990) (prohibiting sex discrimination in any education program or activity receiving federal funds) [hereinafter Title IX].

often recipients of federal funds, and, thus, would have to comply with Title IX's prohibition of sex discrimination. Educators envisioned equal expenditures that would produce equal facilities, equal training, and perhaps even equal salaries for coaches.

However, nearly two decades later—and despite some hard-fought gains—little of that enormous promise has been realized. Title IX, a symbol of hope for women in sports throughout the United States, brought some unanticipated setbacks. Although the number of women and girls participating in athletics increased, the number of women in coaching and athletic administration declined.[2] Title IX enforcement regulations by the Health, Education and Welfare Department, and its successor the Education Department,[3] have never been very tight. In the 1980's, it took congressional passage of a second statute to restore some of the luster to Title IX in the wake of a nearly fatal Supreme Court decision.[4] In the large shadow cast by the massive

---

2. R. Acosta & L. Carpenter, Women in Intercollegiate Sport: A Longitudinal Study—Nine Year Update, 1977-1986, at 1-2 (report on file with *Yale Journal of Law and Feminism*).

3. 45 C.F.R. § 86.1.71 (1989); *see also* Geadelmann, *What Does the Law Say?*, in EQUALITY IN SPORT FOR WOMEN 33, 38-43 (P. Geadelmann, C. Grant, Y. Slatton & N. P. Burke eds. 1977).

4. Civil Rights Restoration Act of 1987 §3, 20 U.S.C. §§ 1687-1688 (1990 Supp.). The Civil Rights Restoration Act, which affected more than women's athletics, was passed in response to the Supreme Court's decision in *Grove City College v. Bell*, 465 U.S. 555 (1984). *Grove City* held that the receipt of federal funds by one school program "does not trigger institution wide coverage under Title IX." *Id.* at 573. Section 1687 of the Civil Rights Restoration Act reads,

> For the purposes of this chapter, the terms "program or activity"
> and "program" mean all the operations of
> (1)(A) a department, agency, special purpose district, or
> other instrumentality of a state or of a local government; or
> (B) the entity of such State or local government that distributes
> such assistance and each such department or agency (and each other
> State or local government entity) to which the assistance is extended,
> in the case of assistance to a State or local government;
> (2)(A) a college, university, or other postsecondary institution,
> or a public system of higher education; or
> (B) a local educational agency[ ], system of vocational education,
> or other school system;
> (3)(A) an entire corporation, partnership, or other private
> organization, or an entire sole proprietorship
> (i) if assistance is extended to such corporation, partnership,
> private organization, or sole proprietorship as a whole; or
> (ii) which is principally engaged in the business of
> providing education, health care, housing, social services,
> or parks and recreation; or
> (B) the entire plant or other comparable, geographi-
> cally separate facility to which Federal financial assistance
> is extended, in the case of any other corporation, partnership,
> private organization, or sole proprietorship; or

effort put into the initial passage and 1988 restoration of Title IX, the women's sports movement[5] has not embraced issues such as racism and drugs that plague all of sport. It has not resolved internal debates about how best to further the goals of women in sports, including whether scholastic teams should be single sex or coed[6] and whether the women's sports movement should embrace the men's model of athletics.[7] Furthermore, it has not been able to gain the support of the broader women's movement.[8]

Title IX also provides a very narrow view of women's sports and the discrimination that women athletes face. The statute bars discrimination on the basis of sex only in educational programs or activities receiving *federal* funding.[9] The focus of Title IX is on discrimination against athletes and not on discrimination against coaches, administrators and other supporting staff.[10] Courts in Title IX cases rarely look beyond such tangible measures of equality

---

    (4) any other entity which is established by two or more of the
entities described in paragraph (1), (2) or (3);
any part of which is extended Federal financial assistance, except
that such term does not include any operation of an entity which is controlled by a religious organization if the application of section 1681 of
this title to such operation would not be consistent with the religious
tenets of such organization.
20 U.S.C. § 1687 (1990 Supp.).

    5. Women's sports movement is somewhat of a misnomer. Just as there are a diversity of interests, needs and problems among women in general, there are a diversity of interests, needs and problems among women involved in sports. *See infra* notes 108-31 and accompanying text and notes 194-95 and accompanying text.

    6. For a view opposing single sex athletic teams, see generally Tokarz, *Separate But Unequal Educational Sports Programs*, 1 BERKELEY WOMEN'S L.J. 201 (1986) (arguing that separate athletic teams for men's and women's sports are inherently unequal). For views supporting single sex athletic teams, see Note, *Where the Boys Are: Can Separate Be Equal in School Sports?*, 58 SO. CAL. L. REV. 1425, 1448-50 (1985) (authored by Virginia P. Croudace and Steven A. Desmarais) (arguing that separate but equal athletic teams are the *best* alternative for furthering participation of women in sport). One of the tensions in the separate but equal approach is that it insists that women athletes often make the choice between individual advancement, as when a female athlete with collegiate or world class abilities tries to gain access to a male team, and advancement of women's sports in general, as when the same female athlete remains with or helps start a women's or girls' team in order to improve the skills and interest of her sister female athletes.

    7. *See, e.g.*, LeMaire, *Women and Athletics: Toward a Physicality Perspective*, 5 HARV. WOMEN'S L.J. 121 (1976); Beck, *The Future of Women's Sport: issues, insights, and struggles*, in S. EITZEN, SPORT IN CONTEMPORARY SOCIETY 401 (2d ed. 1984).

    8. *See infra* notes 98-107 and accompanying text.

    9. 20 U.S.C. § 1681(a) (1990).

    10. The Equal Pay Act of 1963, as amended by the Education Amendments of 1972, guarantees female coaches the same pay as male coaches if the jobs require equal skill, effort and responsibility under similar working conditions. 1972 Amendments to the Equal Pay Act of 1963, 29 U.S.C. § 206(d) (1988).

as funding and facilities.[11] This focus dictates a course of separate but equal athletic teams for women college athletes modeled after men's competitive athletics. The separate but equal approach ignores that men and women are not similarly situated in their relationship to athletics as a social institution.[12] The definition of women's sports produced by Title IX leaves out women who are not collegians; women who play purely for fun rather than to win; women who want to be involved with sport.

While acknowledging the role Title IX played in placing women's sports on the federal agenda, an agenda for women and sports in the 1990's must look beyond Title IX and women's college athletics modeled on men's college athletics. An agenda for women and sports in the 1990's must: (1) eradicate the persistent stereotype that, although society accepts superwomen such as tennis players Chris Evert and Martina Navratilova and sprinter Florence Griffith Joyner, the only roles for ordinary women in the world of sport are as cheerleaders, baseball Annies[13] and football widows;[14] (2) secure a place for itself in the broader women's movement; (3) recognize the diversity of women in and out of the women's sports movement; and (4) address the needs of *all* women in sports, particularly in areas where women can make an impact on the current male model of sport.[15]

The four strains of this agenda are intertwined. By securing a place for itself in the broader women's movement, the women's sports movement will be able to enlist the aid of women in academics and business who may be most capable and qualified to obtain positions as administrators and executives throughout all levels of athletics. The introduction of women who have not yet been involved in the women's sports movement will help eradicate the myth that sports is only for the Chris Everts, Martina Navratilovas and Florence Griffith Joyners. In the world of sport, women need not accept the role of sideline appendage. Moreover, a broader linkage between the general women's movement and the women's sports movement will allow both groups to address the questions of how to meet the needs of diverse groups of women and how

---

11. See, e.g., O'Connor v. Board of Educ. of School Dist. No. 23, 645 F.2d 578, 581 (7th Cir. 1981) (court considered equality of separate teams in terms of funding, facilities, and other "objective" criteria only). These are among the measures outlined in the 1975 HEW regulations. 45 C.F.R. § 86.41(c)(1989).

12. *See* Littleton, *Equality and Feminist Legal Theory*, 48 U. PITT. L. REV. 1043, 1051 (1987).

13. A baseball Annie is a woman who is a professional baseball groupie, who hangs around where players are likely to congregate, including the field and popular night spots.

14. A football widow is a woman who does not enjoy football and whose husband or boyfriend spends much of the fall watching college and professional football games.

15. *See infra* notes 154-59 and accompanying text.

to jointly further women's involvement in sport in the 1990's.[16]

Part I of this paper outlines the history of the women's athletics movement in the United States that produced Title IX. Part II analyzes the areas in which Title IX and the equality model have been inadequate. Part III discusses the importance of the women's sports movement to sports and women. Part IV presents a theory of sport toward which the women's sports movement should direct its agenda. Finally, Part V briefly outlines some initial suggestions and recommendations for a women's sports agenda in the 1990's.

I. FROM RESISTANCE TO A SHATTERED IDEAL

In the twentieth century, the women's sports movement in the United States has been centered in colleges and universities.[17] At least until the passage of Title IX provided the impetus for a more competitive model of women's athletics, colleges and universities emphasized a model of women's sports that was much different from men's sports.

In the early part of the 20th century, women athletes were to engage only in physical activity that allowed them to walk a fine line—exercise was to make them better women without imbalancing their delicate physiques.[18] The myth governing women athletes for most of the twentieth century was that women were simply too fragile to engage in strenuous physical contests. Plenty of groups—of both women and men—were ready to make the myth reality. In 1922, the United States' Committee on Women's Athletics vigorously opposed the entry of American women in the 1922 Paris "Women's Olympics."[19] In the 1928 Olympics, all eleven women who were entered in the 800 meters either withdrew or failed to finish the race. In response, the Women's Division of the National Amateur Athletic Federation petitioned the International Olympic Committee (IOC) to ban all races for women of 800 meters or longer.[20] The IOC, whose president, Baron Pierre DeCoubertin, had himself

---

16. The question of priorities has become particularly complicated in the 1990's by the Supreme Court's decision in *Webster v. Reproductive Health Services*, 492 U.S. ___ , 109 S. Ct. 3040 (1989), making abortion legislation at the state level the focal point of a number of women's groups.

17. Members of the upper-class social elite also participated in sporting games, although mostly as social outings rather than as competitive contests. *See* H. LENSKYJ, OUT OF BOUNDS: WOMEN, SPORT AND SEXUALITY 17 (1986).

18. *See id.* at 21-25.

19. Chandler, *The Association of Intercollegiate Athletics for Women: The End of Amateurism in U.S. Intercollegiate Sport*, in WOMEN IN SPORT: SOCIOLOGICAL AND HISTORICAL PERSPECTIVES 5, 12 (A. Reeder & J. Fuller eds. 1985) [hereinafter WOMEN IN SPORT].

20. *Id.* at 12. The legacy of the 11 women in the 1928 800 meters has taken 60 years to undo. A Ninth Circuit panel declined in 1983 to order the United States Olympic Committee (USOC) to include

been opposed to women's participation in the 1920's, complied.[21]

Most women collegiate physical educators began the twentieth century horrified by the commercial spectacle that men's collegiate athletics had become.[22] These defenders of women's traditional roles as wives and mothers were determined not to let women's college athletics develop along the same lines.[23] Unfortunately, many of these early physical educators' concerns originated more from their perception of the limits of women's physical capabilities than from their disdain of men's collegiate athletics. The focus for women's college athletics was to be the pure pleasure of participa-tion; women athletes were not to be "merely a means to a commercial end."[24]

As women physical educators began to change their views about the ability of women to safely survive strenuous sports,[25] they embraced the noncommercial, process-oriented view of athletics. This was the foundation upon which the Association for Intercollegiate Athletics for Women was built in the early 1970's. The organization, an outgrowth of the Commission on Intercollegiate Athletics for Women,[26] sought to provide female college athletes with a high level of training and competition without the material rewards and excesses available to male college athletes. Restrictions were placed on member universities' recruiting and traveling expenses. Athletes were seen first as

---

the 5,000 and 10,000 meter races for women in their 1984 Olympic trials on the grounds that both the USOC and International Olympic Committee (IOC) were international actors and were not arbitrarily discriminating. Martin v. International Olympic Comm., 740 F.2d 670, 677 (1984). The first women's Olympic marathon, however, was run in 1984 in Los Angeles.

21. Chandler, *supra* note 19, at 12.

22. *Id.* at 8-9.

23. There were, of course, some exceptions. Women's basketball, particularly in Canada, thrived for a time in the early 20th century. *See* W. MOKRAY, THE RONALD ENCYCLOPEDIA OF BASKETBALL I-17 (1963).

24. Chandler, *supra* note 19, at 8. For many commentators on contemporary women's athletics, the goal is the same. *See, e.g.,* Beck, *supra* note 7. Participation for participation's sake has not been exclusively the province of the women's sports movement. *See, e.g.,* Gilbert, *Competition: Is it What Life's All About?*, SPORTS ILLUS., May 16, 1988, at 86.

> The pleasurable and instructive aspects of sport should derive from the competition itself, not from the final score. Traditionally, and perhaps by ancient design, the tangible awards for victory are of little material worth—symbolic trophies of one sort or another—because the only real and lasting value of a game is what's felt and learned during the contest.

Id. at 95. For a discussion of a goal of pleasure of participation in contemporary sports, see *infra* Part IV, notes 143-78 and accompanying text.

25. Women outside the college system were responsible for demonstrating the fallacy of the "fragile female" myth. Chandler points out that in 1932, the IOC added the 80-meter hurdles and the javelin as events for women athletes, both of which were won by Babe Didrickson. Didrickson later was to become one of the premier women golfers in the world. Didrickson, like the African-American women track stars of the 1960's, was not a product of the collegiate system. Chandler, *supra* note 19, at 12.

26. AIAW v. NCAA, 735 F.2d 577, 579-80 (D.C. Cir. 1984).

students. They were not to be viewed as commodities. "College sport was to be an avocation, not a profession; participation, not victory, was the goal."[27]

The lifespan of the AIAW paralleled the first incarnation of Title IX, which prohibited sex discrimination in any program or activity receiving federal funds. For underfunded, underequipped, underestimated women's athletic departments, Title IX appeared as a savior.

Title IX was passed in 1972, the year after the CIAW became the AIAW, and together, the two grew and prospered.[28] In 1971-72, the AIAW sponsored seven national championships for its 278 members. Ten years later, the AIAW had 961 members.[29] A National Association for Girls and Women in Sports survey showed that the number of female athletic participants in 1972 was 300,000 but more than 1.8 million in 1986.[30]

Despite the increased participation and interest in women's sports, the view that women could not be athletes, and female athletes could not really be women, persisted throughout the AIAW-early Title IX era. But as women's collegiate athletic programs blossomed in the 1970's, the women's sports movement began to battle that myth.[31] To assertions that women were likely to be injured engaging in athletics, particularly contact sports, they responded with batteries of studies that indicated that female athletes were no more susceptible to injury than male athletes.[32] To assertions that athletics would

---

27. Chandler, *supra* note 19, at 13 (footnote omitted). Chandler is critical of the AIAW approach for the paternalistic restrictions it placed on women athletes.

> College women were originally kept from competing strenuously because it was believed to endanger their health and their roles as women; now, they were not to be recruited strenuously because that was believed to endanger their mental health and their roles as students. College women's sport had previously been kept free from the taint of commercialism because that was believed to undermine the intrinsic values of sport engaged in for its own sake.

Id. at 15.

28. R. Acosta & L. Carpenter, *supra* note 2. A flurry of equal protection litigation followed quickly on the heels of Title IX's enactment, suggesting that the political act of Title IX's passage was a signal to females everywhere that "ladies' day" at the club was to be every day.

29. AIAW v. NCAA, 735 F.2d at 580.

30. Olson, *A Title IX Paradox: More Female Athletes but Fewer Coaches*, L.A. Times, July 8, 1987, at C3, col. 1. The number of females participating in athletics specifically at the high school level increased 500 percent after the passage of Title IX. In 1972, only 7% of high school females were athletes, but a decade later 35% were athletes. *Miller Lite Report on Women in Sports* 7 (1985) [hereinafter *Miller Lite Report*].

31. *See, e.g.*, Drinkwater, *Myths and Realities of Women's Performance in Sport*, in REPORT ON THE CONFERENCE ON WOMEN IN SPORT 1 (1980).

32. *See, e.g., id.* at 2-10; Tokarz, *supra* note 6, at 222-23; LeMaire, *supra* note 7, at 137-38. Preventing injury to women was among the most common state justifications for prohibiting girls from joining boys' teams when the school did not sponsor a girls' team in the same sport. *See* Note, *supra*

harm women's reproductive functions, they had babies.[33] To assertions that athletics would harm women's ability to be "women," they outlined the psychological benefits of sports for women.[34]

Although the AIAW and Title IX grew together, the AIAW died alone. The AIAW's vision of women's college sports, a vision Chandler argues had been essentially the same paternalistic one espoused by the Women's Division of the National Amateur Athletic Foundation,[35] was a victim of the very success and interest it had inspired. In 1981-82, the National Collegiate Athletic Association (NCAA) began sponsoring championships for women, immediate-ly wooing eighteen of the top twenty women's college basketball teams in the country to play in its championships rather than in those sponsored by the AIAW.[36] The NCAA's entry into the governance of women's sports was opportunistic both for the NCAA and for the women's athletic programs at major universities with successful men's programs. The NCAA had feared Title IX from the beginning, spending "as much money lobbying against Title IX as the [AIAW] spent on seventeen national championship tournaments for women."[37] But when women's collegiate athletic programs took off under Title IX, the NCAA decided that it could better serve its membership by

---

note 6, at 1441-42. The Note's authors describe research that indicates that the risk of serious injury to female reproductive organs and breasts is much less than the risk to male reproductive organs. *See also* Hoover v. Meiklejohn, 430 F. Supp. 164, 169 (D. Colo. 1977).

33. *See, e.g.,* Brownlee, *Moms in the Fast Lane,* SPORTS ILLUS., May 30, 1988, at 57. Although she writes that scientific tests are thus far inconclusive about whether pregnancy actually physically benefits women athletes, Brownlee documents the post-partum athletic success of runners Valerie Brisco, Evelyn Ashford and Ingrid Kristiansen, golfer Nancy Lopez and diver Pat McCormick. In addition, Brownlee outlines the stereotypes women athletes face. *Id.* at 60. Brownlee speculates that these women athletes may well experience psychological benefits from motherhood: women athletes who give birth are reassured that they are, indeed, women. *Id.*

34. Nielsen, *Putting Away the Pom-Poms: An Educational Psychologist's View of Females and Sports,* in WOMEN, PHILOSOPHY, AND SPORT: A COLLECTION OF NEW ESSAYS 287, 289-92 (B. Postow ed. 1983) (participation in sports allows girls to enjoy benefits of self-confidence, control over their lives and enhanced academic achievement through better health) [hereinafter WOMEN, PHILOSOPHY, AND SPORT].

35. *See supra* note 20 and accompanying text.

36. Barnes, *With Gains Come Growing Pains; Weller: 'I Get Tired of the Way They Treat Women's Basketball',* Wash. Post, Mar. 16, 1982, at D1, col. 3.

37. Nielsen, *supra* note 34, at 294. The NCAA continued its fight against Title IX on through the 1970's as the then-Department of Health, Education and Welfare promulgated enforcement regulations for Title IX. In *NCAA v. Califano,* 444 F. Supp. 425 (D. Kan. 1978), *rev'd.* 662 F.2d 1382 (10th Cir. 1980), the NCAA argued that the HEW regulations were not meant to apply to athletic programs that did not receive federal aid. *See* Skilton, *The Emergent Law of Women and Amateur Sports: Recent Developments,* 28 WAYNE L. REV. 1701, 1723-24 (1982). The NCAA argued that equality in women's sports was not at issue since most of its members were state institutions and therefore subject to the equal protection clause. It stressed that many private institutions were subject to nondiscrimination provisions in their state. *Id.* at 1724.

bringing the fledgling women's programs under its wing.[38]

The NCAA's decision to begin sponsoring championships for women made the AIAW's demise inevitable. In the same year that the NCAA entered women's athletics, the AIAW saw its membership revenues drop twenty-two percent and broadcasting and sponsorship revenues nearly evaporate.[39] In 1982, on the brink of bankruptcy, the AIAW folded.[40] The NCAA was simply too big and too powerful. It lured universities to its championships with promises of television coverage and travel funds to the championship events.[41] The AIAW alleged that the NCAA forced the AIAW out of existence by using its monopoly power in men's sports.[42] The D.C. Circuit Court of Appeals rejected the AIAW's arguments that the NCAA's actions violated the Sherman Antitrust Act, sealing the AIAW's fate.

Title IX received its own major blow two years later when the Supreme Court's decision in *Grove City College v. Bell*[43] restricted the application of Title IX to the individual program receiving federal funding. For the growth and success of collegiate women's athletic programs, an expansive reading of "program" and "activity" had been all but a necessity since few college athletic programs directly received federal funding.[44] In a Title IX suit brought by

---

38. For a view more congenial to the NCAA's motives, see Skilton, *supra* note 37, at 1748-49.

39. AIAW v. NCAA, 735 F.2d 577, 580 (D.C. Cir. 1984).

40. *Id.* at 580-81.

41. *Id.*

42. *Id.* at 580. *AIAW v. NCAA* was an antitrust lawsuit in which the AIAW claimed that the NCAA used its "monopoly power in men's college sports to facilitate its entry into women's sports and to force the AIAW out of existence. Specifically, the AIAW asserted that the NCAA's unlawful conduct consisted of predatory pricing, the use of financial incentives to 'link' the sale of competitive services with the sale of monopoly services, and an illegal tying arrangement." *Id.* The D.C. Circuit rejected all of the AIWA's claims.

43. 465 U.S. 555 (1984). In *Grove City*, the college, a private school in Pennsylvania, did not itself receive federal funds, but a number of its students received federal Basic Educational Opportunity Grants. The Third Circuit held that indirect aid, such as that to students, as well as direct aid triggered the application of § 901 of Title IX and made institutions whose students financed their education with BEOG's recipients of federal financial assistance. 687 F.2d 684, 700 (3d Cir. 1982). The Supreme Court rejected the Third Circuit's reasoning and stated that there was no evidence that the federal aid received by Grove City students resulted in the diversion of funds from the College's own financial aid program to other areas within the institution. The Supreme Court also emphasized the program-specific nature of Title IX. *Grove City*, 465 U.S. at 571-72. "In purpose and effect, BEOG's represent federal financial assistance to the College's own financial aid program, and it is that program that may properly be regulated under Title IX." *Id.* at 573-74.

44. The fact that *Grove City* so took the women's athletic movement and the sports media by surprise is itself somewhat of a surprise. For almost a decade—since HEW passed the initial Title IX enforcement regulations—courts, school districts and the NCAA battled over whether Congress intended for Title IX's regulatory and punitive provisions to apply to an entire institution if the institution in any way received federal funds, or to apply only to the specific program that was receiving federal funds. Ironically, the NCAA brought suit against the Department of Health, Education and Welfare, claiming

women athletes at Temple University in Philadelphia, for example, the Third Circuit, relying in part on its own intermediate decision in *Grove City*, ruled that the federal funds received by other parts of the university brought its athletic program under the aegis of Title IX's prohibition of sex discrimination.[45]

Leaders of the women's sports movement blamed the Supreme Court's *Grove City* decision when some colleges and universities began to scale back on women's sports programs while leaving intact or expanding men's programs.[46] They felt that some universities interpreted *Grove City* as license to ignore the letter and spirit of Title IX. For example, in 1986 Southwest Texas State University dropped a successful women's gymnastics program shortly after the football team moved to Division I-AA, a costly shift that produced an 18-26 football record over the next four seasons.[47]

In what the women's sports movement has considered a major victory after a long legislative battle,[48] the *Grove City* decision was overwhelmingly reversed by the Civil Rights Restoration Act.[49] Title IX once again became

---

that its Title IX regulations could not apply to women's sports because college athletic programs do not, as such, receive federal aid. NCAA v. Califano, 444 F. Supp. 428 (D. Kan. 1978), *rev'd* 622 F.2d 1382 (10th Cir. 1980). For a pre-*Grove City* discussion of this debate, see Skilton, *supra* note 37, at 1707-30.

45. Haffer v. Temple University, 688 F.2d 14, 17 (3d Cir. 1982) (when non-earmarked money is received, the institution itself must be the "program"). *Haffer* has enjoyed a long litigation history. In 1980, when the suit was filed, 42% of the athletes at Temple were women, but women's athletic programs were allocated only 13% of the athletic budget. *Id.* at 15 n.1. In 1987, a federal district court in Pennsylvania initially granted summary judgment on three aspects of the Title IX suit—the number of competitors, dining facilities and academic tutoring classes. On motion for reconsideration, however, the court held that final judgment as to those three issues should not have been made because they did not constitute separate claims for purposes of entering final judgment. Haffer v. Temple University, 678 F. Supp. 517, 540-42 (E.D. Pa. 1987). In June of 1988, Temple settled the Title IX suit, promising to allocate a percentage of its athletic budget to women's athletics equal to the percentage of women athletes at the university. *Sports People: Temple Settlement*, N.Y. Times, June 14, 1988, at B14, col. 2. For a discussion of *Haffer* and its importance to Title IX, see Springer, *After 16 Years, Title IX's Goals Remain Unfulfilled*, L.A. Times, Oct. 30, 1988, at C12, col. 1.

46. *See, e.g.*, Boswell, *Women Looking Back, Up*, Wash. Post, Feb. 5, 1987, at C1, col. 1.

47. Neff, *Equality at Last, Part II*, SPORTS ILLUS., Mar. 21, 1988, at 70, 71.

48. At certain points, the Civil Rights Restoration Act was hung up in Congress because many feared that it would force universities that accepted federal funding to fund abortion services. *U.S. Senate Votes to Remove "Abortion Rights" from Civil Rights Bill*, Business Wire, Jan. 28, 1988. Section 1688 of the Civil Rights Restoration Act states that Title IX is neutral with respect to abortion. 20 U.S.C. § 1688 (1989 Supp.). The vote to override the President's veto of the Civil Rights Restoration Act passed the House 292-133 and the Senate 73-24. *Newswire*, L.A. Times, Mar. 23, 1988, at C2, col. 4.

49. Pub. L. No. 100-259, § 6, 102 Stat. 29 (1988). The Civil Rights Restoration Act was also a victory on other civil rights fronts. Also affected by the Act are Title VI of the Civil Rights Act of 1964 (prohibiting discrimination based on race, color or national origin), 42 U.S.C. § 2000d-4a (1990 Supp.); Section 504 of the Rehabilitation Act of 1973 (prohibiting discrimination against handicapped), 29 U.S.C. § 794 (1990 Supp.); and the Age Discrimination Act of 1975 (prohibiting discrimination based

applicable to athletic programs at educational institutions receiving *any* federal funding, regardless of whether that funding reached the athletic program.

Title IX was not the only legal route the women's sports movement pursued in the 1970's. Fourteenth Amendment equal protection litigation aimed at furthering the participation of women and girls in sports secured female athletes spots on men's and boys' interscholastic sports teams at public schools where no comparable teams were offered for female athletes.[50] These suits were useful where public educational institutions did not receive federal funds, but, as state actors, were barred from discriminatory behavior by the Fourteenth Amendment.[51] In addition, in 1978, Melissa Ludtke, a *Sports Illustrated* reporter, won a lawsuit against then-Major League Baseball Commissioner Bowie Kuhn and the New York Yankees for access to Yankee Stadium locker rooms on a level equal to access given male reporters.[52] Ludtke was successful bringing suit against the Yankees because the stadium was, in part, publicly funded, making activities there state action.[53]

Thus, while Title IX provided female college athletes with a legal hook on which to hang allegations of sex discrimination in athletics, equal protection was the primary legal hook for high school athletes and women seeking access to governmentally owned or controlled facilities. No one expected Title IX to immediately eradicate all barriers for women in sport, but Title IX and equal protection litigation together did work a revolution of sorts in women's sports in the 1970's. Title IX meant unprecedented access, but it did not exactly kick

---

on age). 42 U.S.C. § 6107 (1990 Supp.).

50. *See, e.g.,* Brenden v. Independent School Dist., 477 F.2d 1292 (8th Cir. 1973) (holding that school district rules prohibiting girls from participating with boys in cross-country skiing, running and tennis when no teams existed for girls violate the equal protection clause); Bednar v. Nebraska School Activities Ass'n, 531 F.2d 922 (8th Cir. 1976) (upholding preliminary injunction allowing girls to participate on boys' cross-country team when no separate girls' team existed); Gilpin v. Kansas State High School Activities Ass'n, 377 F. Supp. 1233, 1243 (D. Kan. 1974) (invalidating girls' exclusion from cross-country team); Reed v. Nebraska School Activities Ass'n, 341 F. Supp. 258, 262 (D. Neb. 1972) (golf team).

51. For a discussion of the application of equal protection analysis to interscholastic athletics, see Tokarz, *supra* note 6, at 217; Note, *supra* note 6, at 1440-45; Wong & Ensor, *Sex Discrimination in Athletics: A Review of Two Decades of Accomplishments and Defeats*, 21 GONZAGA L. REV. 345, 373-84 (1985). As these three articles point out, courts have analyzed equal protection sex discrimination cases differently depending on a number of factors, including the relationship between the sex of the plaintiff and the sex of the team the plaintiff seeks to join, whether or not the sport is considered a contact sport, and whether the rules for the team of one sex differ from the rules for the team of the other sex. *See generally* Tokarz, *supra* note 6, at 212, 215.

52. Ludtke v. Kuhn, 461 F. Supp. 86 (S.D.N.Y. 1978). However, this strategy has been successful only where the sporting facility was state-owned or publicly funded or activities in the facility could be tied in some other way to state action.

53. *Id.* For a discussion of the impact of Ludtke's lawsuit on the 1990 controversy over women reporters in male athletes' locker rooms, see *infra* notes 93-97 and accompanying text.

in the door for women in sport. In fact, Title IX and equal protection litigation managed barely a toehold—they primarily affected only athletes at public high schools and at colleges and universities receiving federal funds. The participation by women in scholastic sports fostered by Title IX was supposed to produce a trickle-down effect, increasing the participation of women in all aspects of sport. Or so the theory went. The trickle has been a drip.[54] And while the drip may become a flood of women in athletics, the flood will come too late for generations of young women unless the women's sports movement looks beyond Title IX and the equality model.

II. THE WHOLE NINE YARDS

Certainly, Title IX was not meant to be a panacea for the discrimination—both subtle and overt—that had been ossifying for three-quarters of a century in women's athletics. But the women's sports movement's focus on Title IX—implementing it for a decade and then working to restore it for half a decade more—contributed to two unwelcome results. First of all, this focus proved to be too narrow: by centering primarily on colleges and universities as the institutions that received federal funds, Title IX did little to further, and in fact inhibited, the interests of women beyond participating at the college level. Second, Title IX perpetuated an "equality model" of athletics that set as

---

54. Karen Tokarz points out that there are:

virtually no professional opportunities for women in team sports, even on a sex-segregated basis . . . . [T]here are no women athletes or coaches and almost no officials participating in America's professional sports leagues: Major League Baseball, the National Basketball Association, the National Hockey League, the National Football League, the United States Football League, the Major Indoor Soccer League, or the North American Soccer League . . . .

. . . .

The sports-minded male drafters of Title VII even envisioned a possible *bona fide* occupational qualification for professional ball players to be male.

Tokarz, *supra* note 6, at 234-35.

Title VII prohibits discrimination in employment on the basis of race, color, sex, religion or national origin. 42 U.S.C. § 2000e-2 (1988).

In 1988, the only woman to umpire in the minor leagues, Pam Postema, almost reached the majors. Garrity, *Waiting for the call*, SPORTS ILLUS., Mar. 14, 1988, at 26. In 1989, however, Postema was released from her duties as a Triple-A minor league umpire. Most umpires have three years to make the jump from Triple-A to the Major Leagues. Postema, who umpired Triple-A games for seven years, was bitter about her lost opportunity: "[I]f I didn't make it, I don't see how any woman can." *Goodbye to a Pioneer*, SPORTS ILLUS., Dec. 25, 1989, at 24.

In 1989, however, Betty Speziale, a payroll clerk from New York, was selected to be the first woman to umpire in the Little League World Series. *Umpspeak*, TIME, July 17, 1989, at 79.

the standard male athletics.[55] Because implementation of Title IX's prohibition against sex discrimination focused on facilities and funds available to women athletes, universities complied by trying to make their women's programs equal to their men's programs. Men's collegiate athletic programs set the standards; women's athletic programs sought to emulate them. Little time was spent deciding whether the men's programs should set the standard.

While benefitting women college athletes, Title IX actually contributed to a reduction in the number of women in collegiate coaching and athletic administration. Although women's participation in athletics had risen steadily since 1972, a 1986 study by Brooklyn College professors Vivian Acosta and Linda Carpenter found that the number of women coaches at the college level had dropped nearly forty percent.[56] In 1972, ninety percent of coaches in women's intercollegiate athletics were women; by 1986, that number had dropped to fifty percent.[57] In addition, positions coaching men's athletic teams were almost never available to women.[58] Bernadette Locke, a former University of Georgia all-American, became the first woman coach in men's Division I college basketball in the summer of 1990 when Rick Pitino, head coach at the University of Kentucky, named her to his staff.[59] The drop in the number of women's college administrators of athletic programs has been even more dramatic than the drop in the number of women coaches: from more than

---

55. Catharine MacKinnon describes three separate equality models. C. MACKINNON, FEMINISM UNMODIFIED (1987). The first, the sameness approach, defines equality for women as being the same as men. The sameness approach is meant to be gender-neutral and provide a single standard, the male standard. *Id.* at 33-37. The second, the difference approach, defines equality as legal recognition of differences between men and women. The aim of the difference approach is to compensate and value women for what they possess that men do not possess. *Id.* at 33. The third approach, preferred by MacKinnon, is the dominance approach. The dominance approach portrays equality as a fiction created by the sameness/difference approaches. Instead, the dominance approach posits that the relationship between men and women is one of the power exercised by men on the basis of sexual inequality. According to this approach, the sameness approach merely allows some women to exploit other women based on their ability to exercise the kind of power that men as a class have exercised. *Id.* at 14-15, 40-43.

In this article, I use the sameness approach to the equality model to describe the way that Title IX and equal protection litigation have functioned in the women's sports movement. Title IX and equal protection recognize one standard of excellence in athletics—what men are or have been doing. *See id.* at 35. For additional discussion about the various uses of the term "equality model" in feminist jurisprudence, see Littleton, *supra* note 12.

56. R. Acosta & L. Carpenter, *supra* note 2.

57. *Id.* This drop occurred even though the average number of women's sports offered at four-year colleges and universities increased from 5.61 per school in 1977 to 6.48 in 1980 and 7.15 in 1986 at NCAA member schools. *Id.*

58. *See, e.g.,* Potera & Kort, *Are Women Coaches an Endangered Species?*, WOMEN'S SPORTS & FITNESS, Sept. 1986, at 34, 35.

59. Reed, *Here's How It's Done Guys*, SPORTS ILLUS., June 25, 1990, at 12.

90 percent in 1972 to 20 percent in 1980 and 15.21 percent in 1986.[60]

Most Title IX supporters anticipated that the increase in women athletes would produce a long-term increase in women coaches and administrators. Title IX, however, made coaching and administering women's athletics more attractive to men, whose traditional advantage in participating in sports translated into a hiring advantage for coaching positions.[61] In addition, when the NCAA took over the governance of women's collegiate athletics, most of the theretofore separately administered women's collegiate athletic programs were merged with the men's,[62] and the female athletic director became the male athletic director's assistant.[63] Moreover, Title IX did little to help women advance in the officiation and administration of men's professional athletics.[64]

Title IX's narrow focus also created a two-tier structure among women athletes. The real women athletes, those good enough to participate at the college level, gained at least a measure of legitimacy. Recreational athletes, women who participated outside the sphere of competitive college play, gained almost nothing.[65] Title IX focused only on the competitive athlete. It made funding and facilities available for colleges and universities, not for play-grounds and community centers.

In addition to focusing on increased opportunities in athletics by only the elite women athletes, Title IX and the equality model of sport have abandoned the definition of sport to men's athletics. Equality in the Title IX context means equality with *men's* athletics. Those women who could begin to be compared

---

60. Acosta & Carpenter, *supra* note 2.

61. *See* Olson, *supra* note 30 ("It's very easy in looking for qualifications to stack the deck so you hire men even when they aren't the best people," said Margaret Dunkle, director of the Equality Center in Washington. "[Employers] ask, 'Did you play high school and college sports, did you participate on the Olympic team?' Those programs are available to more boys and young men than to girls and young women. If you make that a credential, you're going to exclude a lot of women who could do the job very well.").

62. Acosta & Carpenter, *supra* note 2.

63. Olson, *supra* note 30.

64. Tokarz reports that in 1986, there were no women executives or officials in any of the four major professional sports associations in the United States. Tokarz, *supra* note 6, at 234-35.

65. *See* Addelson, *Equality and Competition: Can Sports Make a Woman of a Girl?*, in WOMEN, PHILOSOPHY AND SPORT, *supra* note 34, at 133, 134. Addelson writes:

> The focus is on "career athletes"—people of considerable ability who are interested in making a major commitment to sport. Through competition, they receive a lion's share of the athletic resources.

Id. at 134.

to their male peers were athletes, all the rest were pretenders.[66] Moreover, as Littleton argues, equality limited by this male standard "has operated to keep most women 'out and down' even as it allows some women a few steps beyond the gate."[67]

Beyond its narrow focus and adoption of the equality model of sport, Title IX—and the women's sports movement's twenty year struggle with it—simply could not begin to reach other obstacles facing women in athletics. Primarily, Title IX did not and could not address three major problems confronting the women's sports movement: (1) the persistent stereotype that women athletes are not normal; (2) the gap between the women's sports movement and the general women's movement; and (3) the diverse needs and problems confronting different portions of the women's sports movement.

A. Women Aren't Athletes—Women Athletes Aren't Women

Of all of these problems, that of overcoming negative stereotypes is perhaps the most intractable because of the strong influence sport has as a socializing agent in American society[68] and the alarming ease with which deprecating views of women athletes are enunciated and widely broadcast.[69] Women athletes face old-fashioned, offensive—yet remarkably durable——stereotypes about their gender and their place—or lack thereof—in the world of sport. Many of these stereotypes of women and athletics are based upon "expert" opinions by psychologists, sociologists, philosophers and physical educators purporting to show the proper sex roles for males and females: "We must clearly identify the characteristics of childhood and adulthood which the

---

66. For a similar analysis, see Littleton, *supra* note 12, at 1058 ("Similarly, in the field of athletics, the usual form of analysis under equal protection or Title IX guarantees is to determine whether the female applicant to the male team is like the guys. If so, then of course, it would be irrational to exclude her.").

67. *Id.* at 1051.

68. George Sage writes in the foreword for an anthology on sports in American society:

Sport is such a pervasive activity in contemporary America that to ignore it is to overlook one of the most significant aspects of this society. It is a social phenomenon which extends into education, politics, economics, art, the mass media, and even international diplomatic relations. Involvement in sport, either as a participant or in more indirect ways, is almost considered a public duty by many Americans.

Sage, *Sport in American Society: Its Pervasiveness and its Study*, in S. EITZEN, *supra* note 7, at 9.

69. Shortly before the 1989 Wimbledon tennis championships began, defending men's champion Stefan Edberg told a British women's magazine that women's tennis is a boring game and that women players do not have to work very hard and do not deserve the money they make—all in comparison with men's tennis. *See Navratilova Deflects Potshots by Edberg*, Wash. Post, June 19, 1989, at C2, col. 1.

American society values as being masculine or feminine . . . We must teach our children . . . through successful participation in games and activities appropriate for proper sex-role identification."[70]

Other stereotypes come from educational materials designed to teach children to read. A well-known 1972 study of the content of the "Dick and Jane" reader series showed that

> in the text illustrations, boys were almost without exception taller, participated in athletics while girls watched, and acted independently while girls did not.
>
> In content analysis it was found that girls were allowed to compete only half as much as boys, but that boys nearly always won. . . . If a girl did win, it was by accident or fluke or because a boy taught her originally. Boys were in positions of power, and to get praise a girl had to play better than a boy. In one instance a girl got on a baseball team, only to be ridiculed by the other team with jests at the team's assumed inferiority since they had a girl as pitcher.[71]

Still other stereotypes are simply manifestations of everyday male and female attitudes about who is knowledgeable about and able to participate in sports. In Texas recently, ten-year-old goalie Natasha Dennis was playing so well in her twelve-and-under girls' soccer league that two fathers of players on an opposing team asked that she go into the ladies' restroom so that an impartial observer could check her sex.[72]

The stereotypes that limit women's roles in sport and that define "woman" out of "woman athlete" often have pressed women to choose between being women and being athletes.[73] In the 1950's and early 1960's, women interested in athletics solved this conflict by competing for a short period of time in a

---

70. Werner, *The Role of Physical Education in Gender Identification*, PHYSICAL EDUCATOR, Mar. 1972, at 28. Seven months later, the same professional journal ran an article which stated: "It is imperative that the masculine concepts of certain sports be retained. . . . Male children, both present and future, cannot afford to be deprived of yet another factor which influences masculine orientation." Fisher, *Sports as an Agent of Masculine Orientation*, PHYSICAL EDUCATOR, Oct. 1972, at 120, 122.

71. Geadelmann, *Sex Role Stereotyping*, in EQUALITY FOR WOMEN IN SPORT, *supra* note 3, at 89, *citing* Women on Words and Images, *Dick and Jane as Victims: Sex Stereotypes in Children's Readers* (1972).

72. Associated Press, *Girl Goalie's Gender Called into Question*, Seattle Post-Intelligence, Oct. 20, 1990, at D1, col. 3. The league suspended four parents following the incident, including the two fathers, Natasha's mother and the mother of one of Natasha's teammates. Natasha told the Associated Press reporter that she permed her hair so she would look more like a girl. *Id.*

73. *See Miller Lite Report, supra* note 30, at ii.

respectable sport for women, such as ice-skating, tennis or golf, and then putting sport aside to get married and have families.[74]

In the 1970's and 1980's, women who participated in high-level competitive athletics often went to extremes to prove that they were indeed feminine—wearing frilly costumes and noticeable amounts of make-up and flaunting their heterosexual relationships.[75] Sportswriter Janice Kaplan reports, for example, that the first time she met Chris Evert, Evert asked her what she thought of Evert's nail polish.[76] When umpire Pam Postema, who in 1988 was considered for a position in the Major Leagues, was released as a Triple-A minor league umpire a year later, sportswriter George Vecsey of the *New York Times* wrote that women who want to be umpires are "trapped in a Catch-22 situation: almost by definition, umpires must be forceful . . . . Most men at least give an appearance of swagger, lest the world walk all over them. Many women have traditionally appeared more considerate than men ("nurturing" is the word often used)."[77]

The struggle to maintain standards of femininity is exacerbated for women who participate in sports such as basketball, where the uniforms display none of the frill of a tennis skirt and in which the style of play involves body contact with other players. Kaplan states that Americans insist that their female sports heroines be dainty and graceful as well as athletic:

> at the 1976 Winter Olympics many people thought that speed skater Sheila Young would emerge as the full-blown media star. She won more medals than Dorothy Hamill, but ultimately, Sheila was like the winning car at the Indy 500—a vehicle to be admired, not loved. Wearing a dark blue uniform which covered every inch of flesh, Sheila depended solely on strength and skill for her victories, not sensuality. Americans have trouble with female athletes who are invulnerable, too competent, too unneeding of affection.[78]

It is little wonder, then, that among the best-known women's basketball players are Cheryl Miller and Jennifer Azzi, both of whom are considered very

---

74. Hall, *Women, Sport, and Feminism: Some Canadian and Australian Comparisons*, in REPORT ON THE CONFERENCE ON WOMEN IN SPORT, *supra* note 31, at 14. The Edmonton Grads, a Canadian team that dominated women's basketball, such as it was, from 1915-1940, required a player to resign as soon as she married. W. MOKRAY, *supra* note 23, at I-17.

75. H. LENSKYJ, *supra* note 17, at 103.

76. J. KAPLAN, WOMEN AND SPORTS ix (1979).

77. Vecsey, *Postema Blazed Trail for Somebody Else*, N.Y. Times, Dec. 17, 1989, at A8, col. 3.

78. J. KAPLAN, *supra* note 76, at 55.

attractive women. Miller parlayed her success on the basketball court into a sports commentating job with ABC, and one New York-based agent estimates that Azzi's looks, talent and skills in dealing with the media may make her the first woman basketball player to land major endorsement deals both overseas and in the United States.[79] In addition, the Ladies Professional Golf Association employs an image and fashion consultant who travels on the tour for five months a year to make sure the players look good for the television camera.[80] The emphasis on physical beauty over athletic talent makes perhaps the biggest difference in the endorsement department where sports figures add extra cash to their earnings.[81]

As the 1990's begin, society continues to demand that women athletes prove their femininity. In April, Steffi Graf, the world's top-ranked woman tennis player, posed for *Vogue* magazine wearing a short black dress and heels and leaning toward the camera to reveal what *Sports Illustrated* delicately termed as her *decolletage*.[82] Graf told the reporter that she had received more congratulations for the photo than she—the first person to do so in two decades—had for winning the tennis Grand Slam in 1988.[83]

The emphasis in sport on women's traditional feminine characteristics—such as beauty—rather than their athletic skills is perpetuated by the media.[84] A 1988 *Sports Illustrated* article about Gabriela Sabatini emphasized

---

79. Telephone interview with Audrey Epstein, sports agent with Bruce Levy Assoc. Int'l Ltd. (April 21, 1990) (transcript on file with *The Journal of Law and Feminism*).

80. Phinney, *Consultant Puts Golfers in the Swing*, Seattle Post-Intelligence, Sept. 15, 1990, at C1, col. 6. Beverley Willey, the tour consultant, explained that she encourages players to continue wearing their visors for on-camera interviews to prevent unsightly visor head. Willey added that the advent of television coverage of the tour made her job possible. *Id.*

81. Becker, *More Career Possibilities for the Elite*, USA Today, Sept. 14, 1990, at C1, col. 3.

82. Wolff, *Ooh La La, Steffi!*, SPORTS ILLUS., Apr. 23, 1990, at 45.

83. *Id.*

84. *See, e.g.*, J. KAPLAN, *supra* note 76, at 55.

Skill has its place in skating, but ultimately image is everything. . . . Possibly the first American skating star with a non-WASP name, [Linda Fratianne] captured her first national championship in 1977 with a performance so exciting that when the lights dimmed because of a power shortage, the word went around that this bright young skater had blown the fuses. Four weeks later she captured the world figure-skating title. Her coach, Frank Carroll, told me shortly afterward that Linda was an all-around superb skater with technical expertise, incredible tricks (including triple jumps), and balletic fluidity. But he was worried. "She needs to improve the performance value of her program," he said. "I want her to give more to the audience." During the next year, Linda worked with a drama coach on how to love an audience and offer kisses, gestures, and smiles. Carroll began picking Linda's clothes and teaching her how to talk to reporters and fans. But although Carroll helped Linda become a champion, he couldn't quite make her a star, and the next year she finished second in the world championships. Athletic excellence wasn't enough.

her continued improvement as a tennis player only as an aid to her vast marketing potential based on her dark, Latin good looks.[85] *Sports Illustrated*, generally considered to be the nation's premier sports magazine, also publishes an annual swimsuit issue, featuring several models in revealing bathing suits. Unsurprisingly, none of the models is a competitive swimmer. The swimsuit issue is *Sports Illustrated*'s biggest seller,[86] and has spawned imitations by two of its chief rivals, *Inside Sports* and *Sport* magazine. Home Box Office also produced a documentary in 1989 for the swimsuit issue's twenty-fifth anniversary.

On the other hand, in order for women athletes to make the cover of *Sports Illustrated*, they have to perform extraordinary athletic feats. In 1988, for example, only four women sports figures were featured on five *Sports Illustrated* covers. Among the four, they had won five Olympic gold medals and tennis' Grand Slam.[87]

At other times, the sports media simply leave women out altogether, reinforcing the notion that the sports world is a men's world. Lyn LeMaire introduced her 1978 article on women and athletics with a random sample of the *Boston Globe* sports section. It contained one small item on women's sports, buried on the back page.[88] In a 1989 editorial-style piece for *Sports Illustrated*, senior writer Frank DeFord decried the absence of sports references from the *Dictionary of Cultural Literacy*, a 1988, self-proclaimed volume about what Americans ought to know.[89] In his own listing of 121 sports items of

---

Id. See also Goldstein & Bredemeier, *Mass Media, Sport and Socialization*, in S. EITZEN, *supra* note 7, at 291, 295 ("Broadcast sports may serve either positive or negative social, psychological, emotional, and intellectual functions. They impart values, especially to the young, and influence spectators' views on the purpose and nature of participation in competitive athletics.").

85. Newman, *Talk About Net Gains*, SPORTS ILLUS., May 2, 1988, at 52, 60 ("When a West German company releases her signature scent next year, Sabatini will become, as far as anyone can determine, the first female athlete in history to have a line of perfume named after her. 'If she should win a Grand Slam event in the next two years, I don't know how high is up,' says [agent Donald] Dell. 'She's one of those rare athletes who have the potential to transcend her sport.'").

86. Margolis, *SI's Swimsuit Issue Exposes Motives, Too*, Chicago Tribune, Feb. 15, 1989, at C1, col. 3 ("At the *Sports Illustrated* offices in New York, a spokesperson who identified herself only as Margo said that the special swimsuit issue was expected to sell 5 million copies, about 2 million more than a standard weekly edition.").

87. Florence Griffith Joyner appeared on three, joined by sister-in-law Jackie Joyner-Kersee on one. SPORTS ILLUS., July 25, 1988, Oct. 10, 1988, Dec. 26, 1988-Jan. 2, 1989. Between them, they won four Olympic gold medals and one Olympic silver medal, setting three world records in the process. Tennis player Steffi Graf made the cover after she won tennis' Grand Slam, the first person—male or female—to do so in two decades. Graf later won a tennis gold medal at the 1988 summer Olympics. SPORTS ILLUS., Sept. 19, 1988. Umpire Pam Postema, who nearly became the first woman umpire in the major leagues, was on one cover. SPORTS ILLUS., Mar. 14, 1988.

88. LeMaire, *supra* note 7, at 121-22.

89. DeFord, *Of Billie Jean and 73-0*, SPORTS ILLUS., Feb. 6, 1989, at 70.

"lasting significance," only three women are listed—track and field star/golfer Babe Didrickson Zaharias, figure skater Sonja Henie and tennis great Billie Jean King.[90] Eighty-seven terms in DeFord's list referred either to male athletes, exclusively male sports or events from men's athletics.[91] The rest, including terms such as "the 1936 Olympics" and "student-athlete" could not be specifically linked with either men's or women's sports.[92]

The stereotypes about the relationship between women and athletics pervade not only the substance of media coverage of women's athletics but also the process of women reporters covering athletics. Sportswriters assumed women had gained equal footing with male writers in 1977 when Melissa Ludtke prevailed in the lawsuit that allowed her to step into Yankee Stadium's locker rooms.[93] Women reporters quickly learned, however, that access and acceptance are two different things. The harassment of *Boston Herald* reporter Lisa Olson in the New England Patriots' locker room,[94] and Cincinnati Bengals coach Sam Wyche's refusal to permit a female *USA Today* reporter into his team's locker room following his team's loss in Seattle[95] within a

---

90. *Id.*

91. *Id.* Male athletics-identified terms in DeFord's list include "home plate," "Say it Ain't So, Joe" (a reference to Chicago White Sox outfielder Shoeless Joe Jackson), "the Long Count" (referring to the heavyweight title bout between Jack Dempsey and Gene Tunney) and Knute Rockne.

92. *Id.* Of course, not all members of the sports media or representations of women athletes in the media conform to stereotypes. Mike Downey, columnist for the *Los Angeles Times*, has been a notable proponent of women's athletics. *See, e.g.,* Downey, *Now, About That Women's Movement...*, L.A. Times, Nov. 5, 1989, at C4, col. 1.

93. *See supra* notes 52-53 and accompanying text.

94. *See, e.g.,* Dvorchak, *Women Scribes Still Fighting for Access 12 Years After Winning It*, Seattle Post-Intelligence, Oct. 3, 1990, at D1, col. 2. Olson, who was in the locker room interviewing a defensive player following a practice, was surrounded by five naked New England players who exposed their genitals only inches from her face. The five taunted her and dared her to touch their genitals, stating that that's what she'd come in the locker room to do. Patriots owner Victor Kiam initially attempted to dismiss the incident, stating that newspapers that send women reporters into locker rooms ought to expect trouble. Kiam also reportedly called Olson a "classic bitch." *See* Lupica, *Pats' Kiam Embarrasses Himself as an Owner, a Man, and a Father*, The National, Sept. 27, 1990, at 2. Scott Ostler, columnist for the *National*, a daily sports journal, pointed out that had the players objected to the reporter because the reporter was African-American or Jewish, the players and owner Victor Kiam would have been treated like former Los Angeles Dodgers executive Al Campanis or CBS commentator Andy Rooney. Ostler, *Patriots Should Be a Rank No. 1 in Locker Room Harass Poll*, The National, Sept. 26, 1990, at 2.

95. *Wyche Pays for Ban on Female Reporter*, Seattle Post-Intelligence, Oct. 6, 1990, at A1, col. 2. National Football League Commissioner Paul Tagliabue fined Wyche $30,000 for violating the league's policy of permitting equal access to women reporters. *Id.* However, the most upsetting aspect of the Wyche incident was the trivialization of the incident by team owner Paul Brown and his son, team assistant general manager Mike Brown. The younger Brown said that "other coaches break a heck of a lot more important rules than that one." Farrey, *Wyche's Act No Big Deal to Bengals*, Seattle Post-Intelligence, Oct. 7, 1990, at C12, col. 3.

two-week period in the fall of 1990 are the latest and most visible reminders that women sportswriters still face discrimination.[96] Perhaps the best lesson women reporters can learn from the fall of 1990 is that their acceptance in the locker room is closely related to women's acceptance in all athletic arenas. Furthermore, these women should utilize their positions as members of the media to paint positive pictures of women athletes.[97]

B. *One Women's Movement—Realigning the Women's*
Sports Movement and the Women's Movement

Although old-fashioned, debilitating stereotypes also plague women in arenas other than athletics, the women's movement and the women's sports movement often have operated as if the other doesn't exist. Title IX's passage and the ensuing litigation it produced naturally captured the attention of women lawyers,[98] but few others have felt that burning bras and sports bras or power lunches and power lifting have anything in common. Quite simply, Title IX, with its energies focused on violations at individual institutions, has been unable to forge a coalition between the women's sports movement and the general women's movement. Women outside sport have been slow to recognize that there are women inside sport.[99] For example Bill Byrne, a sports entrepreneur who has made several attempts to start a U.S. professional women's basketball league over the last decade, said that one of the major problems he has incurred in enlisting financial support is the reluctance of women corporate executives to support women's athletics.[100]

---

96. Dvorchak, *supra* note 94; *see also* Kindred, *NFL Must Take Action and Turn Locker Rooms into Civilized Places*, The National, Sept. 28, 1990, at 2.

97. Some women's groups outside of the women's sports movement responded positively to the Olson incident. When Kiam, also head of Remington products, backed his players, the National Organization of Women called for a nationwide boycott of Remington. Dvorchak, *supra* note 94.

98. The National Women's Law Center in Washington, D.C., handled a significant amount of the litigation for the plaintiffs in Haffer v. Temple University, 688 F.2d 14 (3d Cir. 1982). *See* Springer, *supra* note 45, at C12, col. 1. For a discussion of *Haffer*, see *supra* note 45.

99. *See, e.g.*, Waters & Huck, *Networking Women*, NEWSWEEK, Mar. 13, 1989, at 48. Waters and Huck were addressing the rise of women to executive positions with network television programs and reported the following:

> "Heartbeat" creator Sara Davidson, an acclaimed novelist ("Loose Change") contends that disproportionate male power behind the cameras distorts TV's portrayals of her gender. "You still get men's fantasies of the way women talk and relate," she complains. "The only place I see women playing poker or talking in sports analogies is on television. It just isn't realistic."

Id. at 54.

100. Telephone interview with Bill Byrne (Apr. 17, 1990) (transcript on file with the *Journal of*

According to Canadian women's sports activist Ann Hall,

> Often I ask myself why it is that when reading about women's experience, one never learns anything about sport and when reading about sport, one rarely learns anything about women.
>
> With the former, women's experience is often quite different from men's experience and for many women there is no experience of sport. On the other hand, most girls and women do experience sport in some form or other but [it] is as if the commentators on women's experience have forgotten that entirely.[101]

Unfortunately, most women experience sport from the sidelines either as cheerleaders or as silent spectators rather than as participants. It is this common bond of omission, this common assumption of nonparticipation that allows many in the general women's movement, in defining women's experience, to forget that some women have participated.

Nonalignment between the general women's movement and the women's sports movement may be particularly problematic in the 1990's as both groups face gender gaps between women who fought for access to traditionally male pursuits and younger women who have reaped the benefits of the older women's fight and feel that whatever battle existed has been won.[102] In a *Time* magazine report on the generation of Americans now in their late teens and early twenties, a nineteen-year-old Denver woman studying music and business said of women her age: "It's not that we don't consider feminism important; it's just that we don't see the inequality as much right now."[103]

A 1985 *Report on Women in Sport,* sponsored by Miller Lite, found that women age twenty-five and under tend to be much more likely to have

---

Law and Feminism).

101. Hall, *supra* note 74, at 1. Adds Nancy Theberge,

> Among feminist activists there has been a similar tendency to downplay the relevance of sport to the women's movement. The clearest evidence of this is that the political agenda of women's organizations rarely are concerned with sport and physical activity . . .
>
> Because of the history of sexism in sport, many women have had little opportunity to experience the pleasure and benefits of physical activity. . . . The fact that sport has not been personally rewarding for many women no doubt contributes to their lack of interest in sport as a feminist issue.

Theberge, *Sport and Feminism in North America,* in WOMEN IN SPORT, *supra* note 19, at 46-47.

102. *See, e.g.,* Allen, *Not NOW- It's Time for Consensus, Not Conflict,* Washing. Post, July 30, 1989, at C1 col.4.

103. Gross & Scott, *Proceeding with Caution,* TIME, July 16, 1990, at 56, 61.

participated in organized sport than older women.[104] Unfortunately, however, it is the older women who are also much more likely to identify themselves as feminists.[105] Younger women often fail to realize that those who succeed in formerly all-male bastions such as sports or law firms are still the exception rather than the rule.[106] It may be that younger women have embraced the dominant individualist ideology and do not identify as part of a network of women, where the success of one depends upon the success of others. Rather, they see their own success as an indication that anyone who works hard enough can succeed. They may view themselves as the rule rather than the exception. However, recent studies indicate that in the world of women's athletics, not only do very few succeed, very few even continue to try. A *USA Today*/NBC poll found that fifty-two percent of girls ten to thirteen play unorganized sports at least twice a week, but only twenty-seven percent of girls fourteen to seventeen do.[107]

C. *Time for the Needs of Women of Color and Lesbians*

Perhaps most importantly, Title IX has done little to address the diverse needs and problems of groups within the women's sports movement, including those of women of color and lesbians. If it does not address the needs of all its members, the women's sports movement is a movement without a sense of itself. Despite the visibility of such athletes as heptathlete Jackie Joyner-Kersee, sprinter Florence Griffith Joyner, figure skater Debi Thomas, basketball player Cheryl Miller and tennis player Zina Garrison, the African-American woman has been largely absent from sport in two ways. First, African-American women are an overwhelmingly small proportion of those participating in collegiate sports. Second, when they do participate, African-American women are usually typecast into only a handful of sports.

In 1985, Margaret Dunkle of the Equality Center in Washington, D.C., pointed out that women of color are less likely to participate in intercollegiate or high school athletics than either men of color or white women.[108] A 1982 study by a Johns Hopkins University researcher showed that "athlete" was the last choice as a childhood role model among African-American women but one

---

104. *Miller Lite Report, supra* note 30, at 20.

105. *Id.* at 19. The study also noted that very strong feminism identification increases incrementally with increase in the education level of the individual woman. *Id.*

106. Littleton, *supra* note 12, at 1051.

107. Becker, *supra* note 81 at C1, col.3.

108. Dunkle, *Minority and Low-Income Girls and Young Women in Athletics*, EQUAL PLAY, spring-summer 1985, at 12.

of the top two choices among African-American men.[109] At a 1990 Congressional Black Caucus conference on African Americans in sports, Jackie Joyner-Kersee and ESPN sportscaster Robin Roberts also attributed the paucity of African-American women in sports to an absence of role models. "We need more women who can set the path," said Joyner-Kersee.[110]

The absence of African-American women at the high school and college level can be attributed to the lack of opportunities for African-American women at the professional level.[111] Other researchers have attributed this near absence of African-American women athletes, particularly at the high school and college level, to the "burden of the black woman's work both inside and outside the home. . . . [H]ouse chores, family caretaking, and family income supplementing jobs keep many black girls from honing play skills as do black boys."[112]

In addition, a 1989 Women's Sports Foundation (WSF) report on people of color in sport found that, alone among gender and ethnic/racial subgroups, urban African-American female athletes found problems entering the work force after high school.[113] The WSF concluded that young African-American women who add athletics to the demands made on them in school and at home—demands that are not made as strongly on those in other gender and racial/ethnic subgroups—simply do not have enough time to develop skills and strategies that make it easier for them to obtain employment after finishing high

---

109. *Id.*

110. *Pitfalls of Pro Sports Block Black Athletes*, USA Today, Sept. 28, 1990, at C2, col. 3.

111. Harry Edwards, a sociologist at the University of California-Berkeley, has for several years been at the forefront of addressing racism within American sport. He points out that the African-American male's view of sport as a get-rich-quick scheme has not been productive for African Americans. He says that too many young African Americans have devoted their energies to athletics exclusively and have not developed other skills that will help them either when they fail to attain professional careers, as the overwhelming majority of them will, or when they finish their professional careers.

> What has not been thoroughly understood in Black America is that for all these reasons the overwhelming majority of Black youths seeking sports stardom are foredoomed to be shuttled back into the Black community as noncontributors, undercontributors, and all too often as "mal-contributors" lacking access to any legitimate means of sustaining themselves or their self-respect.

Edwards, *Race in Contemporary American Sports*, in S. EITZEN, *supra* note 7, at 307, 313.

112. BLACK WOMEN IN SPORT 4 (T. Green, C. Oglesby, A. Alexander & N. Franke eds. 1981) (citing Hughley, The Effects of Society on the Black Female's Participation in Sport (1976) (unpublished paper, Black Women in Sport Conference, Temple University)). In addition to the paucity of African-American women in all levels of athletics, in the last decade, there has been a paucity of research on the subject. Dunkle said that she had seen no new data in the last half decade. Interview with Margaret Dunkle (Aug. 1, 1989) (transcript on file with *The Journal of Law and Feminism*).

113. THE WOMEN'S SPORTS FOUNDATION, THE WSF REPORT: MINORITIES IN SPORTS 15 (1989) [hereinafter WSF MINORITIES REPORT].

school.[114]

Moreover, the members of the African-American community who have called attention to racism in sports have not focused on gender. Harry Edwards, a sociologist at the University of California-Berkeley who has been very active in calling for the integration of African Americans at the administrative and coaching level of professional athletics, generally fails to address the possibility of African-American women in those positions.[115]

In the WSF report, the frustration experienced by African-American female athletes was in stark contrast to Hispanic female athletes' success. Of all racial and gender subgroups, young Hispanic women benefitted most from participation in athletics.[116] The differences between the experiences of young African-American and Hispanic female athletes suggest, unsur-prisingly, that women from different racial and ethnic groups also have different needs. The women's sports movement must become as diverse as the society in which it exists and attempt to meet the needs of all its participants.

Among women athletes of color, African-American women who have overcome the barriers to entering athletics next face the barrier of being dragged into only a handful of sports. African-American women have been typecast into sports in which the myth that African-Americans have naturally superior speed and jumping skills stands to become self-fulfilling—track and basketball. As the editors of *Black Women in Sport* point out,

---

114. *Id.* The Women's Sports Foundation study concluded that, in general, high school sports exerted a positive influence on athletes while they were in high school. Specifically, the study found that "sport involvement can be more accurately understood as a means to social and academic ends during high school rather than a guarantee for upward mobility after high school." *Id.*

115. Edwards, *supra* note 111.

Ocania Chalk chose not to discuss the African-American female athlete, stating that "[a]ny effort possibly would have been presumptuous, and certainly would have been inadequate. . . . The writer awaits a definitive treatment on the accomplishments of black women in sports." O. CHALK, BLACK COLLEGE SPORT, foreword (1976). Arthur Ashe, however, did address the significant "firsts" of African-American women such as Debi Thomas, who was the first African-American figure skater to win a senior division singles world championship and the first to win an Olympic medal. 3 A. ASHE, A HARD ROAD TO GLORY: A HISTORY OF THE AFRICAN-AMERICAN ATHLETE 224 (1988). *The WSF Report: Minorities in Sports* also recommended that:

[1] The current debate and research focus on the black male athlete should be expanded to include women and other racial and ethnic groups [2] the relationship between athletic participation and the career patterns of urban black females should be investigated [3] Researchers should gather more data regarding . . . minority athletes' attitudes and perceptions of themselves, their high school experience, and the world in which they live, and how those perceptions mold their future plans.

WSF MINORITIES REPORT, *supra* note 113, at 21.

116. WSF MINORITIES REPORT, *supra* note 113, at 14.

Black women, whether students, teachers, coaches or adminis-trators,
have consistently reported . . . that they feel stereotyped and perceived
as either runners or basketball players. The effects of such perceptions
may reduce the probability that coaches in other sports look to the
black community for new recruits; . . . they may reduce the probability that a successful black tennis coach will be noticed in her high
school position and hired by the local college.[117]

The real reasons behind the concentration of African-American women
athletes in track and basketball, suggest these editors, are the inexpensiveness
of acquiring skills in these sports and the public access to facilities where these
sports can be played.[118] Zina Garrison, one of the top-ranked players in
women's professional tennis, is as much of an oddity in her sport for having
honed her strokes on public courts rather than at expensive private tennis clubs
or instructional camps as she is for being an African-American woman.

Within professional tennis ranks, stereotypes about who watches tennis and
about contemporary standards of beauty have limited Garrison's off-court
earning potential from endorsements. In 1987, while firmly entrenched in the
world's top ten women tennis players, Garrison did not have a major shoe or
clothing endorsement contract.[119] Thus, the poor treatment of women of color
in sports other than track and basketball may provide additional deterrents to
young women athletes of color. Off the track and away from the basketball
court, these athletes lack the support—both financial and emotional—that makes
the track and the basketball court safe havens.[120]

Women of color are not the only portion of the women's sports movement
whose particular problems and needs the Title IX era has not addressed. A
further step in these stereotypes that say women cannot be athletes, athletes
cannot be women, is that women athletes must be lesbians.[121] In fact, it is

---

117. BLACK WOMEN IN SPORT, *supra* note 112, at 9.

118. *Id. See also* Arthur Ashe's discussion of the difficulties encountered by African-American
women athletes in fencing, figure skating and other Olympic sports. A. ASHE, *supra* note 115, at 210-
46.

119. Kornheiser, *Tennis' Black Mark*, Wash. Post, Sept. 12, 1987, at C1, col. 1. Racism has a long
history in women's tennis. In 1950, the United States Lawn Tennis Association finally admitted Althea
Gibson, who eventually won two Wimbledon championships and who in 1957 was the first African
American to win the Associated Press Woman Athlete of the Year Award, to its championships at Forest
Hills. Gibson, *I Always Wanted to Be Somebody*, in OUT OF THE BLEACHERS 130 (S. Twin ed.
1979).

120. There is some indication that African-American women's presence is being felt in greater
numbers at the lower levels of competitive tennis. *See* Williams, *Is Tennis Doing the Right Thing for
Blacks?*, TENNIS, Nov. 1990, at 46.

121. *See, e.g.*, H. LENSKYJ, *supra* note 17, at 95.

this homophobia that goes hand-in-hand with much of the sexism that has barred women from athletics. Stereotypes of lesbians and stereotypes of women athletes are practically identical. Both groups of women are described as masculine, or at least as rejecting traditional standards of femininity.

The problem that the women's sports movement faces in addressing the needs of its lesbian members is twofold. First, the women's sports movement must fight the pejorative use of the lesbian label to denigrate women's athletics and to denigrate lesbians. Second, the women's sports movement must celebrate the contributions, presence and abilities of lesbian athletes as the initial step in that fight.

The pejorative use of the lesbian label has been used to silence lesbian athletes. In an anonymously authored article in a collection of essays about the lives of older lesbians, one former athlete who rose to prominence in the 1940's wrote that she

> was to learn, through a brutal series of lessons, what our society deemed was wrong with being a lesbian, or more accurately, how society exploited the label "lesbian" to brand any woman who engaged in activities threatening to men.[122]

Heterosexual women athletes often have failed to understand the homophobia and the pejorative use of the lesbian stereotype. At times, they have even fueled the homophobia by attempting to distance themselves from the stereotype and to embrace traditional feminine standards. The Ladies Professional Golf Association (LPGA) has been among the most defensive in women's athletics about the lesbian stereotype, mostly for what its executives identify as marketing reasons.[123] Promoters of women's professional golf often have tried to put the sport's most physically attractive players at the forefront of the game. In 1989, the tour's official magazine, *Fairways*, featured a picture of some of the game's top players in bikinis on a golf course in Hawaii.[124] Nancy Lopez' marriages, first to sportscaster Tim Melton and then to baseball player Ray Knight, have been widely reported and followed in the

---

122. Anonymous, *Admissions of Mortality: The Pleasures and Problems of Lesbian Athletes*, in LONG TIME PASSING: LIVES OF OLDER LESBIANS 64, 67 (M. Adelman ed. 1987).

123. Diaz, *Find the golf here?: After 39 years, the women's golf tour is still struggling to find an image that will sell*, SPORTS ILLUS., Feb. 13, 1989, at 58.

124. *Id.* at 58-59. Ray Volpe, LPGA commissioner in the late 1970's and early 1980's, was most adept at promoting physically attractive women players, including Laura Baugh and Jan Stephenson. *Id.* at 63.

media.[125] A recent *Sports Illustrated* article on the LPGA focused on the baby boom among players who increasingly are taking their young children with them to tour events.[126]

In more physically demanding sports such as basketball, women are also pressed to adopt the trappings of a heterosexual lifestyle. Those who are able to do so are role models. Whispers about the lesbian lifestyle follow those who are not feminine, or who are not married or involved with a man. Chris Gobrecht, women's basketball coach at the University of Washington, is touted as a role model because she has been able to combine her career in athletics with a successful marriage and motherhood.[127]

While it is undoubtedly difficult to raise a family on the LPGA tour or to be a mother and a head coach of a major women's college basketball team, lesbian athletes have an even more difficult time combining their personal lives with their athletic careers. The exclusive focus on women athletes' and coaches' family lives reinforces the pejorative lesbian label. The situation involves something of a catch-22. The women's sports movement should develop supportive atmospheres both for women athletes with families and for lesbians; moreover, the two need not be mutually exclusive. But the singular focus on women athletes with families says, in effect, women athletes or coaches who aren't married and don't have children are abnormal. The abnormality in this context is lesbianism. The women's sports movement should not condone such a message.

With the exception of Martina Navratilova, there are few openly "out" lesbians in professional sports. Navratilova's security is in part a product of her status at the top of women's tennis for more than a decade. But even Navratilova is not free from attacks on her sexual orientation. Shortly after Navratilova won her record ninth Wimbledon singles title in July 1990, former Grand Slam winner Margaret Court said that Navratilova is a bad role model because she is a lesbian, claiming that some players do not even go to tournament locker rooms because older players may try to recruit younger players to the lesbian lifestyle.[128] Court's comments did not go unchallenged. *Sports Illustrated* reported that many fans at the U.S. Open in September of 1990 wore pins that said, "Martina is my role model."[129] Also,

---

125. *See* H. LENSKYJ, *supra* note 17, at 103.

126. Steptoe, *Baby Boom in Birdieland*, SPORTS ILLUS., May 14, 1990, at 70.

127. *See* Rockne, *Celebrity Coach*, PACIFIC, Oct. 7, 1990, at 13. In one passage of *Pacific's* feature on Gobrecht, the magazine emphasized that Gobrecht's status as a role model increased when she became a mother. *Id.* at 36.

128. *Court: Navratilova makes poor role model*, Idaho State J., July 11, 1990, at A7, col. 3.

129. Wolff, *Upset Time*, SPORTS ILLUS., Sept. 17, 1990, at 22, 25.

some women tennis players and tennis reporters came to Navratilova's defense. It was, however, defense of Navratilova as a hard-working tennis player, not defense of Navratilova as a lesbian. In *Tennis* magazine, assistant editor Cindy Hahn pointed out that the pejorative lesbian stereo-type was used by people who could not accept women as athletes, but she also wrote:

> Navratilova's lifestyle may not be all right with you. But you'd be hard-pressed to find a woman who is a better model of determina-tion, strength of character and success. That's what Navratilova's all about. And when the match points have all been played, that's what women's tennis is all about, too.[130]

Hahn, and others associated with women's tennis, passed up an opportunity to say that Navratilova as a lesbian has made positive contributions. Instead, they separated her identity as a sexual being from her identity as a player. As heterosexual women athletes who sometimes have attributed their success partially to supportive intimate relationships must understand, no such separation is possible.

Writes one lesbian athlete:

> I concluded there has been only one major change in the lives of lesbian athletes: They have come out to each other en masse . . . . Today lesbian athletes enjoy strong and empathetic support groups. I do not know how we survived without them, almost half a century ago. I do not understand how we coped with the trauma of the rumors, the pursuits of married groupies, the male inquisitions, our crippling existences in our labyrinthian closets, and the trauma of competing against our lovers—without support groups. Indeed, it was remarkable we could exist as lovers at all in the explosive environment.
>
> Tragically, except for the heightened willingness to come out to one's peers, the environment for the lesbian today is very little changed.[131]

To the extent "lesbian" is a term attached to women athletes to denigrate

---

130. Hahn, *Court and the Enquirer: Much Ado About Nothing*, TENNIS, Oct. 1990, at 16. The headline itself, although probably not written by Ms. Hahn, is indicative of the reluctance to acknowledge the positive contributions of women athletes.

131. Anonymous, *supra* note 122, at 67-68.

their abilities and to allow male athletes to assert women's athletic inferiority, it must be challenged—but it must be challenged while embracing the expertise and the excellence of lesbian athletes, coaches, officials and administrators and allowing them to participate in sports without making sacrifices in their personal lives. Moreover, heterosexual women athletes must engage in a dialogue with lesbian athletes and understand that eradicating homophobia both within and outside of athletics is crucial to overcoming sexism. Only when the women's sports movement supports its lesbian members will it be able to confront the sexism in society's sports institutions.

Eradicating stereotypes and building coalitions need not be beyond the reach of legislation. The language of the law can change attitudes and opportunities. Title IX's crafters hoped that it would provide opportunities for all women, yet the task was simply too large for Title IX alone. Its supporters may not have understood in the early 1970's how the intersection of race, gender and sexual orientation combined continue the oppression that has limited women's opportunities in sports.

The time has not come to abandon Title IX. Title IX and the Civil Rights Restoration Act have been a symbolic, substantive and necessary first step toward making room for all women in a more cooperative vision of sport. On the heels of two decades of mixed results under the Title IX and equal protection regimes, however, the time has come for the women's sports movement to reassess where it wants to go and how it plans to get there.

III. Sport, Society And The Oppression Of Women

"The first step along the road to achieving power and personhood in sport is to recognize that the change cannot come from within sport itself. Those interested in changing the sports world for the betterment of women must themselves become part of the more global feminist movement."[132]

Events in sports in the last two years of the 1980's provide a good backdrop against which to reassess the role of Title IX in the women's sports movement and for progress towards implementation of a broader agenda that more closely aligns the women's sports movement with the women's movement generally. When Congress passed the Civil Rights Restoration Act in the spring of 1988, it removed restoration of Title IX as the leading issue for the women's

---

132. Hall, *supra* note 74, at 3.

sports movement.[133] In addition, major drug,[134] crime[135] and college corruption[136] scandals have erupted in sports in the last four years, providing the women's sports movement not only with an opportunity to seize the initiative on how to solve these seemingly intractable problems,[137] but also with an opportunity to redefine competitive athletics.

To date, increased participation in athletics in general and a redefinition of competitive athletics have not been much of a priority for women outside of sport. To women understandably concerned with issues such as daycare,

---

133. Nonetheless, the Women's Sports Foundation has made continued enforcement of Title IX one of its top three priorities. *Scorecard: Equality and Horseshoes*, SPORTS ILLUS., Feb. 20, 1989, at 11. The Department of Education's Office of Civil Rights has reported a dramatic increase in the number of bias claims filed since the passage of the Civil Rights Restoration Act. *Bias charges nearly double*, Am. Sch. Board J., Aug. 1989, at 42. In fiscal 1988, the Office of Civil Rights reported 3,531 bias claims, nearly double the number reported in 1987. The number of sex bias claims was 880. *Id.* In addition, one commentator reports that the June 1988 Temple University Title IX settlement, *see supra* note 45, is likely to encourage other Title IX claimants to push for settlements based on the percentage of women athletes in a university athletic program, a feat not accomplished prior to the passage of the Civil Rights Restoration Act. Steinbach, *Regulatory Issues on Campus: The Handwriting on the Wall*, 53 EDUC. L. REP. 1, 2-3 (1989). Marjorie Snyder, Programs Director for the Women's Sports Foundation, points out, however, that the real challenge may be in encouraging young girls to participate in sports. "What's really happening in the trenches we're not sure. . . Do mom and dad go out and play catch with their daughter to the same degree they do with their son? We don't know, but we expect that's not the case." Becker, *supra* note 81.

134. The problem of performance-enhancing drug use among athletes exploded at the 1988 Summer Olympics in Seoul, Korea, when 100-meter track gold medalist Ben Johnson of Canada tested positive for steroid use. *See, e.g.*, Benjamin, *Shame of the Games*, TIME, Oct. 10, 1988, at 74. Since then, the United States and the Soviet National Olympic Committees have signed an agreement to begin random, out-of-competition drug testing. *See* Wolff, *Playing by the Rules? A Legal Analysis of the USOC- Soviet Olympic Committee Doping Control Agreement*, 25 STAN. J. INT'L. L. 611, 613. The International Amateur Athletic Federation, also passed a random, out-of-competition drug testing program. Mehaffey, *Johnson's World Record Erased by IAAF*, Reuters, Sept. 5, 1989.

135. *See, e.g.* Kirshenbaum, *An American Disgrace: A Violent and Unprecedented Lawlessness has Arisen Among College Athletes in all Parts of the Country*, SPORTS ILLUS., Feb. 27, 1989, at 16; Telander & Sullivan, *You Reap What You Sow: Oklahoma Has Paid the Price for the Anything-goes Attitude That Coach Barry Switzer has Allowed to Take Root*, SPORTS ILLUS., Feb. 27, 1989, at 20; Reilly, *What Price Glory?: Under Coach Bill McCartney, Colorado Football has Taken Off, but so has Criminal Behavior Among the Buffalo Players*, SPORTS ILLUS., Feb. 27, 1989, at 32. In this *Sports Illustrated* special report, not a single incidence of violent behavior by women athletes was discussed, indicating either an extreme respect for the law among women athletes or a narrow definition of athletes by *Sports Illustrated*, or both.

136. *See, e.g.*, Telander & Sullivan, *supra* note 135; Gup, *Foul!*, TIME, Apr. 3, 1989, at 54, 55.

137. Women's athletics have not been completely free from drug and corruption scandals. Several female athletes have been disqualified from international competition for use of performance-enhancing drugs. Moreover, in the wake of the Ben Johnson scandal at the 1988 Seoul Olympics, much speculation about illegal drug use has focused on the American sprinter Florence Griffith Joyner. *See, e.g.*, Brennan, *Lewis 'Sure' Johnson Took Amphetamines at Olympics*, Wash. Post, Jan. 10, 1990, at F1, col. 1; Thomsen, *The Seoul Olympics: Long jump to gold; Another triumph for Joyner-Kersee*, Boston Globe, Sept. 30, 1988, at 70. Griffith Joyner, who has retired from competitive racing, has never tested positive for the use of performance-enhancing drugs.

pornography, abortion, sexual harassment and the career-family struggle, taking time to shoot baskets, call strikes and hit passing shots may seem frivolous. Before dismissing the importance of sport, however, the general women's movement should at least acknowledge that women's relative absence from sport has been a role imposed on women, not one that they have chosen. Moreover, there are three major reasons why improving opportunities for women in sport and redefining sport should be a concern for the general women's movement. First, sports as an institution plays an important role in contemporary society. Sociologist Harry Edwards argues that sport has replaced formal religion as a dominant force in the lives of many Americans,[138] undoubtedly mostly male. The women's movement cannot afford to ignore such a pervasive societal institution, even if the institution seems to want to ignore the women's movement.

Second, many of the struggles women face in general are the same struggles the women's sports movement faces: struggles over how to eradicate outdated stereotypes; struggles over how to gain access to positions of power and economic rewards to which women traditionally have been denied; struggles over how best to advance the position of women; and struggles over how to create a movement that promotes the interests of all women, or at least recognizes the diversity that exists within the women's movement. Hall said at a 1980 conference on women and sport in Australia and Canada,

> But wait! It is no different in society at large. . . Women *do* possess a lower social standing than do men, and their roles, primarily as wife, mother, and often worker, are less highly valued. Women have far *fewer* status alternatives available to them and considerably less access to prestige and power. . . . Sport is no different to the world at large. In fact, it reflects and reinforces that world. Thus to question the sex structure of sport is to challenge the very nature of the sex structure of our society. It is vitally important to ask "why".[139]

Women in and out of sport have much to gain from working together to resolve

---

138. Edwards, *Desegregating Sexist Sport*, in OUT OF THE BLEACHERS, *supra* note 119, at 188.

139. Hall, *supra* note 74, at 3. Nancy Theberge also cautions against assigning priorities within the women's movement, something she thinks is a clear divide and conquer theory. Writes Theberge, "There is, however, a danger in separating and assigning a priority to 'kinds' of feminist issues. That danger lies in failing to recognize the connections among different forms of oppression of women in the manner in which the condition of women in one social sphere, such as sport, has an impact on other spheres." Theberge, *supra* note 101, at 48.

the problems they face. The benefits of a partnership between women in sport and women outside of sport are discussed in part V.

The third reason the women's movement should embrace a partnership with the women's sports movement in the 1990's is simple and functional: athletic activity has a number of positive physical and emotional health effects. As educational psychologist Linda Nielsen points out, exercise reduces depression, produces self-confidence and, perhaps most importantly, makes women feel that they—not men—have personal power and control over their own lives.[140] Lyn LeMaire, a former member of the U.S. National Cycling Team, points out that *Index Medicus* prescribes exercise as the medical profession's remedy for a variety of illnesses and that physical activity increases coordination and body awareness, which can translate into confidence and ease of movement in other spheres of life.[141]

Finally, the women's movement must acknowledge that athletics cannot be defined as an activity outside the feminist perspective. A decade ago, Ann Hall defined feminism as "a perspective, a particular stance one takes if you become angry about the oppression of women. . . . Feminists ask how do we, as women, gain access to the power to accomplish that which is important to us, both individually and collectively?"[142] Feminists should ask these questions in all realms of oppression, including sport.

IV. THE ROAD LESS TRAVELLED

Merely to establish sport—and the benefit it can bring to women— as a part of the women's agenda for the 1990's is not to define a direction for the women's sports movement. The goal of the women's sports movement in the 1990's must be to avoid the mistakes of the past. First, the women's sports movement would be ill-advised to select a path for women's athletics that is

---

140. Nielsen, *supra* note 34, at 290-91. According to Nielsen,

In general, girls have less confidence in their own mental and physical abilities, lower expectations for success, and more inclination to blame failure on their own lack of abilities than boys. . . . Through physical exercise and team sports, players learn that many outcomes are controllable, but that other outcomes are unavoidable.

Id. at 291-92 (footnotes omitted).

141. LeMaire, *supra* note 7, at 134-35 (citing Froelicher, Battler & McKirnan, *Physical Activity and Coronary Heart Disease*, 65 CARDIOLOGY 153 (1980)). *See also* Young, *The Effect of Regular Exercise on Cognitive Functioning and Personality*, BRIT. J. SPORTS MED. (Sept. 1979), at 110; Mathes, *Body Image and Sex Stereotyping*, in WOMEN AND SPORT: FROM MYTH TO REALITY 59 (C. Oglesby ed. 1978).

142. Hall, *supra* note 74, at 23-24.

completely separate from men's athletics. Even a separate path based on a process-oriented, cooperative model, like that espoused by the AIAW in the 1970's,[143] is doomed to fail.

Several commentators over the past two decades have advocated complete separation from men's sports. LeMaire writes that,

> [o]n the one hand, the major contact sports (particularly football), which have traditionally been associated closely with combat, victory, and male glory, should be distinguished from normal athletics. Realistically, the contact sports cannot be eliminated, but they could cease to epitomize our conception of athletics.
>
> One plausible solution to the contact sports problem surfaces if we label these activities what they are: revenue-producing entertainment.[144]

LeMaire is correct when she states that it is realistically impossible to eradicate contact sports. However, her attempt to define them out of the sphere of what women athletes should be concerned about introduces several problems. First, the commercialism that she labels as "revenue-producing entertainment" is the same fault that the AIAW and its predecessors found with men's athletics and tried to avoid for the first three-quarters of the 20th century.[145] The AIAW learned at the expense of its existence as an organization that it could not defeat commercialism in sport simply by ignoring it. Second, abandoning contact sports to men limits the choices of and opportunities for women in sport. These contact sports, hockey, baseball, basketball, and football, produce the highest economic rewards in organized sports.[146] In cities where franchises in these sports exist, participation in the management or administration of the team also opens other economic opportunities. Moreover, in these cities, the franchises themselves have important effects on the economy. For example, most franchises play in publicly supported

---

143. *See supra* notes 26-42 and accompanying text. Chandler writes that there are three main reasons behind the failure of the AIAW's approach in the 1970's: (1) the AIAW had no powerful and logical group of alumni to support it; (2) the AIAW had no prestigious link to professional sports for female physical educators to develop credibility; and (3) the AIAW largely lost control of women's sports to men after the passage of Title IX. Chandler, *supra* note 19, at 14.

144. LeMaire, *supra* note 7, at 140-41.

145. *See supra* notes 18-42 and accompanying text.

146. The major professional leagues in hockey, baseball, basketball and football reap combined gross revenues of more than $1 billion a year. The National Football League in the mid-1980's grossed approximately $600 million a year. 1 R. BERRY & G. WONG, LAW AND BUSINESS OF THE SPORTS INDUSTRIES 40 (1986).

stadiums—at a hefty cost to taxpayers.[147] If such entities are to be publicly supported or are to generate revenue throughout a metropolitan area, women should participate as decision makers in the directions these entities will take. Third, since basketball is among the major contact sports and, at the collegiate level, employs more women coaches than any other sport,[148] abandoning these sports would also abandon a significant segment of the women's sports movement. Finally, LeMaire's approach, like the approach of Title IX and of the equality model, focuses primarily on interscholastic sports and ignores the involvement of women in other areas of sport.[149]

Forging a path for the women's sports movement that is completely separate from the men's sports movement is also unworkable because of the emerging generation gap in women's sport.[150] Younger women, particularly those who have grown up during the Title IX era and consequently have an image of sports as an equal arena for men and women, are less likely than those who fought the battle for Title IX to identify themselves as feminists.[151] The same study shows that young girls whose playmate groups included both boys and girls are much more likely to participate in and watch sports as adults.[152] Based on these findings, the demographic group that is most likely to be active in sport in the next decade may be the least likely to espouse a model of sport that excludes men.

While a completely separate path is unworkable, it would also be a mistake to select the Title IX and equality model course of the 1970's and 1980's. Such a course would not broaden the opportunities open to women in sports but would focus again on those at the college and high school level.[153] Moreover,

---

147. *See* Ross, *Monopoly Sports Leagues*, 73 MINN. L. REV. 643, 646 (1989).

148. R. Acosta & L. Carpenter, *supra* note 2, at 1.

149. LeMaire's focus on interscholastic sports may result from her article's publication in a legal periodical. The legal hooks traditionally used by the women's sports movement are centered on educational institutions. *See supra* notes 50-52 and accompanying text.

150. *See supra* notes 102-07 and accompanying text.

151. *Miller Lite Report*, *supra* note 30, at 19-20.

152. *Id.* at 28.

153. Recent decisions by the Supreme Court with respect to major athletic governing bodies would seem to support the view that existing legal hooks are of limited use beyond the high school and college level (where it is easiest to meet the state action requirement). In two recent cases, the USOC and the NCAA were held not to be state actors, thus insulating them from constitutional equal protection claims. In *San Francisco Arts & Athletics Inc. v. United States Olympic Committee*, 483 U.S. 522, 543 (1987), the Supreme Court held that the USOC was not a state actor, so constitutional provisions of equal protection and free speech did not apply. *Id.* at 543. Although courts in the past had held that the NCAA was in fact a state actor, *see, e.g.*, Howard University v. NCAA, 510 F.2d 213 (D.C. Cir. 1975), in late 1988 the Supreme Court held that the disciplinary actions of the NCAA were not imbued with state action. NCAA v. Tarkanian, 109 S.Ct. 454 (1988). In *Tarkanian*, the court held that the NCAA's participation in the events that led to University of Nevada-Las Vegas basketball coach Jerry Tarkanian's

such a course would continue to let men's sports define what is and is not sport,[154] and, by extension, would continue to let men's sports define who is and who is not to participate.

Sport today—defined by the men who dominate it[155]—focuses on the material rewards participants get from winning, not from playing. In sport today, it is whether you win or lose, not how you play the game. End results determine, at the high school level, whether you win a college scholarship; at the college level, whether you become a professional; and at the professional level, how much money you make.[156] End results determine steps up the athletic hierarchy for coaches and executives as well as for players. Honesty and integrity are valued commodities only in winners.

The current incarnation of commercialism in athletics has been accompanied by drug use and gambling at all levels and, at the college level, where the NCAA and the fiction of amateurism at major universities provide an active regulatory scheme, by illegal recruiting and academic failures.[157]

---

suspension in 1977 did not constitute "state action" and was not performed "under color of" state law. *Id.* at 463-64.

154. LeMaire states that the differentiation between men and women with respect to athletics is valued either positively or negatively. LeMaire, *supra* note 7, at 127. LeMaire writes:

> Once the idea of fundamental difference between women and men with respect to athletics is accepted, the third step of the differentiation process occurs: the application of normative definitions and values to the perceived difference. That boys are strong and girls are weak is a disputable assertion, but is not in itself value-laden. However, at the third step, this facially neutral proposition is transformed: athlete is now *defined* as strong and *valued* as good. Boys are supposed to be vigorous and athletic; girls are not.

Id.

155. Hall points out that in languages where gender is assigned to nouns, sport is always masculine. Hall, *supra* note 74, at 1-2.

156. In 1989, after his team won the Super Bowl, San Francisco 49ers wide receiver and Super Bowl Most Valuable Player Jerry Rice felt that his performance entitled him to more endorsement money than he had made during the first few days after his team's win. He charged racism, an allegation that likely has some merit. Nonetheless, his complaints illustrate that the big moment in athletics comes not when you haul in the pass but when you haul in the endorsement contracts. *See, e.g.,* Fimrite, *The Hero as Huckster,* SPORTS ILLUS., Feb. 13, 1989, at 92.

157. *See supra* note 135. The 1988 NCAA basketball tournament produced $68.2 million in gross receipts. Gup, *supra* note 136, at 55; *see also* Gilbert, *supra* note 24, at 97. Gilbert writes:

> Nowadays, the rewards for winning and the costs of losing are becoming more substantial. This is self-evident at the big-money, big-scholarship, big-celebrity level. But even for young children, succeeding at athletics is more and more often a quick, effective means of gaining status, perks and privileges. As the importance of winning is increasingly emphasized, the competitive process—how one plays the game—becomes further de-emphasized. The worth of the inner rewards declines in comparison with the magnificence of the prizes distributed. Raising the material stakes in contests tends to move competition out of the traditional realm of sport—safe excitement and imaginary risk—and into the real world, a world that

The current model of sport espouses a model of competition that is ugly and undesirable.[158]

> According to traditional usage, *competition* identifies a situation in which two or more people vie for a prize, honor or advantage. However, since it has become a 36-foot-tall pissant of a word, various authorities are suggesting that competition is importantly connected with what should or should not be done about the balance of trade, oil, taxes, dependent mothers, Nicaragua, public schools and the Democratic National Convention. John Thompson, the highly successful Gerogetown basketball coach, summed up a lot of fashionable thinking when he remarked, "Life is *about* competition."[159]

If Title IX and the equality model lead naturally to *this* model of sports, as it is emphasized at the highest levels of competition and on television,[160] Title IX and the equality model are the wrong leaders. The emphasis on competition in this model is an emphasis on end results. The term "competition" becomes defined as a race to succeed by winning. When winning is the only focus, the competition itself becomes secondary.

This male model of sport and competition that focuses on results brands all those who participate in sports as winners or losers. It is this model that discourages the losers from even participating in sports. For men, to whom society often attributes machismo based on sporting prowess or knowledge, this model labels them as abnormal. Nonetheless, for men, those who are the

---

frequently seems so scary and so stressful that we invented games as a means of escaping it.

Many of the authorities expressed concern about the ills bedeviling elite athletes today—substance abuse, cheating and so on. However, the moral lapses of athletes were generally attributed not to the stresses of competition but to those that accompany fame and fortune, that is, the rewards of winning.

Id. at 97.

158. A major textbook on sports and sports industries defines sports as inherently competitive and competition as focusing on successes and failures. R. BERRY & G. WONG, *supra* note 146, at 1.

159. Gilbert, *supra* note 24, at 88.

160. Jeffrey Goldstein and Brenda Bredemeier blame the media for sport's current focus on winning and for all the evils associated with the movement away from a process-oriented vision of sport. Goldstein & Bredemeier, *supra* note 84, at 291. Briefly, Goldstein and Bredemeier assert that: (1) sports broadcasts are zero-sum games that focus on the outcome rather than the process; (2) individual team's broadcast rights increase when the team wins, which focuses teams on winning and has increased the value of professional sports enterprises (as well as the profitability of big-time college athletics); and (3) the values stressed by coaches, players and athletes are "business values of competition, personal success, and corporate obedience to managerial hierarchy." *Id.* at 292-94.

"losers" on the playing field are often able to find an outlet in recreational athletics, where winning is less important, or as sportswriters, executives and officials, where their knowledge of sports allows them to "win" in a different athletic arena.

For women, the competitive model's emphasis on winning is even more destructive. This model of competition prohibits the development of athletics for women at the less competitive playground level that so many men have enjoyed. So few women are involved in sports initially that even fewer are left behind to form recreational leagues.[161] Moreover, those who have sufficient knowledge of sports to serve as coaches, officials, sportswriters and executives don't come in with the experience and playing credentials, even at lower levels, that men have.[162] Perhaps most importantly, women should not aspire to reproduce problems such as drug abuse and corruption that plague men's sports.

While trying to navigate a course between the shortcomings of the separatist and sports-as-men's-sports models, a model for the women's sports movement in the 1990's should be based on the justifications for incorporating the plight of women athletes into the plight of women. It must also recognize that women who participate in sports have diverse interests; they participate for health, competitive and recreational reasons.[163] The process for building a model of sport along these guidelines involves two steps: (1) an orientation toward process not product, even in competitive athletics; and (2) an immediate integration of process-oriented women into influential positions in sport—not just women's sports but sport.

The first step implicitly recognizes women who participate for diverse reasons. Women who participate in sports for health and recreation reasons are generally most intent on the process of participating. Winning does not *a fortiori* produce good physical health. However, for women who participate in athletics because they enjoy testing their skills against other athletes, it is this actual test, the game itself, that is the reason for participation. Thus, the first step in the process for building a new model of sport must incorporate a process-oriented model of competition. Competition need not equal the Social Darwinism that Gilbert described. Some commentators, such as Gilbert himself

---

161. *See* Becker, *supra* note 81.

162. *See* Olson, *supra* note 30.

163. Ann Hall recognized the diversity of women's interests in sports while addressing a 1980 conference on women and sport in Australia. Hall, *supra* note 74, at 5-6 ("Sport, in this sense, means a spectrum of physical activities which range from the more recreational, unorganized pursuits of uncommitted individuals through to competition at the highest level, requiring a high degree of intense commitment and arduous training.").

and Alfie Kohn, simply reject the validity of John Thompson's combative competition model:

> Indeed, it all sounds as if it has a lot to do with the realities of evolution and zoology, but it does not. The trouble with the theory of direct, unrelenting competition as a long-range force in nature is that such a scheme always has fewer winners than losers. Thus the win-or-drop-dead, tennis-tournament model of evolution is at odds with the fact that, through the aeons, life-forms on Earth have become increasingly numerous and various. The multitude of species reflects the evolutionary drive to find a small edge—a niche, zoologists call it—that enables creatures to go about their business without always fighting with others with the same appetites.
>
> Humans have long had a high regard for niches, which allow us to occupy positions in which competition is completely eliminated or greatly reduced.[164]

Kohn argues that competition and success are not the same thing. He defines competition as a method of working toward a goal that prevents others from reaching their goals.[165] Kohn says that "[t]he simplest way to understand why competition generally does not promote excellence is to realize that trying to do well and trying to beat others are two different things."[166]

As other commentators have noted, cooperation—not combat—is the root of competition in athletics. First, for most athletic events even to occur, the participants must cooperate.[167] Tennis rallies are one-shot affairs without cooperation between at least two individuals. Baseball and softball require eighteen to twenty people to be more than games of catch. Pick-up basketball games, even games of h-o-r-s-e, need at least two (one-on-one is fun; one-on-none is just shooting around). Kathryn Pyne Addelson describes this kind of "competiton" as a "cooperative challenge" for each participant.[168] Moreover,

---

164. Gilbert, *supra* note 24, at 88.

165. A. KOHN, NO CONTEST: THE CASE AGAINST COMPETITION 46 (1986). In his book, Kohn goes on to demonstrate the inferiority of competition, compared with cooperation, in learning endeavors. *Id.* at 47-49.

166. *Id.* at 55. Although Kohn maintains that sports are inherently competitive to some degree, *id.* at 79-80, the aim of this section is to introduce a model of competition that incorporates cooperation and social norms of fair play and respect, thus minimizing the all-out competition described by Gilbert. *See supra* text accompanying note 159.

167. There are, of course, several sports that do not absolutely require a second individual, such as golf, archery, aerobics, cycling, gymnastics, swimming, and track.

168. Addelson, *supra* note 65, at 140.

in pick-up basketball games in playgrounds and recreational gymnasiums across the country, the common law of "cooperative competition" prevails. The mere act of participating in the game creates a bond. These pick-up games rarely employ referees or officials; instead, a social self-enforcement mechanism structures the game. Those who don't know the common law of a particular forum don't get to play.[169]

While it doesn't eliminate winning and losing, the cooperative competition model at least focuses on the process before it focuses on the result. Under the cooperative challenge model of competition, sport is a social phenomenon that produces social rather than merely contractual relationships among participants. Each player realizes that without the participation of the other, she would not be able to hone her skills, or even to play.[170]

Lyn LeMaire emphasizes that athletic competition hones skills only if women value athletics as a process, not as purely an end: "An opponent may provide this [external] resistance. Yet we should value the athletic engagement over the final result. Victory over the opponent becomes an incident of, rather than the motivation for, athletic activity."[171]

Sport as cooperative competition is sport at its inception—a joyous diversion from the risks of life and a recognition of the pleasure and beauty that can come from physical exertion.[172] This aspect of sport is symbolized by many of the rituals that take place at the beginning and end of contests: shaking hands at the net in tennis and volleyball; tapping sticks at the end of hockey games. There is a cult of respect among competitors for mere engagement in the game. The rituals symbolize respect for an opponent and for her part in making the sporting contest possible. The challenge for sport in the 1990's is to fill the rituals with meaning, where they largely have become empty.[173]

---

169. Lewis Hyde discusses a similar phenomenon for socially-created bonds in other contexts. Hyde writes that such bonds create community while formal rules and rule systems—such as law—create boundaries. L. HYDE, THE GIFT: IMAGINATION AND THE EROTIC LIFE OF PROPERTY 52-61, 84-88 (3d ed. 1983). The logical extension of the application of Hyde's theory to sport would argue against the use of any formal adjudicators such as referees or umpires.

170. LeMaire, *supra* note 7, at 136.

171. *Id.*

172. This is essentially the definition Kohn gives to play. Kohn would not recognize sport as play because of its high level of structure. *See* A. KOHN, *supra* note 165, at 80-84. Nonetheless, Kohn does recognize what he calls "process competition," which he describes as "the in-the-moment experience of struggling for superiority that is sometimes seen as an end in itself rather than simply a step toward the final victory." *Id.* at 86.

173. After expressing disdain for the crass commercialism that had crept into college athletics, *Sports Illustrated* senior writer Frank DeFord received a letter from—and later visited—then-University of Utah president Chase Peterson. The letter stated:

Chris Evert's retirement from professional tennis in September 1989 was a celebration of a remarkable athlete. Each opponent feared being the one to dispatch her, and when Zina Garrison finally did in the quarterfinals, it was she, not Evert, who was overwhelmed by the enormity of what she had done.[174] The *New York Times* reported Garrison as saying, "When I went over and sat down, I thought what had just happened, that this is the last time we'll see Chris here. She's been so much to the game, she's such a lady."[175]

In team sports, particularly the most highly competitive team sports at the professional and college level, selflessness among team members is considered one of the attributes of a truly great—and often successful—team. For example, the Stanford University women's basketball team, en route to a 17-0 start and, eventually, an NCAA championship, was given high marks by analysts for selfless play, a trait on the basketball court that was defined primarily by players placing team goals ahead of the accumulation of individual rewards.[176]

Making the lore and legend of sport the real life of sport is not an easy task, but it will be a task that can be facilitated by the integration of women into positions of leadership in all sport. It is not presumptuous to suggest that women's integration into sport will produce a process-oriented, cooperative competition model of sport rather than merely perpetuate the current male model. The 1984 *Miller Lite Report* showed that women participate in sports for different reasons than men do.[177] Fifty-four percent of the women in the survey cited improved health as their reason for participation in sport; fourteen percent cited stress reduction; eight percent cited friendship and sociability; eight percent cited competition; and only one percent cited winning.[178]

To achieve sport as a cooperative competition, as something other than money and fame, drugs and corruption, a separate activity for men and women, will not be easy. Cooperation is at the center of women's current, albeit

---

"Well, I [Peterson] believe that football—big-time-sport—fits in there somewhere. The sense of ceremony and community that's inherent in sport can be of value. I don't mean mindlessly screaming 'We're Number 1!' I mean something like the fifth quarter at Wis-consin, where they don't have very good teams but where the band stays after the game and so does the crowd, and they all sing along . . . ."

DeFord, *An Honorable Pursuit,* SPORTS ILLUS., Oct. 17, 1988, at 102.

174. Finn, *Evert Bows Out as Garrison Prevails, 7-6, 6-2,* N.Y. Times, Sept. 6, 1989, at D21, col. 5 ("Evert calmly packed up her racquets on the Stadium Court for the last time, gave a smile and rotating wave of farewell to her fans and put a steadying arm around the shoulders of Garrison, who couldn't suppress a few confused tears.").

175. *Id.*

176. The Stanford Daily, Jan. 25, 1990, at 12, col. 4.

177. *Miller Lite Report, supra* note 30, at 17.

178. *Id.*

limited, association with sport. Emphasizing cooperation in competitive, elite athletics, as well as at lesser skill levels, will allow the women's sports movement to avoid repeating the mistakes introduced by the separate but equal and equality models, neither of which introduced women into positions of responsibility in traditionally men's athletics or reformed the direction and focus of athletics. To develop a model of sport as something other than money, fame, drugs and corruption, women must expand the public perception of sport and sports figures by encouraging participation by women in sport as administrators, coaches, officials and executives at all levels of sport. The final section of this article addresses some of the initial steps the women's sports movement should take toward developing a cooperative competition model of sport.

CONCLUSION: WOMEN AND THE MODEL OF SPORT AS COOPERATIVE COMPETITION

The women's sports movement of the 1990's must be based upon a partnership with the broader women's movement to jointly address overlapping concerns, and present a cooperative view of sport at all levels. An agenda for women and sports for the 1990's must move in a direction that incorporates broad, diverse groups of people for involvement at all levels and in all positions. If the long-term goal is to infiltrate sports and remake them in an image that men and women alike can enjoy, the short-term strategy is to: (1) expose the falsity of stereotypes about women in sport; (2) identify the places where links between the women's sports movement and women who traditionally have not been involved in sport can make an immediate impact; (3) identify places where women can have an immediate impact on the general direction of sport; and (4) address the needs of women of color and lesbians.

A flood of women into sport at all levels, fueled by a partnership between the women's sports movement and the general women's movement, will do much in the short-term to begin to eradicate false stereotypes, forge links between the two groups and have an immediate impact upon the model of sport in American society.

Persistent stereotypes of women in sport can be eradicated by increasing the number of women who are in sport and expanding the variety of positions in which they are involved. In addition, women in the media can take affirmative steps to provide coverage that extends well beyond the traditional stereotypes of women in sport.[179] Women as a powerful demographic market also could affect the presentation of women athletic figures in the media, particularly since the sports media attribute much of the inadequate coverage of women's sports to a "lack of viewer/reader interest."[180]

A partnership between the women's sports movement and the general women's movement could provide broader benefits to both. The women's sports movement can offer the general women's movement some of the most visible women in the world as spokespersons. This may be particularly helpful in convincing younger women, those in their twenties and teens, to abandon individual pursuits long enough to actively engage in some of the most powerful—and even some of the less visible—women's issues of the day. Tennis player Billie Jean King, for example, had an abortion in the early 1970's and is a possible spokeswoman for the pro-choice movement.[181] In addition, tennis player Martina Navratilova, responding to the Supreme Court's decision in *Webster v. Reproductive Health Serv.*,[182] has stated her intention to support Planned Parenthood.[183]

The women's movement can help the women's sports movement by contributing the expertise of those who have organized, networked and lobbied to get women into positions from which they traditionally have been barred. In addition, the women's sports movement could learn a great deal about promoting its top prospects for coaching and administrative positions from such groups as the Coalition for Women's Appointments, which in 1989 was particularly successful in getting women named to cabinet positions in the Bush administration.[184] In their study on women and coaching, Vivian Acosta and Linda Carpenter point out that the old boys' network that exists in athletic coaching and administration is among the factors that has reduced the number

---

179. Jim Spence, a former executive at ABC sports, quotes sportscaster Jim McKay stating that ABC's coverage of figure skating and gymnastics on "Wide World of Sports" made those sports into major spectator sports. J. SPENCE, UP CLOSE AND PERSONAL 77 (1988). If executives like Spence are so certain that their television coverage was responsible for turning these sporting events into hits with spectators, there is no reason why women in the media can't apply their skills to women's athletics.

180. *See, e.g.*, Belliotti, *Sports, Sex-Equality, and the Media*, in WOMEN, PHILOSOPHY, AND SPORT, *supra* note 34, at 96, 98.

181. *See* Bricker, *Take One*, PEOPLE, July 4, 1983, at 29.

182. 109 S.Ct. 3040 (1989).

183. Finn, *Navratilova's Interests Go Beyond Racquet's Reach*, N.Y. Times, Nov. 13, 1989, at C11, col. 1.

184. The Coalition for Women's Appointments, a group of mostly women's and public interest groups, reported in July of 1989 that nearly 40% of women appointed to posts in the Bush administration were women it had recommended. Schwartz, *Coalition's Success*, Wash. Post, July 26, 1989, at A23, col. 1.

of women coaches.[185] Women in coaching and athletic administra-tion need to form their own coalition. They need to have ready a list of top women who can move into positions in coaching and administrations as positions become available. With a ready list of qualified women, a coalition of women coaches and athletic administrators will be able to defeat arguments that the pool of qualified women applicants is inadequate.

While the Women's Sports Foundation has published a guide for women interested in coaching and officiating,[186] its affirmative reach has to be broader. Current athletic administrators and coaches should keep track of the whereabouts of former athletes, particularly those who do not go into coaching right away. In short, the developing "old girls' network" needs to identify those who have stepped away from women's athletics and help them step back toward the sports world.

Moreover, women who have advanced in the corporate world are also the women most traditionally qualified to break the gender barrier at the executive level in men's professional sports. Or, for that matter, in women's profession-al sports. For example, the new commissioner of the Ladies Professional Golf Association selected in November 1988 was a male marketing executive.[187] The position became vacant again in the fall of 1990, but the LPGA has yet to name a new commissioner.[188] In addition, in late 1989, the Women's International Tennis Association named Gerard Smith, a former *Newsweek* publisher, as its executive director.[189]

Women should take the lead in the quest to rid sport of performance-enhancing and recreational drug use. One woman already has. Dorianne Lambelet, a world-class distance runner and attorney in a Washington, D.C. law firm, is counsel to the Athlete's Advisory Committee of The Athletic Congress, which has developed a year-round out-of-competition drug-testing protocol.

---

185. *See* R. Acosta & L. Carpenter, *supra* note 2.

186. Women's Sports Foundation, *A Woman's Guide to Coaching* (1987). Even if its outreach to women is rather narrow, the Women's Sports Foundation's guide is quite broad in describing women's role in sports. *See id.* at 4 ("Boys Need Women, Too").

187. Diaz, *supra* note 123, at 58.

188. Mauro, *New LPGA Commissioner Must Get Corporate America to Cooperate*, Seattle Post-Intelligence, Sept. 12, 1990, at D2, col. 6.

189. Bodo, *The Changing Face of Women's Tennis*, TENNIS, Nov. 1990, at 54, 55. Chris Evert, WITA president, said that several women were considered for the WITA executive directorship, including Phillip Morris vice president Ellen Merlo, but Merlo was out of the WITA's price range. Nonetheless, Women's Sports Foundation president and former professional golfer Carol Mann chastised the WITA, saying that women in athletics "need to examine their own beliefs in women as leaders." *Women's Tennis: 2 Men Left for the Job*, USA Today, Nov. 15, 1989, at C2, col. 1.

The women's sports movement also needs to strive to keep its professional and collegiate sports free from the kinds of recruiting, crime and gambling scandals currently facing men's sports. In its February 1989 special report on corruption and crime in college athletics, *Sports Illustrated* laid much of the blame at the feet of coaches and administrators.[190]

Women coaches and administrators must stand on their records as "clean" coaches, players and administrators in pushing for positions of additional responsibility. For example, women's athletic administrators and coaches at universities such as Oklahoma University and the University of Colorado[191] need to assert the values that their athletic experience would bring to an entire athletic program.[192]

A flood of women into sport at a variety of levels will begin to resolve a number of problems, but it will not automatically meet the needs and resolve the problems in sport of women of color and lesbians unless these two groups are strongly represented in the alignment between the women's sports movement and the general women's movement.

For African-American women, the barriers to actual participation in sport can only be eliminated by addressing the role of the African-American woman in society.[193] In addition, although this paper has been critical of approaches to women's athletics that focus only on the college level, the women's sports movement must recognize that it is at the college level where women of color, because of their greater dependence on financial aid, are most vulnerable.[194] Finally, to eliminate the stereotype that African-American women participants in sport are suited to either track or basketball, the women's sports movement must create opportunities for broader access to other sports and must affirmatively recruit African-American women and girls into sports such as tennis, golf, gymnastics, swimming and figure skating.

Some of the problems lesbian athletes, coaches, administrators and sports executives face will be lessened when "lesbian" is no longer used as a

---

190. Kirshenbaum, *supra* note 135, at 18.

191. For a discussion of the problems at these universities, see *supra* note 135-36 and accompanying text.

192. Ruth Heizer also suggests that employers look to see whether candidates, particularly women, have potential that has gone undeveloped because of discrimination and lack of access to arenas in which training and experience are gleaned, i.e., old boys' networks. Heizer, *Employment for Women in Athletics: What is Fair Play?*, in WOMEN, PHILOSOPHY, AND SPORT, *supra* note 34, at 70, 83-84.

193. For a discussion of the problems facing African-American women in sport, see *supra* notes 108-20 and accompanying text.

194. In 1979, the NCAA reported that, while black women were only 4.7% of all female college athletes, they were 5.6% of those receiving some financial aid, and 8.2% of female college athletes on full athletic scholarships. *See* Dunkle, *supra* note 108.

pejorative label. While it is logical to combat the pejorative use of lesbian in stereotyping women athletes, it is neither logical nor cooperative to ask lesbian athletes to take on a heterosexual identity as part of the battle. The sports arena can be a place for heterosexual women to confront their prejudices about and to begin to understand lesbians. In fact, one of the most sensitive portrayals of lesbians was in the 1982 movie "Personal Best," about two lesbian hept-athletes. Critics praised the film for "making lesbians in sport visible and deemphasizing the stereotyped associations among tomboyism, masculinity and lesbianism."[195] In addition, Martina Navratilova and Judy Nelson, described by tennis broadcasters as Navratilova's "good and great friend," have one of the longest and publicly stable relationships on the women's professional tennis tour.

An agenda for the women's sports movement in the 1990's is necessarily broad. The pinpoint plans of Title IX and the equality model have benefitted too few women over too long a time period. They have focused on women at the elite level, reinforcing the stereotype that only a few super women such as Chris Evert and Jackie Joyner-Kersee are capable of being great athletes. They have done little to open doors for women in other avenues of sport. They have done little to develop a vision of sport that would encourage more women to participate. They have done equally little to address the needs of various groups of women in sport, particularly women of color and lesbians.

Women in sport must pursue careers beyond the playing field, and they must look to the general women's movement as an important and increasingly abundant resource for positions of authority within sport. Sport, with seemingly endless infusions of money and power, is increasingly a culture-shaping and reflecting institution. Sport, then, is clearly something women cannot afford to abandon to men. The cooperative-competition model would allow women to point sport in a new direction and to claim sport as their own.

I spent my eighth summer as I had my seventh—as bat "girl" for my older brother's Little League team. I went to the park again my ninth year. Same cap. Same glove. But the braided pigtails were down. They knew who I was. They knew I could play. And they knew my father was a lawyer. I played little league baseball for three years before abandoning it for a more extensive stint on the Intermountain section junior tennis tour. After four years and paying for four summers of public recreation tennis lessons, my mother was able to convince me that I had more of a future in tennis than in baseball. She was

---

195. H. LENSKYJ, *supra* note 17, at 104 (footnote omitted).

right; I could not have played baseball in college.[196]

---

196. In the spring of 1989, Julie Croteau became the first woman to play on a men's college baseball team when she played for St. Mary's College in Maryland. *Who's on First? On Men's Team at St. Mary's College, It's a Woman*, L.A. Times, Feb. 25, 1989, at C8, col. 2.

Emma Willard's Idea Put to the Test: The Consequences of State Support of Female Education in New York, 1819–67

Nancy Beadie

"Civilized nations have long since been convinced," Emma Willard declared to the New York legislature in 1818, "that education with respect to males, will not, like trade, regulate itself." Thus Willard introduced her famous argument for state support of female education by observing the limits of market principles for promoting good schools.[1]

Willard spoke from experience. She herself headed a female academy in Middlebury, Vermont. As was the case with virtually all the many female academies and seminaries in existence at this time, Willard's institution operated on market principles, that is, as the trade of its master teacher or preceptress. What Willard learned from this experience was the difficulty of enforcing high educational standards on the basis of simple supply and demand.[2]

In proposing a solution to this problem, Willard spoke to the experience of the legislators she addressed. New York already had a system of support for colleges and academies administered by its Board of Regents. A comparative analysis of the status of such institutions with that of female institutions formed the foundation of Willard's

Nancy Beadie is assistant professor in the Department of Educational Leadership and Policy Studies at the University of Washington, Seattle. An earlier version of this paper was presented at the Eighth Berkshire Conference on the History of Women, Rutgers University, 1990. She thanks Joan Burstyn, Jane Hugo, Clare Putala, Laurie Crumpacker, Kathryn Kerns, Natalie Naylor, and an anonymous reviewer for comments.

[1] Emma Willard, *An Address to the Public: Particularly to the Members of the Legislature of New York, Proposing a Plan for Improving Female Education* (Middlebury, Vt., 1918; orig. 1819), 7.

[2] Carl F. Kaestle described independent proprietary schools in "Common Schools before the 'Common School Revival': New York Schooling in the 1790s," *History of Education Quarterly* 12 (Winter 1972): 465–500. According to Kaestle, thirty-one of the ninety-one known proprietors of such schools in New York City in 1796 were women. Ibid., 488, table 3. Natalie Naylor describes early coeducation in New York academies in " 'The Encouragement of Seminaries of Learning': Early Academies on Long Island, New York" (paper presented at the History of Education Society Annual Meeting, Toronto, 1988). On late eighteenth-century schools specifically for women, see Lynne Templeton Brickley's excellent study, "Sarah Pierce's Litchfield Female Academy, 1792–1833"

argument. Essentially she argued that state support and oversight of female education, in the manner of Regents' support and oversight of collegiate and college preparatory education, would improve the quality of female institutions.

The question addressed in this essay is whether Willard was right. Partly in response to her appeal, New York became one of the few states to provide operating funds for female academies and seminaries. It did so under the authority of the Regents. What were the consequences of this support? *Did* it improve the quality of female education? If so, in what ways? The results discussed here suggest that the consequences were mixed. In important ways, state support did promote educational improvement. At the same time, however, some of the state regulation accompanying that support undermined the standards and integrity of female education.[3]

* * * * *

In Willard's analysis, the critical difference between Regents-supported institutions and female institutions was their legal status. As Willard wrote, "Male education flourishes because from the guardian care of legislatures, the presidencies and professorships of our colleges are some of the highest objects to which the eye of ambition is directed. Not so with female institutions. Preceptresses of these, are dependent on their pupils for support, and are consequently liable to become the victims of their caprice."[4]

Lacking the permanency conferred by incorporation, and thus the possibility of endowment, female institutions were "dependent on individual patronage." This meant that even when their preceptresses had the wisdom to make "salutary regulations" regarding the conduct of schools, they had neither the power nor the authority to enforce them.[5]

(Ed.D.diss., Harvard University, 1985); and Sheldon Hanft, "Mordecai's Female Academy," *American Jewish History* 79 (Autumn 1989): 72–93. For general accounts of the state of female education in the early republic, see Nancy F. Cott, *The Bonds of Womanhood: "Women's Sphere" in New England, 1780–1835* (New Haven, Conn., 1977), 101–25; Linda K. Kerber, *Women of the Republic: Intellect and Ideology in Revolutionary America* (Chapel Hill, N.C., 1980), 189–231; Elizabeth Fox-Genovese, *Within the Plantation Household: Black and White Women of the Old South* (Chapel Hill, N.C., 1988), 242–89; David Tyack and Elisabeth Hansot, *Learning Together: A History of Coeducation in American Schools* (New Haven, Conn., 1990), 1–145; and Thomas Woody, *A History of Women's Education in the United States*, 2 vols. (New York, 1966; orig. 1929).

[3] It appears that only New York and Pennsylvania had a system of regular annual state funding of academies which included female institutions. Woody, *History of Women's Education*, 1: 365–66.

[4] Willard, *Address*, 7.

[5] Ibid., 9.

Institutions for young gentlemen, on the other hand, were "founded by public authority," "permanent," and "endowed with funds." Their trustees and instructors were thus invested with the authority "to make such laws as they deem most salutary." They enjoyed the ability, born of their partial independence from tuition-based funding and of their corporate responsibility to the state, to class their students, establish admissions qualifications, and determine the kind and order of their pupils' studies.[6]

What would justify conferring comparable permanence, authority, and funds on female institutions? Justification of state support for collegiate education lay in the public leadership and service for which initiation into the classics, and study of the major questions of moral philosophy, prepared young men. Potentially, the idea of "Republican Motherhood," formulated at the beginning of the early national period, provided a comparable justification for state support of female education.[7]

But to acknowledge the moral value of motherhood was not the same as saying that preparation for it required public assistance. State support of collegiate education was justified not only by the value of the classical curriculum itself, but by the impossibility of sustaining the collegiate tradition any other way. As Adam Smith had noted, the "profit" of a collegiate institution could never repay the expense to any individual or small number of individuals for maintaining it. Employing similar logic, Willard argued that a proper education for Republican Motherhood involved a distinct body of knowledge and a philosophic coherence that could only be maintained with the help of state aid and authority.[8]

To establish this systematic coherence of female education, Willard drew on her own experience. At Middlebury and other high-caliber institutions, leading female educators like Willard and Sarah Pierce had developed a distinct female educational tradition by the mid-1810s. As Lynne Brickley has detailed in her study of Pierce's school in

---

[6] Ibid.

[7] On republican ideology and college founding, see Linda K. Kerber, *Federalists in Dissent: Imagery and Ideology in Jeffersonian America* (Ithaca, N.Y., 1970), 95–134; David B. Robson, "College Founding in the New Republic, 1776–1800," *History of Education Quarterly* 23 (Fall 1983): 323–41; and Douglas Sloan, *The Scottish Enlightenment and the American College Ideal* (New York, 1971). On "Republican Motherhood," see Kerber, *Women of the Republic*; Ruth H. Bloch, "American Feminine Ideals in Transition: The Rise of the Moral Mother, 1785–1815," *Feminist Studies* 4 (June 1978): 100–126; and idem, "The Gendered Meaning of Virtue in Revolutionary America," *Signs* 13 (Autumn 1978): 37–58.

[8] Adam Smith, *An Inquiry into the Nature and Causes of the Wealth of Nations*, ed. Edwin Cannan (New York, 1937), 681, cited in Lawrence A. Cremin, *American Education: The National Experience, 1783–1876* (New York, 1980), 128–33.

Litchfield, Connecticut, this tradition was grounded in a thorough English grammar education, including arithmetic, grammar, and rhetoric. It then was characterized by more than usual attention to geography and history, both ancient and modern, and to written composition. Ornamental studies, such as needlepoint and painting, often reinforced lessons of geography, history, and rhetoric. Most importantly for the development of a self-conscious tradition of female education, the curriculum included studies in natural and moral philosophy. The latter branches of study were introduced in 1814 at both Litchfield and Middlebury.[9]

Natural philosophy encompassed natural sciences, such as chemistry, botany, anatomy, and astronomy, and further involved the integration of scientific knowledge into a larger worldview. In her appeal to the legislature, Willard identified both the scientific and philosophical aspects of these studies as especially appropriate to female education. As a practical matter, knowledge of principles of natural science aided women in improving housewifery and in teaching children about the world around them. Beyond this utilitarian value, natural philosophy would "heighten the moral taste" and "enliven the piety" of young women.[10]

These lessons of natural philosophy were then further developed by the study of moral philosophy. In teaching moral philosophy, Willard followed the example of college presidents, whose senior-year courses in the subject were the culminating experience of the collegiate curriculum. Typically, presidents digressed on a range of topics having to do with questions of ethics, especially in religion, politics, and government. Such discussions of church and state made coherent a collegiate curriculum aimed at educating young men to leadership and public service.[11]

Adapting this tradition to the purpose of female education, Willard addressed moral questions pertinent to the "peculiar duties" of

---

[9] See Nina Baym, "Women and the Republic: Emma Willard's Rhetoric of History," *American Quarterly* 43 (Mar. 1991): 1–23; Brickley, "Sarah Pierce's Litchfield Female Academy," chs. 5 and 6; and Daniel H. Calhoun, "Eyes for the Jacksonian World: William C. Woodbridge and Emma Willard," *Journal of the Early Republic* 4 (Spring 1984): 1–26. On the introduction of natural and moral philosophy at Middlebury and Litchfield in 1814, see Brickley, "Sarah Pierce's Litchfield Female Academy," ch. 7; and Alma Lutz, *Emma Willard: Pioneer Educator of American Women* (Boston, 1964), 24.

[10] See William Paley, *Natural Theology; or Evidences of the Existence and Attributes of the Diety, Collected from the Appearances of Nature* (Philadelphia, 1802; microform, Early American Imprints, no. 21356); and *The Principles of Moral and Political Philosophy* (New York, 1978; orig. 1785); Willard, *Address*, 559–60.

[11] On moral philosophy in American colleges, see Gladys Bryson, *Man and Society: The Scottish Inquiry of the Eighteenth Century* (New York, 1945); Sloan, *The Scottish Enlightenment*; and Wilson Smith, *Professors and Public Ethics: Studies of Northern Moral Philosophers before the Civil War* (Ithaca, N.Y., 1956).

her sex. Her emphasis was less on political philosophy than on what was referred to as "mental philosophy." As represented by Willard's primary source, John Locke's *An Essay Concerning Human Understanding*, this branch of moral philosophy involved study of the operations of the mind, development of perception, acquisition of knowledge, and formation of judgment. While also part of the college curriculum, this subject made particular sense for a course aimed at educating women to exert a reforming influence on men, and to work with children as mothers and teachers.[12]

The idea of educating women for the moral purpose of motherhood was not new. As Linda Kerber has shown, the virtue of Republican Motherhood had been used to justify female education since at least the 1780s. Benjamin Rush used it in 1787. Pierce invoked similar ideas in her exhortations to students as early as the 1790s. In schools like hers and Willard's, connections between the idea of Republican Motherhood and the practice of female education had already been made.[13]

What *was* new was Willard's argument that a *systematic* course of study in the science and philosophy of human improvement required state authority and assistance. Every educated legislator, schooled in principles of political economy as well as classical languages, understood that the collegiate tradition was irreproducible by market forces alone. Just so with female education, Willard argued. A preceptress could teach any collection of subjects she had a mind to offer and her students had the interest to take, but truly to educate her students, to bring them "to the perfection of their moral, intellectual and physical nature," required not only funds adequate to sustain a full course of study, but authority to administer standards of achievement.[14]

What Willard apparently envisioned was a separate system of higher education for women, which paralleled the Regents system of collegiate and college preparatory education for men. With its own body of knowledge and distinct moral purpose, female education could be superintended according to its own set of standards, regulated under its own state authority, and supported with its own permanent fund. King's College (Columbia) had gone from being the sole collegiate institution in the New York colony in 1754, to being a reincorporated insti-

---

[12] John Locke, *An Essay Concerning Human Understanding* (London, 1961; orig. 1690); Willard, *Address*, 551.

[13] Kerber, "Daughters of Columbia," and *Women of the Republic*; Benjamin Rush, "Thoughts upon Female Education, Accommodated to the Present State of Society, Manners and Government in the United States of America" (Philadelphia, 1787), reprinted in Frederick Rudolph, ed., *Essays on Education in the Early Republic* (Cambridge, Mass., 1965); Brickley, "Sarah Pierce's Litchfield Female Academy," 230–31.

[14] Willard, *Address*, 13.

tution at the pinnacle of the Regents system of higher education in 1784, and finally to being one among a number of other chartered colleges in nineteenth-century New York. Such a pattern of development could well have been imagined in 1818 for a female institution established to fulfill Willard's plan.[15]

What Willard actually got was both less than she had envisioned and more than she reasonably could have expected. Willard herself saw her appeal to the New York legislature as a failure. Nonetheless, much of what she requested was eventually achieved in New York.[16]

First, very much in response to Willard, New York did incorporate its first female seminary in 1819. By 1826, six such charters had been granted to female institutions. Incorporation made the institutions "permanent," as Willard desired, and allowed the accumulation of private endowment. At this point, however, female academies still had not received any state funding.[17]

Since 1784, New York had distributed funds to colleges and academies through its Board of Regents. For the first thirty years, all such funding was a matter of special appropriation. In 1813, however, New York established a permanent Literature Fund to complement a similar fund for support of common schools. Income from the fund, which matured in 1817, was to be disbursed on a formulaic basis.[18]

For the first decade of the fund, the Regents disbursed monies on terms that were restrictive with respect to women. Constituted as the governing body of the University of the State of New York, the Regents were ultimately dedicated to collegiate education, and thus the education of boys. Accordingly, when the Literature Fund matured in 1817, the Regents ruled that annual disbursements from the fund should be

---

[15] See George Frederick Miller, *The Academy System of the State of New York* (Albany, N.Y., 1922), 19–23; Thomas Bender, *New York Intellect: A History of Intellectual Life in New York City, from 1750 to the Beginning of Our Time* (Baltimore, 1987), 18–25; "An Act for granting certain Privileges to the College heretofore called King's College, for altering the Name and Charter thereof, and erecting an University within this State," 1 May 1784, *Laws of New York, 1774–1784* (1886), vol. 1, ch. 51, 7th sess., 686; and Ronald Seavoy, *The Origins of the American Business Corporation, 1784–1855* (Westport, Conn., 1982), 12–19.

[16] On Willard's sense that her address was a failure, see Woody, *History of Women's Education*, 1: 345.

[17] The first incorporated female academy was Waterford Female Academy, which Willard headed for two years. "An Act to incorporate a Female Academy in the village of Waterford," 19 Mar. 1819, *Laws of New York*, ch. 52, 42d sess., 59–61; Alma Lutz, *Emma Willard: Daughter of Democracy* (Boston, 1929), 64–66, 80–82; and Lutz, *Pioneer*, 27–29.

[18] "An Act to institute an University within this State and for other Purposes therin mentioned," 13 Apr. 1787, *Laws of New York, 1774–1784*, vol. 1, ch. 82, 10 sess., 434–41; and "An Act to authorize the sale of Lands appropriated for the promotion of Literature," 13 Apr. 1813, in *Laws of New York*, ch. 199, 36th sess., 319–20. The New York Board of Regents is described in Miller, *Academy System*, 19–30.

awarded to Regents academies on the basis of the number of their pupils studying college preparatory subjects. These terms effectively excluded females from earning state funds for their institutions. The first female academies chartered thus belonged to a new category of New York academies which were awarded charters but not Regents status or funding.[19]

In 1828, however, this too changed. New York began awarding funds for enrollment in "the higher branches of English education" as well as in classical studies. Female academies thus became eligible for Regents status and funding. Willard's famous Troy Female Seminary, founded in 1821 with municipal rather than state aid and authority, did not acquire a state charter and Regents status until 1838. Other female academies, however, achieved this position sooner. Three female academies gained Regents status and funding in 1828, and others followed. In the period from 1828 to 1845 the number, size, and influence of female academies increased, as shown by the figures discussed below.[20]

In examining the data for female institutions, it is important to remember that throughout the "age of academies" the overwhelming majority of New York institutions enrolled both men and women. State funds supplied only a part of an academy's financing; otherwise the academy depended on some combination of tuition and voluntary subscription. To attract these sources of funding, academies offered a whole range of more popular subjects on market principles, including vocational studies directed at men, ornamental studies directed at women, and English grammar studies for children of both sexes. In this way, nearly all of New York's chartered academies, from as early as the 1780s, were to some degree coeducational.[21]

Although as many as 24 academies acquired Regents status sometime during the period from 1828 to 1860, the largest number to operate in any single year was 10, in 1845. In that same year, the number of

---

[19] Before 1816 all chartered academies were Regents academies. Under these arrangements, no female academies were ever chartered. In 1816 the legislature chartered its first academy independently of the Regents. That academy was Hartwick Seminary. The Waterford Female Academy was the second institution to receive a state charter without Regents status. Miller, *Academy System*, 24–25; "Acts of Incorporation, Academies," in *The Revised Statutes of the State of New York* (Albany, N.Y., 1829–30), 3: 529–30.

[20] For an account of the origins of Troy Female Seminary, see Lutz, *Pioneer*, 38–40; and Miller, *Academy System*, 96. For a list of state-chartered academies, up to 1830, see "Acts of Incorporation," in *Revised Statutes*. For a complete list of Regents academies, see Miller, *Academy System*, table 17, 86–97.

[21] Theodore R. Sizer, *The Age of the Academies* (New York, 1964). Broadly, the age of academies lasted from 1790 to 1860. For descriptions of these institutions in New York, see William Herring O'Neil, "Private Schools and Public Vision: A History of Academies in Upstate New York, 1800–1860" (Ph.D. diss., Syracuse University, 1984);

all-male academies with Regents status was also 10, and the total number of Regents academies was 152. Data on chartered academies without Regents status are difficult to compile systematically, but it appears that in 1845 non-Regents academies included more female institutions than did Regents academies. In that year, 17 of the approximately 100 total incorporated academies without Regents status were exclusively female.[22]

The growth of female education cannot be measured simply in numbers of institutions, however. Female academies wielded an influence out of proportion to their numbers. From decade to decade, the core female academies remained consistent and were located in commercial hubs. There they attracted large enrollments relative both to academies generally, and to comparable male or coeducational institutions in the same towns and cities.

In 1845, for example, enrollments at the Albany, Troy, Auburn, and Utica female academies exceeded those at the all-male institutions in the same cities. At the same time, no male or coeducational Regents institutions existed at all in the female academy towns of Poughkeepsie and LeRoy. In Rochester, total enrollment at the female academy trailed that at the coeducational collegiate institute, but the total number of advanced female students at the two institutions exceeded that of advanced males. Finally, in New York City, enrollment at Rutgers Female Institute, the largest academy of any kind in the state, totaled 635. This was greater than the combined total enrollments of the two all-male grammar schools in New York City, though the grammar schools together enrolled more advanced students than Rutgers did.

Nancy Beadie, "Defining the Public: Congregation, Commerce, and Social Economy in the Formation of the Educational System, 1790–1840" (Ph.D. diss., Syracuse University, 1989); Kathryn Kerns, "Farmer's Daughters: The Education of Women at Alfred Academy and University before the Civil War," *History of Higher Education Annual* 6 (1986): 11–28; Emily F. Hoag, *The National Influence of a Single Farm Community: A Story of the Flow into National Life of Migration from the Farms*, U.S. Department of Agriculture Bulletin no. 984 (Washington, D.C., 1921); Thomas James, "The Trajectory of a Local School: Community Traditions, State-Building, and the Quest for Educational Authority" (paper presented at the Annual Meeting of the History of Education Society, 26 Oct. 1991, Kansas City, Mo.); and Louis B. Caruana, "Oxford Academy, 1792–1896: The Private Years of a New York State Academy" (Ph.D. diss., Texas A & M University, 1986).

[22] *Annual Report of the Regents of the University of the State of New York* (Albany, N.Y., 1845), 64–73. Figures for the total number of academies chartered by the state, with or without Regents status, compiled from *The Official Index to the Unconsolidated Laws, Being the Special, Private, and Local Statutes of the State of New York, 1778–December 31, 1919* (Albany, N.Y., 1920); "Acts of Incorporation," 13 Apr. 1813, *Laws of New York*, ch. 202, 36th sess., sec. 10—Academies, 563; "Acts of Incorporation," in *Revised Statutes*; and J. H. French, *Historical and Statistical Gazetteer of New York State* (Interlaken, N.Y., 1980; orig. 1860), 130–34. Figures for non-Regents academies are approximate.

Only in Canandaigua did enrollment at a comparable, male institution clearly exceed that at the female seminary.[23]

Statewide, enrollment in female institutions alone represented 11 percent of all Regents students, male *and* female in 1845; and a substantially higher proportion of all *female* Regents students. The Regents broke enrollment information down by sex only for those students who qualified their institutions for per-pupil disbursements by pursuing "higher studies," a qualification favoring males over females. Nonetheless, women constituted just under half of the Regents academy students so designated (48.5 percent). Of these, 23 percent (1,509/6,563) attended the state's ten female academies. In other words, 23 percent of New York's advanced female students in 1845 were concentrated in the 6.5 percent of its academies which were all female. By comparison, 13 percent (920/6,955) of New York's advanced male students attended the 6.5 percent of its academies which were all male in that year.[24]

Since the state awarded funds on a per-pupil basis, the proportionately high enrollments at female institutions translated into proportionately large shares of the annual disbursement from the state's Literature Fund. Due to the structure of the state distribution system, however, this share of the total annual funds was not as great as the female academies' share of total enrollments. Until 1847, the state divided its total annual allotment of funds first among its eight senate districts, and then among the eligible institutions within each district. The proportion of Regents students who attended female academies in each district ranged from 0 to 30 percent. Overall, the 6.5 percent of state Regents academies that were exclusively female earned 12.4 percent of the total Literature Fund disbursement in 1845.[25]

The state support that Willard sought for female education, then, had in some measure been achieved. The question is what the consequences of this support were. In particular, did state funding and oversight of female education promote the higher standards of achievement,

---

[23] Enrollment figures compiled from *Report of the Regents* (1845), schedule no. 2, 64–73.

[24] Ibid., 64–73. Funds were awarded to academies on a per-pupil basis for the students "who are claimed by the trustees to have pursued for four months of said year, or upwards, classical studies, or the higher branches of English education, or both." Quoted from the Regents instructions in Miller, *Academy System*, 26.

[25] An academy earned funds only in proportion to its share of enrollments in its district, not in the state as a whole. In the first senate district, representing New York City, 30 percent of the total Regents students of both sexes attended an all-female academy; that academy therefore received 30 percent of the district's funds. One upstate district had no female academy to receive a share of the state fund. The proportion in other districts ranged from 8.7 percent to 19 percent. State fund figures compiled from *Report of the Regents* (1845), schedule no. 2, 64–73.

greater professional authority, and more systematic study that Willard believed they would?

The consequences of state support and oversight of female education were mixed. Two consequences might be regarded as positive with respect to Willard's objectives, and two as negative.

First, state support did promote the systematic study that Willard advocated. Judging from the course descriptions published in the annual bulletins of academies, Willard's convictions regarding the importance of systematic study were widely shared by female educators by the mid-1830s. By enabling institutions to hire additional teachers, and by providing incentives for teaching the "higher branches," the state reinforced this impulse toward systematization.

The search for order in female education is exemplified by the "system of instruction" published for Albany Female Academy in 1836, at which time the school was one of the largest Regents institutions of any kind in the state. According to the bulletin, the Albany Female Academy was divided into six departments. These six departments were in turn grouped into two sets of three each. The first three covered the equivalent of a good grammar education, while the second three represented the "higher branches" of English education. Studies in the core areas of language and literature, history and geography, and mathematics, progressed in difficulty over the full course. Natural sciences and natural philosophy were introduced in the higher departments, and the whole was capped by study of several branches of mental and moral philosophy.[26]

The vision was of young women undertaking a continuous course of study, lasting perhaps as long as six years, and culminating in graduation, complete with diplomas and honor awards. In describing its program, Albany Female Academy emphasized the systematic quality of the course, and the importance of systematization: "The Institution is designed to be useful and practical. The studies pursued, and the arrangement of the departments are believed particularly to contribute to this end; and from the experience of many years . . . the Trustees flatter themselves that such have been the results of the plan."[27]

Much the same vision and program of study, though less elaborate, could be found at other female academies. At Attica Female Academy in 1835, for instance, Emily Ingham, a former student of Zilpah Grant (a leading Massachusetts educator), described her own teaching simply in terms of the "elementary department" and the

---

[26] The "System of Instruction" for Albany Female Seminary in 1836 is reprinted in Sizer, *The Age of the Academies*, 168–74.
[27] Ibid., 170.

"remaining course of English studies." Nonetheless, the latter course included most of the subjects listed for the upper three departments at Albany. A year later, having become the founding principal of LeRoy Female Seminary, Ingham described her course as having four departments, comprising two divisions of two classes each. This more elaborate classification facilitated inclusion of chemistry and geology in the curriculum, but otherwise the order and content of the course were essentially the same as at Attica. The real difference, which the elaboration of classes and divisions represented, was the presence of additional teachers. At LeRoy, Ingham enjoyed the assistance of a second principal teacher, while at Attica she bore the burden of teaching alone.[28]

In this respect state funding materially advanced systematic study at female institutions. First, since literature funds were dedicated by law to support teachers, these funds facilitated employment of the additional teachers required for classing students and organizing instruction into divisions. Second, New York's policy of awarding funds only for advanced students provided an incentive for institutions to encourage women to complete more thorough courses of study. If more women continued their studies through the higher branches, the institutions they attended would receive more annual state funding.[29]

Thus, insofar as New York's support of female education provided incentives for systematic and higher study, this support raised educational standards for some women. The systematization of female education was part of the larger systematization of schooling, however. The second main consequence of state support and oversight of female education resulted from efforts to standardize teacher education. In this case the exercise of state authority, which Willard believed would promote *higher* educational standards, actually *undercut* standards of female education.

Standardization of teacher education occurred during the reform era of the 1830s and 1840s. The increased moral and political significance attributed to teaching in this era represented the fulfillment of one aspect of Willard's vision. Educated to think of their lives in terms of the larger, public purpose of educating others, female students could find challenges equal to their ambitions as leaders of educational reform. At the same time, however, as the increased importance of

---

[28] "Announcement of Attica Female Seminary, 1835," folder 37, box 1, and "Announcement of the LeRoy Female School and Teacher's Institute, 1836," folder 38, box 1, Ingham University Collection, LeRoy Historical Society, LeRoy, N.Y. For background on Emily Ingham, see Richard L. Wing, "Ingham University, 1857–1892: An Exploration of the Life and Death of an Early Institution of Higher Education for Women" (Ph.D. diss., State University of New York at Buffalo, 1990).

[29] Miller, *Academy System*, 24.

schooling enlarged the educated woman's field of labor in some respects, the standardization of teacher certification compromised the liberal character of her education in others.[30]

As part of the school reform movement, New York experimented with teacher education in existing academies. Beginning in 1834, the legislature granted special funds to selected academies to maintain departments for the certification of teachers. At first the state selected institutions on the basis of political geography: one per senate district. Under these terms no female academies were ever specifically charged with teacher education. From 1838 to 1844, however, the state distributed responsibility for maintaining teachers' departments to those academies already receiving the largest shares of the state's Literature Fund ($700 or more), which included several female academies.[31]

The aim of state support and regulation of teacher education was to improve the quality of teaching in the common schools. Certificates signified to employing school districts that the bearers had successfully completed a three-year English grammar education with some special attention to principles of teaching. At this point, however, certification functioned more as inspiration than regulation. Students could satisfy the certification requirements through the regular courses already offered at the academies, along with attendance at a special set of lectures. In the meantime, the state did not yet have the authority to require that local schools only hire certified teachers, and few school districts set standards so high of their own accord. If they did, a number of academy principals pointed out to the Regents, they would have no teachers, as teachers' salaries and social status were not nearly high enough to justify the investment of time and money which then would be required to become a teacher.[32]

The traditionally low status of common school teaching, already recognized by scholars as shaping a negative response to certification requirements from men, tempered the reactions of female educators to the state's efforts as well. Comments on the prospects for improving common schooling through teacher certification were actively solicited from participating academies and then published in the *Annual Report* of the Regents throughout the experimentation period. From the outset,

---

[30] On how the ideology of female education inspired women as teachers, see Anne Firor Scott, "The Ever Widening Circle: The Diffusion of Feminist Values from the Troy Female Seminary, 1822–1872," *History of Education Quarterly* 19 (Spring 1979): 27–46; David F. Allmendinger, "Mount Holyoke Students Encounter the Need for Life-Planning, 1837–1850," ibid., 27–46; and Polly Welts Kaufman, *Women Teachers on the Frontier* (New Haven, Conn., 1984).

[31] For a survey of New York's actions regarding teacher education, see Miller, *Academy System*, 131–71.

[32] Ibid., 136–40.

both single-sex and coeducational institutions identified the reputation of common school teaching as an obstacle to inducing students to complete such a program.[33]

A report from the all-male Canandaigua Academy summarized the dim prospects for its teachers' department in 1836 by stating "the young men of our county find so many avenues to business more lucrative and more inviting than the life of a teacher, that even after they have commenced a preparation for this employment, they willingly relinquish the object." Similarly, a communication from the coeducational Washington Academy explained its poor enrollment in the teachers' department in 1838 by saying that the common schools were "absolutely *stereotyped,* and the monotonous routine of their dull and unmeaning labors has remained as unbroken as the desert." St. Lawrence Academy, also coeducational, reported in 1837 that "the younger portion of the community . . . think the business of teaching a district school beneath their notice."[34]

Confronting similar conditions in 1842, the principal and trustees of Cortland Academy decided to direct its next course in teacher education specifically to females. At the same time, however, leaders of female academies themselves were expressing resentment that they should be asked to enroll students in courses that were *reduced* to the requirements of common school teaching. Officers of Rutgers, Troy, and LeRoy female seminaries expressed such a sentiment in 1842, with Troy's leaders simply telling the Regents that *all* their students were well qualified to teach common school; and with LeRoy's faculty and trustees explaining that they had higher goals, such as those of educating "thorough scholars, independent thinkers and reasoners, and useful members of society."[35]

This fear that adopting state requirements for teacher certification would somehow compromise students' educations was proved justified by new state regulations instituted in 1849. Under the new legislation, the state drastically reduced certification requirements, thereby bringing them more in line with common practice. Minimum age requirements for admission to teachers' certification programs were set at sixteen years of age for males and fourteen for females rather than at eighteen and sixteen as previously. The list of required studies, formerly consisting of a full English grammar education, was eliminated. In its place the state simply cataloged subjects from which a course of study might be chosen. The only required subject was principles of teaching, which

---

[33] Myra Strober and Audri Gordon Lanford, "The Feminization of Public School Teaching: Cross-sectional Analysis, 1850–1880," *Signs* 11 (Winter 1986): 212–35.

[34] *Report of the Regents* (1836), 124; ibid. (1838), 153; ibid. (1837), 121.

[35] Ibid. (1842), 152, 158, 156, 148.

could be satisfied through observations, lecture attendance, or practice. The whole period of study required for certification was set at only four months—as contrasted with the three-year course demanded under the earlier plan.[36]

In the case of teacher education, then, the consequence of the state's exercise of educational authority was *not* the promotion of a higher educational standard, as Willard had hoped, but the reduction of standards to the virtual minimum of existing practice. Moreover, state regulation trivialized the vocation which female educators had carved out for women as worthy of their talents and dedication, and as requiring the full development of their minds.

Ultimately, this impulse toward standardization threatened the very survival of female institutions. The third main consequence of New York's system of support and oversight of female academies was that it eventually undermined their corporate and financial independence. New state laws induced many coeducational academies to assume the status of tax-supported "high" schools within an increasingly standardized common school system. Female academies, unable to acquire such status, struggled to compete effectively for students and funds under changing conditions.

Changes in the funding arrangements for academies occurred first as a result of simple mathematics. As the number of academies and the size of their enrollments increased between 1820 and 1860, annual disbursements from the Literature Fund were more thinly distributed. Meanwhile, the state began to change the terms of support for "higher" education. In 1853 New York provided for organization of "academical departments" within the district common school system. This meant that in addition to providing elementary education, districts could join forces to offer programs in "higher" studies. As first written, the law allowed for a union district to adopt a local academy for the purpose. In 1864, however, the law required elimination of rate bills for academical departments, and in 1867, it required that departments be fully tax supported. Thus the adopted academies were made dependent on the district school system and subject to its governance.[37]

Faced with these changed circumstances, academies responded in several ways. Many that already served as local "high" schools of choice followed the suggestion of the law and assumed the status of "academical departments" for district schools. Over time, then, these institutions were effectively transformed into what were recognize as tuition-free public high schools.

---

[36] Miller, *Academy System*, 150–55.
[37] Ibid., 34–59.

Local districts were highly unlikely, however, to choose an all-female academy as the basis for their public high school. Nor were local citizens inclined to continue to supply voluntary subscription support once they had to pay taxes to support "academical" education elsewhere. Between 1853 and 1875, sixty-four academies were merged into high schools. None of these was female. In the same period, forty-eight academies closed entirely, to be replaced by new high schools in the same districts. Of those that closed, ten were female.[38]

Those institutions that managed to survive but did not become public high schools were forced to become different kinds of institutions than they had once been. Whether in their own cities or in the towns from which their students migrated, academies now had to compete with tuition-free, tax-supported rivals to attract students. One survival strategy was to become more elite, promising higher standards and greater social status to those students able and willing to pay. Utica Female Academy, Albany Female Academy, and Troy Female Seminary (later the Emma Willard School) all survived by pursuing this course.[39]

Another option was to formally recognize the need to compete at a higher level by reorganizing as a college or normal school. Two well-established female academies pursued this option. The thirty-year-old Rutgers Female Institute of New York City, once the largest Regents institution in the state, became Rutgers Female College in 1867. As a college, however, Rutgers enrolled much smaller student populations than it had as an academy. From a high of over six hundred students per year in the 1840s, Rutgers' enrollment dropped to eighty-one in 1871 and forty in 1880, where it stayed for the next decade and a half. It ceased operations in 1894.[40]

Similarly, the once highly successful LeRoy Female Seminary, first renamed Ingham Collegiate Institute in 1853, became Ingham University in 1857. Both of these changes were made to put the institution on a new financial footing. Neither promises from Presbyterians nor those from local business leaders were fulfilled, however; and a bequest from

---

[38] The female institutions that closed were Albany Female Seminary, Auburn Female Seminary, Batavia Female Academy, Catskill Female Seminary, Cooperstown Female Academy, Cortland Female Seminary, Penn Yan Female Academy, Schenectady Young Ladies' Seminary, Seward Female Seminary of Rochester, and Waterford Female Academy. Ibid., 54–57.

[39] Albany Female Academy and the Emma Willard School (Troy Female Seminary) exist to this day as private secondary institutions. Utica Female Academy was transformed in 1871 into a proprietary institution and closed in 1908. I am indebted to the Oneida County Historical Association for compiling this information.

[40] Rutgers' transformation and decline can be followed through the Report of the Regents (1867–94).

the founding teacher proved insufficient. Having never achieved stability, the university went bankrupt in 1892.[41]

The cases of New York women's colleges that did survive from midcentury reveal the nature of the problem that female institutions faced. Elmira Female College (1855), Vassar (1865), and Wells (1870) were founded with the support of major endowments from individual philanthropists. This means of support differed in scale and character from the communal voluntarism that had attended the founding of most academies in the 1830s and 1840s. Although state funds enabled four coeducational academies to become normal schools in the 1860s, industrial philanthropy and elite clientele were the only viable sources of support for female academies in the post–Civil War era.[42]

State support of female education in New York was thus relatively short lived. Beginning with incorporation charters in 1819 and Regents funding in 1828, this support peaked between 1840 and 1845 and declined along with the academy in the 1850s and 1860s, particularly after 1867. The state did charter new female institutions, and the Regents system continued to exist. The benefits that female institutions received from the state, however, rapidly diminished with the ascendence of the high schools, which dominated "higher" education in New York after 1875.[43]

Willard anticipated these results in some sense when she argued for a separate system of female education. She envisioned two distinct traditions of higher education, one classical and the other female, each funded and administered on its own terms. As it turned out, the two were funded on the same terms and under the same authority. Over time this meant the assimilation of one by the other.

The change was not unidirectional, however. The fourth, and perhaps most important, consequence of state support for female education was that it increased the influence of female education on coeducation. Female educators took the lead in establishing an alternative vision of "higher" education independent of initiation into the classical languages. With state support, the example and success of the female model in turn helped establish other, coeducational alternatives.

---

[41] Folders 24, 31, and 34, box 1, and Minute Book of the Trustees, Ingham University, 1852–82, box 2, Ingham University Collection.

[42] The philanthropists were Simeon Benjamin for Elmira College; Matthew Vassar for Vassar College; and Henry Wells for Wells College. See entries for Matthew Vassar and Henry Wells in the *Dictionary of American Biography* (New York, 1936), 19: 230–31, 639–40; and W. Charles Barber, *Elmira College: The First Hundred Years* (New York, 1955). Miller, *Academy System*, 55.

[43] Miller, *Academy System*, 53. Until 1875 there were still more academies than tax-supported high schools reporting to the Regents.

This model of female education, much like that articulated by Willard in 1818, prevailed among female educators by the mid-1830s. It emphasized systematic study and scientific human improvement. It established the teaching of sciences not simply as electives or subjects squeezed into a standard curriculum of Latin and Greek grammar, but as part of a distinct course of study grounded in history, geography, and English language and literature, and justified in terms of natural and moral philosophy. It did so, moreover, at a time when the place of science in the collegiate curriculum was far from settled; and when other coherent alternatives to the classical curriculum had not yet been established.[44]

This model was not limited to female institutions, however. Maintenance of a special "female department" was common in coeducational academies. It represented an effort to imitate the success enjoyed by female institutions, and to share in the state funds awarded for advanced female students. The coeducational Genesee Wesleyan Seminary, for example, advertised in 1834 that its female department offered instruction "in all the branches, both solid and ornamental, usually taught in female Seminaries." A comparison of male and female enrollment for that institution reveals a greater emphasis on natural sciences and philosophy for women than for men, and on history and modern languages.[45]

At the same time, more systematic plans of study appear to have prevailed for female education than for academy education generally. Having surveyed surviving catalogs for the sixty or so incorporated

---

[44] That Albany Female Academy and LeRoy Female Seminary shared this plan of instruction has already been noted. Thomas Woody's count of the frequency with which various subjects were offered at 162 female academies before 1871 provides a basis for generalization from those cases. After the basic subjects of arithmetic, English grammar, and reading, the 9 most frequent of 161 total subjects listed were natural philosophy (123); rhetoric (121); astronomy (116); geography (113); chemistry (112); plane geometry (110); moral philosophy (106); botany (101); and mental philosophy (100). Woody, *History of Women's Education*, 1: 563–55. On (mostly failed) experiments with science courses at male colleges, see Stanley M. Guralnick, *Science and the Ante-bellum American College* (Philadelphia, 1975). On the strong tradition of science education established at female institutions, see Deborah Jean Warner, "Science Education for Women in Antebellum America," *Isis* 69 (Mar. 1978): 58–67; Sally Gregory Kohlstedt, "In from the Periphery: American Women in Science, 1830–1880," *Signs* 4 (Autumn 1978): 81–96; Margaret W. Rossiter, *Women Scientists in America: Struggles and Strategies to 1940* (Baltimore, 1982), 1–28; and Carole B. Shmurak and Bonnie S. Handler, " 'Castle of Science': Mount Holyoke College and the Preparation of Women in Chemistry, 1837–1941," *History of Education Quarterly* 32 (Fall 1992): 315–34.

[45] The writer of the Genesee Wesleyan annual bulletin for 1836 rebuked parents for the fact that "so few females are permitted to enjoy the privilege of a *thorough* and *entire* course of instruction." "Bulletin of Genesee Wesleyan Seminary, 1836," Genesee Wesleyan Seminary Collection, Syracuse University Archives, George Arents Research Library, Syracuse University, Syracuse, N.Y. Despite the considerably larger number of

academies in Connecticut before 1860, Harvey S. Reed identified just three exceptions to the general lack of sequential and systematic programs of study offered. Two of the three were female academies, though female academies represented only 14.5 percent (9/62), of the total chartered institutions in the state.[46]

Connecticut did not have the same system of per-pupil disbursements as did New York, and so did not offer the same incentive for systematization at the academy level, whether for male or female students. The greater concern for systematization that Reed discovered among female institutions nonetheless reflected a real distinction between female education and general academy education through much of the pre–Civil War period. By 1850 Genesee Wesleyan, then the largest coeducational academy in New York State, had seven departments. "Instruction in all the departments is required to be thorough," the catalog emphasized, but only for ancient languages and the female department did the seminary advertise a specific, graduated course of study.[47]

In the 1850s, however, new conditions favored the assimilation of female education into new, more gender-integrated plans of "higher" schooling. Once "higher" education became subject to popular governance and tax support, taxpayers expected broad access to the goods that such education ostensibly bestowed, and that they were required to subsidize. At the same time, females constituted an increasingly high proportion of the enrollment of "higher" schools. In New York, over half the Regents students were female by 1850.[48]

---

male students than female at Genesee Wesleyan Seminary in that year (232 males, 144 females), female students of natural philosophy exceeded males 85 to 64 in 1834. Similarly, in chemistry females outnumbered males 33 to 20; in botany, 11 to 0; in astronomy, 7 to 0; in rhetoric, 50 to 48; in history, 56 to 11; in ancient geography, 13 to 0; in French, 23 to 10; and females constituted the entire enrollment in the "ornamental branches." Males, by contrast, dominated in Latin, algebra, Greek, Hebrew, bookkeeping, trigonometry, various branches of applied geometry (for surveying), and navigation. "Bulletin of Genesee Wesleyan Seminary, 1834," Genesee Wesleyan Seminary Collection.

[46] Harvey S. Reed, "The Period of the Academy in Connecticut, 1780–1850" (Ph.D. diss., Yale University, 1942), 77–79.

[47] "Bulletin of Genesee Wesleyan Seminary, 1850," Genesee Wesleyan Seminary Collection.

[48] On taxpayers' concerns regarding high schools, see Tyack and Hansot, *Learning Together*, 118–19, 137; M. Lucille Bowen, "The Rochester Free Academy," in *The History of Education in Rochester: Selected Articles on Rochester History*, ed. Blake McKelvey (Rochester, N.Y., 1939), 79, 85; Michael B. Katz, *The Irony of Early School Reform: Educational Innovation in Mid-Nineteenth Century Massachusetts* (Cambridge, Mass., 1968); and Maris Vinovskis, *The Origins of Public High Schools: A Reexamination of the Beverly High School Controversy* (Madison, Wis., 1985). As early as 1848 the academy student population in New York began to shift to being female dominated. *Report of the Regents* (1848), 91. For discussion of higher female enrollment and performance in high schools, see John L. Rury, *Education and Women's Work: Female Schooling and the Division of Labor in Urban America, 1870–1930* (Albany, N.Y., 1991), 11–48; and Tyack and Hansot, *Learning Together*, 114–45.

Institutions responded by developing alternative "graduating" courses of study for both men and women. In developing these alternatives, they drew on the classical and female traditions. At Rochester Central High School (1857), for example, the standard course of study included Latin and French, but no Greek, both natural sciences and higher mathematics, and some study of logic, criticism, and moral science in the senior year. Rochester and other schools also organized special "scientific" and "commercial" courses. While commercial courses were often a male preserve, scientific courses built on a tradition of science education already successfully established by female educators.[49]

The development of alternative courses represented an effort to further systematize "higher education" in the public schools. The new courses were to follow logically from instruction in the common schools, justify a publicly supported high school system, and confer recognition on both male and female students for achievement using something other than the classical model. In this sense, the impulse for systematic higher study, which had long characterized female education, became a model for the system as a whole.

* * * * *

A distinct idea of female education did live on in the new women's colleges of the 1860s, 1870s, and 1880s. Though they also strove to establish foundations in Latin and Greek classics and higher mathematics which conferred collegiate status, the new women's colleges set high standards in the study of modern literature; developed courses and facilities in the natural sciences which rivaled and surpassed those of prestigious male colleges; and educated women in ideas of scientific human improvement and social reform which were rooted in the old moral philosophy, even as they inspired a generation of progressive reform.[50]

This continuity of educational philosophy and curricular emphasis between the antebellum female academies and the postbellum women's colleges suggests that Willard was successful in her plan for improving female education. Female educators did gain authority to uphold a higher standard of achievement for their students, even if ultimately they did so outside the system of state support. It is worth being more precise, however, in identifying which aspects of Willard's plan worked and which did not.

---

[49] Bowen, "The Rochester Free Academy," 88–90.

[50] See, for example, Patricia Palmieri, "In Adamless Eden: A Social Portrait of the Academic Community at Wellesley College, 1875–1920" (Ed.D. diss., Harvard University, 1981).

Willard's argument was that to truly educate women, female institutions and educators had to acquire independence. Institutions that were "founded on public authority," "permanent," and "endowed with funds" provided teachers with the independence necessary to discipline their students, and to avoid becoming "victims of their caprice." Willard emphasized state funding and authority as the means to such independence. The record suggests, however, that the state itself could also undercut teachers' standards, as when New York regulated teacher education. On the other hand, when New York used its resources and authority to provide incentives for advanced study, rather than to maintain minimum requirements, it did help promote high standards for students.

As the fate of female institutions in New York also reveals, however, state support made the long-term survival of alternative educational visions such as Willard's problematic. Different educational visions thrived for a time within the academy system because each institution enjoyed independent corporate legal status and government, and because no institution was completely dependent on one source of support. Once the state had incorporated the majority of academies into a tax-supported common system, however, that foundation of independence was seriously threatened, and the drive for integration and standardization could not be resisted except by moving outside the dominant system.

The results of this experiment merit examination as we consider more recent proposals for reform in education. The historical tendency of systematic requirements to reproduce the minimum and supplant alternative visions is worth keeping in mind. So also is Willard's experience regarding the problems of operating schools on market principles. It was these problems that made Willard first request aid from the New York state legislature in 1818.

Eventually, to maintain the tradition of female education, female institutions had to replace state support with new sources of funding. In one sense this loss of state support represented a failure of Willard's original appeal. In another sense, though, it validated her argument that corporate and financial independence were critical to the realization of an alternative vision of education.

THE LSAT: NARRATIVES AND BIAS

LESLIE G. ESPINOZA*

Fred is tall, dark, and handsome, but not smart.
People who are tall and handsome are popular.
Popular people either have money or are smart.
Joan would like to meet anyone with money.

If the statements above are true, which of the following statements must also be true?

  I. Fred is popular.
  II. Fred has money.
  III. Fred is someone Joan would like to meet.
    (A) I only
    (B) II only
    (C) III only
    (D) I and II only
    (E) I, II, and III[1]

This question is from a recent Law School Admission Test (LSAT) examination.[2] The LSAT is the gatekeeper to the legal profession. The test is used by law schools in combination with undergraduate grade point average as the main criteria for admission to the profession.[3] The test can keep you out of law school, it can determine which law school you attend, and it can greatly affect the way you feel about yourself and your potential for success while in law school.[4]

---

  * Professor of Law, University of Arizona College of Law; Assistant Professor of Law, Boston College Law School, 1992-94.
  1. LSAT, Logical Reasoning, Question 14, June 1988 (all LSAT questions on file with author).
  2. The LSAT is an admissions test administered by the Law School Admission Council (LSAC). The Law School Admission Services (LSAS) administers the LSAC's programs and provides other services to American and Canadian law schools. LAW SCHOOL ADMISSION SERVICES, LSAT 1992-93 INFORMATION BOOK (1992) [hereinafter LSAT INFO. BOOK 92-93].
  3. *Id.* at 6 ("Almost all ABA-approved law schools require both the LSAT and the Law School Data Assembly Service (LSDAS), including undergraduate academic record.").
  4. Despite the obvious limits of a three or four-hour standardized test, research indicates that test takers' self-image is greatly affected by their scores. Studies analyzing the Scholastic Aptitude Test (SAT) indicate internalization of test measures. *See* PHYLLIS ROSSER, CENTER FOR WOMEN POLICY STUDIES, THE SAT GENDER GAP: IDENTIFYING THE CAUSES 22 (1989) ("Unfairly low test scores . . . become a self-fulfilling prophecy for many girls and

Prior to 1979, the LSAT and other standardized tests used for educational admission purposes were shrouded in secrecy.[5] Testing agencies refused to grant access to the tests to test takers, researchers, or state governments.[6] Thus, there was no way to analyze the appropriateness of questions, the correctness of answers, or even the accuracy of scoring of individual examinations.[7] What was known was that women and minorities had substantially lower scores than white males.[8] Additionally, anecdotal tales of biased,

---

young women; lower scores inspire lower expectations and encourage women to apply to less competitive colleges and universities than their grades would otherwise warrant."); *see also id.* at 41 ("Students' overall perceptions are closer to test feedback than to grade feedback, which is beneficial for boys' self image but damaging to girls'."). Despite superior academic records, girls average 19 to 60 points lower on the SAT than boys. Thus, girls judge themselves to be less able than their grades would indicate, and less able than boys. *Id.* at 41-42, 71. *See* Sharif v. New York State Educ. Dep't, 709 F. Supp. 345, 355, 362 (S.D.N.Y. 1989) (finding that the state's sole reliance on SAT scores to award state scholarships is discriminatory because it disparately impacts young women and concluding that the consistent disparity between males' and females' scores cannot be explained through "neutral" variables); William Glaberson, *U.S. Court Says Awards Based on SAT's Are Unfair to Girls,* N.Y TIMES, Feb. 4, 1989, § 1, at 50 (outlining the ruling in *Sharif,* which was the first in the nation to link standardized tests and discrimination against a certain group).

5. *See* Dario F. Robertson, *Examining the Examiners: The Trend Toward Truth in Testing,* 9 J.L. & EDUC. 167, 170-79 (1980) (examining the legislative response to test secrecy in general and discussing the impotence of test takers when attempting to address grievances against the testing services prior to Truth in Testing laws). Robertson claimed that test takers were "defenseless in both the marketplace and the courtroom . . ." because of the secrecy, and that test subjects "ha[d] no cognizable right to receive more information than the test agencies deem[ed] appropriate to provide." (citation omitted) *Id.* Although much of the testing material was kept secret, researchers were able to examine some test questions and forms in order to critique them. *See* David M. White, *An Investigation Into the Validity and Cultural Bias of the Law School Admission Test, in* TOWARDS A DIVERSIFIED LEGAL PROFESSION 66, 132-33 (David M. White ed., 1981) [hereinafter White, *Investigation Into Validity and Bias*] (using samples from the LAW SCHOOL ADMISSION BULLETIN and LSAT preparation material to demonstrate existence of bias in the actual test by inferring that the same biases in the samples will, necessarily, show up in the actual test).

6. Robertson, *supra* note 5, at 167, 174-79 (discussing the difficulty third parties had in obtaining internal studies, financial statements, statistics, or actual questions from the testing services, and other information which was "vital for public review . . ." of the statistical methods used to score exams prior to the Truth in Testing laws).

7. *See* Jocelyn Samuels, Note, *Testing Truth-in-Testing Laws: Copyright and Constitutional Claims,* 81 COLUM. L. REV. 179, 190 (1981) (elucidating some of the purposes behind Truth in Testing laws, which include assuring and encouraging the validity and objectivity of the test, and the accuracy of the scoring and calculating process); *see also* Robertson, *supra* note 5, at 167, 178-79 (discussing the test taker's lack of recourse against the testing companies prior to the Truth in Testing laws when test scores were reported in error, late, or completely lost).

8. *See* Lloyd Bond, *Bias in Mental Tests, in* ISSUES IN TESTING: COACHING, DISCLOSURE, AND ETHNIC BIAS 55, 56 (Bert F. Green ed., 1981) (citing the general fact that white students, on average, receive higher scores on standardized tests than non-whites, and that males, as a group, outperform females); DAVID M. WHITE, NATIONAL CONFERENCE OF BLACK LAWYERS, THE EFFECTS OF COACHING, DEFECTIVE QUESTIONS, AND CULTURAL BIAS ON THE VALIDITY OF THE LAW SCHOOL ADMISSION TEST 73 (1984) [hereinafter WHITE, EFFECTS OF COACHING, QUESTIONS, AND BIAS] (discussing lower minority scores on the LSAT); Cecil R. Reynolds & Robert T. Brown, *Bias in Mental Testing: An Introduction to the Issues, in* PERSPECTIVES ON BIAS IN MENTAL TESTING 4 (Cecil R. Reynolds & Robert T. Brown eds., 1984) (introducing the general controversy that surrounds standardized mental tests and the systematic group performance differences on standardized intelligence and aptitude tests); David M. White, *Culturally Biased Testing and Predictive Invalidity: Putting Them on the Record,* 14 HARV. C.R.-C.L. L. REV. 89,

disturbing questions and actual evidence of bias in the sample questions published in the LSAT Information Book began to be documented.[9]

In 1979, New York State passed a "Truth in Testing" law.[10] It required testing agencies to disclose test questions and answers to the state.[11] The law allowed test takers to request a copy of the test they had taken, the correct answers, and their own score sheets.[12] The law also required test agencies to gather statistical information on the differential performance of women and minorities.[13] The New York law was promptly challenged by the Association of American Medical Colleges (AAMC), the organization which administers the Medical Colleges Admissions Test (MCAT).[14] In 1980, Federal District Court Judge McCurn preliminarily enjoined enforcement of the Truth in Testing law as to the MCAT.[15] However, until 1991, administrators of the other major admissions tests, including the Scholastic Aptitude Test (SAT), the LSAT, and the Graduate Record Examination (GRE), complied with the law during the pendency of the litigation.[16]

114-20 (1979) [hereinafter *Culturally Biased Testing*] (examining the test score gap between non-whites as compared to whites and charting the test score gaps on the LSAT as compared to GPAs of whites and non-whites); David M. White, *Pride, Prejudice and Prediction: From Brown to Bakke and Beyond*, 22 How. L.J. 375, 377, 391-92 (1979) [hereinafter *Pride, Prejudice and Prediction*] (analyzing the implementation of differential admissions programs, instituted because minorities, generally, have lower average LSAT scores and lower average GPAs); *see also* Wade J. Henderson & Linda Fores, *Implications for Affirmative Admissions After Bakke*, in TOWARDS A DIVERSIFIED LEGAL PROFESSION 13, 25-26, 36-41 (David M. White ed., 1981) (discussing the lower LSAT scores of Council on Legal Education Opportunity fellows, all of whom are educationally and economically disadvantaged, and most of whom are minorities); Edward Bronson, *Trial by Numbers: The LSAT and Cultural Bias*, 34 GUILD PRAC. 33 (1977) (charging that cultural and gender bias in the LSAT generally exists because its form is conducive to bias).

9. *See* White, *Investigation Into Validity and Bias, supra* note 5, at 66, 155-56 (discussing reactions of some individuals when they were read a sample question from the *Law School Admission Bulletin* that used a servant as the subject); WHITE, EFFECTS OF COACHING, QUESTIONS, AND BIAS, *supra* note 8, at 35-43 (discussing the results of a National Conference of Black Lawyers' study and the responses of people who were shown various LSAT questions and using anecdotal reactions to questions to explain and reveal forms of bias in testing).

10. New York Standardized Testing Act, N.Y. EDUC. LAW §§ 341-48 (McKinney 1988 & Supp. 1993).

11. *Id.* § 342 (McKinney 1988).

12. *Id.* § 342(2) (McKinney 1988).

13. *Id.* § 341-a (McKinney 1988).

14. Association of Am. Medical Colleges v. Carey, 482 F. Supp. 1358 (N.D.N.Y. 1980) [hereinafter AAMC I], *summary judgment granted*, 728 F. Supp. 873 (N.D.N.Y. 1990) [hereinafter AAMC II], *rev'd sub nom.*, *vacated*, Association of Am. Medical Colleges v. Cuomo, 928 F.2d 519 (2d. Cir. 1991) [hereinafter AAMC III], *cert. denied*, 112 S. Ct. 184 (1991).

15. AAMC I, *supra* note 14.

16. *See infra* notes 224-243 and accompanying text (discussing the testing agencies' compliance with Truth in Testing laws and explaining the subsequent stipulation agreements entered into by the agencies regarding test disclosure pending the *AAMC* litigation); Kevin Sack, *Appellate Panel Grants Reprieve to Law on Tests*, N.Y. TIMES, March 14, 1991, at B3 (examining the Educational Testing Service's national and voluntary policy to disclose test answers).

Between 1979 and 1991, the content of most standardized admission tests was disclosed.[17] Nevertheless, the administrators of the MCAT continued to refuse to disclose, and the preliminary injunction remained in place.[18] The State of New York continued to try to negotiate compliance with all other standardized testing organizations.[19] In 1988, the AAMC moved for summary judgment.[20] It alleged that the Truth in Testing law violated its copyright interest in the MCAT.[21] The district court granted summary judgment in 1990.[22] On appeal, the Second Circuit removed the injunction and remanded the case for trial on the facts.[23]

While the AAMC claimed that disclosure of the MCAT would harm its copyright interest,[24] there is a well established exception to copyright protection known as the Fair Use Doctrine.[25] The applicability of the Fair Use Doctrine is determined by balancing the pub-

---

17. AAMC II, *supra* note 14, at 874, 878 (mentioning specifically the disclosure of the SAT and the LSAT in compliance with the New York Truth in Testing law over the previous ten years).

18. AAMC II, *supra* note 14, at 874. The temporary restraining order that had been issued almost a decade earlier was replaced by a permanent injunction by the district court. AAMC II, *supra* note 14, at 889.

19. *See infra* notes 224-243 and accompanying text (explaining the temporary resolution of the disclosure issue pursuant to stipulation agreements between the agencies and the State of New York).

20. AAMC III, *supra* note 14, at 521.

21. AAMC I, *supra* note 14, at 1361; AAMC II, *supra* note 14, at 874-75; AAMC III, *supra* note 14, at 521-22.

22. AAMC II, *supra* note 14, at 878-79, 889.

23. AAMC III, *supra* note 14, at 521.

24. AAMC I, *supra* note 14, at 1361; AAMC II, *supra* note 14, at 874-75; AAMC III, *supra* note 14, at 521-22.

25. The Fair Use Doctrine establishes that there are certain uses of copyrighted material that are considered non-infringing, "fair" uses. Although it was originally only recognized at common law, the Doctrine has been codified in the Copyright Act of 1976. *See* 17 U.S.C. § 107 (1988 & Supp. II 1990) (setting forth the four factors to be considered in determining whether a use of a work will be an acceptable Fair Use). Section 107 lists examples of uses that might be found fair, including: uses "for purposes such as criticism, comment, news reporting, teaching (including multiple copies for classroom use), scholarship, or research." *Id.* However, this list is not exhaustive. The Fair Use Doctrine and the four factors in the Copyright Act, which shape the use of the defense, have been developed and interpreted through case law. *See, e.g.,* Harper & Row Publishers, Inc. v. Nation Enters., 471 U.S. 539 (1985) (discussing the Fair Use Doctrine and making a distinction between commercial and noncommercial uses of copyrighted works). The Supreme Court has stated:

The factors enumerated in [section 107] are not meant to be exclusive: '[s]ince the doctrine [of fair use] is an equitable rule of reason, no generally applicable definition is possible and each case raising the question must be decided on its own facts.'

Id. at 510 (quoting H.R. Rep. No. 1476, 94th Cong., 2d Sess. 65, *reprinted in* 1976 U.S.C.C.A.N. 5659, 5657).

There has been much commentary regarding the history and development of this exception to copyright protection. *See* MELVILLE B. NIMMER & DAVID NIMMER, NIMMER ON COPYRIGHT § 13.05 (1982) (describing the Fair Use Doctrine and the elements used by courts to determine whether the use of a work is infringing or fair); Pierre N. Leval, *Toward a Fair Use Standard,* 103 HARV. L. REV. 110 (1990) (explaining the development of the Fair Use Doctrine and the general landscape of copyright law in which it is applied); Lloyd L. Weinreb, *A Comment on the Fair Use Doctrine,* 103 HARV. L. REV. 1137 (1990) (exploring the analytical confusion

lic interest in the free flow of information and the private interest of the copyright holder in controlling and being rewarded for her or his work.[26]

The significant public interest in the disclosure of actual test questions was recognized by both the district court and the Second Circuit in reviewing the Truth in Testing law. However, the courts gave significantly more weight to the perceived negative economic impact that disclosure might have, although the circuit court was unclear about the harm in requiring a rehearing.[27]

Despite the concerns raised by the courts, disclosure is the only effective way to monitor the bias of the testing process.[28] It is not enough for the AAMC and other test agencies, such as the Law School Admission Council (LSAC), which administers the LSAT, to disclose statistical and descriptive information about their tests. There is a narrative content to each test question that affects the test taker's ability to analyze that question.[29] More importantly, the narrative content of individual questions creates a discourse, a thematic

---

over the application of the Fair Use Doctrine by a number of courts, despite congressional enactment and interpretation by the Supreme Court).

26. DC Comics Inc. v. Reel Fantasy, Inc., 696 F.2d 24, 27-28 (2d Cir. 1982).

27. The district court recognized and discussed the public interest involved in test disclosure. However, the court found that the other factors to be considered under the Fair Use Doctrine, such as economic injury, strongly supported the plaintiffs (AAMC) in this case. Thus, the court found in favor of the AAMC. AAMC II, *supra* note 14, at 885, 887-88. Perhaps the court did not recognize the full extent of the public interest being served by requiring disclosure of standardized exams and therefore improperly allowed the other factors to overshadow it.

The circuit court also recognized the public interest that is served by the Truth in Testing law. However in support of its holding, it cited Harper & Row Publishers, Inc. v. Nation Enters., 471 U.S. 539 (1985) which elevated the economic interest of the copyright holder above all other Fair Use factors and recognized Fair Use as a privilege. The court could not rule on the issue of injury to the AAMC and therefore could not adequately complete the balancing test between the public interest and the harm. The *AAMC* court stated, "a balance must be struck between the benefit to the public and personal gain the copyright owner will receive if the use is denied." AAMC III, *supra* note 14, at 526 (citing MCA, Inc. v. Wilson, 677 F.2d 180, 183 (2d Cir. 1981)). The case was remanded to the circuit court for further consideration on this issue. AAMC III, *supra* note 14, at 524-26.

28. The importance of disclosure was recognized by the circuit court at one point: "It is clear that the goal of the State Act [,Truth in Testing,] is to subject the MCAT to non-commercial comment and criticism." AAMC II, *supra* note 14, at 884. It could be asserted, however, that although the court recognized the importance of disclosure, it did not fully appreciate its importance, especially with regard to the issue of bias.

29. In order to effectively uncover this narrative content it is important for researchers to have access to various components of standardized tests. See WHITE, EFFECTS OF COACHING, QUESTIONS, AND BIAS, *supra* note 8, at 73-84 (exploring the importance of using the actual text in analyzing test bias and score discrepancies among groups and discussing the obstacles that exist when one is unable to have access to this information); *see also* Lorrie A. Shepard, *Identifying Bias in Test Items, in* ISSUES IN TESTING: COACHING, DISCLOSURE, AND ETHNIC BIAS 79, 81 (Bert F. Green ed., 1981) (explaining that focus on the internal properties of a test is important when ascertaining bias, because testers' development of guidelines aimed at reducing bias are done using the full text of the questions, not just statistical evidence of the results).

content, for the whole test.[30] That discourse has been one that favors the dominant social force in our society, white men.[31] Only through disclosure of actual questions can we begin to understand the relationship between test narratives and bias.

Part one of my article will examine test bias through a narrative analysis of actual LSAT questions. Part two will describe the legal action by test agencies to eliminate mandated disclosure and thus the public's ability to do narrative test analysis. Part three will analyze the need for continuing narrative analysis. The article concludes that it is only through the exposure and disclosure of standardized tests that true eradication of bias can occur. Researchers must be free to examine questions appearing on actual tests in order to expose bias. Additionally, test disclosure highlights the questionable premise of prediction of a student's future academic performance upon which the use of the LSAT and other standardized tests for admission purposes is based.[32] The LSAT only predicts a general correlation between ranges of test scores and first-year law school grades.[33] Should admission decisions be based

---

30. Discourse is the unspoken, assumed viewpoint of the test. *Cf.* Martha Minow, *The Supreme Court, 1986 Term — Foreword: Justice Engendered*, 101 HARV. L. REV. 10 (1987) (analyzing the Supreme Court's approach to racial and cultural differences and noting that differences are created and highlighted through comparisons to what is considered "the norm"; explaining that the Court's attempted use of simple and clear solutions to legal problems exacerbates differences); Leslie G. Espinoza, *Masks and Other Disguises: Exploring Legal Academia*, 103 HARV. L. REV. 1878, 1885 (1990) (exploring the role of Critical Race Theory in identifying and legitimizing the minority experience and explaining that most minorities, especially those in legal academia, face a common social situation that degrades them); Richard Delgado, *Mindset and Metaphor*, 103 HARV. L. REV. 1872, 1874-77 (1990) (discussing the use of metaphors as a standard by which to analyze and measure the law). Delgado states, "One way in which we make sense of the world around us is by means of narrative structures, stories, and metaphors." *Id.* at 1874.

31. Nancee L. Lyons, *FAIRTEST: Nation's Leading Watchdog Over Standardized Tests On a Mission of Fairness*, BLACK ISSUES IN HIGHER EDUC. at 8 (Oct. 12, 1989). Bob Schaeffer, FairTest's Public Education Director, states that, "[t]he very nature of the test itself may be biased because it is a fast-paced, multiple-choice exam with a premium on guessing and being superficial . . . [i]t is . . . a brash white boy's game." *Id.* at 8. Furthermore, FairTest asserts that an important factor in lowering women's scores is that the "reading comprehension passages and other questions feature men and male-oriented sports . . . ." *Id.*

32. *See* Katherine Conner & Ellen J. Vargyas, *The Legal Implication of Gender Bias in Standardized Testing*, 7 BERKELEY WOMEN'S L.J. 13 (1992) (revealing tenuous links between performance on the SAT and actual college performance and stating that the implications and data from one type of standardized test are instructive with regard to other standardized tests, such as the LSAT). Additionally, there is little research focusing on the predictive validity of post-secondary admissions tests for minority females. Conner and Vargyas note, "Differences in the predictive value of test scores also present serious problems for minority students . . . ." *Id.* at 30-31.

33. LSAT INFO. BOOK 92-93, *supra* note 2, at 125. The information book states:
Correlation is stated as a coefficient for which 1.00 indicates an exact correspondence between candidates' test scores and subsequent law school performance. A coefficient of zero would indicate nothing more than a coincidental relationship between test scores and subsequent performance . . . The correlation between LSAT scores and first-year law school grades varies from one law school to another . . .

on first year performance? Should expected first year performance be the primary criterion for predicting who is worthy of admission to the profession, who will be a "good lawyer"?

I.   THE NARRATIVE OF LSAT QUESTIONS

The LSAT is promoted as an essentially objective test.[34] It is lauded as being able to predict which applicant will be a good law student.[35] Recall the LSAT question about Fred and Joan reprinted at the beginning of this article. What did it make you think about? What associations came to mind? The question is from the "Logical Reasoning" section of the test.[36] Did the story which comprises the question have any effect on your ability to discern the objective steps of logic?

The narrative bias of test questions is the atmospheric, sometimes subtle, sometimes blatant, often pervasive bias of stories, manners, sensitivities, and paradigms.[37] It is the same bias confronted in law

---

Correlations between LSAT scores and first-year law school grades ranged from .11 to .64 (median is .41).
LSAT INFO. BOOK 92-93, *supra* note 2, at 125.

34. While the LSAC never actually uses the word "objective," nor claims to be completely infallible, it portrays the exam as broadly applicable and useful. No specific words of caution are issued with regard to certain groups, such as women and minorities, who traditionally score lower on their exams.

When discussing the exam revision process that occurred in the late 1980s, the LSAC states, "We also examined the performance characteristics of various subgroups of LSAT takers to determine whether the test optimally met the measurement requirements of the diverse population of LSAT takers and law school applicants." LAW SCHOOL ADMISSIONS SERVICES, THE LAW SCHOOL ADMISSIONS TEST: SOURCES, CONTENTS, USES 5 (September 1991) [hereinafter LSAT: SOURCES, CONTENTS, USES]. Although it is not stated, the assumption is that they were able to accomplish this task when incorporating changes into the June 1991 version of the LSAT. The LSAC goes on to state that the concern of the Council is that the LSAT be "fair, valid, [and] reliable . . ." *Id.* Later the LSAC states that the new version of the LSAT, instituted in June 1991, functions as well, or better than, the old version in "predicting academic success in the first year of law school." *Id.*

The bulletin further states, in its *Cautionary Policies* section, that "[b]ecause the LSAT is administered to all applicants under standard conditions and each test form requires the same or equivalent tasks of everyone, LSAT scores provide a standard measure of abilities." *Id.* at 26. There is no acknowledgement of any limitations or possible bias within the test or the testing process. The obvious inference is that the LSAT is essentially an objective measure of an individual's aptitude for law school, regardless of the race or sex of the test taker.

35. *Id.* at 5 ("[The] LSAT is designed to perform . . . the task of predicting academic success in the first year of law school.").

36. *See* LSAT INFO. BOOK 1992-93, *supra* note 2, at 52 (describing the Logical Reasoning section and the purpose behind it); *see also* White, *Investigation Into Validity and Bias, supra* note 5, at 137-38 (analyzing and discussing the section in the LSAT BULLETIN 1979-80 that describes the purpose of the Logical Reasoning section).

37. Narrative analysis is increasingly employed by legal scholars to bring new perspective to law in order to reveal hidden bias. *See* Mary I. Coombs, *Outsider Scholarship: The Law Review Stories,* 63 COLO. L. REV. 683, 695-96 (1992) (remarking that outsider scholarship "seeks . . . to cross the boundaries that define [the] community by speaking to the dominant community, but in a different voice . . ." and arguing that the voice often expresses itself through narratives and stories that expose oppression which is overlooked and ignored in mainstream legal

school examinations,[38] moot court questions,[39] casebooks,[40] placement interviews,[41] court procedures, judicial language, and evidentiary conventions.[42]

---

discourse) (citation omitted); Kathryn Abrams, *Hearing the Call of Stories*, 79 CAL. L. REV. 971 (1991) (analyzing and discussing the use of narrative in feminist legal scholarship); Richard Delgado, *Storytelling for Oppositionists and Others: A Plea for Narrative*, 87 MICH. L. REV. 2411 (1989) (examining the use of narratives in legal discourse to challenge the status quo that is perpetuated and protected by dehumanizing mainstream legal discourse).

38. *See* PATRICIA J. WILLIAMS, THE ALCHEMY OF RACE AND RIGHTS 80-95 (1991) (discussing the author's experience with law school faculty and biases after bringing a student complaint of race and gender bias in an exam to their attention).

39. There was a recent controversy at New York University School of Law regarding a moot court question drafted to require an argument about a fictional mother's custody rights. The main issue in the problem was the mother's sexual orientation. New York University School of Law, Moot Court Board, *Subject: Child Custody, Mike Brody v. Carol Brody* (case No. 14-09) *in* 14 MOOT CT. CASEBOOK 381-460 (1990); *see* Jerry Adler, *Taking Offense*, NEWSWEEK, Dec. 24, 1990, at 48 (mentioning, in a general discussion of "political correctness," the controversy surrounding New York University Law School's moot court topic based on the custody rights of a lesbian mother).

40. Traditional law school case books and courses have been criticized as not taking varied perspectives into consideration in their approach to teaching law. *See* Nancy S. Erickson, *Sex Bias in Law School Courses: Some Common Issues*, 38 J. LEGAL EDUC. 101, 104-05, 112-16 (1988) (analyzing the contents of classes, class offerings, and casebooks; finding generally widespread bias in law school classes and materials); Mary I. Coombs, *Crime in the Stacks, or a Tale of a Text: A Feminist Response to a Criminal Law Textbook*, 38 J. LEGAL EDUC. 117 (1988) (condemning the sexism of a particular criminal law textbook and integrating the use of narrative to illustrate the analysis and conclusion of the article). However, attempts have been made to eradicate bias by taking a unique approach to the discussion of traditional legal concepts. *See, e.g.*, Mary Joe Frug, *Re-Reading Contracts: A Feminist Analysis of a Contracts Casebook*, 34 AM. U. L. REV. 1065 (1985) (taking a feminist approach to the analysis of a contracts casebook, finding that readers' views about gender affect their understanding of a law casebook, the law, and themselves).

41. *See* Lisa G. Markoff, *Dean Suspends Baker and McKenzie From 1989-'90 Campus Interviews*, NAT'L L.J. , Feb. 13, 1989, at 4 (relating an incident where a law firm recruiter asked a law student racist questions and the Dean of the University of Chicago Law School responded by suspending the firm from interviewing on campus); *see also* Chris Downey, *Firms Try to Heighten Recruiters' Sensitivity*, N.Y.L.J., March 4, 1991, at 1 (reviewing the many steps that are being taken to help reduce the incidence of discriminatory and improper questions during interviews); Jane Cooperman, *Law Office Management; Recruitment*, NAT'L L.J., July 31, 1989, at 20 (discussing the importance of training law firm recruiters in non-discriminatory interviewing techniques and listing interview "don'ts" to avoid discriminatory interviews); Paula S. Linden, Gail G. Peshel & Jamienne S. Studley, *Recruitment; The Jobs Graduates Grabbed*, NAT'L L.J., March 27, 1989, at 16 (discussing the fact that discrimination against women and minorities in legal employment still exists and may be evidenced in the form of offensive interview questions).

Discrimination in attorney hiring and promotion is also a continuing problem. A 1988 National Law Journal survey found that while 40% of new associates hired were women, only 23% of all lawyers at firms were women and "since 1982, women have increased their share of partnerships by only one percent per year." Indeed, in 1987, only eight percent of partners overall were women. The numbers were far worse for minorities. Doreen Weisenhaus, *White Males Dominate Firms: Still a Long Way to Go for Women, Minorities*, NAT'L L.J., Feb. 8, 1988, at 1. The National Law Journal's 1990 survey confirms that little has changed in the legal profession in recent years. *See* Rita Henley Jensen, *Minorities Didn't Share in Firm Growth*, NAT'L L.J., Feb. 19, 1990, at 1 (listing a breakdown of the number of women and minorities in many of the nation's largest law firms).

42. *See* Elizabeth M. Schneider, *Task Force Reports on Women in the Courts: The Challenge for Legal Education*, 38 J. LEGAL EDUC. 87, 87-88, 92, 95 (1988) (connecting biases in the courts to law schools and addressing the need for changes in legal education because of its critical role in affecting and reforming the legal environment); COMMONWEALTH OF MASSACHUSETTS, REPORT OF THE GENDER BIAS STUDY OF THE SUPREME JUDICIAL COURT (1989), *partially reprinted in*

Bias delegitimizes the whole of the admission test enterprise. Over the years, I collected LSAT questions that I found to be offensive.[43] I have shared these questions with law students for their free associational responses.[44] Their perspective reveals the relationship between narrative test bias and disempowerment.

A.   LSAT Images of Who You Should Be

Remember Fred: "tall, dark, handsome, but not smart. People who are tall and handsome are popular. Popular people either have money or are smart."[45] Next enters the rapacious Joan who would like to meet anyone with money.[46] One student commented, "This question clearly puts down women, making it seem they pursue men with money (any man with money). It also puts down men, making it seem that men who are tall, dark and handsome are not smart."[47] Another student commented that the question reminded her of her mother's puzzlement that she wanted to go to law school, when she could just marry a lawyer.[48]

Test questions are stories. They can also be a form of subtle, unconscious psychological warfare.[49] This tactic is the way that the

---

MARY JOE FRUG, WOMEN AND THE LAW 2-16 (1992) (examining gender bias in the judiciary and making recommendations regarding reforms to ensure equal treatment of men and women in the court system); SENATE COMM. ON THE JUDICIARY, THE VIOLENCE AGAINST WOMEN ACT OF 1991, S. REP. NO. 197, 102D CONG., 1ST SESS. 43-44 & nn.40, 41 (1991) (stating that women often face discrimination and gender bias in the court system, and citing many studies that have been commissioned by the states documenting this pervasive problem).

43. Since 1980, I have collected approximately 100 questions that register from outrageously to highly offensive on my personal meter. The question gathering endeavor was both inspired and assisted by my friend since law school, David White. David White, head of Testing for the Public, is a long-time critic of standardized testing. *See generally* WHITE, THE EFFECTS OF COACHING, QUESTIONS, AND BIAS, *supra* note 8, at 27-73 (criticizing the LSAT generally and specifically addressing bias in testing).

44. Questions were shared with students on an individual basis and in small group settings. Responses to questions have been gathered informally. Students were asked to give voluntary, anecdotal responses to LSAT questions presented both in and out of the classroom setting. Many of the students who participated in these discussions were women and minorities. Student reactions were gathered from 1989 to 1992. Law students in Women and the Law classes, research seminars, and a Law and Literature group from both the University of Arizona College of Law and from Boston College Law School were included. (Results on file with the author).

45. *See supra* note 1.

46. *See supra* note 1.

47. *See supra* note 44.

48. *See supra* note 44.

49. Studies indicate that women do better on test questions that are related to human relationships and humanities rather than the world of practical affairs, especially regarding math questions. Connor & Vargyas, *supra* note 32, at 26 n.67. *See* ROSSER, *supra* note 4, at 43 (examining each question on a given SAT exam and comparing its ease or difficulty for the different sexes; finding that seventeen items were considerably easier for one sex than the other).

Furthermore, it is often overlooked that a defective or biased question will affect a test taker's performance on subsequent questions by interrupting his or her concentration. In this

test reminds "outsiders"[50] that they are indeed outsiders.[51] In a situation of stress and tension,[52] these questions bring out socialized self-doubt.[53] The outsider candidate is reminded of the formidable

---

light, a biased question will negatively impact the test taker's score on more than one question. *See* Shepard, *supra* note 29, at 86 (citation omitted) (discussing the negative "carry-over" effects of an offensive question item to subsequent questions; explaining that this phenomenon affects the test taker's performance on later questions); WHITE, EFFECTS OF COACHING, QUESTIONS, AND BIAS, *supra* note 8, at 75 (supporting the hypothesis that confusion and distraction may result from biased questions and affect the test taker's performance on subsequent questions; criticizing the commonly utilized "item-group" analysis that measures a test taker's reaction only to specific questions).

50. "Outsider" is a term adopted by Professor Mari Matsuda to designate persons of color, feminists, gays, lesbians, and other oppressed groups. Mari Matsuda, *Public Responses to Racist Speech: Considering the Victim's Story*, 87 MICH. L. REV. 2320, 2323 n.15 (1989). In support of this alternative terminology, Matsuda explains that the term "minority" is a misnomer because of the actual large numbers of persons in excluded groups. *Id.* Professor Matsuda also discusses the importance of recognizing outsider perspectives to various legal issues. *See* Mari Matsuda, *Affirmative Action and Plowed-Up Ground*, 11 HARV. WOMEN'S L.J. 1, 2 (1988) (articulating the need to incorporate outsiders' visions to combat racist preconceptions).

51. Two additional examples from the LSAT illustrate the disempowered message of question/stories for women test takers. These passages remind women that examples of their status as outsiders can easily be seen in everyday life. *See* LSAT, Logical Reasoning, Question 22, October 1983:

> Although there are more women working for wages today than ever before, the average wage earned by female workers is only about 59 percent of the average earned by male workers. This is a lower ratio than it was in 1955, when the average income of female workers was 63.9 percent of that earned by male workers. [Answer choices excluded];

see also LSAT, Logical Reasoning, Question 6, March 1984:

> The principle of equal pay for equal work cannot, by itself, eliminate the discrepancy between the earnings of men and women. Women and men are not evenly distributed among ocupations [sic] in our society; men tend to predominate in the higher-paying occupations. Therefore, even if the principle of equal pay for equal work were applied, —— would result. [Answer choices omitted].

52. *See generally* Ray Hembree, *Correlates, Causes, Effects, and Treatment of Test Anxiety*, 58 REV. OF EDUC. RES. 47, 56-58, 60-62, 73 (1988) (compiling results of 562 studies related to test anxiety and finding that anxiety causes poor performance). Hembree shows that females have higher anxiety than males at all schooling levels, that African-Americans have higher anxiety than whites in elementary school, and that Hispanics have higher test anxiety than whites at all ages. *Id.* at 60-62. He concludes that self-esteem and test anxiety have a strong inverse relationship and that low self-esteem causes a high level of test anxiety and thus poorer performance. *Id.* at 73.

53. Standardized tests have a strong impact on an individual's self-evaluation of her or his skills and worth. *See* Connor & Vargyas, *supra* note 32, at 20 ("The evidence strongly suggests that students adjust their college expectations based on their SAT or ACT scores; Lower-scoring females apply to less competitive colleges and universities than their grades would warrant."); ROSSER, *supra* note 4, at 22, 41-42 (discussing findings which reveal that students adjust their expectations of the caliber of school that will accept them based on their scores on standardized tests, rather than grades or other criteria); *cf.* Richard Delgado, *Words That Wound: A Tort Action for Racial Insults, Epithets, and Name-Calling*, 17 HARV. C.R.-C.L. L. REV. 133, 137 (1982) ("The psychological responses to [racial slurs] consist of feelings of humiliation, isolation, and self-hatred . . . . Consequently, it is neither unusual nor abnormal for stigmatized individuals to feel ambivalent about their self-worth and identity.") (citation omitted); Charles R. Lawrence III, *The Id, the Ego, and Equal Protection: Reckoning With Unconscious Racism*, 39 STAN. L. REV. 317, 317-18 (1987) (showing that injury from racial inequality can be profound and severe regardless of the motives behind the action which caused the injury); Espinoza, *supra* note 30, at 1884 (discussing the self-doubts experienced by legal scholars in various situations).

barriers to breaking into the professions.[54]

Take, for example, the following LSAT question:

> The problem with expanding work opportunities for women is that it results in a dangerous situation for our country; fewer children will be born and those children will be less well prepared to perform well in school and in society.
>
> Which of the following presuppositions is (are) necessary to the argument above?
>
> I.   The more education a woman has, the more likely she is to choose to work outside her home.
>
> II. Women who choose to work are better mothers than those who choose to be homemakers.
>
> III. Working women have fewer children than women who do not join the work force.

---

54. *See, e.g.*, LSAT, Logical Reasoning, Question 14, October 1988:
   In order to get good grades, a college student must either have a high IQ or resort to cheating. Unfortunately, a high IQ is something a person is born with; nothing you do in life can help you get a better one. Therefore, if a student who had a low IQ upon entering college ends up getting good grades, he ——. . . . (choices omitted).
This question reinforces the bias of a life-time of standardized tests. It is particularly troublesome because of the long-documented bias of the Stanford-Binet IQ exam and other intelligence tests. *See* STEVEN J. GOULD, THE MISMEASURE OF MAN 146-234 (1981) (tracing the development of the popular Stanford-Binet IQ test, and the uses and misuses of the test throughout the years). Although the Binet test was initially developed to identify children with learning disabilities, and not to rate the intelligence of all children, it was eventually developed into a mass-marketed exam by Dr. Lewis M. Terman, a professor at Stanford University (thus the name Stanford-Binet). Dr. Terman was the "primary architect of its [Stanford-Binet's] popularity." *Id.* at 174-75. The guidelines for narrow and controlled use of the Binet test were disregarded in the United States. *Id.* Furthermore, the widespread use of the Stanford-Binet IQ tests and those modeled after it, often developed out of racist theories of hereditary intelligence, as in the case of Terman. *Id.* at 175. Despite the broad use of IQ exams during the last fifty years, and the reliance upon them, there is no independent confirmation for the proposition that tests accurately measure intelligence. *Id.* at 177.
   Researchers have questioned the legitimacy of intelligence tests. *See* Bond, *supra* note 8, at 63 (breaking down the issues of testing bias, analyzing tests and questioning whether bias exists in the internal structure and criteria of tests, in situational factors, and in the employment and use of tests). Bond discusses a study comparing the results of intelligence tests given to a group of African-American children who had been adopted by white parents to the results of tests given to white adoptee children in the same geographical area. Bond, *supra* note 8, at 64. This study was done to question the theory that intelligence is genetic and to challenge findings which attributed minorities' lower scores on tests to their genetic makeup. The study concluded that the African-American children tested had scores higher than the national white average, above the African-American average, and above other African-Americans reared in the same area. Thus, the results are inconsistent with genetic explanations for differing IQ performance between whites and African-Americans. Bond, *supra* note 8, at 65-66.
   The issue of test bias is a complicated and controversial one. Most academics who have studied the issue have been unable to fully explain the reason for differing outcomes among groups. Bond, *supra* note 8, at 61-62. While many testing agencies have developed formal guidelines and review procedures for spotting and removing biased questions, the most difficult problem is that beyond blatantly biased questions, it is hard to predict ahead of time which questions will be the most difficult for which groups. *See* Shepard, *supra* note 29, at 79, 85-87, 99 (discussing the prediction and analysis of both subtle and statistical bias in test questions and recognizing the difficulty in attributing different meanings in test questions to bias or other "legitimate" reasons).

    (A) II only
    (B) III only
    (C) I and II only
    (D) II and III only
    (E) I, II and III[55]

Now imagine yourself a woman taking the LSAT. If you do not have children, but at least want to leave open the possibility of having children, the question forces you to think of this very difficult and personal choice. If you have children, and are now taking the big step of disrupting your whole life to go to law school, what is this question explicitly telling you? Your children will suffer because you insist on pursuing your own selfish dream of success.[56] In any event, the question makes the test taking personal. It takes the woman reader off-track.[57] The question is gender-related on its face. It is gender-biased in the devious way that it appears to be a neutral question about "logic." However, the question is instead a reminder that for women, the demands that go hand-in-hand with expanded opportunities can leave us with the choice that is no choice at all.[58]

---

55. LSAT, Logical Reasoning, Question 4, October 1982.

56. Women are also reminded that their education will probably be wasted in society's judgment. See LSAT, Logical Reasoning, Question 5, October 1980:

> Mr. Jones argued that money spent on higher education is wasted. He supported his argument by referring to the case of a woman who, at great expense, completed a Ph.D. in English literature only to decide later to move to a remote area and devote her life to meditation, reading no books of any kind. [answer choices omitted]

Many of my women students strongly responded to this question. In their minds, meditation was a metaphor for having and raising children. See supra note 44; see also Leslie G. Espinoza, Constructing a Professional Ethic, 4 BERKELEY WOMEN'S L.J. 215, 226 (1989-90) ("Women students who choose to make quite reasonable compromises internalized their failure to emulate the model of lawyering constructed through the mythology of the institution. Indeed, much of the exclusion of women from the power centers of the law is based far more on their inability 'to maintain the appearance of total dedication to their careers.' ") (citation omitted).

57. See Cathy L. W. Wendler & Sydell T. Carlton, An Examination of SAT Verbal Items for Differential Performance by Women and Men: An Exploratory Study, Paper for the American Educational Research Association Annual Meeting (April 1987) (on file with FairTest, National Center for Fair & Open Testing, Cambridge, Mass.) (discussing the possible reasons for women's lower SAT scores and explaining that one possible factor might be that women are more adversely affected than men "by negative, possibly upsetting, questions."); see also Shepard, supra note 29, at 79, 86 (referring to the negative "carry-over" effects of offensive questions to subsequent questions, implying that test takers are distracted from the intended purpose of the question by questions biased against them); WHITE, EFFECTS OF COACHING, QUESTIONS, AND BIAS, supra note 8, at 75 (supporting the hypothesis that confusion and distraction may result from biased questions, thus taking the test takers off-track and affecting their performance on subsequent questions as well).

58. See Espinoza, supra note 56, at 226 (discussing a woman's difficulty when she must choose between a career and a family or do both with heightened stress and guilt). See generally Susan Gore & Thomas W. Mangione, Social Roles, Sex Roles and Psychological Distress: Additive and Interactive Models of Sex Differences, 24 J. HEALTH & SOC. BEHAV. 300, 301 (Dec. 1983):

> [T]he mental health of employed married women is still poorer than that of employed married men — and not markedly better than that of married homemakers .... From a sex-role perspective, these findings are not surprising. Whereas work is

Women test takers are not being hypersensitive. Nor are they grappling with imaginary hobgoblins. The conflict between career and family is a real one for women.[59] In her controversial "Mommy-track" article in the Harvard Business Review, Felice Schwartz sets forth the common wisdom and the actual facts regarding the work/family conflict:

> Like many men, some women put their careers first. They are ready to make the same trade-offs traditionally made by the men who seek leadership positions. They make a career decision to put in extra hours, to make sacrifices in their personal lives, to make the most of every opportunity for professional development. For women, of course, this decision also requires that they remain single or at least childless or, if they do have children, that they be satisfied to have others raise them. Some 90 percent of executive men but only 35 percent of executive women have children by the age of 40.[60]

The social reality is that for women who are now forty, the decision to become professionals has different consequences and costs than it has for men. Efforts to equalize women's opportunities for career and family continue.[61] These efforts, however, are undermined by the LSAT's reiteration of the discriminatory stereotypes of the past, however much they are couched in the neutral language of Logical Reasoning.[62]

---

compatible with the family-role expectations of men, it is less compatible with the family roles of most women, thus resulting in role stress and the poorer mental health of women (citations omitted).

59. *See* FRUG, *supra* note 42, at 81-133 (devoting an entire chapter of her casebook to the work/family conflict). Frug writes:

Workplace responsibilities often conflict with family duties in ways that produce significant stress and substantial barriers to women as they seek to assimilate and to advance in their labor force jobs.

Id. at 2; Joan C. Williams, *Gender Wars: Selfless Women in the Republic of Choice,* 66 N.Y.U. L. REV. 1559 (1992) (analyzing the pressure on women to take care of their children and parents at the expense of their careers); Deborah L. Rhode, *Perspectives on Professional Women,* 40 STAN. L. REV. 1163 (1988) (examining the barriers to women's career advancement that continue to exist because of the dual burdens women face with work and family responsibilities); Karen Czapanskiy, *Volunteers and Draftees: The Struggle for Parental Equality,* 38 UCLA L. REV. 1415 (1991) (exploring the volunteer father/draftee mother conceptualization in family law and how a reallocation of childcare duties between parents would alleviate part of the conflict women feel in the workplace).

60. Felice N. Schwartz, *Management Women and the New Faces of Life,* HARV. BUS. REV., Jan.-Feb. 1989, at 65, 69.

61. *See* Faye Fiore, *Women's Career - Family Juggling Act,* L.A. TIMES, Dec. 13, 1992, at D3 (discussing the approach taken by some employers to reduce the pressures of the work/family conflict on their female employees); *Work and Women,* BOSTON GLOBE, June 14, 1992, at 86 (reporting the results of a survey which found that women are still suffering from the pressures of the work/family conflict and concluding that more flexible hours are necessary to alleviate pressures).

62. This stereotyping that highlights historical discrimination is evident in one of the few LSAT questions addressing people with disabilities. *See* LSAT Logical Reasoning, Question 14, June 1982:

Lawyers are supposed to rise above the emotions of the problem. Perhaps it is logical that the LSAT should construct an emotional obstacle course. Maybe it should screen out all applicants who cannot objectively apply the rules of logic. However, this is not the intent of the law schools that use the test to make admission decisions. More importantly, the discourse of the test does not challenge the emotional steadiness of white males. The "distractor questions" are discriminatory because they effect only the outsider test taker.[63]

B.   The LSAT Vision of What the Law Should Be

For many students, the LSAT is their first official contact with the study of law and the construction of legal professionalism. The questions within the test often present a social world view that excludes outsider test takers. Frequently the context of the question distorts the content or the meaning of the question for the test taker. For example, one question places us at a dinner party in a mythical land:

> In Evalsland, where it is legal to hold slaves, the guests at a dinner party get into a debate.
>
> One of the guests contends that slavery is a cruel institution. But the host contends that the slaves themselves like it. To prove his point, the host called in the household slaves, all of whom affirm that they do indeed find their condition not simply tolerable but extremely pleasant.
>
> Which of the following would seriously weaken the host's argument in the passage above?
>
> I.   Whenever slaves are offered their freedom they usually take it.
>
> II. There have been numerous slave revolts in recent years.
>
> III. All religions have forbidden one man to be a master over another.
>
> IV. Slavery is an extremely inefficient institution because free labor is much more productive.
>
> (A) I and II only
>
> (B) I and IV only

The demand for bus and subway systems accessible (sic) to and useable by handicapped people in wheelchairs actually discriminates against all but the most athletic of the handicapped, because most people in wheelchairs do not have the physical strength to wheel their chairs from their homes or offices to subway or bus platforms. [question and answer choices omitted].

63.   Distractor questions are those questions that cause the reader to become distracted from the application of logic to find an answer. *See supra* note 50 (defining "outsider" as a term of art); *see also* WHITE, EFFECTS OF COACHING, QUESTIONS, AND BIAS, *supra* note 8, at 88-91 (showing how word choices in LSAT questions have different associations for minority test takers).

(C)   II and III only

(D)   III and IV only

(E)   I, II, III and IV[64]

As one African-American student expressed, first the question reminds you that you are Black, then it forces you to try to divorce yourself from yourself, to pretend that you can look at the question without *you* looking at the question.[65] Furthermore, how can this be called Logical Reasoning when it would be useless to make any logical arguments to the host, who is obviously so blind that he will never see. Logic has no place in this situation at all.[66]

The question begins with the premise that it is legal to hold

---

64.   LSAT, Logical Reasoning, Question 4, February 1986.

65.   *See supra* note 44. The LSAC administers the LSAT and has chosen to allow this type of material to appear on tests without regard to its effect on the test taker. Indeed, the following sample LSAT question was highly criticized in the early 1980's:

> A servant who was roasting a stork for his master was prevailed upon by his sweetheart to cut off one of its legs for her to eat. When the bird was brought to the table, the master asked what had become of the other leg. The man answered that storks never had more than one leg. The master, very angry but determined to render his servant speechless before he punished him, took the servant the next day to the fields where they saw storks each standing on one leg. The servant turned triumphantly to the master, but the master shouted and the birds put down their other legs and flew away. "Ah sir," said the servant, "you did not shout to the stork at dinner yesterday; if you had he too would have shown his other leg."

LAW SCHOOL ADMISSION SERVICES, LAW SCHOOL ADMISSION BULLETIN AND LSAT PREPARATION MATERIAL, Logical Reasoning, Questions 3-4 (1979-80); *see* White, *Investigation into Validity and Bias, supra* note 5 at, 154-55 (commenting that this LSAT question presented is "[p]erhaps the most startling and revealing passage encountered."). The question presents an offensive story which can be critiqued in different ways and can affect readers in varied ways. *Cf.* Robert Williams Jr., *Taking Rights Aggressively: The Perils and Promises of Critical Legal Theory for Peoples of Color*, 5 LAW & INEQ. J. 103, 104-08 (1987) (using a parable about a Native-American "Grandfather" and an elevator to discuss the different positive and negative aspects of Critical Legal Theory for peoples of color).

66.   Logic divorced from content is also evident in the following two LSAT passages:

> By 1670, African slaves took the place of the vanished Native Americans brought to the Caribbean a century earlier from areas farther north. Since many of the Africans were already immune to malaria and yellow fever, relatively few of them died on the island plantations as a result of these diseases. But ultimately the differing immunities of the two slave groups did not matter, for the Africans succumbed to other gastrointestinal and infectious diseases. [answer section omitted].

LSAT, Logical Reasoning, Question 14, December 1984.
The question asks the reader to do a logical comparison of death and disease of oppressed people. It is an example of the same kind of mentality that viewed slavery as an economic calculus rather than a human tragedy. Expression of this viewpoint serves to further alienate outsider test takers. The second passage presents another comparison:

> John Stuart Mill compared the position of married Englishwomen in the nineteenth century to that of slaves. Marital slavery was even worse, he said, because married women had fewer rights than slaves and more onerous duties and were expected to love their masters and their situation. How silly Mill's comparison is can be seen by turning the tables and thinking of husbands as slaves and wives as slaveholders. That makes equal sense, and the analogy collapses. [answer choices omitted].

LSAT, Logical Reasoning, Question 7, February 1989.
These two questions offer a new kind of competition between oppressed groups looking up from the bottom. It forces the test taker to separate logic from the actual content of the question.

slaves.[67] A vision of law is presented that directly contradicts currently held ideals. The law presented in the question validates the institution of slavery. Assessment of slavery now becomes a game of rationality and logic, not a recognition of oppression. This excising of value from the analysis of slavery, as required by the question, obscures the real content and legacy of slavery. The pretense of the question, the way the question pretends that normative judgment is not relevant, is the most relevant and biased aspect of the question.

The outsider test takers are reminded that they are clearly outside, excluded.[68] Not only are they outside, they are subjugated just like the slaves in the question. They have to pretend that the question and the whole test process is not only tolerable, but just and "logical."

In a quest for diversity within test questions, the LSAT only succeeds in objectifying outsiders, not including them. What the white people say is what is important. The outsider remains the object, the subject is the dominant society. This is exemplified in an LSAT question discussing diversity in the academy:

> The universities should not yield to the illiberal directives of the Office of Civil Rights that mandate affirmative action in hiring faculties. The effect of the directives to hire minorities and women under threat of losing crucial financial support is to compel universities to hire unqualified minorities and women and to discriminate against qualified nonminorities and men. This is just as much a manifestation of racism, even if originally unintended, as the racism the original presidential directive was designed to correct. The consequences of imposing any criterion other than that of qualified talent on our educational establishments are sure to

---

67. *See supra* note 64.

68. Examples of LSAT questions excluding outsider test takers also include questions regarding nationality, ethnicity, and stereotyping based on race. *See, e.g.,* LSAT, Logical Reasoning, Question 7, October 1987:

> Few United States high school students achieve fluency in languages other than their native English. Which of the following, if true, would best explain the causes of the situation described above? [answer choices omitted].

Of course, far from all high school students in the United States call English their "native" language. This assumption alienates those test takers who do not agree with the question's premise. *See* LSAT, Logical Reasoning, Question 12, February 1988:

> In a certain mythical community where there are only two social classes, people from the upper class are all highly educated, and people from the lower class are all honest. Maria is poor. If one infers that Maria is honest and uneducated, one presupposes that class status in the mythical society depends upon . . . [answer choices omitted].

Why "Maria"? Is Maria by any chance Hispanic? This is one of a handful of questions using non-Anglo names. The question creates a vision of insiders and outsiders based on ethnicity and class.

be disastrous in the quest for new knowledge and truth, as well as subversive of our democratic values.

Which of the folowing (sic), if true, would considerably weaken the argument above?

   I. The directive requires universities to hire minorities and women when no other applicant is better qualified.

  II. The directive requires universities to hire minorities and women only up to the point that these groups are represented on faculties in proportion to their representation in the population at large.

III. Most university employees are strongly in favor of the directive.

   (A) I only

   (B) II only

   (C) III only

   (D) I and II only

   (E) II and III only[69]

As one student commented, "Why base a question on such controversial racial issues. It is really disturbing."[70] Most of the outsider students who read the question were so upset by the imposing nature of the text that they were unable to focus on arguments that would weaken the statement.[71]

This is diversity askew. Many students commented that they find themselves constantly in the position of justifying affirmative action.[72] There is always the implicit, raised eyebrow, that no matter what they say, they cannot really be logical about the issue, because after all they are certainly the beneficiaries of the policy.[73]

The distracting nature of the question is certainly of concern. The question takes affirmative action and discusses it only from the perspective of white males.[74] Additionally, even the answer

---

69. LSAT, Logical Reasoning, Question 22, October 1988.

70. *See supra* note 44.

71. *See supra* note 44.

72. *See supra* note 44.

73. For a discussion of the stigma associated with affirmative action see Leslie G. Espinoza, *Empowerment and Achievement in Minority Law Students' Support Programs: Constructing Affirmative Action*, 22 U. MICH. J.L. REF. 281, 286-90 (1989) (discussing the stigmas involved as a result of using academic support programs for minority law students) and STEPHEN L. CARTER, REFLECTIONS OF AN AFFIRMATIVE ACTION BABY (1991) (suggesting that affirmative action creates more stigma than help for African-Americans and other racial minorities).

74. LSAT questions continually force outsiders to place themselves in the perspective of white males. *See e.g.* LSAT, Reading Comprehension, Question —, December 1991, *reproduced in* THE OFFICIAL LSAT PREP TEST III, Dec. 1991, form 2LSS13 (discussing Native American diversity and analyzing Navajo weaving from the perspective of Anglo influence).

choices[75] focus on qualifications rather than past discrimination.[76] Rather than being inclusive, it is a diversity that increases exclusion. It requires test takers to justify their inclusion, regardless of qualifications. It increases the sense of "otherness."

II.   CHALLENGE TO TRUTH IN TESTING LAWS

Standardized tests now play an accepted and significant role in admissions for almost all educational levels in the United States.[77] In order to be considered for admission to college, most undergraduate schools require the SAT[78] or its companion test, the ACT. These tests are also required for admission to professional schools. Most medical schools require the MCAT, most business schools require the GMAT, and most law schools require the LSAT.

---

75.   An analysis of questions from the LAW SERVICES INFORMATION BOOK, published after implementation of the LSAC's newest sensitivity review, reveals continued bias. Often this form of bias is more subtle and occurs in answer choices. Certain answer choices are disproportionately attractive to outsiders. For example, one reading comprehension passage analyzes the life and work of Phillis Wheatley, a former slave and early American poet. The first question following the passage asks for the best expression of the main idea in the passage. LSAT INFO. BOOK 92-93, *supra* note 2, at 58-59. Answer choices include: "(B) Although Phillis Wheatley had to overcome significant barriers in learning English, she mastered the literary conventions of eighteenth-century English as well as African aesthetic cannons." and "(C) Phillis Wheatley's poetry did not fulfill the potential inherent in her experience but did represent a significant accomplishment." Answer (C) is the correct answer. LSAT INFO. BOOK 92-93, *supra* note 2, at 58-59. When I first read the question, I chose answer (B)—to me it was the main theme and story of the passage. Similarly, the first question following a reading passage on sex-related wage differentials in the 1991-92 Law Services Admission Book, asks for the best title to the passage. LAW SCHOOL ADMISSION SERVICES, LSAT 1991-92 INFORMATION BOOK 74-75 (1991)[hereinafter LSAT INFO. BOOK 91-92]. Choices include: "(B) Women in Low-Paying Occupations: Do They Have a Choice?; (C) Sex Discrimination in the Workplace; (D) The Roll of Social Prejudice in Women's Careers." *Id.* On my first read, I was certain that (C) or (D) were the correct answers. Wrong again. The correct choice impliedly places the subordinate economic status of women in their own hands.

76.   *See* Richard Delgado, *The Imperial Scholar: Reflections on a Review of Civil Rights Literature*, 132 U. PA. L. REV. 561-63 (1984) (commenting on the lack of minority scholarship on civil rights issues and explaining that this authorship by primarily white males ignores the past history of discrimination by creating a one-sided view of civil rights legal literature).

77.   In 1926, the College Board, a nonprofit organization, introduced the Scholastic Aptitude Test (SAT). The SAT is now administered through the Educational Testing Service (ETS). ETS is the largest test maker in the country. It is a non-profit company which designs standardized tests for over 375 clients. Gil Sewall, *Tests: How Good? How Fair?*, NEWSWEEK, Feb. 18, 1980, at 99-100 (examining different types of standardized testing and criticism about them). ETS currently designs the LSAT. However, during the 1980's the LSAT was at times designed in-house by LSAC and at times by the test designer ACT. *See* LSAT: SOURCES, CONTENTS, USES, *supra* note 34, at 1-4 (giving the history and evolution of the LSAT).

78.   Since its introduction in 1926, the College Board has always described the SAT as a supplementary measure to other admissions criteria. From its inception, the Board warned of a danger in placing too great an emphasis on the test scores. John Elson, *The Test That Everyone Fears*, TIME, Nov. 12, 1990, at 93 (discussing the problems that have arisen with the SAT and the resulting revisions of the test by the trustees of the College Board).

A. Description of Truth in Testing Laws

1. Political Backdrop to Regulation

By 1979, standardized tests, which had been used for decades as admission criteria, were severely criticized.[79] The criticism focused on the secrecy surrounding administration and evaluation of the tests.[80] Secrecy compounded the prevalence of race and gender bias.[81] During this time, Ralph Nader's consumer organization, Congress Watch Public Citizen, issued a study which condemned the Educational Testing Service (ETS), the creator and administrator of the SAT.[82] The six-year Nader study concluded that the SAT successfully predicted college performance in only one out of ten cases.[83] The study found that SAT score correlation to family income was much stronger than the correlation to college performance.[84] Based on new evidence of bias, the 1.8 million member National Education Association campaigned to abolish standardized testing in the public schools.[85] Additionally, studies indicated that the tests were "coachable," and that the results of the tests were not

---

79. Recent commentary has documented over a decade of criticism of standardized testing. *See, e.g.*, Susan Campbell, *Opinions Differ on Suitability, Fairness of Standardized Tests: Standardized Tests Are: A. Needed B. Unfair C. Disputed*, HARTFORD COURANT, October 2, 1992, at B1 (finding, through interviews with high school teachers, that standardized test results do not reflect a logical pattern consistent with a student's achievement); Sean Piccoli, *Charges Persist SATs Biased Against Women and Minorities*, WASHINGTON TIMES, August 5, 1991, at G6 (discussing allegations that the SAT promotes cultural, racial, and gender bias).

80. *See Minutes of Proceedings, New York Joint Public Hearing of the Senate and Assembly Standing Committees on Higher Education* 2-4 (May 9, 1979) [hereinafter *NY Joint Hearing*] (remarks of Sen. Kenneth P. Lavalle, Chairman, Senate Committee on Higher Education) (arguing against the secretive nature of standardized testing); *see also* Robertson, *supra* note 5, at 180-93 (1980) (discussing the legislative response to secrecy in standardized testing and Truth in Testing laws).

81. Because test makers were able to keep test questions secret, the biases in the questions went unchecked by third parties. Nevertheless, some researchers were able to gain access to test forms and sample questions and discovered the presence of bias. *See* Bronson, *supra* note 8, at 33 (1977) (charging that the form of standardized tests is the basis for producing racial bias in testing); White, *Culturally Biased Testing, supra* note 8, at 107 (1979) (showing cultural biases through statistics in LSAT testing); *cf.* David A. Weber, *Racial Bias and the LSAT: A New Approach To the Defense of Preferential Admissions*, 29 BUFF. L. REV. 439 (1975) (discussing the need to reexamine the LSAT to determine if it is unconstitutional based on its inherent racial bias); White, *Pride, Prejudice and Prediction, supra* note 8, at 375 (1979) (exploring the need to continue the legacy of *Brown v. Board of Education* with the integration of professional schools by eliminating the racial bias in LSAT testing).

82. Nader's organization published the results of its six-year study in *The Reign of ETS* (1979). This study was used by the media to expand on the criticism of ETS and standardized testing. *See, e.g.*, Sewall, *supra* note 77, at 99, 100 (using quotes from Nader's ETS study to question the fairness of standardized testing).

83. *See* Sewall, *supra* note 77, at 101 (highlighting the results of the Nader study).

84. *See* Sewall, *supra* note 77, at 101 (discussing the Nader study's commentary on the weaknesses of the SAT).

85. *See* Sewall, *supra* note 77, at 101 (discussing the reaction of the National Education Association to the Nader study). ETS commented that the study was "deliberately fraudulent" in its finding that there was little or no correlation between scores in standardized testing and a student's subsequent grades in college. Sewall, *supra* note 77, at 101.

always an apt indicator of students' later performance.[86]

Legislative efforts to control admissions tests centered on "Truth in Testing," which would, at minimum, require test makers to release their examinations for inspection.[87] California passed a Truth in Testing law in 1979.[88] It was soon followed by a similar law in New York.[89] New York's law, passed after extensive legislative hearings, was a more comprehensive law, requiring disclosure of actual test questions.[90] It became the model for Truth in Testing proposed legislation.[91] In 1979, five other states had legislation pending.[92] By early 1980, fourteen states and the federal government were considering similar laws.[93] Indeed, such politically formidable organizations as the Parent Teacher Association (PTA) and the National Association for the Advancement of Colored People (NAACP) banded together to support the national legislation.[94]

2. New York's Truth in Testing Law

The New York Truth in Testing law, officially entitled the Standardized Testing Act, applies to "any test that is given . . . at the expense of the test subject and designed for use and used in the process of selection for post-secondary or professional school admissions."[95] Rather than taking on the whole world of standardized tests, the law only regulates tests used for college and professional school admissions.[96] The two main provisions of the New York law address the specific concerns enunciated in the Act's legislative

---

86. *See* White, *Pride, Prejudice and Prediction, supra* note 8, at 392-96 (noting that studies on LSAT results show that LSAT scores are better at distinguishing between the races of the test takers than they are at predicting a student's performance in law school).

87. *See* Sewall, *supra* note 77, at 104 (explaining the New York state legislature's support of test disclosure).

88. CAL. EDUC. CODE §§ 99150-99164 (Deering 1993).

89. N.Y. EDUC. LAW § 340-348 (McKinney 1988 & Supp. 1993).

90. *Id.* § 341(1) (McKinney 1988); *see* Samuels, *supra* note 7, at 179-81 (discussing New York's Truth in Testing law and the controversy surrounding its requirements of disclosure of test contents, test scores, and evaluative studies).

91. *See* Sewall, *supra* note 77, at 99 (discussing the reaction of other states to the passage of New York's Truth in Testing law).

92. *See* Joanne Omang, *Making the Grade: Standardized Tests Are Under Attack; Critics Drive for 'Truth in Testing'*, WASH. POST, Dec. 26, 1979 at A10 (noting that in 1979, California, Colorado, Florida, Maryland, Ohio, and Pennsylvania all had legislation pending to regulate standardized testing).

93. *See* Sewall, *supra* note 77, at 99 (noting that New York's Truth in Testing law inspired fourteen other states and the federal government to consider bills requiring test makers to disclose the content of their exams to the public).

94. *See* Sewall, *supra* note 77, at 104 (showing that the supporters of a national Truth in Testing law included influential groups).

95. N.Y. EDUC. LAW § 340 (1) (McKinney 1988).

96. N.Y. EDUC. LAW § 340(1) (McKinney 1988). *But see* Connor & Vargyas, *supra* note 32, at 13 (describing other uses of standardized tests such as employment and elementary school tracking, and detailing the gender bias inherent in this type of testing).

hearings.[97]

The first provision of the Act requires test agencies to file and make public their research information, studies, and evaluations of the tests.[98] This provision allows New York state officials, through the Commissioner of Education, to have a better basis to evaluate the tests.[99] Study disclosure provides more information upon which to examine the evaluations of the tests and claims made about them by the test agencies.[100] The provision also allows outside researchers, like the author of this article, to have access to basic, fundamental information regarding the test and its outcome correlations. It makes available to researchers the LSAC's and ETS's internal studies. In drafting this provision, legislators took into account the testimony, at the New York hearings, of a number of researchers regarding repeated requests to get even simple data from the test agencies which went unanswered or were refused.[101] Prior to the passage of the law, ETS had the ability to suppress internal studies that were critical of the tests, for example those which found bias,

---

97. *See generally NY Joint Hearing, supra* note 80 (discussing the foundations of the Truth in Testing law in a state public hearing).

98. N.Y. EDUC. LAW § 341(1)-(2) (McKinney 1988) provides that:

Whenever any test agency prepares or causes to have prepared research which is used in any study, evaluation or statistical report pertaining to a test operational after January first, nineteen hundred eighty, such study, evaluation or report shall be filed with the commissioner [of Education].

99. *Id.* § 341(1) (McKinney 1988).

100. *See* ANDREW J. STRENIO, THE TESTING TRAP 274 (1981) (commenting on the pre-Truth in Testing world and the extreme importance placed upon the role of standardized testing results in achieving success). Strenio states:

The information available to permit an adequate assessment to be made of these secure tests is quite unsatisfactory . . . . I would like to repeat a statement which I made forty-two years ago; today it is practically impossible for a competent test technician or test consumer to make a thorough appraisal of the construction, validation, and use of most standardized tests being published because of the limited amount of trustworthy information supplied by test publishers and authors . . . . Unfortunately, although some progress has been made, my 1935 complaint is equally applicable today to the majority of existing tests, and especially so for secure tests.

Id.

101. *See NY Joint Hearings, supra* note 80, at 121-23 (testimony of Allan Nairn, speaker for Congress Watch Public Citizen on ETS study) (providing a factual basis to show the merits of the proposed Truth in Testing law). The testimony provides in relevant part: "[E]ntire categories of statistical information and numerous internal reports and critiques of great importance to scholars and the consuming public are now routinely withheld by the testing industry." *NY Joint Hearing, supra* note 80, at 121. In his testimony, Allan Nairn gave three examples of test agencies withholding important data and studies. One example was the refusal by ETS to release a study prepared by Dr. David Loye of the ETS staff. The report was prepared at the request of the president of ETS. The report, entitled "Cultural Bias in Testing: Challenge and Response," discussed the strengths and weaknesses of ETS tests in assessing the performance of minorities and poor people. *NY Joint Hearing, supra* note 80, at 123; *see also NY Joint Hearing, supra* note 80, at 35-36 (testimony of Steven Solomon, New York Public Interest Research Group) (recounting various personal experiences involving repeated requests made to testing agencies for information and reports which were subsequently ignored).

and to release only the studies that were favorable.[102]

The second provision of the law requires test agencies to file with the state a copy of the actual examination administered.[103] This type of test disclosure allows the state and outside watchdog groups to monitor the tests for accuracy and fairness. The law also requires test agencies to release, to test takers who so request, a copy of the test questions, the correct answers and the scoring rules for the tests.[104] In support of this provision, Senator Lavalle explained on the floor of the New York State legislature that disclosure legislation provides fundamental fairness to test takers.[105] He stated that prior to passage of the law, the test agencies refused to return answer sheets, reveal tests, provide raw scores, or tell students how they performed compared to other students.[106] The test agencies provided no method for a test taker to determine if her or his particular test was properly graded.[107] Additionally, there was substantial evidence of mistakes in administration of the tests.[108]

The New York law now also requires test agencies to prepare a statistical report for tests administered between July 1, 1988 and July 1, 1989.[109] The report will relate performance to test takers

---

102. *See NY Joint Hearing, supra* note 80, at 123 (testimony of Allan Nairn, Congress Watch Public Citizen) (explaining that a study of the use and predictive value of the LSAT was deemed "too sensitive" by the LSAC and was withheld from publication and general circulation upon completion).

103. N.Y. EDUC. LAW § 342 (1) (McKinney 1988) (stating in pertinent part that "[w]ithin thirty days after the results of any standardized tests are released, the test agency must file . . . a copy of all test questions . . ., the corresponding correct answers . . . and all rules for converting raw scores into those scores reported to the test subject together with an explanation of such rules").

104. N.Y. EDUC. LAW § 342(1) (McKinney 1988).

105. *Minutes of Proceedings, New York Joint Public Hearing of the Senate and Assembly Standing Committees on Higher Education,* Exhibit-E, at 5321-28 (June 14, 1976) (floor statement of Sen. Kenneth P. Lavalle).

106. *Id.* at 5326-27 (comparing the test agencies' refusal to reveal standardized tests with a hypothetical situation involving a college professor who refuses to return tests to his students in order for them to understand their mistakes).

107. *Id.* at 5327.

108. *See NY Joint Hearing, supra* note 80, at 37-38 (testimony of Steven Solomon, New York Public Interest Research Group) (discussing the imperfections in computer scoring techniques and positing that the notice provision of the law would notify test takers of computer errors so that they could contact law schools). Solomon stated that in the 1975-76 applicant year:

> numerous law school applicants were erroneously designated as unacknowledged repeaters. Unacknowledged repeaters are test takers who have taken the law school admissions test more than once while denying that fact . . . [on] the information sheet filled out prior to taking the test. Law schools that received this information were being told that certain candidates were actually certified liars. No effort was made to inform those students who might have been denied admission because of this error that a mistake had been made.

NY Joint Hearing, supra note 80, at 38.

109. N.Y. EDUC. LAW § 341-a (McKinney 1988).

categorized by race, ethnicity, gender, and linguistic background.[110] Information contained in the report is to be filed with an advisory committee which will then report to the legislature.[111] This report is to provide information about race, gender, and/or ethnic performance differentials in the tests.

Finally, the documents filed under the law are now considered public records.[112] This public record designation assures that the material will be available to all researchers.

B.   The MCAT Court Challenge

One of the prime differences between the New York Truth in Testing law and its predecessor, the California law, is the requirement that actual test questions be disclosed.[113] This provision became the focus for a court challenge to the New York law.[114] In 1979, the Association of American Medical Colleges[115] sued the State of New York claiming that the Truth in Testing law abridged its copyright interest in the MCAT.[116] The AAMC sued in federal district court immediately after passage of the New York Act and prior to the administration of any tests. The Association sought a preliminary injunction in order to enjoin enforcement of the disclosure provisions as to the MCAT.[117] The AAMC informed the court that the MCAT would not be administered in New York if the injunction were not granted.[118]

This threat was not taken lightly. The district court, in granting the injunction, noted,

> [T]he Commissioner of Education of New York has serious misgivings concerning the Testing Law. He has made clear that he questions whether the Law will serve the purposes for which it was enacted [specifically regarding cultural bias], that he fears that many testing agencies will stop giving the tests in New York State,

---

110.   *Id.*

111.   *Id.*

112.   *Id.* §§ 341(3), 342(7) (McKinney 1988).

113.   *Compare* N.Y. EDUC. LAW § 342 (McKinney 1988) (requiring disclosure of "all test questions" used in scoring an examination) *with* CAL. EDUC. LAW § 99162 (Deering 1993) (mandating disclosure of "operational test questions").

114.   AAMC I, *supra* note 14, at 1358.

115.   The Association of American Medical Colleges is a non-profit organization. At the time of initiation of the suit, its members included 125 medical schools, 418 teaching hospitals, 68 academic societies, and over 1,700 individuals. AAMC I, *supra* note 14, at 1359.

116.   *See* AAMC I, *supra* note 14, at 1361 (alleging that sections 341 and 342 of the Truth in Testing law violated both the Federal Copyright Act and constitutional rights to due process and equal protection). *See generally* 17 U.S.C. § 106 (1988 & Supp. II 1990) (enumerating the exclusive rights in copyrighted works).

117.   AAMC I, *supra* note 14, at 1361 n.7, 1368.

118.   AAMC I, *supra* note 14, at 1361.

as threatened, or will decrease the number of test administrations per year, and he is concerned that the price for taking the tests will increase drastically, all to the detriment of the citizens of New York State.[119]

In 1980, when the district court issued the preliminary injunction, it was not unreasonable for Judge McCurn to be concerned about the effect of the law. However, eight years later, in 1988, when the AAMC moved for a permanent injunction, the situation was very different. During the previous eight years, the other test agencies had voluntarily complied with the law.[120] Research studies and disclosure of questions within this time period did affirmatively reveal bias in the tests.[121] The test agencies had changed their "sensitivity review" processes for catching bias.[122] Contrary to the predictions of the testing agencies in the early 1980s, the cost of the tests did not explode as a result of disclosure. Rather, the test agencies prospered financially.[123] The agencies were able to develop and research new questions for future tests. Through the use of "equating" questions, the tests from one year were found to be comparable to those of another.[124]

Nevertheless, in 1990, now Chief Judge McCurn found that the AAMC's copyright interest in the MCAT was greater than the public

---

119.   AAMC I, *supra* note 14, at 1367.
120.   *See* Sewall, *supra* note 70, at 97 (explaining that while the other testing agencies vigorously opposed the New York law, they may have initially cooperated because they feared the passage of comprehensive federal legislation).
121.   *See generally* WHITE, EFFECTS OF COACHING, QUESTIONS AND BIAS, *supra* note 8, at 27-70 (discussing the processes for identifying potential bias and examples of existing cultural bias in the LSAT). Researchers linked bias in the test to the enrollment of minorities in law schools. *See, e.g.,* Eulius Simien, *The Law School Admission Test As a Barrier to Almost Twenty Years of Affirmative Action,* 12 T. MARSHALL L. REV. 359 (1987) (commenting on how the design of the LSAT contributed to the failure to increase enrollment of African-Americans in law schools).
122.   *See* Letter from Lizabeth Moody, President, Law School Admission Services (LSAS), Executive Director, LSAC, to Professor Michael Burns, Editor, SALT EQUALIZER 2 (Apr. 1 1992) (on file with author) [hereinafter Moody letter] (explaining that since 1989 final assembled tests are subjected to a "sensitivity review" to ensure that they comply with *ETS Standards for Quality and Fairness* and are further reviewed for sensitivity by the LSAC test development staff).
123.   *See* Edward B. Fiske, *College Testing is a Hard Habit to Break,* N.Y. TIMES, Jan. 15, 1989, § 4 at, 28 (stating that ETS ended its 1988 fiscal year having earned $226 million).
124.   Equating questions is the process by which test agencies examine and compare questions from previous years in order to develop future questions. This process ensures consistency and prevents the repetition of questions on standardized tests from year to year. *See* LSAT: SOURCES, CONTENTS, USES, *supra* note 34, at 4 (explaining the process of question equating in the context of the LSAT); Edward B. Fiske, *Truth-In-Testing - How's It Working,* N.Y. TIMES, Nov. 23, 1980, § 4 at, 9 (reporting that testing agencies' initial fears that problems in equating questions would destroy the validity of tests proved unfounded). The New York law directly affected the equating process. *See* N.Y. EDUC. LAW § 342 (McKinney 1988) (requiring disclosure of questions actually used in scoring the examination).

interest in the Truth in Testing law.[125] Chief Judge McCurn issued a permanent injunction.[126] The AAMC's primary argument was that disclosure made reuse of test questions impossible. If questions could not be reused, new questions would have to be developed.[127] The AAMC claimed that this would be expensive and that it might well be impossible.[128] The AAMC argued that there was a "finite pool" of possible science and math questions and question stimuli available that must be kept secure.[129] Thus, the AAMC argued that they would be hurt economically because they could not reuse questions and that depleting the pool of possible questions was against the public interest.[130]

On appeal to the Second Circuit, the case was remanded.[131] The Second Circuit found that summary judgment was inappropriate.[132] The effect of the Truth in Testing law on the market value of the AAMC's copyright was a material issue of fact.[133] The trier of fact needed to determine whether questions could be reused and calculate the expense of developing new questions before an injunction could be granted.[134]

C.   Copyright Analysis

The AAMC argued that the New York Truth in Testing law was preempted by the Federal Copyright Act, and thus was invalid.[135] Under the Supremacy Clause of Article VI of the United States Constitution, there are three ways in which state law can be preempted. First, Congress may expressly exclude state regulation.[136] Second,

---

125. See AAMC II, supra note 14, at 889 (finding "that the 'disclosure provisions' of the New York State's Standardized Testing Act, N.Y. Educ. Law §§ 341, 341-a and 342 are preempted due to a direct conflict with Federal Copyright Law"); see also supra note 25 (explaining Fair Use in copyright law).

126. AAMC II, supra note 14, at 873.

127. AAMC II, supra note 14, at 878. However, it was unclear on the record the extent to which the MCAT reuses questions. The state submitted the affidavit of Professor Walter Haney, stating that after a period of years disclosed questions could be reused because the "pool" of those questions would be so large that access to them would not give a test taker an unfair advantage. AAMC II, supra note 14, at 878.

128. AAMC II, supra note 14, at 878.

129. AAMC II, supra note 14, at 878.

130. AAMC II, supra note 14, at 887.

131. AAMC III, supra note 14 (reversing the decision of the district court, vacating the permanent injunction and remanding the case).

132. AAMC III, supra note 14, at 526.

133. AAMC III, supra note 14, at 526.

134. AAMC III, supra note 14, at 525.

135. AAMC III, supra note 14, at 522.

136. U.S. CONST. art. VI, § 2, cl.1 (stating in pertinent part: "The Constitution and the laws of the United States which shall be made in pursuance thereof; and all Treaties made, or which shall be made, under authority of the United States, shall be the supreme law of the land.").

Congress may so extensively regulate an area that federal regulation impliedly leaves no room for, or crowds out, state regulation.[137] Third, state law may be preempted if it actually conflicts with federal law.[138] The third kind of preemption is called "conflict preemption."[139] Conflict preemption occurs when compliance with both state and federal regulations would be impossible, or when the state law prohibits effectuating federal law policies.[140] Congress has neither expressly prohibited state regulation of standardized admissions tests nor comprehensively regulated the tests.[141] Therefore, the AAMC had to argue conflict preemption, the third type of preemption. The AAMC claimed that the Truth in Testing law prohibited accomplishing the policies of the Federal Copyright Act and prevented the copyright holder from receiving the benefits Congress intended.[142]

What then are the policies behind the copyright law? Copyrights are a protected property right.[143] The copyright interest protects intellectual property in order to encourage creativity.[144] Copyright protection is justified because it motivates people to continue to create, to think, to write, to publish, and to exchange information.

What benefits did Congress intend to confer through the copyright law? Authors who hold copyrights receive proper recognition and financial reward for their work.[145] Additionally, publishers can

---

137. *Id.*

138. *See, e.g.* Darling v. Mobil Oil Corp., 864 F.2d 981, 985-86 (2d Cir. 1989) (finding that the Federal Petroleum Marketing Practices Act preempted a similar Connecticut statute because the two laws directly conflicted with each other).

139. U.S. Const. art. VI, § 2, cl. 1; *see, e.g.*, Sears, Roebuck & Co. v. Stiffel Co., 376 U.S. 225 (1964) (holding that a local unfair competition law conflicted with the power of the federal government to grant patents and would preclude implementation of federal policy).

140. *Stiffel*, 376 U.S. at 229.

141. AAMC III, *supra* note 14, at 527 (Mahoney, J., concurring in part and dissenting in part) (explaining that there is "no federal regulation of standardized testing that would displace New York's" Truth in Testing law).

142. AAMC III, *supra* note 14, at 523.

143. *See generally* 17 U.S.C. § 102 (1988 & Supp. II 1990) (enumerating categories of the general subject matter of copyright); Nimmer, *supra* note 25, at 1-44.15 § 103[A] (comparing copyright to the theory of private property).

144. *See* Maxtone-Graham v. Burtchaell, 803 F.2d 1253, 1255 (2d Cir. 1986), *cert. denied*, 481 U.S. 1059 (1987) (holding that verbatim copying of a book was justified as Fair Use under the Copyright Act since the "purpose of fair use is to create a limited exception to the individual's property rights in his [or her] expression - rights conferred to encourage creativity."); *see also* Sony Corp. of Am. v. Universal City Studios, Inc., 464 U.S. 417, 450 (1984) ("the purpose of copyright is to create incentives for creative effort.").

145. *See generally* 17 U.S.C. § 106 (1988 & Supp. II 1990) (explaining authors' exclusive rights in copyrighted works); *see, e.g.*, Mazer v. Stein 347 U.S. 201, 219 (1954) (stating that copyright encourages individual creativity by extending financial personal gain); Harper & Row Publishers, Inc. v. Nation Enters., 471 U.S. 539, 55 (1985) (explaining that one of the primary goals of the Copyright Act is to assure recognition to authors and reporters).

also profit.[146] Profit encourages publication and thus increases availability of information to the public. Without copyright, important ideas might never gain public attention.[147] The concept of copyright protection is founded upon encouraging creativity and enhancing public knowledge.

Copyright protection, however, has never been absolute. There is a tension between reward for creativity on the one hand and availability and public use of copyrighted material on the other. Copyright can be used to monopolize ideas and thus inhibit the exchange of information at a potentially great social cost.[148] In other words, copyright protection at times may be counterproductive to the policies justifying its existence.[149] Because of this potential conflict, exceptions to exclusive copyrights have existed for over 250 years.[150]

1. The Fair Use Exception to Copyright Protection

The most important of the exceptions to exclusive copyright is known as the Fair Use Doctrine.[151] At common law, the Fair Use Doctrine existed as an "equitable rule of reason."[152] The Doctrine allows use of copyrighted material without the copyright owner's consent in circumstances when the use is reasonable, and when the use "would tip the balance between the public interest in the free flow of information and the copyright holder's exclusive control over the work in favor of the public."[153]

This is not an easy balance to strike.[154] Justice Story explicated

---

146. *See Harper & Row*, 471 U.S. at 567 (describing the Copyright Act's focus on the importance of ensuring marketability of copyrighted work).

147. *See, e.g.*, Twentieth Century Music Corp. v. Aiken, 422 U.S. 151, 156 (1975) (stating that the "ultimate aim" of copyright law is "to stimulate artistic activity for the general public good.").

148. *Id.*

149. *See* Iowa State Univ. Research Found., Inc. v. American Broadcasting Cos., Inc., 621 F.2d 57, 60 (2d Cir. 1980) (stating that the "doctrine of fair use permits courts to avoid rigid application of the copyright statute when, on occasion, it would stifle the very creativity which the law is designed to foster.").

150. *See* Gyles v. Wilcox, 2 Atk. 141 (1740) (No. 130) (defining abridgement of the right to use copyrighted material because of public considerations; *see also* Frank D. Prager, *History of Intellectual Property*, 26 J. PAT. [& TRADEMARK] OFF. SOC'Y 711 (1944) (recounting the history of copyright).

151. *See supra* note 25.

152. H.R. Rep. No. 1476, 94th Cong., 2d Sess. 65 (1976), *reprinted in* 1976 U.S.C.C.A.N. 5659 (reporting on the legislative history of the Copyright Act).

153. DC Comics Inc. v. Reel Fantasy, Inc., 696 F.2d 24, 27 (2d Cir. 1982).

154. In 1939, a panel of the Second Circuit, including Judge Learned Hand, called the issue of Fair Use "the most troublesome in the whole law of copyright." Dellar v. Samuel Goldwyn, Inc., 104 F.2d 661, 662 (2d Cir. 1939) (per curiam). It remains so today. *See* Weinreb, *supra* note 25, at 1144 (discussing the difficulty in ascertaining use as a public or private interest); Jay Dratler, *Distilling the Witches Brew of Fair Use in Copyright Law*, 43 U. MIAMI L. REV. 233, 250 (1988) (addressing the conflict between the public's right to know and privacy interests).

the operation of the doctrine in 1841: "We must often look to the nature and objects of the selections made, the quantity and value of the materials used, and the degree in which the use may prejudice the sale or diminish the profits, or supersede the objects of the original work."[155]

In 1976, Congress passed a comprehensive, new Copyright Act[156] that codified existing statutory copyright law and the substantial body of common law.[157] At the same time Congress formalized copyright protection, it also recognized the fundamental tension between monopoly and access in copyright law by codifying the Fair Use Doctrine in section 107 of the Copyright Act.[158] This section was intended to "restate the present judicial doctrine of fair use, not to change, narrow or enlarge it in any way."[159]

Section 107 is basically a restatement of Justice Story's description of Fair Use. In its entirety it reads:

> Not withstanding the provisions of sections 106 and 106A, the fair use of a copyrighted work, including such use by reproduction in copies or phonorecords or by any other means specified by that section, for the purposes such as criticism, comment, news reporting, teaching (including multiple copies for classroom use), scholarship or research is not an infringement of copyright. In determining whether the use made of a work in any particular case is a fair use the factors to be considered shall include—
>
> (1) the purpose and character of the use, including whether such use is of a commercial nature or is for nonprofit educational purposes;
>
> (2) the nature of the copyrighted work;
>
> (3) the amount and substantiality of the portion used in relation to the copyrighted work as a whole; and
>
> (4) the effect of the use upon the potential market or value of the copyrighted work.[160]

The criteria set out in section 107 should be applied on a case-by-case basis.[161] Although the contextual nature of the Fair Use Doc-

---

155. Folsum v. Marsh, 9 F. Cas. 342, 345 (C.C.D. Mass. 1841) (No. 4, 901).

156. Copyright Act, Pub. L. No. 94-533, 90 Stat. 2541 (codified at 17 U.S.C. §§ 101-810 (1988 & Supp. III 1991)).

157. *See* Notes of Committee of the Judiciary House Report No. 94-1476, Single Federal System, Historical Note, 17 U.S.C.A. § 301 (West 1977) (explaining that the Copyright Act had changed what had been a "dual system of 'common law copyright' for unpublished works, . . . the system in effect in the United States since the first copyright statute in 1790 . . . .").

158. 17 U.S.C. § 107 (1988 & Supp. II 1990).

159. H.R. Rep. No. 1476, *supra* note 152, at 66, *reprinted in* U.S.C.C.A.N. at 5679.

160. 17 U.S.C. § 107 (1988 & Supp. II 1990).

161. *See* Harper & Row Publishers, Inc. v. Nation Enters., 471 U.S. 539, 560 (1985) ("The factors enumerated in [section 107] are not meant to be exclusive: '[s]ince the doctrine is an equitable rule of reason, no generally applicable definition is possible, and each case raising

trine has always been a challenge,[162] there is ambiguity in using specific case analysis. It is difficult to predict if the exception will apply in any given situation.[163] Nevertheless, case-by-case analysis is essential. The Doctrine arises in varied situations and there must be flexibility in its application. Rote application of the Fair Use criteria is too dangerous. However, regardless of the difficulty in applying the Fair Use Doctrine, its goal of resolving the conflict between the monopoly granted to the owner of the copyright and the free flow of information, serves to foster a creative and informed society. This goal is important in the arena of standardized testing.

a.) The Purpose of the Use

Section 107 lists "the purpose of the use" as the first criterion for claiming Fair Use exemption from copyright.[164] When applying this first prong of the Fair Use Doctrine the distinction between commercial use and non-profit use must be recognized. There is no doubt that Truth in Testing laws fall within the parameters of the exception for non-profit use. The disclosure provisions are aimed at teaching, scholarship, and research. Truth in Testing laws were passed because of the need for meaningful comment and criticism in this area with regard to standardized tests. The Truth in Testing law provides for the use of copyrighted material for non-profit, educational purposes only. It is not for commercial purposes, profit, or exploitation.[165]

b.) The Nature of the Work

The second criterion for determining Fair Use is the nature of the copyrighted work.[166] The AAMC, like most test agencies, regularly

---

question must be decided on its own facts.' "); *see also* Iowa State Univ. Research Found., Inc. v. American Broadcasting Cos., Inc., 621 F.2d 57, 60 (2d Cir. 1980) ("[The] resolution of a fair use claim 'depends on an examination of the facts in each case' ")(citation omitted).

162.   *See generally* Weinreb, *supra* note 25, at 1137 (1990) (commenting on the "confused" Doctrine of Fair Use).

163.   *See* Maxtone-Graham v. Burtchaell, 803 F.2d 1253 (2d Cir. 1986) (exemplifying the unpredictability of the Fair Use Doctrine where verbatim copying of interviews published in a pro-choice book by an author of an antiabortion book was justified).

164.   17 U.S.C. § 107(1) (1988 & Supp. II 1990).

165.   *See* AAMC III, *supra* note 14, at 524 ("The State does not seek to exploit disclosed MCAT materials commercially . . . . This conclusion is essentially uncontested by the parties . . . ."). Though disclosure might result in commercial use of questions by test preparation services or test "coaching" businesses, this would be a commercial use also subject to copyright protection. Additionally, hypothetical infringing uses should not render the non-profit, Truth in Testing use a copyright infringement either. *See* Sony Corp. v. Universal Studios, Inc., 464 U.S. 417, 454-56 (1984) (stating that the possibility that VCRs are capable of infringing uses does not support a finding of copyright infringement because the VCRs are also capable of substantial non-infringing uses).

166.   17 U.S.C. § 107(2) (1988).

files for and receives copyrights for its tests.[167] The MCAT consists of science and math questions.[168] The factual nature of the MCAT material generally would afford it less copyright protection because a higher value is placed on copyrighted fiction than on nonfiction. As one court noted, "Factual works such as biographies, reviews, criticism and commentary are believed to have greater public value and, therefore, uses of them may be better tolerated by the copyright law."[169] Normally, "no author may copyright facts or ideas."[170] Yet, while the MCAT, like other admissions tests, is less than great literature, it is more than pure fact.[171] The test involves compilation and presentation of facts within the vehicle of the question stimulus or fact pattern. Questions are ordered by design. There is, therefore, a creative aspect to the test. This creative aspect must, however, be balanced with the public interest in disclosing the "objective" test questions and test agency factual, research reports.

Test agencies have successfully argued that their tests are protected by copyright because of the "secure" nature of the test material.[172] The AAMC in 1983, and ETS in 1986, sued for commercial infringement of their "secure" admissions tests.[173] However, both these law suits involved use of tests by commercial test "coaching"

---

167. AAMC III, *supra* note 14, at 521.

168. *See* AAMC III, *supra* note 14, at 521 (explaining that the MCAT consists "of some 300 questions and is designed to measure a test-taker's knowledge in chemistry, biology, and physics, as well as his or her reading and quantitative skills.").

169. Basic Book, Inc. v. Kinko's Graphic Corp., 758 F. Supp. 1522, 1532-33 (S.D.N.Y. 1991) (holding that a duplication business had infringed publishers' copyrights by copying excerpts from books without permission and compiling them into university report packets).

170. Harper & Row Publishers, Inc. v. Nation Enters., 471 U.S. 539, 547 (1985). *See* American Geophysical Union v. Texaco Inc., 61 U.S.L.W. 2066, 2067 (S.D.N.Y. July 22, 1992) (stating that the factual nature of a work weighs in favor of Fair Use, but finding that the commercial nature of the user and harm to profits led to copyright infringement).

171. *See American Geophysical Union*, 61 U.S.L.W. at 2066 (explaining that less protection is afforded work that is non-fiction to the extent that non-fiction work does not require creativity, but finding even purely factual work may be creative and protected by copyright where the compilation and presentation are creative).

172. *See* National Conference of Bar Examiners v. Multistate Legal Studies, 692 F.2d 478, 484 n.6 (7th Cir. 1982) (interpreting Congress's intent in creating the Copyright Act to "afford protection to confidential creative material such as secure tests . . . ."); *see also* 37 C.F.R. § 202.20(c)(2)(vi) (1991) (obviating the need for the Copyright Office to retain a copy of "secure" tests after the administration of the exam).

173. *See* American Assoc. of Medical Colleges v. Mikaelian, 571 F. Supp. 144, 155 (E.D. Pa. 1983) (commenting that the reuse of old secured test questions saves expense to AAMC and its member medical schools and granting a preliminary injunction to prevent a test preparation business from using AAMC questions in its materials), *aff'd without opinion*, 734 F.2d 3 (3d Cir. 1984); *see also* Educational Testing Serv. v. Katzman, 631 F. Supp. 550 (D.N.J. 1986) (holding that the court had jurisdiction over a review course corporation officer); Educational Testing Serv. v. Katzman, 793 F.2d 533 (3d Cir. 1986) (upholding an injunction against a test preparation course). The legal battles between Katzman and ETS date back to 1983, when ETS discovered that Katzman was registering for and taking several ETS examinations in order to become more familiar with them. *Id.* at 536.

groups. In *AAMC v. Mikaelian*,[174] the defendant's coaching classes used verbatim questions from MCAT tests that were thought to be secure.[175] The defendant had taken the MCAT on numerous occasions. His answer sheets for the tests were virtually empty. It appeared that he would sign up to take the test for the purpose of copying actual test questions and then would use them in his coaching classes.[176] The students in the defendant's coaching courses benefitted from an obvious advantage.[177] The court in *Mikaelian* refused to apply the Fair Use exception because of the commercial nature of the use and the unfairness to test takers who were not in the coaching course.[178]

Likewise, in *ETS v. Katzman*,[179] the test agency sued a commercial defendant who had somehow obtained a copy of various standardized tests before they were used for actual testing.[180] Again, the courts found that such a use was not a Fair Use at all, but rather against public policy.[181] It was unfair to students not in the course, and indeed distorted the whole testing process.[182]

Truth in Testing Fair Use is very different from selected exploitation of tests for commercial benefit by coaching services. The nature of the MCAT as a secure copyrighted work should be viewed in relationship to the Truth in Testing law. Certainly test agencies should be able to use copyright laws to protect themselves from use of tests such as that in *Katzman*. Copyright protection is needed to safeguard the tests as unpublished works prior to their administration.[183] The tests are more than raw facts. If a test taker knew exactly what questions would be asked and the order in which they would appear, answers could be memorized and the test would not be a test at all. On the other hand, disclosure after the test has been

---

174. 571 F. Supp 144 (E.D. Pa. 1983).

175. *Id.* at 148 ("Many of the Multiprep [Mikaelian's company] test questions are not only word-for-word reproductions of the MCAT test question, but also have the same typeface and graphic irregularities [e.g. an uneven line] found on the MCAT question.").

176. *Id.* at 147-48.

177. *Id.* at 153.

178. *Id.*

179. 631 F. Supp. 550 (D.N.J. 1986).

180. *See id.* at 551 (explaining that in 1982, Katzman obtained copies of the English and Math Achievement tests before the exams were administered and distributed them, causing ETS to cancel all students' scores and readminister the tests); *see also* Daniel S. Hinerfeld, *Cheating Time*, ROLLING STONE, Mar. 19, 1992 at 74 (postulating that Katzman and his cohorts would make use of time zone changes to transmit questions and answers from East Coast to West Coast test takers).

181. *Katzman*, 793 F.2d at 543.

182. *Id.*

183. *See Mikaelian*, 571 F. Supp. at 153 ("[T]he development, testing, and administration of the questions [are] performed under strict scrutiny. The very purpose of copyrighting the MCAT questions is to prevent their use as teaching aids . . . .").

given has distinct fairness advantages. The primary disadvantage is that if questions are disclosed, there is a potential that the questions cannot be used in subsequent tests.[184] Yet, if the pool of previously used questions was large enough, it would be nearly impossible to memorize all the answers if the questions were disclosed.[185] The format and order of the questions could be changed in order to alter the test.[186] Additionally, new questions could be written and kept secure until their use.

c.)   The Extent of the Use

The third factor of the Fair Use Exception, the amount of the protected material used, also has to be viewed within the context of the Truth in Testing law.[187] The Truth in Testing law requires that all test questions and answers actually used in scoring must be disclosed.[188] On the other hand, questions used for equating or development purposes do not have to be disclosed.[189] Likewise, the Truth in Testing law does not require disclosure of the test before it is given.[190] In this way, the law strikes a balance between strong public interest in monitoring this widely used type of test and the equally strong interest in fairly developing and administering admissions tests. In utilizing these balancing factors the law does not seek to ban the tests, but strives to make them better.

d.)   The Economic Effect of the Use

The final factor in the analysis of Fair Use is the effect of the use on the potential market value of the copyrighted material.[191] This factor is viewed by courts as the most important in determining Fair Use.[192] A copyright holder can argue against Fair Use by showing

---

184. AAMC III, *supra* note 14, at 525.

185. AAMC III, *supra* note 14, at 525 (discussing a study on disclosure of standardized testing questions finding that, over time, the effect of test disclosure on test scores becomes negligible).

186. AAMC III, *supra* note 14, at 525 (describing how mathematical adjustments in the value of test questions reduces any scoring deviations).

187. 17 U.S.C. § 107(3).

188. N.Y. EDUC. LAW § 342(1) (McKinney 1988).

189. N.Y. EDUC. LAW § 342(1)(a) (McKinney 1988). For the test taker, these questions might be as distracting and biased as questions used for scoring. Nevertheless, this exemption in the Truth in Testing law seems a reasonable balance with the interests of the agencies developing and administering standardized tests. This may also help the testing agencies to discern which types of questions, in fact, are distracting to the test taker if they are allowed to add non-scored experimental questions.

190. *Id.* §§ 340, 341(1) (McKinney 1988).

191. 17 U.S.C. § 107(4).

192. *See* Harper & Row Publishers, Inc. v. Nation Enters. 471 U.S. 539, 566 (1985) (describing the impact on the potential market as "undoubtedly the single most important element of Fair Use."). There has also been a scholarly critique of the Court's emphasis on

that the excepted use would have a negative effect on the profitability of the copyrighted work.[193] However, negative effect alone is not enough. To prevent application of the Fair Use exception, any adverse effect on the value or profitability of the work must outweigh any benefit to the public if the Fair Use is permitted.[194]

Test agencies must demonstrate that the Fair Use would cause profit loss.[195] In evaluating the impact on profits of any Fair Use of copyrighted material the commercial/nonprofit distinction is again important.[196] The Supreme Court has stated, "If the intended use is for commercial gain, that likelihood [of economic harm] may be presumed. But if it is for a non-commercial purpose, the likelihood must be demonstrated."[197] It is not enough for test agencies to demonstrate profit loss under their current way of operating. In response to this assertion a court might hold that they would have to alter their business operations to mitigate the Fair Use harm.[198]

To challenge the Truth in Testing law, the AAMC brought forth several claims. They argued that Truth in Testing harmed the value of their copyright because questions could not be reused.[199] They also claimed that the cost of writing new questions would be excessive.[200] As a direct result of implementation of truth in testing procedures, they claimed that their profit would be effectively eroded.[201] The AAMC also asserted that disclosure might eliminate the ability to produce even a very expensive test because there is a

---

economic factors to the exclusion of equity and policy issues. *See* Weinreb, *supra* note 25, at 137 (posing a broader, contextualized approach for Fair Use analysis and rejecting the limited utilitarian type of analysis); Leval, *supra* note 25, at 1105 (presenting a traditional utilitarian analysis of Fair Use concepts).

193. *Harper & Row*, 471 U.S. at 539. The Court provided an example of this type of Fair Use analysis where former President Ford claimed that a portion of his yet unpublished memoirs printed in The Nation Magazine violated the Copyright Act by reducing the potential market value of his memoirs. *Id.* at 548-55.

194. MCA, Inc. v. Wilson, 677 F.2d 180, 183 (2d Cir. 1981).

195. *See* AAMC III, *supra* note 14, at 525-26 (describing the court's reaction to the claim of loss of profits asserted by AAMC). The court stated, "Moreover, we reject the district court's conclusion that a copyright owner, such as AAMC, should not be 'required to change its operations when another individual or entity is interfering with its ownership rights under the Federal Copyright Act in order to make the fair use exception fit.'" AAMC III, *supra* note 14, at 525-26 (citation omitted). Additionally, courts have also held that a copyright owner may be required to take certain steps to avoid profit loss. AAMC III, *supra* note 14, at 525-26.

196. *See* AAMC III, *supra* note 14, at 523 (citing section 107 of the Copyright Act as requiring assessment of whether the use is for commercial or non-profit educational uses).

197. Sony Corp. v. Universal Studios, Inc., 464 U.S. 417, 451 (1984).

198. *See* AAMC III, *supra* note 14, at 525-26 (describing situations where the copyright owner might be required to make accommodation for Fair Use).

199. AAMC III, *supra* note 14, at 522. *But see* AAMC III, *supra* note 14, at 525 (disputing the AAMC's claim that reuse of MCAT test questions was impossible).

200. *See* AAMC II, *supra* note 14, at 887 ("The plaintiff also maintains, and defendants do not dispute, that the development of effective questions costs a good deal of both time and money—an investment which would be lost with disclosure.").

201. AAMC II, *supra* note 14, at 887.

finite number of possible science and math questions that could be asked.[202] This would both hurt the public interest in having admissions tests and eliminate the market for their test.

The AAMC's assertion of economic harm is difficult to fathom. The AAMC and the other test agencies are monopolies. They can charge whatever they choose for the costs of administering admissions tests.[203] The market for medical school standardized admissions tests is absolutely captive. A person wishing to be admitted to medical school can go nowhere else to obtain this necessity. The AAMC, like the LSAC which administers the LSAT, gives itself a monopoly when acting for individual member schools. The same educational institutions which use the test information for admission purposes have banded together to form the AAMC and the LSAC.[204] Furthermore, the cost of question development and new test production for each series of administrations[205] may not be high.[206] Certainly the ten years of experience with disclosure would seem to indicate that new questions can be drafted without excessive cost.[207]

---

202. AAMC II, *supra* note 14, at 878.

203. *See* David M. White, Brief of Testing for the Public, Puerto Rican Legal Defense and Education Fund, United States Students Association, and the Equality in Testing Project as Amici Curiae, U.S. Court of Appeals for the Second Circuit, at 18-20, AAMC v. Cuomo 928 F.2d 519 (2d Cir. 1991) (No. 90-7269) (stating that standardized test makers have a monopoly over this type of testing and thus have the ability to regulate prices at their discretion); *see also*, AAMC III, *supra* note 14, at 521 (noting that almost all medical schools in the United States require applicants to take and pass the MCAT which is produced by AAMC).

204. *See* AAMC I, *supra* note 14, at 1359 (explaining that the AAMC is comprised of over 125 medical schools, 418 teaching hospitals, 68 academic societies, and over 1700 individuals); *see also* LSAT INFO. BOOK 92-93, *supra* note 2 (describing the history and composition of standardized testing and explaining that virtually every ABA and AALS accredited and unaccredited law school in the United States is a member of the LSAC).

205. A new test would not have to be developed for each administration of the MCAT. *See* N.Y. EDUC. LAW § 342(1) (McKinney 1988) (explaining that admissions tests are usually administered in clusters over the calendar year in coordination with professional school application processes, and providing that substantial delay in reporting of scores after administration must be disclosed). The New York law established that disclosure of test questions by the test agency does not have to occur until 30 days after announcing test *results. Id.* This lag time allows for a number of administrations of the same test before it is disclosed.

206. *See* Fiske, *supra* note 124, § 4, at 9 (reporting that an ETS official indicated that the additional cost of disclosing the SAT nationwide could be kept to 30 cents per test given). Additionally, during the Joint Hearings on New York's Truth in Testing law, there was testimony that test questions generally cost between 21 cents and 42 cents per candidate to develop. *See NY Joint Hearing, supra* note 80, at 127-131 (testimony of Allan Nairn, Congress Watch Public Citizen) (noting that internal industry estimates for test development costs were inconsistent with the studies of cost disclosure done by ETS); AAMC I, *supra* note 14, joint app. at 15 (affidavit of Karen Mitchell, Director, MCAT Program) (on file with FairTest, National Center for Fair & Open Testing, Cambridge, Mass.) (explaining that each MCAT test forms costs $215,000 to develop; each question on a test form costs $705 for multiple choice and $39,000 for essay questions).

207. Not only have test agencies been able to draft new questions at little expense, but they have also profited by the publication and sale of disclosed tests. *See* Mark J. Sherman, *The College Board Joins Publishers of S.A.T. "Cram" Books*, N.Y. TIMES, January 8, 1984, § 12 at 8

The policy behind copyright protection is encouragement of creativity and increased information.[208] The anomaly of the AAMC's claim for protection is that it is founded on a desire not to be creative. If questions are disclosed, the AAMC urges, they cannot be reused. They seek copyright protection to avoid any further creativity. The purpose of disclosure is to encourage the continued creation of better tests. The AAMC wants to have a static test, given without outside scrutiny.

Disclosure will not hurt the test agencies' profits or creativity. Additionally, it serves a significant public purpose. Disclosure leads to better tests, particularly in terms of confronting race, ethnic, and gender bias. For example, the LSAC has had a sensitivity review process for decades.[209] In 1989, after the exposure of offensive questions,[210] the LSAC instituted a new sensitivity review process.[211]

2. Judicial Treatment of Fair Use in Truth in Testing

The Fair Use Doctrine is to be applied contextually. The courts should examine the public interest in any individual case to the same extent that they examine potential harm to the copyright

---

(revealing the College Board's reluctant admission that preparation for standardized testing can be beneficial to the test takers and discussing the Board's profitable sale of test preparation material). The financial hardiness of the LSAC and the LSAT post-Truth in Testing is evident by the efforts made in the late 1980s by for-profit entrepreneurs to purchase and operate the LSAT. *See* Victor G. Rosenblum, *Complementary Concerns About Legal Education: No Buyout or Sellout*, ASSOCIATION OF AMERICAN LAW SCHOOLS NEWSLETTER, June 1987 at 2 (discussing the attempted purchase of Law School Admission Services, Inc., a subsidiary of LSAC, and the ensuing resolution by LSAC which rejected this offer of purchase).

208. *See* Sony Corp. v. Universal Studios, Inc., 464 U.S. 417, 429 (1984) (stating that the purpose of the Copyright Act is *not*, ". . . primarily . . . to provide a special private benefit," but is to benefit the public by, "motivat[ing] the creative activity of the authors and inventors by the provision of special reward, and to allow the public access to the products of their genius . . . ." and discussing the intention of monopoly privileges authorized by Congress through the Copyright Act).

209. *See* Moody letter, *supra* note 122, at 1:
    "[From the early 1980s], [i]n addition to the standard item-bias and other psycho-metric reviews, test specialists, minority consultants, and a Test Question Review Committee of law school volunteers conducted reviews of test items; however, once assembled into a test form, these questions did not receive additional sensitivity review."

210. *See, e.g., supra* notes 51, 54, 55, 64, 68 and accompanying text (providing examples and analysis of offensive questions).

211. *See* Moody letter, *supra* note 122, at 2:
    "[Since 1989], LSAS has broadened the test-review process beyond the basic item-bias review to ensure that tests do not include inappropriate or offensive material and that they do include a balance of material recognizing the diversity of our society and the contributions of women and minorities."

owner.[212] Neither the district court[213] nor the Second Circuit[214] in the AAMC case acknowledged the nexus between disclosure and amelioration of race and sex bias in standardized tests. In order to eliminate these biases, it is necessary to disclose actual test questions and internal test agency research reports.

Chief Judge McCurn, in the district court opinion, recognized the state interest in eliminating race and gender bias in testing only regarding the mandated data collection in section 341-a.[215] In detailing the provisions of the New York law, Chief Judge McCurn noted that the law was amended in 1987 to include section 341-a "[d]ue to a concern that standardized tests may be *biased in some manner* . . . ."[216] The provision requires that test agencies collect data and file statistical reports correlating performance with race, language, ethnicity, and gender.[217] However, this section of the law has nothing to do with disclosure of copyrighted questions.[218] Chief Judge McCurn was silent regarding race and gender bias and the disclosure of test questions and research reports.

Like Chief Judge McCurn, Judge Altimari, writing for the Second Circuit, focused mainly on the effect of the law on the AAMC.[219] His discussion of the state's interest is presented in the vaguest terms. Judge Altimari noted that the law was enacted "in order to open the standardized testing process to public scrutiny."[220] He asserted that its purpose is to review the validity and objectivity of the tests, to assure accuracy in scoring and to aid in development of better future tests.[221] However, there was no discussion of the leg-

---

212. *See* United States v. Paramount Pictures, Inc., 334 U.S. 131, 158 (1948) (quoting Chief Justice Hughes in Fox Film Corp. v. Doyal, 286 U.S. 123, 127 (1931)). Justice Hughes stated, "The sole interest of the United States and the primary object in conferring the [copyright] monopoly lie in the general benefits derived by the public from the labors of authors." *Id.* at 158.

213. AAMC II, *supra* note 14, at 873.

214. AAMC III, *supra* note 14, at 519.

215. AAMC II, *supra* note 14, at 884-85 (citing N.Y. EDUC. LAW § 341-a (McKinney 1988)).

216. AAMC II, *supra* note 14, at 875 (emphasis added).

217. N.Y. EDUC. LAW § 341-a (McKinney 1988).

218. Indeed, under copyright analysis it is difficult to see how section 341-a was even properly under review by the district court. This section mandates that *data* be collected and disclosed, not that independently created and copyrighted material be disclosed. Judge Mahoney makes this point in his concurrence to the circuit court opinion. AAMC III, *supra* note 14, at 536 (Mahoney, J., concurring in part and dissenting in part).

219. AAMC III, *supra* note 14, at 519 (reversing the summary judgment and permanent injunction and remanding case for a determination of whether disclosure of STA [Standardized Testing Act] affected the "potential market for or value of MCATs . . . .").

220. AAMC III, *supra* note 14, at 521.

221. AAMC III, *supra* note 14, at 524.

islative history of the Act[222] nor any mention of the relationship between disclosure and efforts to eliminate race and gender bias in the examinations.[223] Both the district court and the Second Circuit should have noted that section 341-a expresses the significant legislative concern about bias. It bears on interpreting the public interest in the test and research report disclosure provisions of the law.[224]

The Truth in Testing law is not just about computer scoring errors. It also was passed because test agencies failed to address concerns of race and gender bias on their own.[225] Yet, the public interest in equality of opportunity for education was ignored by the courts responsible for reviewing the law.

III.   THE NEED FOR CONTINUED DISCLOSURE.

A.   Test Agencies Should Be Forced to Open the Test Process.

The Truth in Testing law was the impetus for disclosure.[226] When the Truth in Testing law became effective in 1980, the Educational Testing Service (ETS), the leader in standardized admissions tests, did not challenge the law in court.[227] ETS complied by disclosing all required tests and answers.[228] The LSAC, like most other test agencies, also complied with the law.[229]

Nevertheless, the test agency commitment to full test disclosure is tenuous. For some testing agencies, the issuance of the permanent injunction by the New York District Court in 1990 led to a return to secret testing. The Graduate Management Admission Council (GMAC), which develops the admissions tests used by business schools, was one of five testing agencies that challenged New York's Truth in Testing law in 1990 and sought to permanently enjoin en-

---

222. Additionally, in the district court opinion, Judge McCurn also ignores the context in which the Act was passed. *See* AAMC II, *supra* note 14, at 877-81 (discussing only the administration and security of the MCAT and the alleged inability to reuse questions).

223. AAMC III, *supra* note 14, at 519. Judge Mahoney at least notes that the issue of reuse of questions is unrelated to this provision of the law. AAMC III, *supra* note 14, at 526 (Mahoney, J., concurring in part and dissenting in part).

224. N.Y. EDUC. LAW § 341-a (McKinney 1988).

225. *See supra* notes 95-112 and accompanying text (discussing the background and development of New York's Truth in Testing law).

226. Kevin Sack, *Judge Strikes Down Law Forcing Release of College Tests*, N.Y. TIMES, Jan. 19, 1990, at B1.

227. *Id.*

228. *Id.*

229. *Cf.* Jonathan Rowe, *A Tale of Two Tests: SAT vs. LSAT*, THE CHRISTIAN SCIENCE MONITOR, July 27, 1987, at 21 (discussing the different philosophies of ETS and LSAC regarding disclosure).

forcement of the law as applied to them.[230] Following initiation of this suit, all of the plaintiffs, except the GMAC, moved for a preliminary injunction.[231] This motion was then resolved by a stipulation specifying which tests, or test questions, would be disclosed.[232] The stipulation, however, did not represent full compliance with the Truth in Testing law.[233] The stipulation was to expire at the end of the 1990-91 test year or when the *AAMC* litigation was completed.[234] Due to the length of the *AAMC* proceedings, the issue was extended into the 1991-92 test year.[235] All of the plaintiffs, except the GMAC agreed to an extension of the stipulation.[236] The GMAC chose to file a motion for a preliminary injunction instead.[237]

Chief Judge McCurn, ruling after the Second Circuit remand of the *AAMC* case, refused to preliminarily enjoin the law.[238] Chief Judge McCurn found that the state had raised triable issues about the applicability of the Fair Use Doctrine.[239] However, the outcome of the original action, *AAMC v. Carey*,[240] which was remanded to the district court after the decision was appealed in the Second Circuit, may bring the return of secret testing. The case, on the remand, is still in the discovery stage.[241]

Test agencies which have not directly challenged the law, like ETS and LSAC, may jump on the bandwagon if the law is struck down with reference to the AAMC. When interviewed, Stanford H. von Mayrhauser, General Counsel for ETS, stated that the testing service continues to believe that "in general, disclosure is a positive

---

230. College Entrance Exam. Bd. v. Cuomo, 788 F. Supp. 134, 137-38 (N.D.N.Y. 1992) (reviewing the history of the case). The other plaintiffs in the case were the Graduate Record Examination Board, the Test of English as a Foreign Language Policy Council, and the Educational Testing Service. *Id.* at 134.

231. *Id.* at 137-38.

232. *Id.* at 138 (citing the Stipulation Agreement of Parties, dated May 11, 1990). The stipulation expressed the plaintiffs' agreement to disclose a certain percentage of tests administered. *Id.* The GMAC, although it was not a moving party, also agreed to the stipulations. *Id.*

233. *See Id.* at 138, n.4 (noting that the plaintiffs did not agree to disclose all of their tests).

234. *Id.*

235. *Id.*

236. *Id.* (citing Stipulation Agreement of Parties, dated January 12, 1992). The stipulation reflected the plaintiffs' agreement to continue disclosing their tests at the same rates as they had done in the 1990-91 test year. *Id.*

237. *Id.*

238. *College Entrance Exam. Bd.*, 788 F. Supp. at 134 (denying GMAC's motion for a preliminary injunction for failing to show a likelihood of prevailing on the merits of a claim preempted by the Federal Copyright Act; holding that the use of the test was not within the Fair Use exception).

239. *Id.* at 140-43.

240. AAMC II, *supra* note 14, at 873.

241. Discovery in this case has been extended to May 1, 1993. As of publication of this article, no trial date has been set.

concept."[242] Mayrhauser implied that it is still possible that ETS could change its national policy: "If you're looking for a categorical denial that we won't seek to avail ourselves of any remedies made available to us by this ruling, I won't deny that . . . ."[243]

The LSAC, which did not join the GMAC in its direct challenge to the law, has also entered into a stipulation with the State of New York.[244] The LSAC stipulated to defer disclosure and filing of LSAT tests it administered in December 1992 and December 1993, along with any studies, evaluations, and reports, for two years from the date the tests are administered.[245] The LSAC entered into this stipulation at about the same time that it began using a new LSAT format.[246] The format is even more important now because, at the time of the format change, the LSAC also changed the scoring of the test.[247]

In the last eight years, there have been three different methods used by LSAC to score the LSAT.[248] There is no doubt that scoring affects admissions. The test appears to be a sensitive measure between students with small score differentials. Depending on the year the students took the examination, a comparison of two students with very similar scores might appear very different. With the new scoring of 120 to 180,[249] the increase in calibrations makes small score differences appear more significant. The LSAC itself has acknowledged that a three digit scoring system is misleading.[250]

The distinctions between any of these score groupings is deceptive. Any individual score reflects a broad range of accuracy, called

---

242. Sack, *supra* note 226, at B1.
243. Sack, *supra* note 226, at B1.
244. *See* Stipulation of Parties, dated January 21, 1992 (on file with FairTest, National Center for Fair & Open Testing, Cambridge, Mass.) (articulating the provisions of the agreement between LSAC and the State of New York).
245. *Id.*
246. *See* LSAT: SOURCES, CONTENTS, USES *supra* note 34, at 5 (describing the new LSAT format introduced in June, 1991).
247. *See* LSAT: SOURCES, CONTENTS, USES, *supra* note 34, at 10 (discussing the change in the scoring of the LSAT; stating that the revised version of the test cannot be equated with the previous version because the new format "does not test exactly the same qualities in the same way as they were tested by earlier versions.").
248. Until 1982, scoring was on a 200 to 800 scale. In 1982, scoring changed to a scale of 10 to 48. In 1990, it changed a third time to a scale of 120 to 180. The LSAC distributes guides to the law schools for comparing scores for years with different scoring tables. LSAT: SOURCES, CONTENTS, USES, *supra* note 34, at 9-10.
249. *See* LSAT: SOURCES, CONTENTS, USES, *supra* note 34, at 10 (explaining the new scoring system).
250. *See* Beth Bogart, *Law Schools Adjust to New LSAT Scoring System,* LEGAL TIMES, Dec. 31, 1984, at 6 (quoting LSAC Deputy Executive Director, Paul Richard). Richard stated that the LSAC changed in 1982 from a three-digit scoring to a two-digit scoring in part because the three-digit scoring gave a "misleading appearance of precision." *Id.; see also* LSAT: SOURCES, CONTENTS, USES, *supra* note 34, at 9 (acknowledging that a three digit score scale created "an impression of precision that was not warranted.").

the measurement error. The Standard Error of Measurement (SEM) for the LSAT is approximately 2.5 scaled points.[251] The LSAC describes the accuracy of the score as follows:

> The chances are 2 out of 3 that an individual's test score is within one SEM of his or her hypothetical "true" score and nine out of ten that it is within two SEMS. A test taker's true score is the score he or she would obtain on a perfectly reliable test. When the SEM is approximately 2 scaled score points, . . . *a test taker who has a true score of 35* [on the 10 to 48 scale] *would obtain an observed score between 30 and 40 nine times out of ten.*[252]

The controversy surrounding the composition of questions and scoring of the LSAT reveals that test development should be open, subject to criticism, and reflect the broad legal community. Unfortunately, this has not been the test agency tradition.[253] The latest change in LSAT scoring, introduced in 1990, received criticism for being done in a rush and without proper consultation with the law school community. As one law school dean pointed out, "[T]he precipitous way in which the Board [of the LSAC] has sought to make changes in the LSAT makes it appear that we are dealing with an instrument that is so delicate and so finely tuned that any delay in correcting it would cause havoc."[254]

B.   Test Secrecy Perpetuates Test Bias

Test agencies vigorously opposed Truth in Testing. They argued that bias would be increased because reusing questions would give students who previously saw the questions an unfair advantage over those who had not.[255] However, the real unfairness is the failure to disclose. If all test questions were available, perhaps through local libraries, then all test takers would, at minimum, have the opportunity to read the questions.[256]

---

251. LAW SCHOOL ADMISSION SERVICES, INTERPRETIVE GUIDE FOR LSAT SCORE USERS (Feb. 1990).

252. *Id.* (emphasis in original).

253. Muriel Cohen, *Secrecy on Questions Becomes Issue in Standardized Tests*, BOSTON GLOBE, Oct. 18, 1990, at 9 (citing EDUCATIONAL TECHNOLOGY CENTER, HARVARD UNIVERSITY, SECRET (1990) and explaining that test agencies are still not disclosing the information base from which they develop their test questions despite Truth in Testing laws).

254. Howard A. Glickstein, Dean, Touro College, Jacob D. Fuchsberg Law Center, President, Society of American Law Teachers, Address before the Board of Trustees of the Law School Admission Council 2 (Sept. 8, 1990) (on file with the author).

255. AAMC II, *supra* note 14, at 887. Additionally, the AAMC flatly stated that no disclosed questions or portions of disclosed questions would be reused in the MCAT. *Id.*

256. The test agencies publish preparation material for the tests. Unfortunately, they do not seem to be the best judge of what constitutes helpful test preparation material. *See* DONALD E. POWERS, PREPARING FOR THE SAT: A SURVEY OF PROGRAMS AND RESOURCES, College Board Report No. 88-7 (1988) (stating that SAT test takers surveyed rated SAT preparation programs outside of school to be the most helpful activity in raising their scores and

Secrecy exacerbates economic discrimination between test takers.[257] Students with money, who are connected to the right networks to know the best preparation courses, have access to the secrets of the tests. The AAMC tells us that the MCAT is a secure test because it has never been released.[258] This rhetoric is used to keep the test secure from bias scrutiny by educators and researchers. Meanwhile, test preparation coaching courses have used verbatim copies of the MCAT.[259] The AAMC sued and stopped this verbatim use of previous MCAT questions.[260] Nevertheless, it is clear that the test, in reality, is not "secure."

The difficulty in obtaining actual test questions does not make it impossible.[261] There is no such thing as an absolutely secure test.[262] The result is that the cost of the best test preparation

---

reporting that test takers judged the College Board booklet, TAKING THE SAT, to be the least helpful).

257. For example, with the SAT, "studies done over the last 20 years prove that coaching courses can raise a student's score by 100 points . . . ." Anthony DePalma, *SAT Coaching Raises Scores, Report Says*, N.Y. TIMES, Dec. 18, 1991, at B9. However, "FairTest argues that minorities, low-income students and those students whose first language is not English often score too low to qualify for admissions or scholarships because they cannot afford coaching classes available to more affluent candidates." Muriel Cohen, *Testing Firm Said to Hide Coaching Benefits on SATs*, BOSTON GLOBE, Dec. 18, 1991, at 78.

258. AAMC III, *supra* note 14, at 521.

259. *See* AAMC III, *supra* note 14, at 521 (noting that a previously administered MCAT exam, "compromised by unauthorized disclosure," is available to applicants to use as a practice exam); *see also* AAMC v. Mikaelian, 571 F. Supp. 144 (E.D. Pa. 1983) (detailing AAMC's copyright infringement action where a test preparation agency's materials contained verbatim questions from previously administered exams).

260. *See Mikaelian*, 571 F. Supp. 144 (granting the AAMC's request for a preliminary injunction to enjoin a test preparation agency from using verbatim MCAT questions in its test preparation materials).

261. At the testimony in favor of the Truth in Testing law, Senator Halperin explained what everyone who is part of the right network knows:

> I was the beneficiary of one of these [coaching] courses . . . . I had seen those questions [for both the LSAT and the Multistate Bar] and the reason I had seen them is not because anybody saw the test ahead of time, but because over the years the same questions are used, and the people who put together these courses have a little system worked out where they select certain people to remember certain questions and they come back and they actually have a list of all the questions that are asked year after year . . . . I already had an advantage because I was able to afford the cost [of the course] . . . . [O]ne reason for disclosing the questions is to put everyone on equal footing since really the questions are not as secret as some would be led to believe.

NY Joint Hearing, *supra* note 80, at 23-25 (Testimony of Senator Halperin).

262. *See* Hinerfeld, *supra* note 180, at 72 (describing a coaching service employee's test taking on the East Coast and telephoning of test information to test takers on the West Coast on the day of the exam). In his article, Hinerfeld states,

> O]rganized academic fraud is on the rise and apparently beyond the knowledge or control of authorities. Most of these students seem to know at least one person who cheated on the SAT, and the variety of ingenuity of their methods is astounding — from the buddy system, in which friends swap answers during breaks to the surrogate approach to the use of wristwatch-size data banks that can store vocabulary words and formulas. Says one college freshman: "It's easier to cheat on the SAT than to get a six-pack of beer."

Hinerfeld, *supra* note 180, at 76.

courses, the ones with close facsimile questions, will be high. Thus, those medical school applicants with money, will have a distinct advantage over other students.[263] Indeed, if MCAT questions are now routinely reused, the validity of the current MCAT is questionable.

Finally, the Association of American Medical Colleges argued that MCAT questions need to be reused because there is a limited pool of these questions.[264] This argument places a mask of neutrality on the test. How can there be bias subject to correction if there is an Aristotelian definiteness to MCAT questions? The MCAT is comprised of approximately 300 questions on math and science.[265] The AAMC gives the MCAT to thousands of persons with pre-med, undergraduate science backgrounds. These test takers have attended hundreds of different undergraduate colleges and had many different science and math professors, all of whom gave examinations which we can assume contained many thousands of different questions. The AAMC now asks us to believe that, contrary to the obvious experience of the whole of the academic world, the universe of possible test questions is a small, "finite pool."[266] Similar "limited

---

263. *See* Joshua Hammer, *Cram Scam: Fighting Educational Injustice for Fun and Profit; Princeton Review Course,* THE NEW REPUBLIC, April 24, 1989, at 15 (interviewing John Katzman, founder of the Princeton Review). Katzman says he based "more than 50 percent . . ." of his teaching on having students "get inside the heads of the test makers and figure out how to get the right answers, or at least improve their odds, without actually learning much of substance." *Id.*

In the Logical Reasoning section of the LSAT certain test "coaching" tricks became insider, elitist knowledge well before official release of actual tests through the Truth in Testing law. In 1984, because of Truth in Testing legislation, David White of Testing for the Public, analyzed long-used coaching tricks based on actual LSAT forms. *See* WHITE, EFFECTS OF COACHING, QUESTIONS, AND BIAS *supra* note 8, at 6-7. For example, White found that two out of three items designated as "Major Objective" began with a gerund (a verbal noun ending in "-ing"). He stated:

> Thus, by merely remembering this rule, the candidate would be correct in the selection of 2/3 of the Major Objectives after merely reading the first word of the statement to be classified . . . The most disturbing aspect of the LSAT trick may be its origins. The gerund rule was first discovered by this author through a third hand report from a former administrator of the Stanley H. Kaplan LSAT Preparation Course. Once LSAT forms were released, this author applied the rule with success. Later, widespread knowledge of the gerund rule was confirmed in conversations with students attending some of the most prestigious, selective law schools in the nation—students who had previously taken a coaching course which taught the gerund trick."

WHITE, EFFECTS OF COACHING, QUESTIONS, AND BIAS *supra* note 8, at 6; *see also* Stuart Katz et al., *Answering Reading Comprehension Items Without Passages on the SAT,* 1 PSYCHOLOGICAL SCIENCE 122, 126-27 (1992) (suggesting that SAT verbal scores are heavily influenced by factors other than real verbal ability and that examinees in their study answered a substantial number of reading comprehension questions correctly without reading the passage).

264. AAMC II, *supra* note 14, at 878.

265. *See* AAMC III, *supra* note 14, at 521 (describing the composition of the MCAT and stating that its purpose is to measure the test taker's quantitative and reading skills and knowledge of biology, physics, and chemistry).

266. *See* American Assoc. of Medical Colleges v. Mikaelian, 571 F. Supp. 144, 147 (E.D. Pa. 1983) (stating AAMC's claim that there exists a finite number of potential questions due to

pool" arguments are often made by agencies and institutions that want to avoid claims that they are biased and exclusive.[267] Secret tests are the best insulation from scrutiny. An absolute, finite pool of questions is the best protection from responsibility for race and sex bias.

CONCLUSION

The Educational Testing Service, constructing the LSAT for the LSAC, understands bias and corrects for it in the same way that bias is addressed by law schools and courts. There have been consistent efforts in the past ten years to be inclusive, to be diverse. The test makers acknowledge that the older tests only reflected white, male life experience. The test now includes issues about women and other cultures.

While I laud efforts to diversify, I am concerned that diversity too often means, as Leslie Bender has so aptly stated, "Add women and stir."[268] Too often people with institutional power, like ETS, law professors, and judges, are not careful of what they say or how they say it. They are insensitive to the whole of their audience, including the historically disempowered.

The faculty and administrators of law schools who comprise legal academia have a responsibility to assure that the LSAT is a meaningful measure of admissibility to the profession.[269] It is not enough that a correlation to law school performance be demonstrated. Fundamental fairness demands more. For example, suppose there was compelling statistical evidence of a nearly complete correlation be-

---

the limitation of questions to "basic science course knowledge . . . ," in order to avoid asking highly sophisticated questions which would unfairly advantage students with extensive education in a particular area tested over those students who took basic science courses in preparation for medical school). This is the most audacious use of the "pool" argument I have seen.

267. For example, law school faculties argue that there are so few minorities in teaching because the "pool" of qualified candidates is limited. *Compare* Randall L. Kennedy, *Racial Critiques of Legal Academia*, 102 HARV. L. REV. 1745, 1762 (1989) (challenging Derrick Bell's race-based exclusion argument in *The Unspoken Limit on Affirmative Action: The Chronicle of the DeVine Gift, in* AND WE ARE NOT SAVED 140-61 (1987) and suggesting that Bell does not sufficiently address the fact that the paucity of minority professors on law school faculties is due to the lack of minority applicants possessing the necessary qualifications) *with* Espinoza, *supra* note 30, at 1882 (critizing Kennedy's assessment of Bell's argument by citing to an interpretation of statistics, compiled by the American Association of Law Schools, which found the "credentials of the majority of minority candidates hired to law schools' faculties to be comparable . . ." to other candidates).

268. Leslie Bender, *Sex Discrimination or Gender Inequality*, 57 FORDHAM L. REV. 941, 950 (1989).

269. *See* Glickstein, *supra* note 254, at 8 ("I believe that it is only the law schools that should be allowed to decide whether we [through the LSAT] separate people into 39 different groups or 61 different groups when we decide who deserves to be admitted to law school and to the legal profession.").

tween income of the applicant's parents and success in law school. Would law schools be justified in using parental wealth as a basis for admission?[270]

We need to force our institutions and ourselves to be careful in the use of language. Language is powerful. The effort to choose correct language, to try to root out bias, is not about magic formulae. Discussing law school examinations, Professor Patricia Williams writes: "This brings me back to my original issue — how to distinguish the appropriate introduction of race, gender, class, social policy, into law-school classrooms . . . I think such discussion should be ongoing, constant, among faculties willing to hear diverse points of view — as difficult as such conversations are, and as long-term and noisy as they may have to be."[271]   Disclosure of admissions tests through Truth in Testing will continue this conversation.

---

270. Grades and references are less subject to fraud than are SAT scores. " 'It's one more example of how one three-hour test on a Saturday morning is a lot easier to scam than a grade-point average,' says Sarah Stockwell of the nonprofit student-advocacy group FairTest." Hinerfeld, *supra* note 180, at 76.

271. WILLIAMS, *supra* note 38, at 90.

UNITED STATES v. VIRGINIA: THE CASE OF COEDUCATION AT VIRGINIA MILITARY INSTITUTE

JULIE M. AMSTEIN*

Virginia Military Institute ("VMI"), a state-supported school of higher education, was founded in 1839 as a four-year military institute. Many men who graduated from this prestigious school have become generals and leaders of the country.[1] The Board of Visitors, whose members are appointed by the Governor, is the primary governing body for the school.[2] Since its founding, this Board has maintained the objective of providing VMI's education to males only.[3] This admissions policy, which denies women the opportunity of VMI's unique education, has been under attack as unconstitutional. The attack began in 1989 when a Virginia woman's application was rejected based on her gender.[4]

---

* J.D. candidate, Washington College of Law at The American University, 1995; A.B., Dartmouth College, 1992.

1. United States v. Virginia, 976 F.2d 890, 892-93 (4th Cir. 1992), *vacating*, 766 F. Supp. 1407, 1409 (W.D. Va. 1991), *cert. denied*, Virginia Military Inst. v. United States, 113 S. Ct. 2431 (1993), *and on remand*, United States v. Virginia, 852 F. Supp. 471 (W.D. Va. 1994).

2. United States v. Virginia, 766 F. Supp. 1407, 1409 (W.D. Va. 1991), *vacated by*, 976 F.2d 890 (4th Cir. 1992), *cert. denied*, Virginia Military Inst. v. United States, 113 S. Ct. 2431 (1993), *and on remand*, United States v. Virginia, 852 F. Supp. 471 (W.D. Va. 1994).

3. *Virginia*, 766 F. Supp. at 1415.

4. John F. Harris, *Ghosts of Old Virginia Haunt VMI Biased Trial*, WASH. POST, Apr. 5, 1991, at C1. The Citadel has been facing the courts on the same issue as the Virginia Military Institute. On February 15, 1990, The Citadel rejected its first woman, who applied to the academy despite the all-male admissions policy. *The Citadel Rejects Woman as Cadet*, WASH. POST, Feb. 15, 1990, at A18. Three years later, a federal appeals court blocked Shannon Faulkner from enrolling until it could hear further discussion concerning whether the military college should be required to admit women. *Around the Nation*, WASH. POST, Aug. 25, 1993, at A9. In January, 1994, U.S. Supreme Court Chief Justice William Rehnquist ruled that Faulkner could attend The Citadel as a civilian, but could not live on campus, wear a uniform, or take part in any cadet activities. Henry Eichel, *Citadel Trial Nears End; Appeal Likely; Faulkner Reflects Women-*

The United States Department of Justice issued an ultimatum in early February, 1990 that VMI must change its all-male admissions policy by February 20th of that year, or the Justice Department would file a federal lawsuit.[5] On March 1, 1990, the United States Justice Department filed suit against VMI, claiming the admissions policy violated the Equal Protection Clause of the Fourteenth Amendment and the Civil Rights Act of 1964.[6] The United States District Court for the Western District of Virginia heard the case and issued a decision in 1991, holding that VMI's policy was not unconstitutional.[7] The following year, the United States appealed to the United States Court of Appeals for the Fourth Circuit. It contended that Virginia's objective of diversity in education, asserted by the state in the district court, was not legitimate. Therefore, the state could not justify VMI's admissions policy.[8] The court found the objective of the school to be permissible, but found the exclusion of women, without providing them the same opportunity, questionable. The judgment was vacated, and the case remanded to the district court.[9] Therefore, the court of appeals required VMI to take measures necessary to satisfy the Fourteenth Amendment.[10] The choice of measures included admitting women, abandoning state-support of the institution, or developing a remedial plan that would create a parallel program and that would address the constitutional concerns expressed by the Justice Department.[11]

VMI chose to establish a separate, parallel program for women. The plan, proposing a separate leadership institute at Mary Baldwin College—a neighboring, all-female school—was submitted to the district court in September, 1993. On November 15, 1993, the Justice

---

Only Option, WASH. POST, May 27, 1994, at A1.

U.S. District Judge C. Weston Houck will issue his decision in July as to whether women must be admitted to the Citadel. Chris Barritt, *Around the South Sex Bias Case Judge Berates Lawyer, Vows Citadel Ruling Soon: A Ruling on the Sex Bias Suit is Vowed by Mid-July*, ATLANTA J. & CONST., June 17, 1994, at A3. See *infra* note 262 and accompanying text.

5. Peter Baker, *Women Cadets? VMI Hears a Call to Battle*, WASH. POST, Feb. 4, 1990, at D1.

6. Peter Baker, *U.S. Files Its VMI Lawsuit; Action Seeks to Force Admission of Women*, WASH. POST, Mar. 2, 1990, at C1; United States v. Virginia, 766 F. Supp. 1407 (W.D. Va. 1991), *vacated by*, 976 F.2d 890 (4th Cir. 1992), *cert. denied*, Virginia Military Inst. v. United States, 113 S. Ct. 2431 (1993), *and on remand*, United States v. Virginia, 852 F. Supp. 471 (W.D. Va. 1994). The Department of Justice also joined the Citadel case. *What if The Citadel Lost its R.O.T.C. Funds?*, N.Y. TIMES, June 5, 1994.

7. United States v. Virginia, 766 F. Supp. 1407, 1415 (W.D. Va. 1991), *vacated by*, 976 F.2d 890 (4th Cir. 1992), *cert. denied*, Virginia Military Inst. v. United States, 113 S. Ct. 2431, *and on remand*, United States v. Virginia, 852 F. Supp. 471 (W.D. Va. 1994).

8. *Virginia*, 976 F.2d at 891.

9. *Id.* at 891.

10. *Id.* at 900.

11. *Id.*

Department responded to the plan, stating that it did not provide an adequate alternative to admitting women to VMI.[12] A hearing in early 1994 allowed the district court to consider all arguments concerning the plan.[13] On April 29, the district court held that the plan was constitutional and gave VMI permission to begin implementation.[14]

The situation with VMI exemplifies the continuing struggle the courts face regarding the issue of gender-based classification and equal protection. The Constitution is constantly being re-interpreted to ensure that citizens' rights are protected. Equality, under the Fourteenth Amendment, has been a highly pronounced area of the law for race and gender. These classifications are particularly evident in the education field. Consequently, the Supreme Court has heard numerous equal protection arguments, concerning race and gender-based classifications, and the denial of benefits in education because of these classifications. In related decisions, the Court has struggled to determine how to best provide equal protection and has relied on two levels of judicial review: strict scrutiny for race, and intermediate scrutiny for gender. The recent case, in which the United States challenges VMI's all-male admissions policy, provides an excellent basis for analyzing this constitutional doctrine.[15] This piece

---

12. Robert O'Harrow, Jr., *U.S. Decries VMI Plan for Women*, WASH. POST, Nov. 16, 1993, at E6.
13. *Id.*
14. United States v. Virginia, 852 F. Supp. 471 (W.D. Va. 1994).
15. Two statutes have been considered in previous analyses of military academies and coeducation. First, a federal mandate was issued in 1975, and was amended in 1988, requiring United States Service Academies to admit women. Marcia Berman, *An Equal Protection Analysis of Public and Private All—Male Military Schools*, 23 U. CHI. LEGAL F. 211 n.1 (1991) (citing 10 U.S.C. §§ 2009, 4342); *see also* Lucille M. Ponte, *Waldie Answered: Equal Protection and the Admissions of Women to Military Colleges and Academies*, 25 NEW ENG. L. REV. 1137-38 n.3 (1991). Yet, as of September 15, 1994, two military colleges, the Virginia Military Institute and The Citadel in South Carolina, still remained all male. In addition, no female military colleges have been established. Berman, *supra*, at 211 n.2. The academies' reluctance to become coeducational confirms that "[c]ertain military colleges and academies have been either slow to accept or obstinately opposed to the admission of women." Ponte, *supra*, at 1139.

Second, Title IX of the Education Amendments of 1972 prohibits sex discrimination for all "institutions of vocational education, professional education, and graduate higher education, and . . . public institutions of undergraduate higher education." Bennett L. Saferstein, *Revisiting Plessy At The Virginia Military Institute: Reconciling Single-Sex Education with Equal Protection*, 54 U. PITT. L. REV. 637, 673 (1993) (citing 42 U.S.C. §§ 2000c-2000c-9 (1988)). However, the legislative provision does have an exception that where single-sex schools already exist, "all the benefits available to one sex [must] be made available to the other sex." *Inner-City Single-Sex Schools: Educational Reform or Invidious Discrimination?*, 105 HARV. L. REV. 1741, 1754 (1992) [hereinafter *Inner-City Schools*]. As a result of these two clauses, the question has arisen whether mandatory coeducation was the aim of the legislation. Saferstein, *supra*, at 673-74. One response is that the statute does not require coeducation, but it does forbid discrimination. Jones *ex rel.* Michele v. Board of Educ., 632 F. Supp. 1319, 1322 (E.D.N.Y. 1986) (holding that converting an all-girl high school into a coeducational school did not violate Title IX). "In enacting Title IX, Congress sought to avoid the use of federal resources to support discrimina-

will focus on whether VMI's policy presents a constitutional violation of the Equal Protection Clause, regardless of any statutory remedy that may exist.

Section I of this article presents the formulation, rationale, and early application of the separate but equal doctrine. This theory, applied initially to discrimination based on race, was applied in the educational context to justify the establishment of separate educational institutions. However, since the 1950s, the theory of separate but equal has been erased from areas that directly or indirectly implicate race. As will be discussed, it has been determined that separation in education is inherently unequal when race is concerned. The inequality derives from the denial of intangible factors to certain members of society. Although the doctrine of separate but equal has not been completely eradicated in terms of gender-based classifications, it is important to consider because parallels can be seen between the judicial decisions on race and gender-based classifications.

Section II considers cases that trace the development of equal protection in the realm of gender and education. These cases can be viewed as analogous to the separate but equal line of cases. Although the result for gender has not yet been that the concept of separate is inherently unequal,[16] the denial of intangible factors is recognized

---

ry practices, and to provide individual citizens effective protection against such practices." *Id.* (citing Cannon v. University of Chicago, 441 U.S. 677, 704 (1979)). In conjunction with Title IX, the Equal Educational Opportunity Act seems to support single-sex education as long as equal single-sex and coeducational alternatives exist and "the separation of the sexes is not a smokescreen used to disguise some other illegal motivation." *Inner-City Schools, supra,* at 1755 (citing Note, *The Constitutionality of Sex Separation in School Desegregation Plans,* 37 U. CHI. L. REV. 296, 325-26 (1970)).

The Court addressed the issue of statutory violations in Mississippi Univ. for Women v. Hogan, 458 U.S. 718 (1982). Its analysis in that case emphasized that statutory compliance does not necessarily guarantee that constitutional compliance also exists. The Court held that the portion of Title IX, §901(a)(5), which exempts schools that traditionally have a policy of admitting only students of one gender, applied to Mississippi University for Women. However, the Court further found the provision provided the state no solace. *Hogan,* 458 U.S. at 733. "[A] statute apparently governing a dispute cannot be applied by judges, consistently with their obligations under the Supremacy Clause, when such an application of the statute would conflict with the Constitution." *Id.* (citing Younger v. Harris, 401 U.S. 37, 52 (1971) (citing Marbury v. Madison, 1 Cranch 137 (1803))). Congress may exempt the institution from a statutory violation, but it did not intend the provisions of Title IX to exempt schools from their constitutional obligations. *Hogan,* 458 U.S. at 732-33.

Although the ramifications of these legislative enactments are worthy of consideration, the possible statutory violations of Virginia Military Institute's all-male admissions policy will not be addressed in this paper.

16. In fact, counterarguments to the application of this line of reasoning assert that single-sex institutions do not even attempt to be separate but equal. Many women's colleges are founded on the belief that an all-female environment is distinct and superior. *See generally* Ruth Schmidt, *The Role of Women's Colleges in the Future, in* WOMEN AND HIGHER EDUCATION IN AMERICAN HISTORY: ESSAYS FROM THE MOUNT HOLYOKE SESQUICENTENNIAL SYMPOSIA 198 (John

as part of the equal protection consideration involving gender. This section also develops the relationship between the Supreme Court's level of review for gender-based classifications, intermediate scrutiny, and equal protection arguments. These first two sections lay the foundation for the rest of the article, which focuses on VMI's all-male admissions policy and the proposed remedial plan that allegedly provides women equal opportunity and equal protection.

Section III presents the two courts' decisions regarding VMI. Section IV discusses the subsequent plan proposed by VMI to remedy the consequences of its all-male admissions policy in line with the courts' decisions.

Section V applies court decisions regarding gender-based classifications in education to the remedial plan. In this discussion, the argument is made that VMI's plan is not sufficient to afford equal protection to women who seek admission. Applying the analogy from racial cases and the doctrines established in the gender cases, it is argued that VMI's all-male admissions policy denies women equal protection because it makes certain intangible factors inaccessible on the basis of gender. Moreover, the proposed plan, under standards established in gender-based classification precedent, does not constitute means substantially related to the important governmental interest of developing future leaders of society.

Section VI presents arguments that, in order to meet its burden under intermediate scrutiny, VMI must integrate women. Coeducation is the substantially related means. It allows both men and women to benefit equally from the intangible factors offered by an education at VMI. In light of this analysis, the latter part of Section VI addresses the ongoing VMI appeal and the important implications this case may have on the Citadel case, also within the Fourth Circuit.

I. "SEPARATE BUT EQUAL" AND EDUCATION—ITS HISTORY:
FROM START TO FINISH

The Supreme Court has a long history of interpreting the Fourteenth Amendment, specifically the Equal Protection Clause. A substantial number of decisions, prior to the 1970s, focused on racial equality. However, gender has now become a prominent area of the equal rights discourse. In order to fully examine VMI's admissions

---

Mack Faragher & Florence Howe, eds., 1988); M. Elizabeth Tidball, *Women's Colleges: Exceptional Conditions, Not Exceptional Talent, Produces High Achievers*, in Educating The Majority—Women Challenge Tradition in Higher Education 157 (Carol S. Pearson et al. eds., 1989); David B. Truman, *The Women's Movement and the Women's College*, in WOMEN IN HIGHER EDUCATION 56 (W. Todd Furniss & Patricia Albjerg Graham, eds., 1974). *See also infra* note 172.

policy and remedial plan, the historical basis of the separate but equal doctrine and its subsequent rejection in racial education cases will be discussed. As the notion of separate but equal weakened and was replaced by the concept that separate was inherently unequal, standards of scrutiny[17] became the means the Court employed to ensure that racial classifications did not result in further separation that violated the Equal Protection Clause. Section II will expand this discussion, concentrating on how these constitutional theories have developed and how they apply to gender cases.

A. *Separate But Equal*

In 1896, the United States Supreme Court handed down its decision in *Plessy v. Ferguson*.[18] The Court's holding stated that although the undoubted intent of the Fourteenth Amendment was to ensure absolute racial equality before the law, "it could not have been intended to abolish distinctions based upon color, or to enforce social, as distinguished from political equality, or [to enforce] a commingling of the two races upon terms unsatisfactory to either."[19] The Court seemed to recognize that arbitrary discrimination would not pass a constitutional test; thus, part of the decision is based on whether segregation passed a reasonable test.[20] In order to decide that separation of accommodations based on race was reasonable, the Court referred to "established usages, customs, and traditions of the people" and considered "their comfort and the preservation of the public peace and good order."[21] The Court refused to require commingling because it believed "[i]f the two races are to meet upon

---

17. The Court has articulated three levels of scrutiny that can be applied in constitutional cases. First, strict scrutiny requires there be a compelling governmental interest, and the means employed to achieve that interest must be narrowly tailored. Second, intermediate scrutiny necessitates that the government interest be important, and that the state's means of achievement be substantially related. Third, rational basis requires that the state have a legitimate interest, and that its means of achievement have a fair and substantial relationship to its interest. The origin of strict scrutiny's application to race was based on the notion that racial minorities had been subject to invidious discrimination and must be protected in the future. Intermediate scrutiny's origin in relation to gender will be discussed in more detail in this article, but was based on the notion that gender was a suspect class and warranted some protection, although not the same necessitated by invidious discrimination. *See infra* note 59.

18. Plessy v. Ferguson, 163 U.S. 537 (1896), *overruled by* Brown v. Board of Educ. of Topeka, 347 U.S. 483 (1954) (holding that the Equal Protection Clause was not violated where separate accommodations were provided for black train passengers because, although separate, the accommodations were equal).

19. *Plessy*, 163 U.S. at 544. The Court placed a great deal of emphasis on the argument that blacks now had equal political rights and social separation did not infringe on that essential equality. *Id.* at 545.

20. *Id.* at 550 (stating that all acts of police power must be reasonable and must be used for the promotion of the public good, and not to oppress a particular class).

21. *Id.*

terms of social equality, it must be the result of natural affinities, a mutual appreciation of each other's merits, and a voluntary consent of individuals."[22] Legislation cannot eliminate distinctions that are made based on physical differences; and if legislation tries to abolish classifications premised on these differences, the result will only be to emphasize those differences.[23] The Court, pointing to segregated schools for support, reasoned that separating people based on race did not necessarily imply inferiority.[24]

Justice Harlan dissented, expressing the view that the Constitution is color-blind and recognizes no classes among citizens.[25] Recounting the history of the Thirteenth, Fourteenth, and Fifteenth Amendments, Justice Harlan stressed the inconsistency of the Court's decisions. The same Court, which had just found in *Plessy* that separate but equal did not violate the Constitution, had previously found the following:

> The words of the [Fourteenth] amendment . . . . contain a necessary implication of a positive immunity or right, most valuable to the colored race,—the right to exemption from unfriendly legislation against them distinctively as colored; exemption from legal discriminations, implying inferiority in civil society, lessening the security of their enjoyment of the rights which others enjoy . . . [26]

Justice Harlan's contention with *Plessy* was that separate but equal did not exemplify the freedom protected in those amendments because it resulted in the degradation of a large class of fellow citizens.[27]

Since *Plessy*, the preservation of equal rights based on race has been challenged a great deal. The majority's opinion in *Plessy* now seems archaic and Justice Harlan's dissent has become a prevailing view among advocates of racial equality. Courts began combatting discrimination by holding that schools must provide equal opportuni-

---

22. *Id.* at 551, *overruled by* Brown v. Board of Educ. of Topeka, 347 U.S. 483 (1954).

23. *Id.*

24. *Id.* at 544. The Court cites the case of Roberts v. City of Boston (citation omitted), to support its contention that equality does not mean men and women have the same civil and political powers; rather, that equality means everyone is "equally entitled to the paternal consideration and [paternal] protection of the law." *Id.* at 544.

25. Plessy v. Ferguson, 163 U.S. 537, 559 (Harlan, J., dissenting).

26. *Id.* at 556 (Harlan, J., dissenting) (referring to decisions that held that prohibiting citizens from becoming jurors because of their race violated the Fourteenth Amendment). Justice Harlan also warned that the majority's decision would promote a belief that state legislation could be used to defeat the purposes of the Fourteenth Amendment and, specifically, the Equal Protection Clause. *Id.* at 560 (Harlan, J. dissenting).

27. *Id.* at 562 (Harlan, J., dissenting).

ties to all students.[28] Eventually, the doctrine of separate but equal was held to be inherently unequal.

B. Intangible Factors and the Eradication of Plessy

The Court, in reviewing racial segregation cases after *Plessy*, began to formulate a new racial equality doctrine, specifically in education. The doctrine rested on the concept that minorities — in separate but equal facilities—were denied intangible factors, thereby making those facilities inherently unequal and violating the Equal Protection Clause. The Court did not have a preconceived idea of what constituted intangible factors. Thus, the list developed over several years, based on specific cases.

McLaurin v. Oklahoma State Regents for Higher Education,[29] decided four years before *Brown v. Board of Education,*[30] began to establish the importance of intangible factors in considerations of equal protection. The Court in *McLaurin* started to delineate intangible factors, holding that even segregation within an integrated school denied an individual the ability to study, to discuss and exchange viewpoints, and to learn.[31]

McLaurin offers an excellent basis for comparison with the Virginia Military Institute case because the Court specifically addressed the significance of isolating members of society who seek to become leaders. McLaurin sought to obtain a doctorate in education, a degree that would invariably make him a leader of others. "Those who will come under his guidance and influence must be directly affected by the education he receives. Their own education and development will necessarily suffer to the extent that his training is unequal to that of his classmates."[32] The Court held that by requiring the state to remove barriers to equal opportunities, it may not eradicate all forms of prejudice, but it will ensure that an individual

---

28. These cases indicated that the application of a separate but equal doctrine would no longer withstand judicial scrutiny. The cases that implicated the *Plessy* decision concerned specifically the issue of education. *See* Brown v. Board of Educ. of Topeka, 349 U.S. 294 (1955) (Brown II); Brown v. Board of Educ. of Topeka, 347 U.S. 483 (1954) (Brown I) (holding that separate is inherently unequal); McLaurin v. Oklahoma State Regents For Higher Educ., 339 U.S. 637 (1950) (holding that when a black student is admitted to a traditionally white school, that student must be given equal treatment in the school); Sweatt v. Painter, 339 U.S. 629 (1950) (providing a clear statement that the court neither reaffirmed nor overruled Plessy); Sipuel v. Oklahoma, 332 U.S. 631 (1948) (holding that when there is only one state-sponsored law school in a state, blacks must be admitted); Missouri *ex rel.* Gaines v. Canada, 305 U.S. 337 (1938) (holding that the state must remove barriers that deprive the opportunity for peer acceptance).
29. 339 U.S. 637 (1950).
30. Brown v. Board of Educ. of Topeka, 347 U.S. 483 (1954) (Brown I).
31. *McLaurin,* 339 U.S. at 641.
32. *Id.*

is not deprived of the chance to earn peer acceptance based on individual merits.[33] By having the opportunity and by not being automatically classified and placed in a separate group, the level of training and ability to lead will most likely improve.

Sweatt v. Painter[34] also advanced the importance of intangible factors. In *Sweatt v. Painter*, a black man's application to law school was denied solely based on race. The Supreme Court held that the University of Texas Law School possesses—to a far greater degree than the State law school established for Blacks—those qualities which are incapable of objective measurement, but which make for greatness in a law school.[35] The Court highlighted such intangible factors as reputation, administrative experience, position and influence of alumni, standing in the community, traditions, and prestige.[36] Furthermore, the Court stated that few students would choose to study in an environment that excludes the exchange of viewpoints and that excludes from its population a large percentage of citizens with whom those students must deal after graduation.[37] The Court's decision also emphasized that the rights to equal protection are individual rights, not group rights; thus, the number of Black applicants seeking admission to the law school should not be relevant in the Court's consideration.[38]

Brown v. Board of Education reinforced the decisions of *McLaurin* and *Sweatt.* In *Brown I,* Black students sought to attend the white elementary schools and high schools because the segregated schools were not equal and deprived the students of their Fourteenth Amendment rights.[39] The Court described education as the "very

---

33. *Id.* at 641-42.

34. 339 U.S. 629 (1950).

35. *Id.* at 634. Compared to the University of Texas Law School, the law school established for blacks had a faculty of five full-time members (versus 16), a library of 16,500 volumes (versus 65,000), 23 students (versus 850), and only one alumnus who was a member of the Texas Bar. *Id.* at 632-33.

36. *Id.* at 634.

37. *Id.*

38. *Id.* at 635. *See also* Missouri *ex rel* Gaines v. Canada, 305 U.S. 337, 351 (1938) (reasoning that equal rights is based on the individual). The *Gaines* Court would not consider the limited demand for legal education among Blacks in Missouri as a means to justify discrimination by whites. *Id.* at 350. The Court specifically found the argument that a constitutional right depends on the number of persons discriminated against was without merit because the essence of a constitutional right is that the right is personal. *Id.* at 351 (discussing McCabe v. Atchinson, Topeka & Sante Fe Ry. Co., 235 U.S. 151, 161 (1914)). The Court furthermore held that unconstitutional discrimination, concerning the legal right to enjoy opportunities throughout the State, cannot be resolved by requiring the individual to resort to another option, such as attending school in another state; that resort may be mitigating, but it does validate the constitutional violation. *Id.* at 350.

39. Brown v. Board of Educ. of Topeka, 347 U.S. 483, 486-88 (1954) (Brown I).

foundation of good citizenship"[40] and crucial to fulfilling public duties, including military service.[41] Moreover, education prepares students to succeed in life and to adapt to environments in which they are placed.[42] The Court held that in public education separate was inherently unequal because it denied all students access to intangible benefits, such as those expressed in *Sweatt* and *McLaurin*.[43] In light of this constitutional violation, the Court ordered desegregation.[44]

II. GENDER AND EDUCATION: ANALOGY TO THE RACIAL DECISIONS

Brown's adoption of and assertion regarding the importance of intangible factors did not end the judiciary's grappling with this issue in its constant protection of equal rights. *Brown* addressed race; but race is only one area affected by the denial of intangible factors due to constitutional violations. Gender has joined race in the quest to attain equal protection. Jurisprudence in the area of gender has followed a similar developmental history as race, but with some variations.[45]

Gender presented the courts with a new dimension for interpreting the separate but equal doctrine. Regardless of the indication by previous decisions that separate but equal was no longer applicable, the courts, including the Supreme Court, continued to vacillate in the area of gender, from recognizing that the denial of intangible factors invalidated separate but equal, to permitting exceptions to this standard.[46] The Court's formulation of intermediate scrutiny for

---

40. *Id.* at 493.

41. *Id.*

42. *Id.* Although the people to whom the Court's concern was addressed were elementary and high school students, the principles of education apply uniformly to elementary school, college, and post-graduate programs.

43. *Id.* at 493-95 (preventing the denial of intangible factors, such as the ability to study, to discuss, to learn, as well as to gain the benefits of leadership opportunities, reputation and tradition).

44. Brown v. Board of Educ. of Topeka, 349 U.S. 294, 301 (1955) (Brown II).

45. In looking at the history of the Equal Protection Clause, the argument is seldom put forth that any part of the original purpose of the Clause was to prevent discrimination based on gender. The protection gender receives from the Equal Protection Clause is a result of "a judicially created extrapolation" from the body of law regarding racial discrimination. Allan Ides, *The Curious Case of the Virginia Military Institute: An Essay on the Judicial Function*, 50 WASH. & LEE L. REV. 35, 40 (1993). The incorporation of gender into the realm protected by the Fourteenth Amendment was a result of the Court's interpretation of the Constitution based on its perception of current societal values. "[T]he Court forced the preferences and innovations of an evolving society into the Constitution, creating a new constitutional text that conformed to emerging ideas about the proper roles of men and women." *Id.* at 42. The Court, however, did not act inappropriately because the strength of the Constitution comes from the ability to interpret it to resolve contemporary problems. *Id.*

46. *See* Jon Allyn Soderberg, *The Virginia Military Institute and the Equal Protection Clause: A Factual and Legal Introduction*, 50 WASH. & LEE L. REV. 15, 22 (1993) (indicating that despite *Brown's* declaration that the separate but equal doctrine has no place in the educational sphere

gender-based classifications indicated the necessity of close judicial review to prevent a return to the days when separate but equal was promoted unquestionably and when inherent inequalities were ignored.

A. Intangible Factors and Gender

Most of the cases involving gender, education, and equal protection surfaced after the Court's decision in *Brown*. In 1958, a woman sought admission to the all-male Texas A & M University on the basis of convenience, not on the basis of wanting to pursue one of its courses of study.[47] The Court, in *Heaton v. Bristol*, ignored the intangible factor that the most prestigious schools with the broadest academic programs were usually all-male institutions;[48] these intangible factors, however, were addressed in a later case, *Kirstein v. Rector and Visitors of the University of Virginia*.[49] *Kirstein* challenged the University of Virginia's all-male admission policy, eventually resulting in the court ordering the University to admit women.[50] The court, considering the intangible factors in *Sweatt* and *McLaurin*, held that denying a qualified female admission to the most prestigious school in Virginia violated equal protection.[51]

Williams v. McNair,[52] decided twelve years after *Heaton*, relied on the *Kirstein* court's approach. In *Williams*, the Supreme Court found the exclusion of males from admission to Winthrop College was not in violation of the Equal Protection Clause and held that states can create schools with different missions in order to promote educational

---

suggests that the doctrine is banned at all educational facilities, later decisions allowed continued application of the doctrine when the classification was based on gender); William A. Devan, Note, *Toward A New Standard In Gender Discrimination: The Case of Virginia Military Institute*, 33 WM. & MARY L. REV. 489, 511 (1992) (explaining how the logical extrapolation would be to deny single-sex schools from existing, the *Brown* decision was issued before the Court recognized gender discrimination). *See also* Mary Jordan, *Citadel's Ramparts Unbreached*, WASH. POST, Jan. 13, 1994, at A1, A7 ("'It's time for women, [cadet Von Mickle] went on. Twenty years ago, blacks couldn't go here.' Mickle said that as a black American, he felt he had to support Faulkner . . . .").

47. Heaton v. Bristol, 317 S.W.2d 86 (Tex. Civ. App. 1958), *cert. denied*, 359 U.S. 230 (1959) (cited in Bennett L. Saferstein, *Revisiting Plessy At The Virginia Military Institute: Reconciling Single-Sex Education with Equal Protection*, 54 U. PITT. L. REV. 637, 647, n.48 (1993)).

48. Saferstein, *supra* note 15, at 648.

49. 309 F. Supp. 184 (E.D. Va. 1970).

50. Phillip Comer Griffeth, *The Beat Goes On: District Court Upholds Virginia Military Institute's All-Male Admissions Policy in United States v. Virginia*, 43 MERCER L. REV. 767, 779 (citing Kirstein v. Rector & Visitors of the Univ. of Va., 309 F. Supp. 184, 185-87 (E.D. Va. 1970)). This order however, did not require all state-supported colleges to become co-educational. *Id.*

51. Saferstein, *supra* note 15, at 649 & n.59 (citing *Kirstein*, 309 F. Supp. at 186).

52. 316 F. Supp. 134 (D.S.C. 1970), *aff'd per curiam*, 401 U.S. 951 (1971).

diversity.[53]   The Court, however, did not give the states unqualified power. The Court held that the state's objective could be achieved using gender classification *only if* no denial of tangible or intangible factors occurred.[54]

Furthermore, the Court held that although the Equal Protection Clause does not require identical treatment for all citizens, it does prohibit classifications that are arbitrary and wanting in any rational justification.[55] This principle is reminiscent of the reasonable test articulated in *Plessy*.

> [T]he maintenance of two institutions for the sexes in South Carolina, one for male warriors [the Citadel] and the other for female domestics [Winthrop College], is different [from racially segregated institutions] only in that the assumptions it reflects about individual capabilities and aspirations are more widely shared. The role of a housewife or a secretary is an honorable and productive one; so of course is the role of a champion athlete or a tenant farmer. To attack the attitudes reflected in the *Williams* decision is not to denigrate the individuals for whom such stereotypes happen to be accurate; it is to attack the arrogant assumption that merely because these stereotypes are accurate for some individuals, the state has a right to apply them to all individuals—and, indeed, to shape its official policy toward the need that they shall *continue* to be accurate for all individuals.[56]

---

53. Williams v. McNair, 316 F. Supp. 134, 138 (D.S.C. 1970) (stating that "flexibility and diversity in educational methods . . . often are both desirable and beneficial; they should be encouraged, not condemned").

54. Saferstein, *supra* note 15, at 650. The Court demonstrated in *Kirstein* and *Williams* that the notion of "separate but equal," with regard to race, but not necessarily gender, inherently violates the Equal Protection Clause because of a similar consideration of intangibles. As an explanation for why a parallel argument could not be made here, the Court stated that at the time of the *Williams* decision, the Court was not ready to adopt that rationale for gender. Therefore, "[appellants] must build up the cases that all illustrate cogently just how unequal *in fact* are the opportunities for women." Susan C. Ross, *The Rights of Women, in* SEX DISCRIMINATION AND THE LAW: CAUSES AND REMEDIES 995 (Barbara Allen Babcock et al. eds., 1975).

55. Williams v. McNair, 316 F. Supp. 134, 136 (D.S.C. 1970) ("[T]he Constitution does not require that a classification 'keep abreast of the latest' in educational opinion, especially when there remains a respectable opinion to the contrary; it only demands that the discrimination not be wholly wanting in reason.").

56. Johnston & Knapp, *Sex Discrimination By Law: A Study in Judicial Perspective,* 46 N.Y.U. L. REV. 657, 723-26 (1971), *in* SEX DISCRIMINATION AND THE LAW: CAUSES AND REMEDIES 1010-11 (Barbara Allen Babcock et al., eds., 1975). *See also* Catherine S. Manegold, *Save the Males Becomes Battle Cry In Citadel's Defense Against Woman,* N.Y. TIMES, May 23, 1994, at A10 (describing the federal case that the U.S. Justice Department and a female applicant named Shannon Faulkner are bringing against the state of South Carolina in opposition to the all-male admission standard at The Citadel, the state's public military institution. In the district court's decision, Judge C. Weston Houck referred to the VMI case when he stated that The Citadel must show that "South Carolina's education policy is inherently different from Virginia's and [in doing so,] should not be bound by the appellate court ruling [in the VMI case]").

The *Williams* Court went on to give two related reasons why men were not being denied equal protection and the benefit of intangible factors. First, Winthrop was only one part of the entire system of state-supported higher education and, thus, could not be viewed in isolation.[57] Second, no unique feature was connected with Winthrop that gave its students more of an educational advantage over any student at another state-supported institution.[58] As will be discussed below, these two rationales are still asserted today. However, in the case of VMI, they are not compelling.

B. The Development of Intermediate Scrutiny for Gender-Based Classifications

About the same time the Court affirmed *Williams*, it began to recognize gender as a suspect class and to apply heightened scrutiny to instances in which equal protection was denied.[59] The three major equal protection cases are *Reed v. Reed*,[60] *Frontiero v. Richardson*,[61] and *Craig v. Boren*.[62] Over the next several years, the use of intermediate scrutiny, which requires an important government goal achieved by substantially related means, was developed by the Court to ensure equal protection based on gender.

Classifications cannot be arbitrary; they must have a fair and substantial relationship to the goal of the legislation in order to ensure that all similarly situated individuals receive equal treatment.[63] Giving mandatory preference to members of one sex over

---

57. *Williams*, 316 F. Supp. at 137.

58. *Id.* at 138 (stating that the convenience of the proximity of a school is not a reason on which to base a decision of whether to allow both sexes admission).

59. Race, on the other hand, has received strict scrutiny continuously. *See, e.g.*, Korematsu v. United States, 323 U.S. 214 (1944); United States v. Carolene Products, 304 U.S. 144 (1938). Race and gender are subject to different levels of scrutiny based on the distinction that racial discrimination is usually the result of invidious stereotyping and animus, whereas gender discrimination can be the result of genuine psychological and physiological differences. Soderberg, *supra* note 46, at 20. "Through many battles in the courts, legislatures, and businesses of America, women have made unprecedented progress in securing equal rights under the law in the past thirty years. Society and the courts, however, have failed to reach the same consensus regarding the place of gender under our Constitution as they have with respect to race." Devan, *supra* note 46, at 489.

60. 404 U.S. 71 (1971) (holding that a statute giving preference to men over women, when both apply to be administrator of an estate and have equal entitlement, violates equal protection).

61. 411 U.S. 677 (1972) (plurality opinion) (holding that not allowing male spouses of female military officers the same benefits as those given to female spouses violates the Equal Protection Clause).

62. 429 U.S. 190 (1976) (holding that a statute that prohibited males under the age of 21 from buying alcohol, but that prohibited females only until they reached 18, violated equal protection).

63. *Reed*, 404 U.S. at 76 (*citing* Royster Guano Co. v. Virginia, 253 U.S. 412, 415 (1920)).

members of the other, simply to eliminate having to decide an issue based on the merits, is exactly the kind of arbitrary legislative choice that the Equal Protection Clause prohibits.[64] In these two declarations, the Court restated its concern with arbitrariness initially expressed in *Plessy.* However, the Court no longer employed a reasonableness standard as a solution, but required a higher level test: an articulated relationship between legitimate goals and related means.

In *Frontiero,* the Court raised the level of scrutiny. The Court agreed that sex-based and race-based classifications were both inherently suspect; and thus gender, like race, must be subjected to close judicial scrutiny.[65] Moreover, the Court declared sex and race to be immutable characteristics that evidence no relation to the ability to perform or contribute to society.[66] Brennan took these similarities to their logical conclusion: if race is subject to strict scrutiny, gender classification must be subjected not only to close, but strict, judicial scrutiny.[67] This standard, however, prevailed for only a few years.

Three years later, in *Craig v. Boren,* the Court stated that "classifications by gender must serve important governmental objectives and must be substantially related to the achievement of those objections."[68] The Court relied extensively on *Reed,* stating that the 1971 decision was the foundation to invalidate other statutes that used gender as a means for germane bases of classification.[69]   The rationale applied in *Reed,* and subsequently adopted in *Craig,*

---

64. *Id.* (rejecting the Idaho Supreme Court's decision that a legislative method of avoiding probate hearings was valid when it did not allow a woman to be the administrator of an estate, when a man was also qualified for that position).

65. *Frontiero,* 411 U.S. at 682 (plurality opinion).

66. *See id.* at 686 (stating the immutable characteristics of sex and race should not be a basis for the imposition of a disability because "legal burdens should bear some relationship to individual responsibility" (quoting Weber v. Aetna Casualty & Sur. Co., 406 U.S. 164, 175 (1972)).

67. *Id.* at 688. It is suggested, however, that Justice Stewart's vote and concurrence, based on the invidious discrimination standard set out in *Reed,* struck down the notion of applying strict scrutiny in favor of applying a lower, yet heightened standard, to these cases. Griffeth, *supra* note 50, at 769; *see also* Frontiero, 411 U.S. at 691 (holding "[c]lassifications based upon sex, like [those] upon race, alienage, and national origin, are inherently suspect and must therefore be subjected to close judicial scrutiny"). (Justice Ginsberg, however, has arguably raised the issue again).

68. 429 U.S. 190, 197 (1976). The dissent in *Craig* expressed the sentiment that gender-based discrimination should be reviewed under rational scrutiny. *Id.* at 217-18 (Rehnquist, J., dissenting).

69. *See id.* at 198 (explaining that governmental entitlements could not be determined by characterizations, such as the financial positions of service women in Frontiero v. Richardson, 411 U.S. 677, 689 n.23 (1972), and working women in Weinberger v. Wiesenfeld, 420 U.S. 636, 643 (1975)).

promoted the rejection of loose-fitting characterizations based on outdated misconceptions of the role of women in the home and away from the marketplace. *Craig* further asserted that laws based on weak relationships between gender, and the stereotypical characteristics or traits associated with that gender, were no longer tolerable.[70] Thus, the intermediate scrutiny became the standard of review for gender classifications and, as it is the scrutiny applied today, it will be used in Section V to evaluate VMI's Plan.

C. Application of Intermediate Scrutiny and Intangible Factors to Gender Cases in the Field of Education

In the previous cases that held single-sex schools did not violate the Constitution, the Supreme Court did not express a view on the appropriate level of scrutiny to use in gender classification cases.[71] Within the next decade, however, the Court articulated its decision to apply intermediate scrutiny for gender classifications. As a result, other federal courts followed the heightened standard of review and applied it in the context of education.

In *Vorchheimer v. School District of Philadelphia*,[72] a female high school student who was denied admission to an all-male academic high school brought an action to challenge the constitutionality of the exclusion. The female student was interested in an academic school, which by definition offered only college preparatory courses, but only two such schools existed.[73] One was for males; the other was for females.[74] The student's primary contention was that the academic reputation at the male school exceeded that of the female school.[75] The district court issued an injunction, requiring that females be admitted to the male school, based on the conclusion that the gender-based exclusion lacked a fair and substantial relationship to the government's interest.[76] In considering the constitutional issues and determining that the test to be applied was based on the notion of a fair and substantial relationship between means and ends, the

---

70. *Id.* at 199.
71. In both *Williams* and *Heaton*, the intermediate scrutiny test had not been articulated and, therefore, was not applied. Griffeth, *supra* note 50, at 780; *see also* Devan, *supra* note 46, at 513 (referring to the rejection of the separate but equal theory in *Brown*).
72. 532 F.2d 880 (3d Cir. 1976), *aff'd per curiam*, 430 U.S. 703 (1977).
73. *Id.* at 881. Philadelphia has four types of senior high schools, which can be categorized as academic, comprehensive, technical, and magnet.
74. *Id.*
75. *Id.* at 882.
76. *Vorchheimer*, 532 F.2d at 882. (finding the gender-based classification was not substantially related to the government's interest in offering the educational alternative of sexually-segregated high schools).

district court reviewed *Reed* and *Frontiero*.[77] The court of appeals, rejecting plaintiff's reliance on cases that address race and education (because race is held to strict scrutiny whereas gender is not), looked instead to the Supreme Court's decision in *Williams v. McNair*. The court of appeals regarded that case as controlling on the issue of denying the injunction.[78] The *Williams* standard of scrutiny was a rational basis, since *Reed* had not been decided at that time.[79] The court articulated, in *Vorchheimer*, that a legitimate educational policy existed and could be served by means of single-gender schools, based on the respected theories that adolescents may study more effectively when they are separated.[80] Thus, no constitutional violation existed.

The dissent, in criticizing the majority's holding, paraphrased from *Plessy* to demonstrate the similarity between the 1896 opinion and the 1976 decision.[81] The parallel is drawn between the two cases to emphasize the dissent's concern that the majority has reverted back to accepting separate but equal, even though that analysis in the field of education had been eliminated from Fourteenth Amendment jurisprudence with *Brown*.[82] The dissent continued the parallel between *Vorchheimer* and *Plessy* by emphasizing that the majority's characterization of petitioner's choice as voluntary is equivalent to Plessy's "voluntary" choice to ride the train.[83]

Since affirming *McNair* in 1971 and *Vorchheimer v. School District of Philadelphia* in 1977, the Supreme Court did not address another

---

77. Vorchheimer v. School Dist. of Philadelphia, 532 F.2d 880, 886 (3d Cir. 1976), *aff'd per curiam*, 430 U.S. 703 (1977) (distinguishing *Reed* and *Frontiero* because they involved situations in which a female is deprived of a benefit that cannot be obtained elsewhere. In the case at bar, however, the female student could have attended Girls High.).

78. *Id.* at 886-87 (justifying the intermediate scrutiny of gender classifications and the stricter scrutiny of those based on race, the appeals court notes that "there are differences between the sexes which may, in limited circumstances, justify disparity in law").

79. *Id.* at 887 (quoting the Supreme Court's opinion in *Williams* which stated that the Constitution only requires a classification be "not wholly wanting in reason").

80. Vorchheimer v. School Dist. of Philadelphia, 532 F.2d 880, 888 (3d Cir. 1976), *aff'd per curiam*, 430 U.S. 703 (1977).

81. *Id.* at 888 (Gibbons, J., dissenting) (citing Plessy v. Ferguson, 163 U.S. 537, 544 (1896) (inserting semantical changes to make the decision in *Plessy* read as if it were written in 1976 by the *Vorchheimer* majority)).

82. *Vorchheimer*, 532 F.2d at 889 (Gibbons, J., dissenting). "The majority opinion, in establishing a twentieth-century sexual equivalent to the *Plessy* decision, reminds us that the doctrine can and will be invoked to support sexual discrimination in the same manner that it supported racial discrimination prior to *Brown*." *Id.* The Court's rationale in *Brown* that the educational arena had no room for separate but equal should also apply to the realm of military education. Mary M. Cheh, *An Essay On VMI and Military Service: Yes, We Do Have To Be Equal Together*, 50 WASH. & LEE L. REV. 49, 55 (1993).

83. Vorchheimer v. School Dist. of Philadelphia, 532 F.2d 880, 889 (Gibbons, J., dissenting), *aff'd per curiam*, 430 U.S. 703 (1977). "The train Vorchhemier wants to ride is that of a rigorous academic program among her intellectual peers . . . . Her choice, like Plessy's, is to submit to segregation or refrain from availing herself of the service." *Id.*

gender and education case until the Court revisited the issue in *Mississippi University for Women v. Hogan.* In *Hogan,* a male nurse who applied to the University's school of nursing was denied admission based solely on gender.[84] The Court's decision solidified the use of intermediate scrutiny.[85] In articulating this test in an educational context, the Court addressed the prevention of continuing stereotypes through classifications.[86] If protecting members of one gender based on the presumption that they are inherently handicapped is the statute's objective, the statute would not pass the first prong of judicial scrutiny.[87] In making the determination, intermediate scrutiny itself, "must be applied free of fixed notions concerning the roles and abilities of males and females."[88]

Under *Hogan,* in the area of gender and education, the purpose of intermediate scrutiny, making the important goals and means substantially related, is to ensure that reasoned analysis is used to determine whether a gender-based classification is valid. Any other kind of analysis would risk a "mechanical application [and consequent perpetuation] of traditional, often inaccurate, assumptions about the proper roles of men and women."[89] The Court affirmed the court of appeals' decision that the State did not meet its burden under intermediate scrutiny. "The State had failed to show that providing a unique education opportunity for females, but not for males, bears a substantial relationship to that interest."[90]

Although the Court did not expressly state any reliance on an idea of intangible factors, its decision reflects such consideration. As the Court noted in *Hogan,* by guaranteeing that more women than men are provided opportunities at state-supported nursing schools, it reinforces old stereotypes suggesting that women, not men, should be

---

84. 458 U.S. 718, 719-23 (1982).

85. *Id.* at 724 (stating that the party seeking classification based on gender has the burden of showing an exceedingly pervasive justification, a burden met only by establishing that the discriminatory means are substantially related to the achievement of an important governmental objective). Justice O'Connor set forth the issue in gender discrimination cases as "not whether the benefitted class profits from the classification, but whether the State's decision to confer a benefit only upon one class by means of a discriminatory classification is substantially related to achieving a legitimate and substantial goal." *Id.* at 731 n.17.

86. "Care must be taken in ascertaining whether the statutory objective itself reflects archaic and stereotypic notions." *Id.* at 725.

87. Mississippi Univ. for Women v. Hogan, 458 U.S. 718, 725 (1982) (concluding that, despite the University's claim that its policy compensates for discrimination against women, the actual effect of the policy is to perpetuate the stereotyped image of nursing as a woman's job).

88. *Id.*

89. *Id.* at 726. *Contra* Plessy v. Ferguson, 163 U.S. 537, 550 (1896) (describing the rationale of separating people based on usage, customs, and traditions).

90. *Hogan,* 458 U.S. at 722 (citing the Fifth Circuit's opinion, 646 F.2d 1116, 1119 (5th Cir. 1981)).

nurses.[91] The intangible factor realized and preserved by admitting men to the university is the eradication of similar stereotypes. Thus, in the area of gender, intangible factors have been given weight in an equal protection analysis and separate facilities have been found to be unconstitutional.[92]

A recent case that also addressed gender segregation in education is *Garrett v. Board of Education of the School District of Detroit*.[93] *Garrett* concerned the opening of three male academies designed to offer special programs emphasizing male responsibility.[94] The academies had individual counseling and mentors, extended classroom hours, and uniforms.[95] The goal of the academies was to decrease high unemployment rates and dropout levels and to help eliminate homicide among urban males.[96] The academies were challenged on the basis that these goals, while important, did not necessitate an all-male environment because they addressed issues that face all students, male and female.[97] In striking down the constitutionality of the schools, the district court relied on *Craig v. Boren* which disallowed the use of gender as "a proxy for other, more germane bases for classification."[98] Under heightened scrutiny, the curriculum's emphasis on providing men with a vision and a plan for living, helping them master their emotions, and assisting them in acquiring skills and knowledge to overcome life's obstacles were found to be important governmental interests; but, the exclusion of women was not found to be a means substantially related to this objective.[99] The goal of keeping adolescents alive and out of prison was also impor-

---

91. *Hogan*, 458 U.S. at 730.

92. It is important to note that Justice Powell makes a direct reference to *Plessy v. Ferguson* in his dissent: "Sexual segregation in education differs from the tradition, typified by the decision in Plessy v. Ferguson [citation omitted], of separate but equal racial segregation. It was characteristic of racial segregation that segregated facilities were offered, not as alternatives to increase the choices available to blacks, but as the *sole* alternative." *Hogan*, 458 U.S. at 741 n.9 (Powell, J., dissenting). As I will argue later, these two bases for segregation may not be that different because, even in the gender context, segregated facilities may be an individual's sole alternative.

93. 775 F. Supp. 1004 (E.D. Mich. 1991).

94. *Id.* at 1006. The programs included "rites of passage," an Afro-centric curriculum, and lessons geared toward 21st century careers.

95. *Id.*

96. *Id.*

97. *See id.* (also challenging the stated goals on the basis that "at-risk" males were not targeted).

98. Garrett v. Board of Educ. of Detroit, 775 F. Supp. 1004, 1007 (E.D. Mich. 1991) (quoting Craig v. Boren, 429 U.S. 190, 198 (1976)).

99. *Id.* The defendant, however, argues that the schools have tried coeducation and that it has failed to improve male performance. *Id.* The court did not support this argument because, in the case where the schools succeeded, the success would be focused on the absence of girls and not on the educational factors that are more likely to be responsible. *Id.*

tant; but, again, the existence of all-male schools was not substantially related to this goal.[100] Nothing has shown that the failure of the education system to meet its goals is connected to the fact that males and females attend school together.[101] Thus, relying on the standard expressed in *Hogan*,[102] the establishment of these schools cannot pass intermediate scrutiny.

The judicial system has struggled to formulate a clearcut way to analyze cases involving gender classification and education. Although *Hogan* provides a more solid foundation for analysis, a close examination of all of the principles involved—equal protection, judicial scrutiny, and intangible factors—is still needed. The rest of this article will discuss the case of *United States v. Virginia*[103] and will analyze VMI's proposed plan in terms of these elements.

III. VIRGINIA MILITARY INSTITUTE: DISTRICT COURT AND COURT OF APPEALS' DECISIONS

As indicated previously, the case of VMI's admissions policy has been in the judicial system for several years. The case was first heard in 1991, and since then has reached the appellate level and has been remanded back to the district court where it was heard in January, 1994.[104]

A. *The Adversative Educational Model*

In 1991, the United States District Court of Virginia found that VMI's all-male facility and admissions policy did not violate the Equal Protection Clause.[105] The facts giving rise to this action were set forth in the District Court's opinion.[106] A female high school student wanted to be considered for admission to VMI, but was

---

100. Garrett v. Board of Educ. of Detroit, 775 F. Supp. 1004, 1008 (E.D. Mich. 1991).

101. *Id.*

102. *See id.* at 1006 (describing the standard as requiring that any gender-based classification must serve an important governmental interest, and the means used must be substantially related to those interests).

103. 766 F. Supp. 1407 (W.D. Va. 1991), *vacated and remanded,* 976 F.2d 890 (4th Cir. 1992).

104. O'Harrow, *supra* note 12, at E6. The result of this hearing was a decision issued by Chief Judge Kiser on April 29, 1994. United States v. Virginia, 852 F. Supp. 471 (W.D. Va. 1994).

105. United States v. Virginia, 766 F. Supp. 1407 (W.D. Va. 1991).

106. Facts concerning the public versus private nature of Virginia schools and the cost of attending either kind are not discussed in this article. Such concerns are not fundamental to the core of the equal protection argument being addressed. Moreover, the issue of the possibility of allowing a private college to run a VMI-like program, and remain immunized from equal protection challenges because the college is not part of the State, are resolved by provisions in the plan proposed by VMI. *See* VMI Defendants' Proposed Remedial Plan, United States v. Virginia, 976 F.2d 890 (4th Cir. 1992), *reh'g, reh'g en banc denied and cert. denied,* 113 S. Ct. 2431 (1993) [hereinafter VMI Plan].

denied on the basis of her gender.   Historically, VMI resisted becoming coeducational in an effort to preserve its unique educational method.[107]   VMI's method is based on the adversative model, which involves "physical rigor, mental stress, absolute equality of treatment, absence of privacy, minute regulation of behavior, and indoctrination in desirable values . . . ."[108]   Except at VMI, this system of education is not offered anywhere in the United States; and the school is often sought out by applicants because of its reputation as the most challenging military school in the country.

The adversative model relies on several interdependent facets.   The class system's objective of developing leadership qualities is reached through a program of privileges and responsibilities.   Each cadet is given specific responsibilities such as writing the standard operating procedures for the first year students, supervising the "rat line,"[109] serving as a disciplinarian,[110] and acting as a mentor to a specific first year student.[111]   A system of peer pressure is used to instill VMI's values.[112]   The VMI Honor Code controls all aspects of life, and violations are penalized by one sanction: expulsion.[113]   Another central aspect of the unique VMI experience is the barracks arrangement, which provides the environment for cross-class relationships, peer interaction, and administration of the class system and honor code.[114]   The barracks are designed with stark rooms, and the windows and doors are always open.   The purpose is to reduce all cadets to the lowest level, and then instill the values and attitudes expected from VMI's graduates.[115]   The anticipated change in the

---

107. In promoting its uniqueness, VMI relied in part on its history and tradition, being founded in 1839 and patterned after West Point. United States v. Virginia, 766 F. Supp. at 1427. However, West Point changed its traditions to accommodate the integration of women; therefore, if VMI prides itself on being like the academy on which it was patterned, the logical conclusion would be for VMI to change, also. *See infra* note 129 and accompanying text.

108. United States v. Virginia, 766 F. Supp. at 1421. The adversative model is employed to its extreme through the "rat line," in which first year students are treated, as the name "rat" suggests, as the lowest creature on earth. The training is comparable to Marine Corps boot camp, declared to be more strenuous than Army boot camp. *Id.* at 1422.

109. See *infra* note 165 for a description of the "rat system."

110. This assignment is often considered part of the "dyke system," which seeks to create cross-class bonding and give a model for leadership and support. United States v. Virginia, 766 F. Supp. 1407, 1423 (W.D. Va. 1991), *vacated by*, 976 F.2d 890 (4th Cir. 1992), *cert. denied*, Virginia Military Inst. v. United States, 113 S. Ct. 2431, *and on remand*, United States v. Virginia, 852 F. Supp. 471 (W.D. Va. 1994).

111. *Virginia*, 766 F. Supp. at 1422-23.

112. *Id.* at 1423.

113. *Id.*

114. United States v. Virginia, 766 F. Supp. 1407, 1423-24 (W.D. Va. 1991).

115. *Id.* at 1422. The conditions, which also include many cadets assigned to one room, poor ventilation, and gang bathrooms, is intentional in order to place each cadet under constant scrutiny, with no privacy, and to induce stress. *Id.* at 1424.

barracks' culture is an additional and frequently stated explanation for VMI's resistance to coeducation.[116]

At trial, one expert testified how the adversative model forces a student to know everything about himself: how far he can go with his anger, and how much he can take when he is exhausted physically and mentally.[117] Through this model, an individual completely comprehends his limits and his capabilities, which is the basis of leadership.[118] "All of the experts agreed that the components which make up the VMI system of encouraging leadership and character development must be understood holistically. If any of the individual systems were altered, it would affect the educational experience as a whole."[119]

The mission of VMI states the following:

> It is the mission of the Virginia Military Institute to produce educated and honorable men, prepared for the varied work of civil life, imbued with love of learning, confident in the functions and attitudes of leadership, possessing a high sense of public service, advocates of the American democracy and free enterprise system, and ready as citizen-soldiers to defend their country in time of national peril.[120]

In order to accomplish the desired results, the education at VMI is of the highest quality. Regular undergraduate courses in liberal arts, science, and engineering are complimented by military ROTC programs as well as the unique system of military discipline.[121] In conjunction with its mission, VMI stresses how its primary objective is not only to teach men who foresee a career in the military, but rather to develop character, and to prepare men for leadership positions in any domain.[122]

VMI considered its single-gender status prior to the present case. In 1983, a committee was formed to examine the advantages, disadvantages, and general effects of admitting women to VMI by

---

116. United States v. Virginia, 766 F. Supp. 1407, 1438 (W.D. Va. 1991). VMI contends that the barracks would have to change to allow for privacy, which would contradict the notion of community scrutiny. The honor code would, therefore, have less meaning because cadets could act more secretly. On the contrary, I argue that the honor code would have more meaning based exactly on the opportunities that secrecy makes available. The honor code is not tested to its fullest if there is no opportunity to be dishonest based on an individual's fear as a result of constant scrutiny by his peers.

117. *Id.* at 1421-22.

118. *Id.*

119. *Id.* at 1422.

120. *Id.* at 1425.

121. United States v. Virginia, 766 F. Supp. 1407, 1424-1425 (W.D. Va. 1991).

122. *Id.* at 1426-27 (describing VMI's commitment to developing the "citizen-soldier").

comparing VMI to other similar education institutions.[123]   West
Point, upon which VMI was originally based, presented eleven factors
that favored coeducation:

(1) Attrition occurs for the same reason, regardless of gender;

(2) resentment is not prevalent and individual achievement forms
the basis of acceptance;

(3) VMI graduates will be at a disadvantage in the military, after
graduation, because the military is coed and they are accustomed
only to the single-gender military environment;

(4) the admission of women to West Point did not significantly
change the academy;

(5) women perform and compete as well as men in all training
programs;

(6) training can be altered to account for gender-based physical
differences without disrupting the character of the academy;

(7) physical education courses are the same for men and women
with the one exception of self-defense for women and box-
ing/wrestling for men;

(8) the cost of education was not affected by admitting women;

(9) going coeducational did not require changes in the curriculum,
procedures, or facilities;

(10) women have not encountered problems with the honor code;
and

(11) women have excelled at all levels of the West Point experience.[124]

The examination of the United States Naval Academy revealed very
similar information to that provided by West Point.[125] A comparison
to Washington & Lee University provided the same result. Women
succeeded and, in fact, their admittance resulted in attracting better
qualified students that improved the overall quality of life at the
University.[126] This comparison went on to recognize that changes
would inevitably have to occur if VMI became coeducational, but

---

123. *Id.* at 1427.

124. *Id.* at 1428.

125. United States v. Virginia, 766 F. Supp. 1407, 1428 (W.D. Va. 1991). The Air Force
Academy (AFA), however, which was not considered in the committee's study, found opposite
results. Although the AFA was originally supportive of the idea of coeducation, this support was
replaced by resentment based on the fact that women, due primarily to the nature of their
housing apart from their squadron, were spared interruptions and harassment. Devan, *supra*
note 46, at 525. In addition, the Naval Academy, although favoring coeducation, did recognize
the fine line that must be drawn between hazing that forms class bonding and conduct that
forms sexual harassment. *Id.* at 527.

126. United States v. Virginia, 766 F. Supp. at 1429 (providing a statement by Dr. John D.
Wilson that the admittance of women at Washington & Lee was generally positive, while
admitting that such a change at VMI would necessitate certain modifications).

those changes would not destroy the entire system.[127] The committee gained further insight by looking to the University of Virginia, which indicated that coeducation was a positive experience resulting in the strengthening of the school.[128] Yet, even with this information, the committee found nothing that warranted VMI to admit women. VMI held steadfastly to the argument that admission of women would alter its mission.[129]

At the district court level, Virginia emphasized the physical and developmental differences between men and women to justify maintaining a single-sex policy. Physical comparisons were made based on aerobic and lifting capacity, body fat, push-up and pull-up capabilities, and susceptibility to injury.[130] Physical education, VMI contended, would have to be altered based on inherent differences, which would result also in the alteration of rat training.[131]

Developmental differences were explored in more detail, emphasizing different needs and different means of learning.[132] According to VMI, males tend to need an adversative atmosphere, in which the teacher is a disciplinarian and competitor, whereas females need a cooperative atmosphere, in which the teacher emotionally connects with the students.[133] Although this theory seems to dominate the findings of facts, one expert conceded that some women can thrive in an adversative environment.[134] VMI also argued that a single-gender environment, for men, eliminates sexual tension that would be created with the presence of women.[135] Relationships between the sexes would affect the nature of the VMI experience because it would lead to jealousies and aspirations that work against the central notion of complete equality.[136] As VMI further contended, in general, single-gender education has been shown, through research, to benefit both sexes based on increased academic involve-

---

127. *Id.*

128. *Id.* (demonstrating how "contrary to expectations, female students at the University [of Virginia] tend to enroll in the strongest departments and superior programs including engineering and architecture").

129. *Id.* at 1429-30 (considering the reasons that other institutions changed to coeducational, VMI found that none of the motivating factors of other institutions applied to them).

130. United States v. Virginia, 766 F. Supp. 1407, 1432-33 (W.D. Va. 1991).

131. *Id.* at 1438 (describing a physical education program as a part of a proposed remedial plan).

132. United States v. Virginia, 852 F. Supp. 471 (W.D. Va. 1994).

133. *Id.* at 1434.

134. *Id.* The expert, however, remarked how women who thrive under an adversative model are the exception.

135. United States v. Virginia, 766 F. Supp. 1407, 1435 (W.D. Va. 1991). The opposite gender is implicated as a distraction and a source of dissipating energy that could be otherwise spent pursuing educational opportunities. *Id.*

136. *Id.* at 1440.

ment, faculty interaction, and increased self-esteem.[137] Furthermore, the research used by VMI also indicated additional benefits, namely that careers of men who graduated from single-gender schools tended to focus on law, business and college teaching, thus positively affecting their starting salaries. It further alleged that women who graduated from single-gender schools assumed leadership positions and aspired to advanced degrees, presumably increasing their starting salaries.[138]

Because some minor accommodations would have to be made with the admission of women, VMI argued that absolute equality of treatment would also be changed to a standard based on fairness of treatment due to the physiological, psychological, and sociological differences of the two genders.[139] VMI maintained that these changes would drastically alter the VMI experience, and that gender-based classification to preserve this element was appropriate.

B. The Opinion of the District Court of Virginia

Applying the Supreme Court's intermediate scrutiny test—requiring an important governmental objective be met by substantially related means—the District Court seemed to reason that preventing the alteration of key elements of VMI's educational system because of the admittance of females was a governmental goal sufficient to satisfy the first part of the test.[140] Moreover, the diversity provided by the single-gender experience offered at VMI was seen as a second governmental goal that could withstand intermediate scrutiny.[141] The means, single-sex education, by which these goals were achieved was, according to the district court, substantially related and survived constitutional scrutiny.[142]

---

137. *Id.* at 1435. (citing Alexander Astin, Four Critical Years, (1977)). These factors may be considered by some proponents of the plan to be intangible aspects of single-sex education that would be denied if VMI was forced to integrate women. To the contrary, these benefits can still be taken advantage of at coeducational institutions. Although they may not be attained to the same degree, if the current system is left intact with the additional separate program, other intangible benefits exist that are not available to any degree through the proposed segregated system.

138. *Id.* Another study indicates that students from single-sex colleges may be more likely to pursue careers traditionally associated with the opposite sex. United States v. Virginia, 766 F. Supp. 1407, 1435 (W.D. Va. 1991) (citing Marvin Bressler & Peter Wendell, *The Sex Composition of Selective Colleges and Gender Differences in Career Aspirations*, 51 J. OF HIGHER EDUC. 650 (1980)).

139. United States v. Virginia, 766 F. Supp. at 1439.

140. *Id.* at 1411. The district court relied heavily on the Supreme Court's articulation of intermediate scrutiny in Mississippi University for Women v. Hogan, 458 U.S. 718 (1982), which will be discussed in further detail in Section V. The court also refers to *Williams v. McNair* to support its opinion that gender segregated institutions may be permissible.

141. United States v. Virginia, 766 F. Supp. 1407, 1412-13 (W.D. Va. 1991).

142. *Id.* at 1414-15. In fact, Judge Kiser states that the means can benefit both genders. *Id.*

C. The Opinion of the Fourth Circuit Court of Appeals

In 1992, the United States Court of Appeals for the Fourth Circuit reviewed the issue of single-gender education at VMI.[143] The court of appeals also recognized VMI's unique educational method as an important governmental objective and upheld the single-gender admissions policy as a substantially related means.[144] The court, however, added an important distinction. It did not agree that the existence of this objective warranted limiting this opportunity to only the single gender of males.[145] Ultimately, the case was remanded to the district court. The Commonwealth, consequently, was required to choose one of three alternatives: admit women; give up its state support of VMI; or develop a plan that would meet the principles of equal protection set forth in the court of appeal's decision.[146] The Commonwealth decided to develop the plan and submit it to the district court for adoption and implementation.[147]

In reaching a decision, the court of appeals established its perception of equal protection principles by stating that the Equal Protection Clause did not intend to eliminate all differences between individuals.[148] In undertaking an equal protection analysis, the court had to decide whether the class of persons targeted by a state regulation is defined so that the class' relationship to the purpose of the regulation is fair and substantial.[149] The court of appeals determined that "[i]t is not the maleness, as distinguished from femaleness, that provides justification for the program. It is the homogeneity of gender in the process, regardless of which gender is considered, that has been shown to be related to the essence of the education and training at VMI."[150] Thus, the court of appeals seemed to suggest that single gender institutions could pass intermediate scrutiny, but only if both genders had substantially the same opportunity available to them.

The diversity argument, advanced by the lower court's decision—that VMI allowed an additional and different educational opportunity—did not satisfy the court of appeals. A policy of diversity which aims to provide an array of educational opportunities, including

---

143. United States v. Virginia, 976 F.2d 890 (4th Cir. 1992).
144. *Id.* at 892.
145. *Id.*
146. *Id.*
147. *Id.*
148. United States v. Virginia, 976 F.2d 890, 895 (4th Cir. 1992).
149. *Id.* (relying on Mississippi Univ. for Women v. Hogan, 458 U.S. 718 (1982)).
150. *Id.* at 897.

single-gender institutions, must do more than favor one gender.[151] In other words, VMI had not established how limiting this experience to men, without providing any opportunity—single-gender or coeducational for women—was substantially related to achieving its goals. The court of appeals, therefore, remanded the case to the district court and allowed VMI the option of admitting women, giving up its state support, or formulating a similar program for women.

IV. VIRGINIA MILITARY INSTITUTE'S PROPOSED REMEDIAL PLAN

In September, 1993, VMI chose the option of establishing a parallel program for women and submitted its remedial plan ("the Plan") to the United States District Court, Western District of Virginia.[152] The Plan proposed means to provide college-age women a state-supported, single-gender educational program that would resemble VMI in its preparation of leaders for civilian and military life. The program, however, would be located off-site at Mary Baldwin College in Staunton, Virginia.

The creation of a separate educational program for women under the Plan is based on the court of appeals' perception that single-gender education may be justified when an institution such as VMI offers its program in a holistic educational environment and the inevitable destruction of that environment would result if VMI were to admit women.[153] The Plan further relies on the notion that single-gender programs particularly benefit women, who otherwise may be denied leadership opportunities in coeducational institutions.[154]

---

151. *Id.* at 899.

152. VMI Plan, *Supra* note 106. In a South Carolina case in which a 19-year-old woman sued to be the first female student in the military college's all-male corps, the Citadel was ordered to allow Shannon Faulkner to attend classes starting January, 1994, while it develops a plan for a parallel program for housing, clothing and feeding a woman at their academy. The Citadel, the only other all-male, public military college in the nation besides VMI, initially indicated it would propose a program similar to that of the Mary Baldwin Institute for leadership proposed by VMI. The Court has requested a final proposed plan from the Citadel by the end of July, 1994. Eichel, *supra* note 4, at A1. *See also Citadel's Fallback Position: No Females in Cadet Corps*, WASH. POST, Apr. 3, 1994, at A10 (describing the Citadel's ten-page plan which suggested three options: sending students to military institutions out-of-state, giving support to private women's schools, or having co-educational cadet corps at another state school).

153. VMI Plan, *supra*, note 106, at 1. The court of appeals remarked on (and the Institute reiterated in its proposed Plan) the Catch-22 situation that is presented to VMI because the members of the opposite sex who desire the VMI experience, would—by the nature of their presence—alter that experience due to the accommodations that would have to be made. United States v. Virginia, 976 F.2d 890, 897 (4th Cir. 1992); VMI Plan, *supra* note 152, at 2.

154. VMI Plan, *supra* note 152, at 3. The U.S. government argued in the course of this action that VMI is a state-supported school and thus is subject to certain requirements in the interest of equal protection. Mary Baldwin, however, is a private college and some commentators suggest this immunizes Mary Baldwin from equal protection claims. This status does not

VMI's Plan proposes to establish a unique, innovative, and state-supported leadership program at Mary Baldwin College, an all-female, private school. The underlying mission of this leadership program parallels VMI's mission: to produce women as citizen-soldiers through physical and mental rigor and other unspecified components.[155] To further simulate VMI, the proposed program would offer women the chance to partake in a co-educational military component through Virginia Polytechnic Institute and State University.[156] The Plan is designed to provide women a comparable physical and mental single-gender program. The program is also specifically designed to develop women as leaders and to give women a coeducational military experience similar to that which would be offered by VMI, if VMI became coeducational.[157]

The Plan is based on the establishment of a four-year residential undergraduate program at Mary Baldwin College, entitled Virginia Women's Institute for Leadership ("Institute for Leadership").[158] The mission of the Institute for Leadership purports to be "comparable to and derived from" VMI's mission.[159] However, to achieve the mission, Mary Baldwin will adopt only some of VMI's educational systems, and with gender-based differences within some of those

---

change VMI's obligation to ensure that women are given equal rights because Mary Baldwin will be contracting with the state to receive funding for this program, thereby intertwining itself with the state and becoming subject to its constitutional requirements. Educating students in both educational curriculum and in military training constitutes a dual function that is traditionally a governmental function, indicating that such schools are state actors regardless of their private status. Berman, *supra* note 15, at 228-29. This paper does not address whether Mary Baldwin is immunized from the requirements of the Equal Protection Clause; it is assumed that the college is not (based on Berman's argument alone). *See also* Note, *State Action, Private Colleges, and Sex Segregation, in* Sex Discrimination and the Law: Causes and Remedies, *supra* note 54 at 997, 998 (stating that if a private college is intermingling with a public institution or with the state—such as through receiving financial support or by exercising a traditionally governmental power—it can be considered public for the purpose of reviewing certain policies). *See also supra* note 138 and accompanying text (discussing the assumption of leadership positions by women graduates of single-gender schools).

155. VMI Plan, *supra* note 152, at 3.

156. VMI Plan, *supra* note 152, at 3. The Plan suggests that this offering further ensures that women could participate in a holistic program.

157. VMI Plan, *supra* note 152, at 3.

158. VMI Plan, *supra* note 106, at 6. VMI will give Institute for Leadership brochures and application forms to females who are interested in VMI and will forward these inquiries to Mary Baldwin. Mary Baldwin, in turn, will provide VMI admissions information to any males who express an interest in Mary Baldwin College. *Id.* at 14. However, Dr. Cynthia Tyson, president of Mary Baldwin College, stated they have never had inquiries from male applicants. Telephone Interview with Dr. Cynthia Tyson, President, Mary Baldwin College (Oct. 11, 1993).

159. VMI Plan, *supra* note 152, at 7. The mission is to produce "citizen-soldiers who are educated and honorable women, prepared for the varied work of civil life, qualified to serve in the armed forces, imbued with love of learning, confident in the functions and attitudes of leadership, and possessing a high sense of public service." *Id.*

systems.[160] These systems include a curriculum of traditional liberal arts and sciences, as well as course offerings that focus on leadership in business, government service, volunteerism, interpersonal communication, organizational behavior, ethics, and mediation.[161] The Institute for Leadership will also adopt the following: military training through cross-enrollment with other ROTC programs, an honor code, a mentoring system, physical training,[162] a residential system,[163] extracurricular programs, orientation programs, and externship opportunities.[164]

One of the major differences between VMI and the proposed Plan at Mary Baldwin is the elimination of the "rat system."[165] This adversarial model is not included for women because it was determined to be unsuitable for the majority of female students, even though it is conducive to the development of confidence and self-esteem in men.[166] The Institute for Leadership maintains that the mental toughness objective achieved at VMI through the rat system will be attained at Mary Baldwin through the combination of its other programs.[167]

In the Plan, VMI emphasizes that it does not seek to achieve a separate but equal program, but strives to provide a distinct and superior program for women using methods that meet their specific

---

160. See VMI Plan, supra note 152, at 8-12.

161. VMI Plan, supra note 152, at 8.

162. Although the requirement of eight semesters of a physical education program would be the same for men at VMI and women at Mary Baldwin, the level of rigor that must be met for women is different from that of men, based on gender-based differences. This training will also include confidence-building exercises and an obstacle course. VMI Plan, supra note 152, at 10.

163. The residential system, however, is altered to promote esprit de corps, leadership, and mentoring not gained through the military atmosphere associated with barracks. VMI Plan, supra note 152, at 11.

164. See VMI Plan, supra note 152, at 8-12.

165. The court of appeals described the rat system as "the harsh orientation process to which all new cadets ('rats') are subjected during their first seven months at VMI. Designed to be comparable to the Marine Corps' boot camp in terms of physical rigor and mental stress, the rat line includes indoctrination, minute regulation of individual behavior, frequent punishments, rigorous physical education, and military drills." United States v. Virginia, 976 F.2d 890, 893 (4th Cir. 1992).

166. VMI Plan, supra note 152, at 4-5. The Plan argues that a program based on the adversarial model would attract few females and would benefit even fewer of them. Id. at 5. This consideration, however, does not have merit as will be discussed in section V.

167. VMI Plan, supra note 152, at 10 (specifying the Institute for Leadership's cadre week, rigorous physical training program, student-regulated residence hall life, honor code, ROTC program, and intensive academic program). However, if all the other systems are so similar to VMI as to make the experience equal at both institutions, it is unclear why VMI is so concerned about maintaining its own rat system? "The combination of these systems will achieve the same results . . . as the rat training system in the development of mental discipline and the capacity to solve problems . . . ." VMI Plan, supra note 152, at 10.

needs.[168]   Virginia contends that the Plan solves the problem created by the absence of a VMI-type program for women and represents a creative option that not only provides women a superior eduction, but also achieves the State's goal of diversity in higher education and of training future leaders.[169] As such, VMI maintains that the Plan does not violate any element of equal protection.[170]

V. GENDER, EDUCATION, INTANGIBLE FACTORS, AND INTERMEDIATE SCRUTINY: APPLICATION TO VIRGINIA MILITARY INSTITUTE'S REMEDIAL PLAN

The Plan does not resolve VMI's violation of the Equal Protection Clause. A close examination of the proposed Plan will show that the separate institution at Mary Baldwin denies women from receiving equal benefits of intangible factors based on gender classification, and it does not meet the standards of intermediate scrutiny.   The following analysis flows from the historical and parallel trend—in cases of race-based segregation in education—that practices once considered separate but equal are now found to be inherently unequal.[171] Additionally, the analysis takes into account the differences between the two constitutional approaches. In the context of gender, the focus is two-fold: whether separate institutions deny women intangible factors[172] that are provided to men, and whether gender-based segregation passes intermediate scrutiny.

---

168. VMI Plan, *supra* note 152, at 4; Telephone Interview with Dr. Cynthia Tyson, President, Mary Baldwin College (Oct. 11, 1993).

169. VMI Plan, *supra* note 152, at 19.

170. VMI Plan, *supra* note 152, at 2, 19. The U.S. Department of Justice ("DOJ") objects to the Plan based on violations of equal protection; specifically, DOJ argues that the plan "omits the essential components and benefits of the unique VMI experience" and "it designs programs based on gender stereotypes." United States' Opposition and Response to the VMI Defendants' Proposed Remedial Plan 1, 1, United States v. Virginia, 976 F.2d 890 (4th Cir. 1992), (No. 90-0126-R) (filed Nov. 15, 1993) [hereinafter Opposition]. DOJ concludes its argument by stating that because VMI has failed to demonstrate a constitutionally adequate alternative to its present program, VMI should be required to fully integrate women. *Id.* at 2-3.

171. *See supra* notes 45-70 and accompanying text. It is important to reiterate that Mary Baldwin does not assert this plan creates a separate but equal facility. On the contrary, the Plan is considered to establish a "distinct and superior" program for women. VMI Plan, *supra* note 152, at 4. On remand, the District Court rejected the proposition that the Court of Appeals would be satisfied with a Plan that offered a separate but equal alternative. "[I]f 'separate but equal' is the standard by which the Commonwealth's plan must be measured, then it surely must fail because, as the United States pointed out time and time again during the trial, even if all else were equal between VMI and the Virginia Women's Institute for Leadership (VWIL), the VWIL program cannot supply those intangible qualities of history, reputation, tradition, and prestige that VMI has amassed over the years." 852 F. Supp. 471, 475 (W.D. Va. 1994). Regardless of the different labels, equal or superior, the consequences are the same: women are separated from men based solely on gender.

172. In United States v. Virginia, 766 F. Supp. 1407 (W.D. Va. 1991), the court relied on research indicating that certain benefits can be derived from single-sex education that cannot be gained from coeducation. *Id.* at 1411-12, *vacated by*, 976 F.2d 890 (4th Cir. 1992), *cert. denied*,

A. *Intangible Factors and Virginia Military Institute*[173]

"[A]s courts have recognized in other contexts, educational quality

---

Virginia Military Inst. v. United States, 113 S. Ct. 2431, *and on remand,* United States v. Virginia, 852 F. Supp. 471 (W.D. Va. 1994). Although proponents of sexual segregation deny the similarities between the race equivalent cases, the court's reliance on this social science research is strikingly similar to the sociological evidence used in *Brown I* to determine that racially segregated schools were inherently unequal and that segregation effected intangible factors. Saferstein, *supra* note 15, at 640 n.13; *see also* Brown v. Board of Educ. of Topeka, 347 U.S. 483, 495 (1954) (Brown I) (emphasizing the importance of intangible factors in Equal Protection case analysis). It seems ironic, however, that in *Brown I* a study was used to show the negative effects of segregation and to support the contention that desegregation was necessary; yet, in VMI, an empirical study is being used to show that segregation, based on gender, is more beneficial. *Brown I,* 347 U.S. at 493-94. *See* United States v. Virginia, 766 F. Supp. 1407, 1412 (W.D. Va. 1991); *see also* Saferstein, *supra* note 15, at 657. By viewing single-sex education as beneficial for both men and women, the court in VMI did not consider that women's goals of higher education might be due to exceptional academic experiences, and men's goals of career opportunities might be the result of 'old boys' networks." Saferstein, *supra* note 46, at 657 n.99.

173. Two cases have specifically addressed the issue of gender-based classification as it relates to admission to military academies. These cases sandwich the Court's decision in *Hogan,* 458 U.S. 718 (1982), which set intermediate scrutiny as the level of review for gender-based discrimination. Waldie v. Schlesinger, 509 F.2d 508 (D.C. Cir. 1974), preceded *Hogan* and United States v. Massachusetts Maritime Academy, 762 F.2d 142 (1st Cir. 1985), succeeded it. The governmental interest at issue in these cases was upholding the policy that women could not undertake combat positions; the means was excluding them from military schools. *Waldie,* 509 F.2d at 509; *Massachusetts Maritime Academy,* 762 F.2d at 153. This interest is not a concern in the VMI case, but a brief look at the two decisions reinforces the use of the intermediate scrutiny test in the context of gender, education, and military academies.

Waldie presented three issues involving gender-based discrimination in a military context: 1) the proper level of deference the courts should give Congress on military affairs; 2) the adequate protection of constitutional guarantees despite military concerns; and 3) the level of review that should be used for gender-based distinctions. Ponte, *supra* note 15, at 1141. The United States Court of Appeals for the District of Columbia Circuit, focusing on the constitutionality of single-sex admission policies at military academies, rejected the district court's application of the rational basis test. *Id.* However, it did not apply a heightened scrutiny because no such standard had been clearly articulated. *Id.* at 1140-41 n.20 (citing *Waldie,* 509 F.2d 508, 509 (D.C. Cir. 1974)). The *Waldie* court suggested that the standard for testing sex-based equal protection claims was still developing and depended on the facts of each particular case. Ponte, *supra* note 15, at 1143 n.31. As a result, the facts were essential to determine whether distinctions were based on sex-stereotypes or on justifiable government objectives. *Id.* at 1143.

Massachusetts Maritime Academy, in admitting women, rejected both the argument that women could not be involved in combat and the argument their exclusion from military academies furthered the important government objective of national defense. 762 F.2d at 153; *see also* Ponte, *supra* note 15, at 1158. Due to the statutory and regulatory revisions from Congress that required federal military academies to admit women, men and women were now similarly situated for recruitment, admissions, training, and commissioning at the academies and colleges. Ponte, *supra* note 15, at 1159; *Massachusetts Maritime Academy,* 762 F.2d at 153. *Massachusetts Maritime Academy* is important in the development of gender-based standards to determine discrimination, especially in military colleges and academies. It signifies a merger between the heightened scrutiny test and legislative revisions. Ponte, *supra* note 15, at 1160. In *Massachusetts Maritime Academy,* the court applied heightened scrutiny and held that this same standard of review should be applied in gender-based claims regardless of whether the academies are federal or state. Ponte, *supra* note 15 at 1158; *Massachusetts Maritime Academy,* 762 F.2d at 152-53. In light of the developing case law and legislative changes, the argument has been made that all military academies should be coeducational; and thus, those colleges that have not yet admitted women are in violation of equal protection guarantees. Ponte, supra note 15, at 1160.

rests on a host of intangible and to some extent incommensurable factors regarding reputation, learning environment, and socialization patterns."[174] Although previous analyses of the current Virginia case speculated that intangible factors consist of the prestige and strength of the alumni of VMI as well as the tradition and history of the school,[175] these are no longer as questionable given the reputation, alumni strength, tradition, and history of Mary Baldwin College. Nonetheless, other intangible factors exist which are not provided equally to men and women under the Plan.

Courts are continuously engaged in defining what constitutes an intangible factor. Generalized terms, such as learning environment and socialization patterns, provide some guidance. Considering these broad categories, the Court should recognize the following intangible factors: the benefit of a holistic experience; informal learning and interaction among classmates; the elimination of, and the prevention of perpetuating traditional gender stereotypes; and the realization of empowerment. These factors are equally as important as those factors listed in the Supreme Court's previous decisions. Consequently, these intangibles warrant the application of heightened scrutiny to ensure that they are provided equally to members of both sexes. Under intermediate scrutiny, therefore, VMI's proposed plan should fail.

1. Holistic Experience

The idea of gaining a complete educational experience often lies at the heart of an equal protection analysis examining the benefits of intangible factors in the educational context. No court decision has considered a school's holistic experience in and of itself an intangible factor. In the present case, however, the holistic educational experience of VMI is a separate intangible factor that women do not receive under the exclusionary admissions policy nor under the proposed plan.

A holistic experience emphasizes the importance of the entirety and focuses on the interdependence of the parts; the primary concern lies on the whole and does not concentrate on the dissection of that whole into its separate components.[176] The VMI experience offers a unique combination of an adversative model of education, an

---

174. Deborah L. Rhode, *Association and Assimilation*, 81 Nw. U. L. REV. 106, 138 (1986) (citing Sweatt v. Painter, 339 U.S. 629, 634 (1950)). The author also argues that consideration of intangible factors can explain why the court's decision in *Vorchhemier* is inadequate. *Id.*

175. *See generally Cheh, supra* note 82, at 51; Griffeth, *supra* note 50, at 772-74; Ides, *supra* note 45 at 45; Saferstein, *supra* note 15, at 659-66; Soderberg, *supra* note 46 at 17-18; Devan, *supra* note 46, at 494.

176. WEBSTER'S II DICTIONARY 587 (1988).

egalitarian ideal of absolute equality of treatment, an intense physical program, an absence of privacy, and strict regulation of behavior through military discipline and through the honor code.[177] These elements exist in conjunction with a strong extra-curricular program and a unique residential system. Moreover, VMI's faculty and facilities are dedicated completely to the success of the program. VMI's resources are invested solely in this program; The one and only objective with which the entire VMI community is concerned is developing leaders, citizen-soldiers.[178]

Women cannot experience VMI's unique combination of factors elsewhere because no other institute provides the same military, educational, and developmental experience.[179] The Plan suggests that the new program at Mary Baldwin provides this same holistic program by providing opportunities for both a strong education at Mary Baldwin and military training at Virginia Polytechnic Institute,[180] and by placing emphasis on leadership development.[181] The Plan does not, however, remedy the unconstitutional infringement of equal protection because it does not provide the crucial combination of the many facets of a VMI education that is the crux of this intangible factor. First, the Plan specifically excludes the adversative model and the absence of privacy from its program.[182] In addition, the Plan's structure, by its very design, separates the curriculum, disciplinary procedures, leadership development, extra-curricular activities, mentoring, residence requirements, and the honor code into distinct spheres.

The curriculum, as it relates to specific courses, is important at VMI; but it encompasses other elements. The VMI educational curriculum is "conducted in, and facilitated by, the unique VMI system of military discipline."[183] In addition, VMI's leadership

---

177. *See* United States v. Virginia, 766 F. Supp. at 1412-13; Griffeth, *supra* note 49, at 772-74; *Saferstein, supra* note 15, at 659-66;

178. VMI Plan, *supra* note 152, at 1 (stating the purpose of the VMI Proposed Remedial Plan).

179. *See* Berman, *supra* note 15, at 221 (arguing that the lack of access to VMI for females was not the true issue, rather the issue was the lack of an all-female counterpart to VMI).

180. VMI Plan, supra note 152, at 3 (describing the purpose of the Plan: to provide women with the educational choices of a single-gender program designed exclusively for women, or a coeducational program at Virginia Polytechnic Institute and State University).

181. Again, one argument in support of the Plan contends that the leadership program at Mary Baldwin does not strive to be separate but equal, rather it strives to be distinct and superior. VMI Plan, *supra* note 152, at 4. Telephone Interview with Dr. Cynthia Tyson, President, Mary Baldwin College (Oct. 11, 1993).

182. VMI Plan, *supra* note 152, at 4-5, 10-11 (discussing how the adversative model and the constant scrutiny of a barracks is not conducive for developing self-esteem in women).

183. Opposition, *supra*, note 170, at 22 (quoting Virginia Military Institute 1993-1994 Catalogue at 3).

development is achieved through its holistic method that cuts across specific courses.[184] The Plan, on the other hand, proposes that students must complete core and elective courses in leadership.[185] Mary Baldwin's approach places the focus of leadership development mostly in the classroom whereas VMI's method focuses on leadership development in all aspects of the student's life.[186]

At VMI, extra-curricular activities are a serious part of the curriculum.[187] Extra-curricular activities at Mary Baldwin, however, would include students who are not part of the program. These activities must then cater to the needs of a student body which is not immersed in the leadership program. Furthermore, it is likely that other students would not undertake these activities with the same degree of seriousness as the cadets at VMI, thereby depriving the Institute for Leadership students of a comparable experience. This emphasizes, again, that at Mary Baldwin this program is only one of a vast number of activities being offered.[188]

The structured mentoring process at Mary Baldwin is also not the same as the systems imposed at VMI. Without the rat line or dyke system, the same degree of pressure and stress is not present. It is these elements that lead to self-control, self-discipline, and selflessness for the good of a unit that VMI contends is necessary for leadership in combat.[189]

Men at VMI live together in stark, uncomfortable barracks, arranged so every movement can be seen. Although the Plan recognizes the need for women enrolled in the program to live together, the character of dormitory life does not equal the character of barracks life. Women, therefore, are deprived of another element

---

184. Opposition, *supra* note 170, at 23.

185. VMI Plan, *supra* note 152, at 8 (highlighting topics under consideration including "Issues of Leadership in Business, Government and Voluntary Service; Interpersonal Communication; Organizational Behavior; Ethics; Mediation; and Issues of Women and Leadership.").

186. Opposition, *supra* note 170, at 24 (discussing the stark contrast between providing leadership training on-post the way VMI does versus relegating a large component of leadership training to the classroom the way Mary Baldwin's approach would).

187. Opposition, *supra* note 170, at 30-31 (explaining the significance of "extra curricular" activities at VMI). In addition, as part of the entire training, VMI houses unique physical training facilities that it has offered to share for one week of orientation. During the rest of the year, Mary Baldwin students do not have access to them. *Id.* at 20.

188. Opposition, *supra* note 170, at 30-31 (listing examples of "non-serious" activities offered at Mary Baldwin such as "Apple Day, Junior Dad's Weekend, Parents' Weekend and Commencement Ball").

189. Opposition, *supra* note 170, at 27.

of the entire experience—the constant scrutiny and minute regulation of behavior considered essential to the VMI system.[190]

The honor code also differs. At VMI, one violation of the honor code results in expulsion. At Mary Baldwin, however, students who violate the honor code are subject to varying degrees of punishment, not automatic expulsion.[191]

The lack of a holistic experience is also exemplified by the allocation of resources at Mary Baldwin. Mary Baldwin College would offer the leadership program as only one of the many undergraduate programs available to its students. Resources and administrative energy cannot be focused solely on this leadership program. It is merely one aspect of the vast curriculum offered by the college. Mary Baldwin's course curriculum focuses on literature, arts and science, and does not offer any engineering course, which VMI does provide. The creation of this separate program does not meet the requirements of equal protection.[192] Again, it is the combination and interdependence of these factors that provides the foundation of the intangible benefit of a holistic VMI education.

The holistic experience is undeniably an important benefit of VMI, as indicated by the numerous references made by VMI itself to the holistic nature of its education.[193] Furthermore, the justification for creating a program at Mary Baldwin College is premised on the opinion that making VMI coeducation would "tear at the fabric of the college's holistic educational methodology."[194] Thus, rather than destroy the benefit for men, women are excluded and denied the equal opportunity of that holistic experience. As a result women do not receive the intangible benefits of a VMI education—that unique combination of developmental factors and complete devotion of the faculty and other students to their experience.

---

190. Opposition, *supra* note 170, at 29. The argument in support of dormitory living is that barracks living would be inappropriate for women. *See supra* notes 116 and 165.

191. Opposition, *supra* note 170, at 25-26 (explaining that Mary Baldwin's program separates violations into "major" and "minor" categories with such categorization to be determined by the students on a case-by-case basis).

192. *See generally Inner-City Schools, supra* note 15, at 1746-49 (discussing intermediate scrutiny under the Equal Protection Clause and *Vorchheimer* and the idea that allocation of resources poses the danger of unfair treatment). Resources at Mary Baldwin College would not be allocated in the same manner as at VMI, even considering its contract with the State.

193. *See generally* VMI Plan, *supra* note 152 *passim* (emphasizing throughout the importance of the holistic program at VMI).

194. VMI Plan, *supra* note 152, at 2 (stating the court's opinion that "members of the opposite sex who are denied the opportunity to attend a college such as VMI, cannot obtain the educational benefits of that college's program because their admission would destroy the single-gender environment which is the key to the success of the educational program").

2. Informal Learning From and Interaction With Peers

McLaurin, Sweatt, and *Brown*[195] recognized informal learning and interaction as important intangible factors that cannot be achieved through separate institutions, even if the premise is that the schools are equal. Virginia initially claimed that VMI's all-male institute provided diverse educational choices within the system of higher education to its students, thereby promoting an important governmental aim. That aim is not met, however, by segregating men and women based on gender. Segregation deprives students of the benefit of informal learning among classmates who are themselves diverse.[196] The rationale that coeducation better prepares students for the real world is legitimate and important.[197] Coeducation is important because it provides "an educational environment that mirrors the diversity of modern society."[198] If VMI became coeducational, it would allow women and men to benefit equally from the advantages of learning among a student body diverse in views.

The nature and ambiance of classrooms would unquestionably change upon the admission of females to a previously all-male environment; but if women continue to be excluded, a distinct quality is lost in everyone's educational experience.[199] One of the criteria established in *McLaurin* was that being separated diminished the student's ability to discuss different viewpoints with other students.[200]

"If VMI claims a military mission, it should prepare its cadets to deal with realities of a mixed-gender military."[201] If women are going to be leaders in a society in which they must associate with men, and vice versa, then their ability to engage in discussions and exchange views with other future leaders should not be infringed because of VMI's unwillingness to become coeducational.

---

195. 339 U.S. 637, 640-41 (1950); 339 U.S. 629, 633-34 (1950); 347 U.S. 483, 493-95 (1954).

196. Berman, *supra* note 15, at 214 (citing Regents of the Univ. of Cal. v. Bakke, 438 U.S. 265, 312-13 n.48 (1978)).

197. Jones *ex rel.* Michele v. Board of Educ. of N.Y., 632 F. Supp. 1319, 1324 (E.D.N.Y. 1986). "The attainment of a diverse student body . . . clearly is a constitutionally permissible goal for an institution of higher education." *Id.* (quoting Regents of the Univ. of Cal. v. Bakke, 438 U.S. 265, 311-12 (1978)).

198. *Jones,* 632 F. Supp. at 1324. "[T]here is no constitutional right to the best education possible." Although a single-sex school may enhance some individuals' academic experiences (i.e., men), this consideration is irrelevant to the inquiry of whether the right to education, with all its intangible factors, has been infringed. *Id.*

199. Devan, *supra* note 46, at 530. *But see id.* (stating also that the inclusion of both sexes may result in a loss of quality).

200. McLaurin v. Oklahoma State Regents for Higher Educ., 339 U.S. 637, 641 (1950).

201. Saferstein, *supra* note 15, at 663 (arguing for coeducation at VMI).

3. Elimination and Prevention of the Perpetuation of Stereotypes

Socialization patterns have been regarded as intangible factors related to education. A current socialization pattern is seen by the way an individual develops based on preconceived ideas of who he or she should be. Separating men and women tends to perpetuate stereotypes about their proper roles in society. Individuals who are stereotyped based on one characteristic, such as sex, are unable to break traditional roles because of being separated. The legal theory of equal rights, however,

> [c]hallenges biological determinism by asserting that there is substantial overlap between women and men as to most characteristics relevant to social roles and career options. Therefore, . . . individuals should be free to choose among social roles and careers on the basis of their individual inclinations and talents, rather than be channeled into particular roles and careers on the basis of rigid and inaccurate notions about female and male capacities.[202]

Therefore, the elimination of stereotypes is one intangible benefit that is closely related to another intangible benefit: making choices free of preconceived ideas.[203]

In *Hogan*, for example, the Court suggested that if the all-female admissions' policy was upheld, men would be denied equal protection because they would not receive the intangible benefit of pursuing their own career choices and breaking the traditional roles of men and women (i.e., women are better nurses).[204] The recent district court decision in *Garrett* lends further support to the idea that equal protection is necessary to ensure that no one, regardless of gender, is denied the benefit of learning and developing free from preconceived notions of who he or she is. The court cautioned against justifications for single-gender educational institutions predicated on "unsubstantiated notions" of the differences between gender groups.[205]

Cases that advocate special programs designed to compensate for sex differences—such as Mary Baldwin's Institute for

---

202. Ann E. Freedman, *Sex Equality, Sex Differences, and the Supreme Court*, 92 YALE L.J. 913, 916 (1983).

203. Some of the reasons historically used to limit women in their educational pursuits consisted of such factors as their brains were too light and their ability to reason was not adequate enough for rigorous academic programs. Rhode, *supra* note 174, at 290.

204. Mississippi Univ. for Women v. Hogan, 458 U.S. 718 (1982).

205. *Inner-City Schools, supra* note 15, at 1750. This conclusion is based on the precedent of Craig v. Boren, 429 U.S. 190 (1976), which established that even though reasons may be statistically measured, if they are loose-fitting generalities about gender, they will not provide the necessary justification. *Id.*

Leadership—"have been more ideologically denigrating than materially helpful. While some situations have been improved, the conditions of inequality that made compensation seem necessary have been altered virtually not at all."[206] In this particular situation, VMI's plan simply emphasizes the stereotypes that women cannot succeed in an adversative environment and that they require some form of paternal nurturing.

Allowing VMI to legally implement its Plan and continue to exclude women imposes generalized traits or characterizations, based on what may be true for some individuals in a group, onto the entire group (i.e., women cannot handle the adversative model, the lack of privacy, or the physical rigor). Further, the atmosphere at many all-male colleges encourages the admitted tendency to view women as sex objects.[207] As a result, misrepresentation occurs that not only can be trivializing, but also perverse.[208] The danger is "when sexist stereotypes dictate associational policy they tend to become self-reinforcing."[209] *Hogan* specifically stated that excluding males from admission to Mississippi University for Women perpetuates stereotyped views of who should be a nurse, and, in enforcing that presumption, makes it a self-fulfilling prophecy.[210] The *Hogan* decision presented examples of legislative attempts to keep women in a subordinated position based on the generalized belief that women could not perform a particular function as well as men.[211] The Court specifically cautioned that objectives based on the presumed innate inferiority of one gender are illegitimate.[212]

The court of appeals' adoption of the argument that the introduction of women into VMI would change the VMI experience is based on speculation of how VMI would offer an inferior experience if

---

206. Catharine A. MacKinnon, *Reflections on Sex Equality Under Law*, 100 YALE L.J. 1281, 1292 (1991). In her article, which discusses primarily sexual assault and reproduction, she suggests that the law of discrimination, focusing on accuracy of classification and categorization, "has targeted inequality's failure of perception such that full human variety is not recognized . . . [and] is not permitted to exist." *Id.* at 1293.

207. Rhode, *supra* note 174, at 142. Coeducation may help eliminate these stereotypes and may help promote a new view of women as potential equals in the post-graduation business and professional world. *Id.*

208. MacKinnon, *supra* note 206, at 1293.

209. Rhode, *supra* note 174, at 123.

210. Mississippi Univ. for Women v. Hogan, 458 U.S. 718, 729-30 (1982).

211. *Id.* at 725 n.10 (listing Myra Bradwell's attempt to challenge legislation that prohibited women from practicing law because they were seen as unfit; the upholding by the Court of a legislature's right to preclude women from bartending with the aim of preventing moral and social problems; and the enactment of early labor laws designed to protect females, the weaker sex).

212. *Id.* at 725.

women were admitted.[213]　The court did not rely on existing evidence that the integration of women into the United States military academies such as West Point and the Naval Academy has been positive.[214]　The speculative changes the court foresaw were based on stereotypes of women: the adversative model would have to be abandoned because women could not handle it; the nature of dormitory life would have to change because women have a heightened need for personal privacy; and the physical education requirements would have to be altered because women would not be able to pass.[215]　Although some real differences admittedly exist, many of the stereotypes that appear in the Plan are premised on the idea that women require a nurturing and supportive environment.[216]　As a result, "VMI's all-male policy perpetuates outdated notions about men and women's military capabilities by denying women consideration for admission based on a strict gender classification."[217]

VMI's Plan allows stereotypes to dictate how the leadership program is structured, as outlined in Section IV.　Consequently, women will develop in a way that reinforces preconceived ideas, such as their need for a more nurturing environment, or their inability to survive a high stress environment.　Women will be steered in particular directions and will not be free to choose their own paths.

Denying women the intangible factor of being free from stereotypes in their educational environment has significant repercussions. Legitimizing separatism in private institutions has the ramification of entrenching it in public institutions.[218]　Women's exclusion from private spheres contributes to their exclusion from public spheres.[219] "As long as women do not 'fit in' in the private worlds where

---

213. Berman, *supra* note 15, at 217. Women, historically, were kept out of institutions of higher education because "[n]ot only were women thought generally incapable of intellectual self-discipline and rigor, but the attempt to impose it on them was thought debilitating to both mind and body." Jencks & Riesman, *Feminism, Masculinism and Coeducation, in* THE ACADEMIC REVOLUTION 291-311 (1968), *reprinted in* SEX DISCRIMINATION AND THE LAW: CAUSES AND REMEDIES, 1001.

214. Berman, *supra* note 15, at 217 & n. 27 (noting the argument of the proponents of the bill directing the U.S. Service Academies to admit women in 1975; namely, that Service Academies did not have as their sole purpose training leaders for combat and, therefore, exclusion of women denied them equal opportunity for successful careers in comparison to male officers).

215. Berman, *supra* note 15, at 218.

216. Berman, *supra* note 15, at 218 (noting one stereotype that women would be "uncomfortable in VMI's stark and unattractive barracks").

217. Berman, *supra* note 15, at 214-15.

218. Rhode, *supra* note 174, at 109.

219. Rhode, *supra* note 174, at 120-21 (discussing how club membership has led to enhanced individual status for men in their firms and/or their communities, while the exclusion of women involves lost opportunities for informal exchanges, social status, and personal contacts that generate career opportunities and lead to prestigious positions).

friendships form and power congregates, they will never fully 'fit in' in the public sectors with which the state is justifiably concerned."[220] This broad statement has been narrowly applied in a military context.

> If military training or education is constructed so that it is a problem for women "to fit," then the answer is to reconstruct the military and military service so that both men and women "fit." Only women and men together, with whatever rearrangements that fact requires, can define what military service is. Side-by-side arrangements will only enshrine the male model . . . and consign the female experience to be judged as inferior. That inferiority will then be attributed to . . . women's nature . . . . Differences can be accounted for and privacy can be accounted for . . . all in the context of equal power and equal service.[221]

The Plan, by infringing upon women's rights under the Equal Protection Clause, denies women (as well as men) the intangible factor of developing free of the reigns of tradition in both education and society. If the Plan is implemented in this private educational sphere, women will be denied the intangible benefit of being free of stereotypes in the private domain, and of "fitting in" in areas of the public world.

Women who attend Mary Baldwin under the Plan are paying a high price.[222] By attending a separate institution, women—as proposed by the Plan—may have the equal opportunity to receive intangibles such as support, solidarity, and self-esteem. At the same time, the Plan encourages stereotypes of women and their inability to succeed at VMI. Consequently, women are denied the intangible benefit of deciding for themselves if they can succeed in the rigorous environment of VMI.

4. Empowerment and Leadership

Realizing one's full potential, strength, and power in the educational and societal spheres is still another intangible factor that should not be denied to either gender. Education has the ability to empower an individual; this opportunity of empowerment should be provided equally to men and women.[223] As shown through research, women

---

220. Rhode, *supra* note 174, at 123-24.

221. Cheh, *supra* note 82, at 56.

222. "Separatist education, like other forms of separatist affiliation, offers the vices and virtues of a ghetto: it provides support, solidarity, and self-esteem for subordinate groups, but often at the price of perpetuating attitudes that perpetuate subordination." Rhode, *supra* note 174, at 143.

223. Many women students indicated that they were most empowered and developed leadership skills through programs designed primarily for women. Mary Ann Danowitz Sagaria, *The Case for Empowering Women as Leaders in Higher Education, in* EMPOWERING WOMEN:

approach leadership development differently than men.[224] Studies indicate women value commitment, affiliation, caringness, responsibility to others, and balancing work with relationships.[225] Segregating the sexes to develop leaders, however, may not be the solution to accommodate the differences; expanding leadership models to incorporate the values of women into models based on male values may be better.[226] To help women develop as leaders, institutions of higher education must create experiences that are closely related to the world women will experience.[227] *McLaurin* confronted this issue and required the removal of barriers so that individuals could be judged based on their merits, and develop into leaders on the same basis as any peer.[228]

Although the benefits of achieving individual autonomy and fostering collective goals may be derived from sex-segregated institutions, these educational establishments perpetuate collective subordination.[229] Dominant groups often reinforce their privileged positions in society and the corresponding stereotypes by choosing specific forms of institutional separatism.[230] Separatism imposed by dominant groups differs significantly from separatism chosen by subordinate groups.[231]

Empowerment is closely related to other intangible factors. For example, because men and women have the same responsibility to empower women students as leaders,[232] informal learning and the elimination of stereotypes are equally necessary.

LEADERSHIP DEVELOPMENT STRATEGIES ON CAMPUS 9 (Mary Ann Danowitz Sagaria ed., 1988). However, the author advocates a view of leadership that is integrated into women's lives and does not necessarily advocate women colleges. *Id.* at 10.

224. *See* Sagaria, *supra* note 223, at 6.

225. *See* Sagaria, *supra* note 223, at 6.

226. Sagaria, *supra* note 223, at 7.

227. Sagaria, *supra* note 223, at 7. One suggestion is to provide a setting that helps women develop the ability to relate to many different people. *Id.*

228. McLaurin v. Oklahoma State Regents for Higher Educ., 339 U.S. 637 (1950).

229. Rhode, *supra* note 174, at 108-09.

230. Rhode, *supra* note 174, at 122 (relating the explanations given by private club members for why they exclude women). One club manager explains, "If a man has a business deal to discuss, he doesn't want to sit next to a woman fussing about how much mayonnaise is in her chicken salad." *Id.* (citing Calvin Trillen, *U.S. Journal: Tampa, Florida; Four People Who Do Not Lunch at the University Club,* NEW YORKER, Apr. 11, 1977, at 101).

231. Rhode, *supra* note 174, at 122.

232. Sagaria, *supra* note 223, at 7 (asserting the special importance of women as professionals empowering women students as leaders, because of their influence by virtue of the fact that they themselves are women).

B. Intermediate Scrutiny

The courts have made progress in the area of racial equality by preventing the establishment of separate institutions claiming to be equal. The premise that these institutions are inherently unequal because they infringe on an individual's opportunity to receive certain intangible benefits is now part of race-based equal protection jurisprudence. In racial cases, strict scrutiny ensures the courts' maintenance of the doctrine.

In the area of gender, however, courts still vacillate, and single-gender institutions continue to exist. As a result, the racial "inherently unequal" doctrine has not been incorporated completely into the analysis of gender-based classification. Instead, courts have concentrated on how race-based and gender-based classifications differ and thus warrant different protection. Regardless of their differences, courts must not ignore that the consequences are substantially the same for racial and sexual segregation: the denial of intangible factors and the denial of equal protection.

The courts' use of intermediate scrutiny helps to eliminate some of the gender-based separations. The exclusion of women from admission to VMI must be examined under this level of scrutiny. Under intermediate scrutiny, the proposed plan submitted by VMI violates equal protection.

The important government objective at issue is the development of young adults into future leaders. For VMI, the objective is specifically to develop citizen-soldiers who will have the ability to be leaders after graduation—an important governmental goal. The substantially related means to achieve that goal, however, cannot be segregation, as the Plan suggests. The substantially related means, which would allow VMI to meet both prongs of intermediate scrutiny, must be coeducation.

The ultimate goal of equal protection is often forgotten as courts become preoccupied with articulating important goals and substantial relationships.[233] The *Hogan* Court expressed concern for the unique educational opportunity provided to one gender and the institution's failure to show any substantial relationship between the important goal (a unique educational experience) and the means (not providing the other sex that same unique opportunity).[234]

---

233. "When unique and valuable educational opportunities are made available to only one sex, the nebulous intermediate scrutiny standard can be used to obscure this prima facie denial of equal protection." Saferstein, *supra* note 15, at 640.

234. Mississippi Univ. for Women v. Hogan, 458 U.S. 718, 722 (1982).

VMI contends its Plan offers the same kind of education to women that they would receive if admitted to VMI. The Institute also contends that by its segregation of men and women, both sexes would benefit. This rationale is precisely the mask, under intermediate scrutiny, that contributes to a continued denial of equal protection. VMI's Plan does not provide equal protection when the mask is removed.

VMI also asserts that the Plan, with its continuous segregation of the sexes, is a substantially related means to several components of its important goal, developing leaders. First, it protects women from the harsh nature of the VMI training (because they are not capable of surviving a stressful, physically rigorous, non-private environment) and allows them to develop in an atmosphere suited for women. However, the Court stated in *Hogan* that this rationale would not even pass the first prong of intermediate scrutiny because protecting members of one gender based on the assumption that they are inherently handicapped is not a valid objective.[235]

Second, VMI contends its Plan is substantially related to the goal of leadership development because, by employing the means of sex segregation, men can concentrate on becoming leaders and not be distracted, sexually, because women are present. *Garrett v. Board of Education of the School District of Detroit* addressed the same argument and held that the single-gender policy did not pass intermediate scrutiny. The success or failure of the education system to meet its goal has not been shown to be related to whether males and females attend the same institution.[236] Thus, creating separate institutions—one program at VMI and one at Mary Baldwin—is not a substantially related means to reach the goal of successfully training leaders.

VMI may attempt to rely on *McNair* and *Vorchheimer*, which used *Williams* as controlling authority, because the courts held single-gender institutions did not violate the Fourteenth Amendment. *Williams* specifically held that states can legitimately create schools with different missions in order to achieve a goal of educational diversity. This reliance does not apply to the present Plan because it ignores the *Williams* court's restriction that segregation is allowed only if no intangible factors are denied. As discussed previously, the Plan denies women four intangible factors. Moreover, the court held in *Williams* that no unique feature was being given to one gender and

---

235. *Id.* at 725.
236. Garrett v. Board of Educ. of Detroit, 775 F. Supp. 1004, 1008 (E.D. Mich. 1991).

not to the other.[237]   Under the Plan, in contrast, women are still being denied the unique combination of education, military training, and leadership development that exists at VMI.

More importantly, it must be remembered that both *Williams* and *Vorchheimer* were decided before the Court expressly adopted intermediate scrutiny in educational cases in *Hogan.* Since that time, the cases involving the issues VMI presents have found that single-gender schools infringe on rights guaranteed by the Fourteenth Amendment.

In addition, the opinion that "the nonexistence of a market for such schools [like VMI] ought to tell us something about the reasonableness of VMI's admissions policy . . . ."[238] suggests that the courts should revert back to a time when scrutinization by the Court did not exist in the realm of gender or race discrimination.[239] Since *Plessy*, and throughout the development of both strict and intermediate scrutiny in education, the Court has determined that the number of people openly expressing a denial of rights is immaterial to the issue of whether the Equal Protection Clause has been violated. Equal rights are based the individual, not on how many people want that right.   Thus, the protection afforded by intermediate scrutiny of gender-based classifications remains unaffected by the fact that VMI can point to only one woman who has judicially contested its admissions policy.

The parallels between the line of cases leading to *Brown* and the development of precedent in gender-based classification decisions are crucial.   The Court, rejecting the separate but equal doctrine and developing strict scrutiny as it was applied to race, did not create any new right.   Rather, the Court ensured that an already established right would operate successfully in the context of the 1950s, a decade in which education played a significant role, and in which racial segregation greatly impeded citizens' full enjoyment of civil rights.[240] Critics argued that the Court's decision in *Brown* was wrong because it contradicted the current social practices of the 1950s; "but it was

---

237. Williams v. McNair, 316 F. Supp. 134, 137-38 (D.S.C. 1970), *aff'd per curiam*, 401 U.S. 951 (1971).

238. Ides, *supra* note 45, at 45-46.

239. *See supra* note 38 and accompanying text (discussing the Court's finding that the essence of a constitutional right is personal, so that it does not matter how many people have been discriminated against in order for the Court to find an Equal Protection violation).

240. Ides, *supra* note 45, at 43.

those practices and not the Court that were out-of-touch with fundamental constitutional principles."[241]

In rejecting a separate institution and in applying intermediate scrutiny for gender, no new right would be created. Although admitting women to VMI might run contrary to the current social practices within the boundaries of that campus, the courts should not endorse these practices, which are clearly counter to equal protection. "The pluralistic argument for preserving all-male colleges is uncomfortably similar to the pluralistic argument for preserving all-white colleges . . . ."[242] It would be a more defendable argument if these all-male colleges existed in a society where women were completely equal to men; but they do not.[243] Therefore, allowing them to continue to exist would encourage unspoken assumptions about male superiority and would require women to continue to be perceived as inferior; this must not happen.[244] "Colleges and universities have a moral responsibility to critique our social order and to provide models to be emulated by other institutions, so that women can participate more fully and equitably in society."[245]

VI. CONCLUSION: INTEGRATION OF WOMEN AT VIRGINIA MILITARY INSTITUTE

Coeducation is a means that is substantially related to the important governmental interest of shaping the leaders of tomorrow's society. Leadership programs for women and men together approximate the reality that women and men must work together.[246] Coeducational programs highlight characteristics that women and men must explore in order to discover similarities and differences among themselves, and in order to appreciate and respect both how they differ and what they share.[247] Men and women, in order to develop into leaders, cannot be excluded from exposure to the unique perspectives the

---

241. Ides, *supra* note 45, at 43. Ides goes on to suggest, however, that gender discrimination cannot be considered in the same manner because in this area the Court has been more creative. I disagree; the social practices are still out-of-touch. Ides states that "but for the creative, and somewhat nonjudicial impulses of the Supreme Court during the 1970's, VMI's all-male admissions policy would be plainly constitutional. In this manner, the district court's resolution of the controversy reflected the normal, acceptable, indeed, constitutionally required conservatism of the judicial function." *Id.* at 44.

242. Jencks & Riesman, *supra* note 213, at 1003.

243. Jencks & Riesman, *supra* note 213, at 1003.

244. Jencks & Riesman, *supra* note 213, at 1003.

245. Sagaria, *supra* note 223, at 6.

246. Mary Ann Danowitz Sagaria & Lisa L. Koogle, *Greater Than the Sum of Its Parts: Strategy and Resources, in* EMPOWERING WOMEN: LEADERSHIP DEVELOPMENT STRATEGIES ON CAMPUS, *supra* note 223, at 89, 91.

247. *Id.*

other sex brings to developing solutions for contemporary societal problems.[248] Coeducational institutions provide excellent opportunities to apply these new understandings to leadership roles.[249] As a result, coeducation makes it more likely that the government will attain its goal of developing leaders who can function successfully in a gender-integrated society.

If society permits institutions to establish separate programs for women who achieve in nontraditional (i.e., nonfemale) ways, individuals' efforts to meet their potential are seriously impeded, and their ability to improve society is limited. Although men and women often take different approaches to moral or political issues, men and women who choose to join a particular group will not necessarily differ in those approaches.[250] Thus, organizations should not exclude a gender based on the mere attitudinal characteristics attributed to that sex.[251] "The court erred . . . by failing to realize that the women who apply to VMI will want the VMI experience, as is. These will be women who seek the whole VMI challenge, not a relaxed, special program."[252] The choice offered to women of attending Mary Baldwin's Institute for Leadership is a mirror attempt to deflect the underlying constitutional violation. "[T]he danger of sustaining paternalistic classifications [is not] mitigated by the fact that women can accept or reject, as a matter of personal choice, the 'benefits' offered by the state."[253] Often the voluntary nature of a program only masks an underlying sexual oppression and women's passive acceptance of sexual stereotypes.[254]

The need for single-gender environments decreases greatly as the level of education increases.[255] Although in the past an all-female institute of post-secondary education may have been especially supportive of women "by providing role models, leadership opportuni-

---

248. *See generally id.*; *but see supra* note 223 and accompanying text.

249. Sagaria & Koogle, *supra* note 246, at 91. The counterargument is that social norms and expectations continue to influence the way women perceive themselves and their abilities, and shape their aspirations; thus, to some extent, programs designed solely for women are still essential. *Id.* Furthermore, opponents of coeducation still argue that "coeducation ignore[s] 'natural' differences in the sexes' mental capacities and social roles. Joint instruction would compromise traditional academic standards and coarsen feminine sensibilities. Related concerns involve[] the decline in athletic achievement, alumni contributions, and academic inquiry that would reportedly follow from female intrusion; women could scarcely be expected to hold their own on the football field or in rigorous analysis of 'delicate' subjects." Rhode, *supra* note 174, at 292-93 (citations omitted).

250. Rhode, *supra* note 174, at 120.

251. *Id.*

252. Berman, *supra* note 15, at 218.

253. *Constitutional Law: The Supreme Court, 1981 Term*, 96 HARV. L. REV. 62, 119 (1982).

254. *Id.* at 120 (footnote omitted).

255. Saferstein, *supra* note 15, at 673 n.166.

ties, and positive faculty/student interaction, such characteristics [of an all-female setting] should become more dominant in coeducational environments as well."[256]   Indeed, in contemporary society, as the remedial role of all-female schools is decreases, one goal of today's women's colleges should be to create an environment that no longer necessitates their . compensatory function.[257]   Therefore, Mary Baldwin College should not encourage the continuing separation of the program, nor should VMI be allowed to continue to violate the Equal Protection Clause.

EPILOGUE

On November 15, 1993, the United States Justice Department filed its opposition to VMI's Proposed Remedial Plan.[258]   The Justice Department asserts that the only way VMI could meet its requirements under the Fourteenth Amendment was to admit women.[259]   Two days later, on November 17, 1993, the Fourth Circuit ordered the Citadel to allow Shannon Faulkner to attend classes while her lawsuit was pending.[260] She, too, challenged an all-male academy's admission policy on the basis of equal protection.[261]

The most recent line of cases—from *Hogan* in 1982, *Garrett* in 1991, VMI in 1992, to the Citadel case in 1993—indicates that single-gender institutions are finding it increasingly difficult to pass intermediate scrutiny and are finding it harder to provide alternatives that do not infringe on one gender's access to intangible factors. Following this trend, VMI's Plan should be rejected, and integration, as the Justice Department has urged, should be implemented.

---

256. Rhode, *supra* note 174, at 144.

257. Rhode, *supra* note 174 at 144. *Compare* Jencks & Riesman, *supra* note 213, at 1005-09 (presenting the benefits of all-women colleges and tracing their development through the schools' strengths and successes, but, at the same time, surmising the decline of women attending these colleges).

258. Opposition, *supra* note 170.

259. Opposition, *supra* note 170, at 2-3.

260. *Woman to Attend Citadel Classes*, WASH. POST, Nov. 18, 1993, at A17. While Faulkner has been allowed to attend day classes at the Citadel since January 1994, she is not allowed to wear the military uniform, cannot march as a cadet, and must live off campus. *Id.* Such full integration at the Citadel is the focus of her current law suit.

261. *Id.* Shannon Faulkner was accepted into the all-male core at the Citadel in 1993 after asking that reference to her gender be deleted from her high school transcripts. After the Citadel learned that Shannon was a female, they revoked her acceptance. *Citadel Told to Devise Plan for Woman Student*, LOS ANGELES TIMES, May 29, 1994, at A18. However, one writer noted that although Faulkner has indicated she is interested in attending the Citadel in part because of its discipline, she has "already violated the school's most sacred tenet, the honor code, by misleading admissions officers about her sex when she applied." Linda Chavez, *Single-Sex Schools: Why We Need Them*, USA TODAY, June 1, 1994, at News Section.

On April 29, 1994, the United States District Court ruled to endorse VMI's and Virginia's efforts to create a similar program for women at Mary Baldwin College.[262] The district court judge agreed with Virginia's position that an all-female program furnishing women "an outcome . . . comparable" to what VMI gives men would satisfy the demands of the appeals court and the Constitution, without adopting methods the same as or similar to those used at VMI.[263] The Justice Department has appealed this decision.[264]

In the parallel case involving the Citadel, also in the Fourth Circuit,[265] the federal district court judge in Charleston, South Carolina, requested both parties to restrict their arguments to the issue of why South Carolina's education policy is inherently different from that of Virginia's. Otherwise, the Citadel should be bound by the U.S. Court of Appeals for the Fourth Circuit's recent decision that VMI's policy of excluding women is discriminatory.[266]

The Citadel trial continued through May, 1994. Faulkner, as well as two other women who seek admission to the Citadel, have renounced the option of attending a similar all-women's program, reflective of VMI's attempt to establish such a program at Mary Baldwin.[267] On July 22, 1994, the Citadel was ordered to admit Faulkner; however, the court did not decide if the Citadel would be required to admit women in the future.[268] Faulkner's triumph, however, was short-lived. The Friday before she was scheduled to become the first female cadet, the United States Forth Circuit Court of Appeals granted the Citadel's motion to prevent her from matriculating as a full cadet until December, 1994, when the court will hear a formal appeal.[269] Thus, women's fights for equal protection at both VMI and the Citadel have not ended.

---

262. *See* United States v. Virginia, 852 F. Supp. 471 (W.D. Va. 1994). The court ordered VMI to have the plan operational by Fall, 1995. *Id.*

263. Martin Weil, *Judge Backs Males-Only VMI Policy: Alternative Program is Ruled Acceptable,* WASH. POST, May 1, 1994, at B3.

264. Mary Jordan, *Appeals Court Keeps Faulkner Out of Citadel,* WASH. POST, Aug. 13, 1994 at A3 (outlining briefly the history of the parallel VMI case).

265. Faulkner v. Jones, 10 F.3d 226 (4th Cir. 1993).

266. Catherine S. Manegold, *Arguments Begin at Trial on Citadel's Male Policy,* N.Y. TIMES, May 17, 1994, at A16.

267. Henry Eichel, *supra* note 41, at A1.

268. Mary Jordan, *Citadel Ordered to Admit Women; Shannon Faulkner to Be First Female Cadet at the Military School,* WASH. POST, July 23, 1994 at A1. "U.S. District Judge C. Weston Houck . . . has left open the possibility that the school could establish a parallel program for women in 1995 at another college." *Id.* (indicating that this solution would protect Faulkner's Equal Protection rights and reserving his opinion on whether a parallel program would offer the same protection).

269. Mary Jordan, *supra* note 264, at A3.

Where Coeds Were Coeducated: Normal Schools in Wisconsin, 1870–1920

Christine A. Ogren

More than two decades of interest in the history of American women as college students have recently culminated in a trio of notable books. Barbara Miller Solomon's *In the Company of Educated Women: A History of Women and Higher Education in America*, Helen Lefkowitz Horowitz's *Campus Life: Undergraduate Cultures from the End of the Eighteenth Century to the Present*, and Lynn D. Gordon's *Gender and Higher Education in the Progressive Era* all use a rich variety of sources to bring to life the experiences of generations of women undergraduate students, mainly at prestigious colleges and large state universities. While the authors have different emphases, they share a commitment to making sense of college experiences through alumnae memoirs, letters, yearbooks, and works of fiction, as well as more conventional sources. Their inquiries intersect in their analyses of life for women on coeducational campuses during the Progressive Era and earlier years. Together, Solomon, Horowitz, and Gordon present a cohesive picture of "coeds" whose lives were entirely controlled by the Victorian notion of separate gender spheres. The "outsiders" of the first generation espoused traditional values, studied hard, and remained on the sidelines during extracurricular activities. Beginning in the 1890s, women of the second generation proclaimed that, like men, they could devote themselves to "college" life; adhering to a separate spheres ideology, they created student government, clubs, and activity groups for women only. Solomon, Horowitz, and Gordon portray a form of education in which male and female students stayed entirely apart—education that did not warrant the prefix "co."[1]

While this widespread image of female exclusion and subordination is no doubt accurate for elite colleges and large, highly visible state

Christine Ogren is a doctoral candidate in Educational Policy Studies at the University of Wisconsin–Madison. She would like to thank Jurgen Herbst, Clif Conrad, Bill Reese, *HEQ*'s anonymous reviewers, and David Brandt for their helpful comments on drafts of this essay.

[1]See Barbara Miller Solomon, *In the Company of Educated Women: A History of Women and Higher Education in America* (New Haven, Conn., 1985); Helen Lefkowitz Horowitz, *Campus Life: Undergraduate Cultures from the End of the Eighteenth Century to the Present* (Chicago, 1987); and Lynn D. Gordon, *Gender and Higher Education in the Progressive Era* (New Haven, Conn., 1990).

universities, it is not the complete picture. Solomon, Horowitz, and Gordon exclude less-prestigious institutions, such as state normal schools. Ostensibly teacher-training schools, many normal schools functioned as all-around institutions of higher learning, especially in the Midwest and West. In the mid-nineteenth century, they resembled sophisticated academies; in the late nineteenth century, junior colleges; and in the early twentieth century, small liberal arts colleges. Almost always coeducational, state normal schools were especially significant institutions for women, who had limited opportunities at other colleges and saw teaching as a viable vocational option. Women constituted the majority of normal students; in 1898–99, ratios of females to males ranged from 14:1 at Fitchburg Normal in Massachusetts to 1.3:1 at Oklahoma Normal, but the gender ratio at most normal schools was squarely between these two extremes. Normal schools affected a remarkable number of students, both female and male; attendance grew from 10,000 nationwide (16 percent of the total enrollment in higher education) in 1870 to 76,000 (30 percent of the total enrollment in higher education) in 1900. In addition, normal schools were very widespread; at least thirty-seven states had one or more normal schools as of 1890, and state-supported normal schools numbered 48 in 1872, 135 in 1892, and 172 in 1917. This article extends the inquiry into women's experiences in higher education to these important institutions.[2]

The state of Wisconsin was a microcosm of the nationwide system of renowned state universities surrounded by normal schools that were only slightly recognized as institutions of higher education. Wisconsin established nine state normal schools from the 1860s through the 1910s. While the university's enrollment varied from 316 to over 500 (of whom the majority were men) between the mid-1870s and the mid-1880s, the

---

[2]Richard J. Altenbaugh and Kathleen Underwood, "The Evolution of Normal Schools," in *Places Where Teachers Are Taught*, ed. John I. Goodlad et al. (San Francisco, 1990), 163; Colin B. Burke, *American Collegiate Populations: A Test of the Traditional View* (New York, 1982), 216, 222; Thomas Woody, *A History of Women's Education in the United States* (New York, 1929), 1: 482–83.

Several historians have argued that our understanding of the history of higher education is incomplete without including normal schools in the analysis. See Burke, *American Collegiate Populations*; Geraldine Jonçich Clifford, "No Shade in the Golden State: School and University in Nineteenth-Century California," *History of Higher Education Annual* 12 (1992): 35–68; Jurgen Herbst, "Nineteenth-Century Normal Schools in the United States: A Fresh Look," *History of Education* 9 (Sep. 1980): 219–27; and Jeff Wasserman, "Wisconsin Normal Schools and the Educational Hierarchy, 1860–1890," *Journal of the Midwest History of Education Society* 7 (1979): 1–9.

Historians of teacher education are responsible for much of the current research on the history of normal schools in the United States. While they have undoubtedly made important contributions, their focus has caused them to overlook the concerns of historians of higher education for women, such as coeducation. See Altenbaugh and Underwood, "The Evolution of Normal Schools"; Geraldine Jonçich Clifford and James W. Guthrie, *Ed School: A Brief for Professional Education* (Chicago, 1988); John I. Goodlad, *Teachers for Our Nation's Schools* (San Francisco, 1990); and Jurgen Herbst, *And Sadly Teach: Teacher Education and Professionalization in American Culture* (Madison, Wis., 1989).

1879–80 enrollment of just one—the oldest—of the normal schools was 219 (130 women and 89 men). Thus, normal school enrollments were not overshadowed by the university's enrollment. "Coeducation" at the University of Wisconsin in Madison was typical of the colleges described by Solomon, Horowitz, and Gordon during this time. The university segregated women in a separate building called the Female College from 1867 to 1871. Although the Madison institution officially became coeducational in 1874, "practice did not necessarily follow theory. Segregation, and the attitudes which had created it, continued to influence the college experience of women" into the early twentieth century. Women shared classrooms and some activities with men but often felt like outsiders. Women-only campus organizations that began during the 1890s took second place to men's groups, which were considered the only "university" organizations, and male and female students rarely mixed socially. Life inside and outside the university classroom hinged on gender differences, but campus life was very different at the state's normal schools.[3]

Wisconsin is also a fruitful setting for research because its network of normal schools left a trail of alumnae memoirs, literary magazines, and yearbooks. These and other sources speak to the issue of gender in intellectual and social affairs and in matters of campus leadership and teamwork. They create a picture of educational institutions very different from the state university. At Wisconsin's normal schools, female and male students shared in the intellectual life. Side-by-side in class, they followed the same courses of study, under the tutelage of male and female professors. Men and women were enthusiastic about, and involved in, literary societies and debating contests. Normal schools provided a rich social life with social groups of mixed genders and varying degrees of formality. Women and men both took part in student government, athletics, school publications, and many other activities. In many, if not quite all, aspects of college life, the experiences of normal students inside and outside the classroom did not hinge on gender differences.

The following pages demonstrate how the tenor of Wisconsin's normal schools markedly contrasted with that of the University of Wisconsin in the late nineteenth and early twentieth centuries. The state's normal schools offered shared educational experiences in which both men and women actively participated—education that deserved the prefix "co." Of course, these schools did not exist in a perfect world. Florence Howe reminds us that true coeducation requires total equality and exists only "in our dreams of a more

---

[3]Wisconsin established nine normal schools, named for their host cities, during these years: Platteville (1866), Whitewater (1868), Oshkosh (1871), River Falls (1875), Milwaukee (1885), Stevens Point (1894), Superior (1896), La Crosse (1909), and Eau Claire (1916). Merle Curti and Vernon Carstensen, *The University of Wisconsin: A History, 1848–1925* (Madison, Wis., 1949), 1: 364, 369; Herbst, *And Sadly Teach*, 130; Amy Hague, "'What If the Power Does Lie Within Me?' Women Students at the University of Wisconsin, 1875–1900," *History of Higher Education Annual* 4 (1984): 78.

perfect future society," even in the late twentieth century.[4] Nevertheless, different aspects of normal school life offered students implicit lessons in how gender relations could move beyond separate spheres. Intellectual life taught students that men and women could be intellectual equals, while mixed social groups fostered social familiarity between males and females. In other activities, women and men learned that they could lead individuals of either gender and could work as members of both single-sex and mixed teams. These were important lessons in a society permeated by notions of separate gender spheres. During the 1920s, normal schools achieved the status of colleges and also began to adopt the instructional procedures and forms of social life practiced in the colleges, giving up their distinctive brand of *co*education for women and men. It is a fair question to ask whether American education gained or lost when the lowly normal schools advanced to collegiate status.

* * * * *

Victorian notions of separate spheres assigned rigorous academic pursuits to men. As women defied these notions and entered classrooms at the University of Wisconsin, they were constantly reminded that they "had entered a male world." Their professors were almost always male and passed knowledge "from man to man." In the early 1870s, men and women recited separately in some subjects, and in 1907 and 1908, President Charles Van Hise proposed that classes in some subjects be separated by sex. As late as 1909–13, female students were segregated in the back of some classrooms. A student's diary noted: "'There are three times as many fellows [in chemistry class] as girls but girls get the back seats.'" The unofficial message was that women students were intellectual outsiders.[5]

As elective courses greatly expanded the curriculum on American university campuses during the late nineteenth century, women generally did not share the new classes with men. At Wisconsin, undergraduate courses in surveying, navigation, and agriculture appeared in the general science course during the 1870s, the pharmacy school was well established by the mid-1880s, and the most rapid academic growth during the 1890s was in the engineering college. Largely vocational, these new courses were not suited to women's traditional societal roles. In the 1880s and 1890s, women mainly studied in the "modern classical" and "English" liberal arts courses and were absent from the new technical courses. After 1908, women also had the option of studying home economics—another sex-segregated

---

[4]Florence Howe, *Myths of Coeducation: Selected Essays, 1964–1983* (Bloomington, Ind., 1984), 209.

[5]Student's diary quoted in Ellen D. Langill, "Women at Wisconsin, 1909–1939," in *University Women: A Series of Essays: They Came to Learn, They Came to Teach, They Came to Stay*, ed. Marian J. Swoboda and Audrey J. Roberts (Madison, Wis., 1980), 16; Hague, "'What If the Power Does Lie Within Me?',", 90; Jean Droste, "Coeducation, 1849–1909: They Came to Stay," in *University Women*, ed. Swoboda and Roberts, 5, 7.

subject. At Wisconsin, like other universities, a stigma made courses pursued by high concentrations of women appear inferior to those in which men were the majority. Historian Frederick Rudolph explains: "One tendency of these developments therefore was the growth of the idea that the liberal arts programs and courses were essentially feminine. Coeducation helped to divide the subjects of the curriculum and the courses of study into those which were useful, full-bodied, and manly, and those which were ornamental, dilettantish, and feminine." President Van Hise's proposal of separate classes for men and women was a reaction to this stigma; he wished to make the liberal arts more attractive to men. Although Van Hise also lent his support to coeducation, his proposal contributed to the sense that women were outside the mainstream of the Madison campus.[6]

Of course, the classroom was not the only setting for intellectual life. At many state universities, including Wisconsin, students joined literary societies and debating clubs for cultural and philosophical exploration. Not welcome in the all-male societies, women students at Wisconsin formed the Castalian society in 1864 and Laurea in 1873. These all-female societies had many positive effects on women's intellectual development, but there were no mixed-gender groups and there was minimal interaction between the all-male and the all-female societies. Furthermore, women were excluded from the Joint Debate between men's societies, a major event each year. Female students thus received the message that they could challenge each other intellectually but were not welcome in the sphere of male intellectual debate. Women were not treated as intellectual equals to men at the University of Wisconsin.[7]

Gender stigmatization was largely absent from the intellectual life of normal students, and this absence conveyed the message that women and men could function as intellectual equals. As the "advanced" normal course changed and grew into baccalaureate work, men and women studied it, side by side (although not necessarily in equal numbers), and under the tutelage of male and female teachers. They also enjoyed the opportunity for intellectual growth in single-sex and mixed literary societies, and they debated important questions in mixed-gender settings. The Wisconsin normal school law of 1866 stated: "The exclusive purpose of each normal school shall be instruction and training of persons, both male and female, in the theory and art of teaching, and in all the various branch-

---

[6]Helen R. Olin, *The Women of a State University: An Illustration of Working Coeducation in the Middle West* (New York, 1909), 58–59; Curti and Carstensen, *University of Wisconsin*, 1: 660 and 2: 404, 82; Amy Hague, "'Give Us a Little Time to Find Our Places': University of Wisconsin Alumnae, Classes of 1875–1900" (M.A. thesis, University of Wisconsin, 1983), 80; Frederick Rudolph, *The American College and University: A History* (New York, 1968), 324.

[7]See Curti and Carstensen, *The University of Wisconsin*, 1: 423–38; Hague, "'What If the Power Does Lie Within Me?,'" 84–87.

Students studying in Whitewater Normal School Library, circa 1904. Scrapbook, 1902–5, 73. Courtesy of University of Wisconsin–Whitewater Archives.

es that pertain to a good common school education; also to give instruction in agriculture, chemistry, in the arts of husbandry, the mechanic arts, the fundamental laws of the United States and of this state, and in what regards the rights and duties of citizens."[8] Although the normal schools did not develop courses in agricultural chemistry or husbandry, the message that women and men would share varied opportunities for intellectual growth was heeded during the next several decades.

According to somewhat limited sources, the atmosphere in Wisconsin's normal school classrooms was relatively gender-neutral, at least on the surface. Though the Whitewater chapel's "broad central aisle separated the men from the women" during the early years, no such separation appears to have occurred in classes. Separate study rooms for men and women continued, at least at Oshkosh, into the 1910s. But the study halls were overshadowed by "the arrangement of classes for rhetorical exercises." Oshkosh's *The Normal Advance* explained in 1895: "Not only may the young men sit in the same room with the ladies, but even by their side, some being so fortunate as to have a fair one to right and a fair one to left."[9]

---

[8]Conrad E. Patzer, *Public Education in Wisconsin* (Madison, Wis., 1924), 148.
[9]Janette Bohi, "Whitewater, a Century of Progress, 1868–1968," in *History of the Wisconsin State Universities*, ed. Walker D. Wyman (River Falls, Wis., 1968), 63; "Tabulation of Building and Contents at Oshkosh Building of 1869," 12 Dec. 1913, Theodore Kronsage Papers, State Historical Society of Wisconsin Archives, Madison; *The Normal Advance* (Oshkosh, Wis.) 2 (Sep.–Oct. 1895): 11.

Teachers of both sexes guided these normal students, although male and female professors sometimes dominated different disciplines. In 1868, Platteville and Whitewater had mixed faculties; male teachers were concentrated in math and Latin, and female teachers were in the English, history, drawing, and model departments. Three years later, Oshkosh opened with a similar faculty, except that a woman taught math. By 1876, River Falls Normal had opened as well; the four schools employed forty-seven faculty members, nineteen of whom were male and twenty-eight female. When a later historian singled out highly revered teachers at Oshkosh, three of the four he profiled were women: Jennie Marvin was the principal of the grammar department beginning in 1889; and Emily Webster (who "'never felt the heaviest load . . . a burden'") and Rose Swart ("a teacher of rare ability") had careers spanning most of the last quarter of the nineteenth century and the first quarter of the twentieth.[10]

In the second decade of the twentieth century, women continued to be a strong force on normal faculties. Ruth Engebretsen Dorr, who attended both Whitewater and the university in Madison during that time, later remembered: "'I had many good women teachers at Whitewater, but none in Madison.'" The historians who told her story reflected: "Whitewater Normal had a tradition of women educating women." When Eau Claire Normal opened in 1916, its faculty was comprised of fifteen women and six men. Perhaps the most outstanding was Laura Sutherland, who "taught history with distinction. . . . 'When she came into the classroom, day after day, she was so completely prepared that she never carried a note with her. . . . She held her classes spellbound year after year.'" Learning from a faculty that included men and women such as Marvin, Webster, Swart, and Sutherland, normal students experienced a coeducational faculty.[11]

Did this faculty of mixed gender treat male and female students differently? This is a difficult question to answer, but scattered recollections indicate that the faculty engaged and challenged both male and female students in normal classrooms. At Oshkosh, Webster "'was as searching and relentless as a lawyer in cross-examination of a witness. Tears on the part of a girl, or bluff on the part of a boy, was never accepted as legal tender for the correct method or answer for a problem in arithmetic.'" Norah Halverson (Howe), who graduated from River Falls in 1916, remembered entering Professor Lewis Clark's math class knowing she would "get along fine" if she showed him that she could "stand on" her "own two feet." When called on the first day of class, she, with shaking knees, explained

---

[10]Albert Salisbury, *Historical Sketch of Normal Instruction in Wisconsin* (1876), 51, 53, 57, 96; Edward Noyes, "Oshkosh—From Normal School to State University, 1871–1968," in *History of the Wisconsin State Universities*, ed. Wyman, 102.

[11]Agate Krouse and Harry Krouse, "Educated Daughters and Sisters: Three Graduates Comment," in *University Women*, ed. Swoboda and Roberts, 100; Ellen Last, "Voices from Three Generations of Women at Eau Claire, 1916–1970," in ibid., 107–8.

a problem on the blackboard; he replied, "'Good, sit down.'" Public speaking, an activity traditionally restricted to men, was an integral aspect of normal education for all students. Sally Birkenwald graduated in 1880 with a volume full of recitations she had delivered, and Fred Short, who graduated in 1910, recollected that a "feature of the English Department was 'the Rhetoricals' which every student was required to present to the whole school once each year." Male and female professors who challenged both male and female students, as well as relatively relaxed seating arrangements, created the backdrop for intellectual equality in Wisconsin's normal classrooms.[12]

From 1868 to 1892, the normal curriculum was closer to that of an academy than a college, but Wisconsin educators were proud of its academic rigor and made no distinctions along gender lines. Between 1869 and 1876, seventy-five men and ninety-seven women graduated from the three-year advanced "full course" at all of the normals combined. Beginning in 1874, Wisconsin normals offered a four-year advanced course of study. Albert Salisbury reported in 1876 that the third and fourth years of study consisted of higher algebra, geometry, trigonometry, Latin, rhetoric, English literature, "Chemical Physics," chemistry, zoology, astronomy, geology, "Universal History," political economy, "Mental and Moral Science," and the theory and practice of teaching. These courses represented a move toward a college curriculum. Salisbury stated that the male to female ratio in the normal schools at the time of his report was two to three, but he made no references to gender in relation to the curriculum; the advanced course existed for men and women alike. During the next several years, gender issues did not influence adjustments in the advanced course. In the mid-1880s, an editorial in the *Wisconsin Journal of Education* spoke of "a gratifying unanimity of opinion that nothing should be done to lower the standard of scholarship" in the normal schools. Advocates of high standards fostered an atmosphere that enabled women to pursue rigorous scholarship without experiencing considerable gender discrimination.[13]

By 1892, the state of Wisconsin offered elective courses in the normal schools, without the stigma that accompanied courses aimed at women in the state university. That year, students were allowed to choose between different four-year courses of study. Among the requirements for each course were mathematics, English, natural sciences, "United States history and civil

---

[12]Kathy Greathouse, "Emily Webster: Math and Maxims, 1849–1933," in *University Women*, ed. Swoboda and Roberts, 31; "Memories of School Days," undated, Norah Halverson Howe Papers, State Historical Society of Wisconsin Archives; Recitations and Two Volumes of Class Notes, undated, Sally Birkenwald Papers, State Historical Society of Wisconsin Archives; "Recollections of River Falls," 19 Feb. 1974, p. 2, Fred Short Papers, State Historical Society of Wisconsin Archives.

[13]Salisbury, *Historical Sketch of Normal Instruction in Wisconsin*, 69, 63, 99; anonymous editorial, *Wisconsin Journal of Education* 15 (May 1885): 206.

"Biological Laboratory," Platteville State Normal School, *State Normal School Catalog,* 1900–1901. Courtesy of University of Wisconsin–Platteville Archives.

government," general history, and professional work in education. The English course had more extensive English language requirements, and the Latin course included less natural science in order to make room for Latin study. A third course was essentially created when students were allowed to substitute German for Latin in the Latin course. Unlike university students, normal students were not able to take courses that prepared them for exclusively male professions, such as pharmacy and engineering. All normal courses of study provided liberal arts backgrounds that would be useful to both men and women as teachers or in other future pursuits. Accordingly, there is no evidence that students' gender affected course choice or reputation. It is also important to note that women took advantage of the normals' expanding technical facilities during this time. Whitewater, for example, added to its science laboratory "such modern accessories as a Toepler-Holz machine, an 8-cell plunge battery, a dynamo, a dissecting microscope, and a host of other implements." Later in the decade, a Whitewater student wrote in her diary: "In Phys. [physiology] the [*sic*] morning we looked at nerve and cartilage fiber and cells through the microscope. Very wonderful."[14]

[14]Charles McKenny, ed., *Educational History of Wisconsin: Growth and Progress of Education in the State from Its Foundation to the Present Time* (Chicago, 1912), 158–59; M. Janette Bohi, *A History of Wisconsin State University, Whitewater, 1868–1968* (Whitewater, Wis., 1967), 92; Louise Bailey, personal diaries, 1893–1914, 15 Sep. 1898, State Historical Society of Wisconsin Archives.

Also by 1892, graduates of the two-year advanced courses of normal schools could officially graduate from the university with the degree of B.S. or B.L., in just two years. Many normal graduates accordingly began to matriculate as juniors at the University of Wisconsin. The normals thus essentially functioned as junior colleges, *but* teacher training remained their official purpose. This was an important distinction as normal elective offerings increased during the next couple of decades, because the new courses were ostensibly preparation for teaching—a career pursued by women and men alike. When Platteville began an industrial arts program in 1902, when Stevens Point established its domestic science department in the same year, and when La Crosse opened in 1909 with an emphasis on physical education, these varying courses lacked gender stigmatization because they shared the same goal. One sex may have outnumbered the other in certain courses, but no course was elevated above others because of its gender composition. And women were often able to venture beyond conventional boundaries; for example, women at Whitewater participated in manual training as part of practice teaching—"the young ladies who a few weeks before hardly knew 'a plane from a drawshave' were turning out beautiful work." Female normal students were relatively unhindered by gender discrimination in these elective classes.[15]

In 1911, the Wisconsin state legislature recognized the junior-college function of normal schools and authorized them to include two years of college work as an advertised offering.[16] This meant that, for the first time, teacher training was not the overriding function of normals. They had many options for academic expansion. The schools embarked upon this new phase with a firm and solid legacy of academic equality for male and female students. The first generations of students were basically treated as intellectual equals in normal school classrooms.

Unlike University of Wisconsin students, these normal students also functioned as intellectual equals in their primary extracurricular intellectual activity, literary and debate societies. Single-sex as well as mixed societies arose on virtually every campus. While mixed societies increased in number, men's and women's societies not only remained strong but had equal status; male and female students had equal opportunities for involvement in the societies. Platteville's first men's group, called the Philadelphian Society, began during the fall of 1866. That December, the members invited women to attend a meeting, and a society for women called the

---

[15]Patzer, *Public Education in Wisconsin*, 277; Richard G. Gamble, "From Academy to University: Wisconsin State University-Platteville, 1866–1966," in *History of the Wisconsin State Universities*, ed. Wyman, 31; William C. Hansen, "History of Wisconsin State University-Stevens Point, 1894–1966," in ibid., 177; George R. Gilkey, "LaCrosse: A Half-Century of Higher Education in Wisconsin's Coulee Region, 1909–1966," in ibid., 280; Bohi, *A History of Wisconsin State University, Whitewater*, 91.

[16]McKenny, ed., *Educational History of Wisconsin*, 163.

Athenaeum was soon under way. This group's "purposes and activities" were "closely intertwined with those of the Philadelphians." Men at Whitewater formed the Lincolnian Literary Society in 1868 to focus on "'reading, writing, and debate.'" In 1869, the Young Ladies Literary Society formed there; its members intended "to improve in elocution, composition, and debate and to enlarge their fund of general intelligence." After a coeducational society called Athenaeum lasted only from 1884 to 1886, Whitewater established a long-lasting mixed group just after the turn of the century. This organization, called Aureola, aimed "to furnish opportunity to men and women alike to practice in all lines of literary work; debate, extemporaneous speaking, oratory, elocution, music, etc." Oshkosh also had both single-sex and mixed groups. Dating back to 1871, its Lyceum was the oldest mixed group; still going strong in 1895, the society provided "some solid work in mental gymnastics." The other normal schools followed similar patterns.[17]

Within these groups, students wrestled with subjects that interested them, ranging from current events to philosophical issues. Different permutations of inter- and intra-group relations usually assured that the opinions of women and men on the varying subjects had equal validity. For example, Oshkosh's Phoenix, a mixed group, had separate debates for male and female members in 1895; the men debated the question of whether "war is inconsistent with Christianity," and the women debated woman's suffrage. Meanwhile, the mixed society at River Falls had a completely integrated forum in which men and women presented similar orations. The September 1896 meeting included "a paper by Miss Anna Dodge, entitled 'Bells,'" and Mr. George Schwartz's "short resume of his visit to Puget Sound." At Platteville, joint meetings of the Athenaeum and Philadelphian societies included debates on topics of current interest. A student publication reported that at a 1901 "Joint Session": "The most interesting number in the program was the debate upon the phenomenal subject: 'Resolved that the "Bachelor Girl" is a greater power in the world than the "Bachelor Boy."' This was argued by two young ladies defending the affirmative and two young men supporting the negative." The writers were "impressed by the master effort that was displayed in its defense." Another "Joint Session" in 1902 included a debate on the resolution "that the victory of Japan over China was for the interests of civ-

---

[17]Milton Longhorn, ed., *During Seventy-Five Years: A History of the State Teachers College, Platteville, Wisconsin, 1866–1941* (Platteville, Wis., 1941), 26–27; Gamble, "From Academy to University," 47; Bohi, *A History of Wisconsin State University, Whitewater*, 48, 101–2; Bertha Schuster Beach, "The Literary Societies," in *Historical Sketches of the First Quarter Century of the State Normal School at Whitewater, Wisconsin: With a Catalogue of Its Graduates and a Record of Their Work, 1868–1893* (Madison, 1893), 90; *The Royal Purple* (Whitewater, Wis.) 1 (June 1902): 21; *The Normal Advance* 2 (Sep.–Oct. 1895): 16.

ilization." Miss Weller defended the affirmative against Mr. Ruble, and she won.[18]

Beginning in the 1890s, normal school societies focused on big schoolwide contests. Female and male students were active participants at this level as well; Bertha Schuster Beach reported at Whitewater in 1893: "The contest, declamatory and oratorical, is the striking feature of recent times. The ladies entered the lists with the gentlemen and have carried off their share of the honors." At Oshkosh, the Inter-Society Debate League organized yearly contests between Lyceum teams and Phoenix teams, beginning in 1894. In 1898, two men and one woman composed each team and debated the question, "'Resolved, that Congress take immediate steps for the withdrawal of all legal tender notes.'" Two women and four men competed in an all-school oratorical contest organized by the Oshkosh Oratorical Association in 1896. Five women and one man were the 1897 contestants, and their subjects ranged from "Booker T. Washington" to "Rural Libraries" to "Independence of Cuba."[19]

Contests between schools became increasingly widespread. The teams for debates between two schools were often exclusively male—an indication that normal schools were not immune to Victorian notions of separate spheres. But yearly statewide inter-normal oratorical contests organized by the Inter-Normal League beginning in 1897 included women and men and were the focus of most of the attention. In April 1899, Stevens Point's *The Normal Pointer* printed a special issue covering the state oratorical contest, including a photograph of each of the six finalists, as well as his or her speech. The only woman of the six, Elizabeth Shepard of Oshkosh, entered with a speech entitled "Grant." At the 1902 state oratorical contest, men represented River Falls, Platteville, Stevens Point, and Superior, while Whitewater and Oshkosh sent women. Charlotte D. Ray of Oshkosh won with her speech, "A Plea for Shylock." In 1906, male orators spoke on behalf of Platteville, Whitewater, and Oshkosh, while females represented River Falls, Stevens Point, Milwaukee, and Superior. There was room for both women and men in even the most public, competitive outgrowth of literary society activity. The inherent message of normal school intellectual life, in literary and debate societies as well as in the classroom, was that men and women could function as intellectual equals.[20]

---

[18]*The Normal Advance* 2 (Sep.–Oct. 1895): 16; *The Normal Badger* (River Falls, Wis.) 2 (Sep. 1896): 5; *The Normal Exponent* (Platteville, Wis.) 1 (Jan. 1901): 10 and 3 (Jan. 1902): 7–8.

[19]Beach, "The Literary Societies," 91; *The Quiver* (Oshkosh, Wis., 1898), 69; *The Normal Advance* 2 (Mar.–Apr. 1896): 71–73 and 3 (Jan.–Feb. 1897): 61.

[20]*The Normal Pointer* (Stevens Point, Wis.) 4 (Apr. 1899): 81 and 7 (15 May 1902): 74–80; *The Royal Purple* 5 (Mar. 1906): n.p.

June Contest, June 22, 1909

MARGARET E. GODFREY
Oration
"Our Duty to the Italian Immigrant."
First Place

J. B. WITHERS
Oration
"Abraham Lincoln."
Second Place

CORA FISHER
Oration
"Nathan Hale."
Third Place

Winners of the June 1909 oratorical contest at Whitewater Normal School. *The Minneiska* 10 (1910): 53. Courtesy of University of Wisconsin–Whitewater Archives.

Campus social life complemented the life of the mind. Gender-segregated social life was very common at coeducational universities. Resentful of coeducation, many male students excluded women from campus life. At the same time, discomfort due to unequal treatment caused many members of the first two generations of college women to retreat, creating their own social world. Following a class party, the wife of a University of Wisconsin professor wrote in an 1891 letter: "'You can't imagine how grateful some of the students were to me! One young man confessed that he had been here over two years, and had never in all that time known a woman well enough to exchange a word with her. Another had been here four years with a similar experience, and this in a coeducational institution!'" After the turn of the century, interest in dating dissolved some of the social barriers, but virtually all interaction between the sexes then revolved around dating. Wisconsin women fought to be more than just the objects of romantic interest. University rules and regulations tended to reinforce social segregation, as women were often subject to stricter rules and guidelines than male students. From 1885 into the twentieth century, Ladies Hall was the only dormitory at the University of Wisconsin. Living in separate social spheres, male and female students at the University of Wisconsin generally did not get to know each other in the late nineteenth century.[21]

Conditions at the state university were not mirrored in campus life at Wisconsin's normal schools. Men and women at these institutions were like-minded in their approach to campus social life and were treated similarly outside the classroom. Relaxed social interaction in both more- and less-structured settings enabled men and women to become friendly with each other. Activity groups, most notably the literary societies, often organized events. "Reunions" between the Philadelphians and Athenaeums at Platteville included "social intercourse," singing, and toasts. Oshkosh's all-male Philakean reported in 1900: "Occasionally, as a denial of the character of confirmed woman haters, the members entertain the ladies, and great has been the enjoyment therefrom. It has been the custom to give an annual banquet . . . and these revels of wit and feasting are looked forward to each year with many pleasant emotions." The Philakeans also enjoyed inviting women students on a sleigh ride each winter. Supporting the school's contestant in statewide oratorical competitions fostered the bonds of school spirit among normal students of both sexes. For the 1899 contest, a delegation of 180 from Oshkosh traveled to Stevens Point in "a train load of fun, school songs, and school yells." In addition to encouraging intellectual interaction, literary societies nurtured social familiarity between men and women.[22]

---

[21]Solomon, *In the Company of Educated Women*, 99; Hague, "'What If the Power Does Lie Within Me?'," 82–84, professor's wife quoted on 82; Curti and Carstensen, *The University of Wisconsin*, 1: 664.

[22]Longhorn, ed., *During Seventy-Five Years*, 26–27; *The Quiver* (1900), 57; *The Normal Pointer* 4 (Apr. 1899): 96.

Whitewater Normal School outing to a bluff near campus, circa 1899. Scrapbook, 1899–1900, 55. Courtesy of University of Wisconsin–Whitewater Archives.

Other activities focused exclusively on social interaction. Gatherings with varied themes were popular throughout the period. While dances, such as a "Leap Year Hop" at River Falls in 1896, were oriented toward couples, numerous mixed parties focused more on friendship. When a Platteville student had a party for the whole senior class at her home in 1889, "everybody was glad to go, and the time and the students were filled with conversation, games and refreshments." Students wore ghost costumes to a "Phantom Social" in 1899 at River Falls, and the program included "Goblin Song (by female ghosts) . . . Peter Gray (by male ghosts)," games, and a contest to see who could identify the most people under their costumes. Class parties were popular on the Whitewater campus after the turn of the century. On a Friday evening in February 1906, a party hosted by the senior class honored Earl Rohr and Rachel Smart, winners in the Whitewater-Platteville debate. And at a Junior-Senior party in 1913, female and male students entertained each other with imitations of professors. Picnics and outings were less formal still; at Platteville, for example, "mixed groups . . . congregated at Fountain Bluffs, the Mound, Tufa Falls, and the Powder Mills." At parties and picnics, men and women were able to get to know one another as friends.[23]

---

[23]*The Normal Exponent* 1 (Dec. 1889): 13; *The Normal Badger* 4 (Jan. 1899): 1; *The Royal Purple* 5 (Feb. 1906): 7 and 12 (Feb. 1913): 6–7; Gamble, "From Academy to University," 49.

Normal school rules and regulations tended to reinforce social familiarity by providing common ground; men and women were, for the most part, subject to the same maxims. All students were generally expected to follow prescribed study hours. Students—of both sexes—were "urged to '. . . attend regularly to sleep, diet, ablution [bathing], and exercise." Early in the 1890s, Platteville's President Duncan McGregor required students to submit weekly reports on their attendance and conduct directly to him. Herman Landschulz wrote: "Have been at school every day, have not been tardy, studied hard, I think. I am making better progress than I did at the first of the term." Sarah Jones submitted a similar note: "I have been present each day this week and punctual at all times. My deportment has been some better this week. I have not been very successful at my work this week." In the middle of the same decade, Mrs. Emily M. B. Felt spoke to groups of males and females at Platteville "on the social and moral standards of the school and society in respect to dating, etiquette, courtship, and matrimony." Meanwhile, Whitewater's president, Albert Salisbury, used "morning talks" to instruct all students in manners and morals. Although such regulations may have echoed female seminaries, they contributed to common social ground between the sexes at normal schools.[24]

Residential life also placed the two sexes on common ground at Wisconsin's normal schools. The residences of all normal students were carefully regulated. Rules stipulated that students live only in rooming houses or homes approved by the school, and "proper family oversight" was an important criterion for approval. For a time, normal presidents themselves oversaw "arrangements for suitable living quarters." Restrictions pertaining to living quarters remained virtually the same into the 1900s, and there were no dorms for the normal schools until the 1910s. Men and women occasionally lived under the same roof. John Staack wrote of his Platteville living situation: "The group of young people constituting the boarders was a mixed collection of three women and three men students. . . . It was a sociable and refined group of young people with whom I had affiliated." Female and male students were not subject to separate residential spheres.[25]

Literary society gatherings, various parties and outings, and universal regulations allowed for cross-gender familiarity among normal students. The result was a playful spirit and much friendly teasing. For example, when Sally Birkenwald predicted the futures of her fellow graduates in 1880, neither men nor women were exempt from her good-

[24]William Harold Herrmann, "The Rise of the Public Normal School System in Wisconsin" (Ph.D. diss., University of Wisconsin, 1953), 355; "Student Notes to President McGregor," 1890s, University of Wisconsin–Platteville Archives, Platteville; Gamble, "From Academy to State University," 46; Bohi, "Whitewater," 66.

[25]Herrmann, "The Rise of the Public Normal School System in Wisconsin," 353; John G. Staack, autobiography, undated, 114–15, State Historical Society of Wisconsin Archives.

natured barbs. She wrote: "we see Monsieur Wahl in the 5th story of his Technical Institution in Oshkosh (the very one he used to ridicule) . . . [and] the former Miss Martha Schmitt, a follower of Susan B. Anthony, discussing Women's Rights in the kitchen." The composer(s) of a "Physician's Chart" in 1911 at Whitewater likewise knew both men and women well enough for friendly teasing. Some of the students and their supposed ailments were: "Donald McLachlin—Swell Head. . . Steve McNally—Love Sickness. . . Hattie Noel—Insomnia. . . [and] Lilal Eberle—Hysteria (caused by giggling)."[26] Campus social life made men and women familiar to each other in Wisconsin's normal schools.

In addition to forming friendships and growing intellectually, college students acquired leadership and teamwork skills through all sorts of organized activities. In clubs and on sports teams, some students had opportunities to lead, and all worked together for a product or result. At many coeducational universities, gender issues hindered full participation in such activities by women. They had limited opportunities for leadership and teamwork, and the few they had were mainly in women-only settings. As student organizations grew in number at the University of Wisconsin between 1885 and 1901, men had many more options than women had. When the university built a new gymnasium in the mid-1890s, "A notable case of quite forgetting the girls was shown in the equipment of the splendid new gymnasium, one of the finest in the United States, where with everything that modern ingenuity has devised for the physical culture of men not the slightest provision was made for women," according to the *Wisconsin Journal of Education.* "The regents evidently quite forgot that there was a woman student in the University." Women did not have access to an athletic facility until Lathrop Hall was built in 1909. In addition, a significant number of the new organizations before and after the turn of the century were single-sex. Women's groups took second place to male-only organizations, which were assumed to represent all students. The Women's Self-Government Association allowed female students to be active in student government, but not in the all-male structure that already existed. Similarly, during the first decades of the 1900s, women wrote for and edited the *Coed Cardinal* once per year, while men used the newspaper facilities to produce the *Wisconsin Cardinal* on a regular basis. Through athletics, student government, and many other activities, women at the University of Wisconsin had fewer opportunities than men to lead and work in teams, and the few chances they had were usually in women-only groups.[27]

---

[26]Recitations and Two Volumes of Class Notes, June 1880, Birkenwald Papers; *The Royal Purple* 10 (Feb. 1911): 10.

[27]Hague, "'What If the Power Does Lie Within Me?'," 88; "Co-Education in Wisconsin," *Wisconsin Journal of Education* 25 (Aug. 1895): 176; Langill, "Women at Wisconsin," 11–13, 17.

At Wisconsin's normal schools, on the other hand, gender equality characterized not only intellectual and social relations but also the development of teamwork and leadership skills; like men, women enjoyed ample opportunities to lead and work with groups of their own sex, as well as groups of mixed gender. The literary societies and the Young Women's Christian Association allowed women to gain leadership and teamwork experience in both settings. Female students naturally served as officers in women-only societies and in the YWCA chapters that were active on normal campuses. The officers and group members also worked as teams to plan meetings and, in the literary societies, to prepare each other for debates and oratorical meets. Teamwork in YMCA chapters included "aiding new students in finding boarding places" and studying the Bible. In the YWCA, leadership and teamwork experiences in a women-only setting extended beyond campus boundaries. In October 1895, for example, Emma Blood represented Oshkosh Normal at the YWCA state convention in Milwaukee. Women like Blood in the societies and Christian Association gained valuable experience as leaders and team players in women-only groups.[28]

In addition, women-only literary societies planned and ran events with men-only societies, and YWCA chapters often undertook joint activities with Young Men's Christian Association chapters. YW- and YMCA "joint devotional meetings" were common in the 1890s and 1900s. This meant that leaders of male and female groups shared responsibility for planning and directing meetings, gaining valuable experience in mixed-gender leadership and teamwork. Men and women also shared leadership positions in mixed literary societies. More often than not, group presidents were male, but it was possible for women to hold the position—Whitewater's Aureola had female presidents and male vice presidents in 1904 and 1906. Both sexes served as society secretaries, treasurers, and vice presidents. Women, as well as men, also led and planned statewide oratorical activities. The Inter-Normal Oratorical League, for example, had a female secretary in 1897–98, and a female president and secretary in 1905–6. Women gained valuable leadership and teamwork skills in mixed-gender, as well as single-sex, settings through literary societies and Young Women's Christian Association chapters.[29]

Athletics was the area of activity perhaps most touted for fostering leadership and teamwork skills. In contrast to students at the university, at normal schools women as well as men had access to sports, as long as they did not cross gender lines. Athletics gave women an important chance to

---

[28]*The Normal Advance* 1 (Sep.–Oct. 1894): 13 and 2 (Sep.–Oct. 1895): 17.

[29]*The Normal Badger* 2 (Sep. 1896–Nov. 1899); *The Royal Purple* 1 and 8 (June 1902–Oct. 1908); Bohi, *A History of Wisconsin State University, Whitewater*, 104; *The Royal Purple* 3 (Apr. 1904): 24 and 6 (Sep. 1906): 10; *The Normal Advance* 3 (Mar.–Apr. 1897): 73; *The Royal Purple* 5 (Mar. 1906): 20.

Platteville Normal School gymnasium during the 1890s. Courtesy of iconographic collection, University of Wisconsin–Platteville Archives.

Women's basketball team, Whitewater Normal School, 1912–13. *The Minneiska* 13 (1913): 100. Courtesy of University of Wisconsin–Whitewater Archives.

learn leadership and teamwork in a single-sex setting, although the ideology of separate spheres remained in the background. The first step to participation in sports was physical development. Early on, normal school presidents
encouraged calisthenics for both sexes. A Whitewater alumnus remembered,
"The school exercises were given in the Assembly room, the pupils standing
in the aisles and marching up and down and around. A leader stood at the
head of each aisle and whatever her fancy devised those behind executed. There
were some funny effects, pupils standing on one heel, one toe, both toes, or
both heels." Physical education classes were part of the curriculum by the late
1880s and early 1890s. Athletic facilities differed between schools, with
requirements varying occasionally by sex, but women always had access. At
Superior in the late 1890s, "all students spent several hours a week in the gymnasium, swinging dumbbells, whirling Indian clubs, vaulting, sprinting, turning cartwheels, and cavorting on parallel bars." And Whitewater's *The Royal
Purple* reported in the fall of 1902 that "the young ladies are to have a
punching bag of their 'very own.' Next spring shapely arms, well-rounded
throats and queenly carriage of heads will show the benefit of such exercise." These women were well prepared for team sports.[30]

The 1890s was the decade when intramural, and even some internormal,
sports competition mushroomed. While men focused mainly on baseball
and football, women formed all sorts of basketball teams. Students at
Oshkosh were especially enthusiastic about basketball. "The indoor gymnasium is entirely devoted to basket ball except during regular class peri-
ods," stated the yearbook. "Members of the foot-ball team are often found
watching the game from some good safe position, but only the ladies are
allowed to participate. There are many good teams in the school and the
games are often very close. . . . True there were no games played with
teams representing other schools, but that was not the fault of the Oshkosh
bloomer brigade, for several challenges were sent to teams of other institutions." In 1904, female basketball teams had use of the Platteville gymnasium after four o'clock each Wednesday and Friday. There was also
speculation at Whitewater in 1906 that the faculty women would organize
a basketball team, "to meet the girls' champion team." These women and
the "bloomer brigade" learned the value of depending on one another and
the importance of doing their own part for the good of the whole team, as
they practiced and competed on the basketball courts.[31]

---

[30]Herrmann, "The Rise of the Public Normal System in Wisconsin," 388; Charles M.
Gleason, "Physical Training at Whitewater," in *Historical Sketches of the First Quarter
Century of the State Normal School at Whitewater*, 84; Bohi, *A History of Wisconsin State
University, Whitewater*, 88; John C. Haughland, "Wisconsin State University–Superior,
1896–1966," in *History of the Wisconsin State Universities*, ed. Wyman, 207; *The Royal
Purple* 2 (Sep. 1902): 10.
[31]See Ronald A. Smith, "Athletics in the Wisconsin State University System: 1867–1913,"
Wisconsin Magazine of History 55 (Autumn 1971): 2–23. *The Quiver* (1898), 113; *The
Normal Exponent* 4 (Jan. 1904): 10; *The Royal Purple* 5 (Jan. 1906): 11.

As normal school sports diversified and grew in popularity for both male and female students after the turn of the century, women's mechanisms for developing their teamwork and leadership skills with other women became more varied. For instance, tennis and "association football" appeared along with basketball in the Whitewater yearbooks for 1912 and 1913, and pictures of junior and senior hockey teams appeared a few years later. The 1915 Oshkosh yearbook described the "Happy Hunting Ground of retired athletic trophies" in a female student's cabinet: "Hockey clubs and baseball bats threatened the more delicately constituted tennis rackets." Women thus worked together to score touchdowns, goals, and runs, as well as baskets. They also organized their own leagues and games; Whitewater had a Girls' Athletic Association by 1915, Platteville by 1916, and Oshkosh by 1920. Normal school athletics enabled female students to develop themselves physically, as well as develop teamwork and leadership skills in single-sex arenas.[32]

Countless short- and long-lived normal organizations also provided mixed-gender settings for developing aptitudes for leadership and teamwork. These ranged from the "Sketch Club" at Stevens Point, which had male and female officers, to River Falls' Orchestra and Dramatics Club, which relied on all members for quality performances. Probably the most long lasting and enduring of such organizations were student government and school publications. Most graduating classes elected officers to represent them, and student magazines appeared beginning in 1889. By the early 1900s there were multiple monthly magazines and yearbooks; *The Royal Purple* at Whitewater even became a weekly in 1913. *The Normal Advance* at Oshkosh reported that junior class elections for the class of 1897 brought men "face to face with the ever present woman question." The possibility that women were elected class president because of a disproportionate number of women voters is less important than the fact that men and women in student government and on the *Advance* staff could grow as leaders and teammates in mixed-gender settings.[33]

Men and women shared leadership positions in student government and campus publications. For instance, Whitewater's classes of 1903, '04, '07, '08, '09, and '10 elected a total of four male and two female presidents, two male and four female vice presidents, one male and five female secretaries, and four male and two female treasurers. Students at Oshkosh Normal noted the importance of such leadership experiences: "two or three years of experience in class meetings will be valuable to any student

---

[32]*The Minneiska* (Whitewater, Wis., 1913, 1914, 1917, 1918); *The Quiver* (1915), 156; Bohi, "Whitewater," 72; *The Normal Exponent* 17 (Nov. 1916): 10; *The Quiver* (1920), 109.

[33]*The Normal Pointer* 5 (15 June 1900): 103–5; *The Meletean Annual* (River Falls, Wis., 1915), 73; *The Normal Exponent* 1 (Oct. 1889); *The Royal Purple* 12 (Apr. 1913): 1; *The Normal Advance* 2 (Sep.–Oct. 1895): 14.

who expects to become a teacher, and who at any time may be called upon to organize or preside over a meeting." Women and men also shared the various editorial positions on normal school magazines and year-books, including the post of editor-in-chief. For instance, Margaret Ashman served as literary editor under Jay S. Hamilton, editor-in-chief on *The Normal Pointer* staff in 1895–96; the following fall, she was editor-in-chief. Students like Ashman and Hamilton faced the challenges of directing the actions of writers and editors of both sexes toward the final product of a quality publication.[34]

Women and men also worked together as teammates on class councils and magazine and yearbook staffs. Oshkosh seniors recognized the advantages of working as a team: "The responsibilities, about which we have heard so much, should be met by us as a class rather than as individuals." Likewise, the 1915 River Falls yearbook staff saw itself as a cohesive team, presenting as the staff picture a cartoon of sorts, in which actual photographs of only editors' heads appeared atop cartoon bodies in settings to represent their particular functions in the production of the book. The woman editor-in-chief and man associate editor sat together behind a formal desk, while the male and female sports editors sat together on a giant football, both wearing football jerseys, and a man and woman each held one cover of an open book labeled "Jokes." Publication teams such as this one covered virtually all aspects of normal school life in columns and articles. There were no great distinctions in subjects covered by female as opposed to male writers. For example, Gertrude Preston authored "Some Evils of American Slum Life and Methods of Dealing with Them," the lead article in *The Royal Purple* of November 1906, and Hubert Chaffee's "The Progress of Sanitation" was prominent in the January 1911 edition. By working together, women and men reported thoroughly on normal school life and effectively carried out their class duties.[35]

Diversified student organizations provided normal students with multiple channels for developing aptitudes for leadership and teamwork in both single-sex and mixed settings. In athletics, they combined energies with others of their own sex to compete against other teams. On class councils and publication staffs, they represented the experiences of all normal students, male and female. And in literary societies and Christian Associations, students organized single-sex as well as mixed meetings and competitions. It is not surprising, therefore, that the 1915 River Falls yearbook expressed confidence in the abilities of women students to lead and work with teams; the book mentioned editor-in-chief Hazel Hansen's

---

[34]*The Royal Purple* 2 (Sep. 1902): 10, 3 (Sep. 1903): 10, 6 (Sep. 1906): 10, 7 (Sep. 1907): 9, 8 (Sep. 1908): 10, and 9 (Sep. 1909): 10; *The Normal Advance* 2 (Sep.–Oct. 1895): 14; *The Normal Pointer* 1 (Dec. 1895): 4 and 2 (Sep. 1896): 78.

[35]*The Normal Advance* 2 (Sep.–Oct. 1895): 14; *The Meletean Annual* (1915), 102; *The Royal Purple* 6 (Nov. 1906): 1–3 and 10 (Jan. 1911): 3–5.

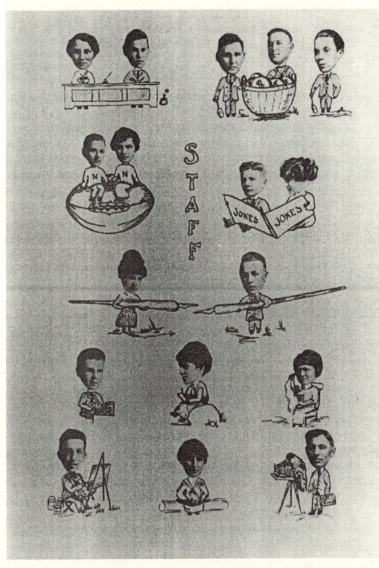

The River Falls Normal School yearbook staff's representation of itself, 1914–15. *The Meletean Annual* (1915), 102. Courtesy of University of Wisconsin–River Falls Archives.

"power to command" and sports editor Jessie Reynolds's abilities in edit-
ing as well as "in the gymnasium."[36] These normal women took advantage of opportunities to become leaders and team players.

* * * * *

Wisconsin's normal schools entered the decade of the 1910s with a legacy of relative gender equality—in intellectual life, in social activities, and
in settings that promoted leadership and teamwork. Each of these areas
related to a single official purpose, teacher training. In 1911, the state
legislature authorized these institutions to begin offering two years of
general baccalaureate work. During the following decade and a half, the
normal schools began to modify their original exclusive concentration on
teacher preparation and to clarify their position as collegiate institutions.
In 1925, the state legislature authorized the normals to offer four-year
bachelor's courses for the first time, and beginning in 1927, the schools
were known as State Teacher Colleges. As the normal schools transformed
themselves into institutions with collegiate status, they also began to modify their unique lessons in gender equality.

In the intellectual sphere, Wisconsin's normal schools developed elective courses that encouraged gender differentiation. New departments of
instruction prepared students for careers pursued unequally by the sexes.
A commercial department began operations at Whitewater in 1913; by
1915, "two types of curricula developed which divided the efforts of the
department between producing teachers and office workers." Oshkosh's
Department of Industrial Education was part of the school's "broadening
mission" in 1912; Stevens Point had "seven different courses of study for
Domestic Science and Domestic Art" by the same year, and River Falls's
facilities for agricultural education were "excellent" by 1917. At the same
time, single-sex literary societies and debating clubs became more prominent on normal campuses. During the late 1910s, Whitewater students
debated in the all-female Burke Debating Club and the all-male Salisbury
Debating Club. In 1920, Oshkosh's previously mixed societies called
Phoenix and Lyceum were all-women and all-men, respectively. Developments in the curriculum and societies threatened intellectual equality.[37]

Nonromantic social familiarity between men and women also
decreased somewhat. Dating, rather than friendship, was increasingly the
focus of stories in student magazines. In 1911, the following poem signaled
the beginning of the change:

---

[36]*The Meletean Annual* (1915), 103.
[37]Bohi, "Whitewater," 77; Noyes, "Oshkosh," 108; Hansen, "History of Wisconsin
State University-Stevens Point," 177; John Lankford, "A History of Wisconsin State Uni-
versity-River Falls, 1874–1966," in *History of the Wisconsin State Universities*, ed. Wyman,
154; *The Minneiska*, 7–12 (1915–19); *The Quiver* (1920), 64–67.

Says the Normal girl to the Normal boys:
When you're in heaps of trouble,
And don't know what's to be done;
Just try to travel double,
And you'll find it's lots of fun.
(That is, if you don't get stung).[38]

And a short story in 1920 called "A Normal Romance" described the woman who attracted "languishing glances as she peers into her vanity-case mirror while in the library" and "the hero and his muscular arms."[39] Women's, but not men's, dormitories appeared on several of the normal campuses during the 1910s; women and men were thus subject to different levels of behavioral scrutiny for the first time. By the 1920s, changes in normal school life made men and women increasingly foreign to one another.

In leadership and teamwork as well, men and women began to appear somewhat less equal. Not only were mixed-gender literary and debate activities less common, but they were overshadowed by athletic activities. Although women were also quite active in sports, men's sports received the attention that internormal oratorical contests had received in the past. In 1912, the normal school presidents decided to begin an "internormal basketball championship," as well as informally to prohibit internormal basketball games for women. Men's football and basketball were gaining prestige. Women and men continued to have many opportunities to develop leadership and teamwork skills, but men were more often in the limelight.[40] Gender equality in leadership and teamwork, as well as in the intellectual and social spheres, was disappearing on normal school campuses during the 1910s and 1920s.

The twentieth-century shift toward greater gender *in*equality at Wisconsin's normal schools highlights the remarkable environment that these schools provided during earlier decades. Students at Wisconsin State Normal Schools between 1868 and the mid-1910s generally experienced *coed*ucation; their lives inside and outside the classroom did not hinge on gender differences. Normal students thus received implicit lessons in gender relations. Their classroom and literary society activities sent the message that women and men could be intellectual equals, campus life fostered social familiarity between the sexes, and student organizations demonstrated that females and males were equally capable of leadership and teamwork in single-sex and mixed-group settings. These lessons sharply contrasted with the experiences of students at the University of Wisconsin. Student life at this more prestigious institution was characterized by gender separation and lower status for women.

---

[38]*The Royal Purple* 11 (Nov. 1911): 7.
[39]*The Quiver* (1920), 139.
[40]Smith, "Athletics in the Wisconsin State University System," 16–17.

The investigation of coeducation at Wisconsin state normal schools in the late nineteenth and early twentieth centuries suggests two important areas for further research. First, we need to understand better why coeducation at normal schools, at least in Wisconsin, was so different from coeducation at the institutions described by Solomon, Gordon, and Horowitz. This study of Wisconsin points to two important factors that differentiated the two types of institutions: prestige and purpose. Unable to grant baccalaureate degrees until the 1920s, the normal schools clearly had less prestige than the universities; in status, they were perhaps closer to high schools, where coeducation was not as contentious.[41] While the universities prepared students for various futures, normal schools shared the distinct official purpose of teacher preparation, a pursuit equally acceptable for male and female students. Prestige and purpose were two characteristics of normal schools that changed along with the erosion of gender equality in the 1910s and 1920s. Was there a cause-and-effect relationship between prestige level and purpose, on the one hand, and gender equality, on the other, or were they unrelated characteristics that happened to change simultaneously? Further exploration of these and other factors will help us understand why coeducation at Wisconsin's normal schools was different from coeducation at other institutions of higher education.

Second, we need to understand more clearly whether Wisconsin's normal schools were characteristic of normal schools across the nation. Other states duplicated the Wisconsin system, which relied on several normal schools to offer all-around higher education in the shadow of the state university. This similarity suggests that normal schools in other states also offered lessons in gender equality. Future research should explore the universality of the type of coeducation offered at Wisconsin's normal schools and possible reasons why it was different from coeducation at other institutions of higher education. Given the sizable number of students trained in normal schools, the influence of these schools on gender relations should not be overlooked.

---

[41]On coeducation in the high schools, see David Tyack and Elisabeth Hansot, *Learning Together: A History of Coeducation in American Schools* (New Haven, Conn., 1990); and John L. Rury, *Education and Women's Work: Female Schooling and the Division of Labor in Urban America, 1870–1930* (Albany, N.Y., 1991).

Acknowledgments

Harvard Educational Review. "An Interview on Title IX with Shirley Chisholm, Holly Knox, Leslie R. Wolfe, Cynthia G. Brown, and Mary Kaaren Jolly." *Harvard Educational Review* 49 (1979): 504–26. Reprinted with the permission of the Harvard University, Graduate School of Education.

Berkeley, Kathleen C. "'The Ladies Want to Bring About Reform in the Public Schools': Public Education and Women's Rights in the Post-Civil War South." *History of Education Quarterly* 24 (1984): 45–58. Reprinted with the permission of the author.

Wong, Glenn M. and Richard J. Ensor. "Sex Discrimination in Athletics: A Review of Two Decades of Accomplishments and Defeats." *Gonzaga Law Review* 21 (1985–86): 345–93. Reprinted with the permission of the *Gonzaga Law Review*.

Rury, John and Glenn Harper. "The Trouble with Coeducation: Mann and Women at Antioch, 1853–1860." *History of Education Quarterly* 26 (1986): 481–502. Reprinted with the permission of John Rury.

Brown, Victoria Bissell. "The Fear of Feminization: Los Angeles High Schools in the Progressive Era." *Feminist Studies* 16 (1990): 493–518. Reprinted with the permission of the publisher, FEMINIST STUDIES, Inc., c/o Women's Studies Program, University of Maryland, College Park, MD 20742.

Olson, Wendy. "Beyond Title IX: Toward an Agenda for Women and Sports in the 1990s." *Yale Journal of Law and Feminism* 3 (1991): 105–51. Reprinted with the permission of the *Yale Journal of Law and Feminism*.

Beadie, Nancy. "Emma Willard's Idea Put to the Test: The Consequences of State Support of Female Education in New York, 1819–67." *History of Education Quarterly* 33 (1993): 543–62. Reprinted with the permission of the author.

Espinoza, Leslie G. "The LSAT: Narratives and Bias." *American University Journal of Gender and the Law* 1 (1993): 121–64. Reprinted with the permission of the Washington College of Law.

Amstein, Julie M. "*United States* v. *Virginia*: The Case of Coeducation at Virginia Military Institute." *American University Journal of Gender and the Law* 3 (1994): 69–115. Reprinted with the permission of the Washington College of Law.

Ogren, Christine A. "Where Coeds Were Coeducated: Normal Schools in Wisconsin, 1870–1920." *History of Education Quarterly* 35 (1995): 1–26. Reprinted with the permission of the author.